The Chief Justiceship of
Warren Burger, 1969–1986

CHIEF JUSTICESHIPS
OF THE UNITED STATES SUPREME COURT

Herbert A. Johnson, Series Editor

The Chief Justiceship of
Warren Burger, 1969–1986

Earl M. Maltz

University of South Carolina Press

© 2000 University of South Carolina

Published in Columbia, South Carolina, by the
University of South Carolina Press

Manufactured in the United States of America

04   03   02   01   00   5   4   3   2   1

Library of Congress Cataloging-in-Publication Data

Maltz, Earl M., 1950–
    The chief justiceship of Warren Burger, 1969–1986 / Earl M. Maltz.
      p.   cm. — (Chief justiceships of the United States Supreme Court)
    Includes bibliographical references and index.
    ISBN 1-57003-335-8 (cloth : acid-free paper)
    1. Burger, Warren E., 1907–   2. United States. Supreme Court—History.
    3. Judges—United States—History.   I. Title.   II. Series.
    KF8745.B76 M35   2000
    347.73'2634–dc21   00-008049

CONTENTS

ILLUSTRATIONS

TABLES

VOTING PATTERNS

SERIES EDITOR'S PREFACE

Surveying the work of the United States Supreme Court under Chief Justice Warren Burger is a complicated task. Many of the issues that emerge in the Burger era date back to the Roosevelt "revolution" of 1935 to 1937, when judicial nullification of New Deal legislative programs pitted the justices against the political branches of government. From that struggle emerged not only a different emphasis in constitutional adjudication, but also the potentiality for rapid expansion of judicial power and activism. Chief Justice Burger succeeded to the Court's central seat after a long and extremely active time of Supreme Court adjudication under Chief Justice Earl Warren. In retrospect the Warren years may now be viewed as the high tide of liberal constitutionalism. The Burger Court from its very inception was believed to mark a time of transition from liberal constitutionalism to conservative ideological views that would gain predominance under the chief justiceship of William H. Rehnquist. Yet, as Professor Maltz amply shows in this volume, the transition was far from immediate, and certainly not regular or universal in its process. Quite the contrary, there is good evidence here that in several critical areas of constitutional law, the Burger Court was as liberal in its decision making as its predecessor.

Scholars examining the Burger Court differ sharply in their interpretations. As Professor Maltz points out in his brief introductory chapter, the Burger Court has been seen to be an essentially centrist institution, involved in limiting or reversing some of the more radical or innovative positions taken by the Warren Court. A variant of this interpretation points out that the Burger Court was guided by a need to apply distinctive legal principles in its constitutional analysis. In doing so it is said to have abandoned the broader ideological and philosophical approach of the Warren Court, and held more closely to traditional common-law methods. A third analysis, which Professor Maltz accepts with some qualification, is that on core constitutional issues the justices divided on the basis of their political ideology. Finally, scholars have considered the Burger Court's jurisprudence to adhere to no particular pattern, but rather to represent the pragmatic conclusions emerging from the deliberations of thirteen independent judicial contractors who formed a variety of loose and temporary coalitions over a period of time.

While Maltz freely admits the complexities of decision making in the Burger Court, he insists that discernible patterns explain the doctrinal position adopted by the majority in any given case. He advances the controversial thesis that Burger Court activism occurred almost entirely in a liberal political direction. That was particularly the case prior to 1974 when the appointment of Justices Blackmun, Powell, and Rehnquist (1970–1971) began to incline the majority toward conservative positions. Maltz also notes a pattern of conservatism in regard to statutory construction, but, on the other hand, he suggests that on civil-rights constitutional issues, the Court followed a distinctly conservative trend. Although his views may well stimulate strong dissents in the scholarly community, they provide a new and thought-provoking approach to historical interpretations of the Burger Court.

In terms of Court administration, Professor Maltz points out the chief justice's strenuous, but unsuccessful, effort to reduce Supreme Court dockets by the creation of a national court of appeals. Chief Justice Burger was also an active voice for increased standards of preparation and performance in the legal profession. He was a powerful advocate for the improvement of lawyerly skills in the presentation of cases and the argument of appeals. Viewing himself as the leader of the entire legal profession, and not simply of the federal bench and bar, Burger played a significant role in the establishment of the National Center of State Courts. Internally, in the conferences of the court and in forming coalitions, Chief Justice Burger was much less effective. In part this may have been attributable to a lack of intellectual leadership; Maltz rates Burger as less than a great chief justice. On the other hand, he points out that even Earl Warren would have experienced difficulty in achieving consensus when faced with such a diversity of opinions as characterized the justices of the Court during Burger's chief justiceship.

Valuable insights emerge from the author's close analysis of the diverse and sometimes conflicting positions taken by the Burger Court. Its conservatism led to more vigorous use of the principle of standing, thereby limiting ready access to the Supreme Court's dockets. A probusiness trend when dealing with statutory issues in the antitrust field indicates a tendency toward conservative positions. In addition, the Court was willing to exercise a broader review of administrative regulation, insisting that agencies provide adequate reasons for their regulations. Under Warren Burger, federal principles began to emerge once more in regard to electoral reapportionment cases, and most notably in the localization of obscenity case jurisprudence.

By way of contrast, Maltz argues that in dealing with religion cases, the Burger Court moved existing doctrine to the left of the political spectrum, and in ruling on affirmative action programs, the Court found itself more liberal than the Warren Court at the end of the Burger Era. In nonracial discrimination cases the Court moved in a liberal direction except when the privacy rights of gay or lesbian couples were involved.

Not content to merely delineate the doctrinal positions of the Burger court, Professor Maltz focuses upon the personalities and complex pattern of political attitudes among the justices. He wisely observes that conservative members of the Court were hampered in institutionalizing their ideology because they were restrained by their rejection of judicial activism. They had greater respect for stare decisis than was typical of Warren Court hold-over justices. Maltz reminds us that until 1974 the Burger Court remained a fairly active and liberal tribunal, reflecting the continuance of Warren Court justices on the bench and their persistent influence.

Through a vigorous examination of the work of the Burger Court, and particular attention to the doctrinal rationale of its opinions, Professor Maltz has provided a comprehensive summary and thoughtful analysis of the impact of Warren Burger and his Court upon American law and government. His study provides a new basis for the historical argument that legal institutions and their ideological foundations change very slowly; it also points out that some aspects of constitutional and private law change more slowly than others. For this reason, there is much to be learned from careful attention and study of transitional periods in the Supreme Court's history. The chief justiceship of Warren E. Burger was undoubtedly one of the most interesting times in the Court's history. Rather than seeing change by revolution, we can trace a fascinating mosaic of gradually altering constitutional thought, superimposed upon many Warren Court values and liberal principles. In the Burger Court change came slowly, if at all, because of inertia inherent in the concept of stare decisis. This was augmented by the natural reticence of many of the conservative justices to engage in judicial activism that had been so characteristic of the Warren period.

Herbert A. Johnson

PREFACE

Any author seeking to write a brief account of the chief justiceship of Warren E. Burger faces a daunting task. The years in which Burger led the Supreme Court witnessed an explosion of doctrinal developments whose magnitude surpassed even that of the regime of his predecessor, Earl Warren. These developments occurred in many different areas, ranging from the law of race relations to that of sex discrimination, freedom of speech, privacy, criminal procedure, regulation of interstate commerce and business, generally, to name only a few. The evolution of Burger Court jurisprudence in any one of these areas could easily merit book-length treatment; indeed, a number of excellent books discussing Burger Court analyses of particular subject matters have already appeared. One important challenge lies in compressing the full range of material into a single volume of manageable size.

In order to meet this challenge, a number of difficult choices had to be made. First, in order to provide space for a reasonably broad range of coverage of the doctrinal developments of the Burger era, this book focuses primarily on the doctrinal developments and interactions that are reflected in the cases decided by the Burger Court. Second, I had to decide which specific doctrinal developments should be covered and which cases within those areas were the most important. Some of these decisions are by their nature idiosyncratic and will no doubt be controversial. Nonetheless, taken together, the selections should provide the reader with a good overall picture of the basic structure of Burger Court decision making.

Parts of this book have appeared previously as articles in scholarly publications. Much of chapter 1 is taken from "The Prospects for a Revival of Conservative Activism in Constitutional Jurisprudence." This article was originally published in 24 *Ga. L. Rev.* 629 (1990) and is reprinted with permission. A substantial portion of chapter 3 is adapted from "The Impact of the Constitutional Revolution of 1937 on the Dormant Commerce Clause—A Case Study in the Decline of State Autonomy," *Harvard Journal of Law and Public Policy* 19 (1995): 121–45, reprinted with permission of the *Harvard Journal of Law and Public Policy.*

In writing this book, I have been fortunate to receive help from many talented people. Judy Weinstock not only was an excellent research assistant, but also made valuable editorial comments. The secretarial staff at the Rutgers University School of Law performed ably in preparing the manuscript. The librarians at Rutgers and the Library of Congress were invaluable resources. John Jacob, the custodian of the Lewis Powell Papers at the Washington and Lee University School of Law, was particularly helpful, providing assistance that went well beyond what one would normally expect from a reference librarian. Steve Wermeil generously shared his insights into Justice Brennan.

Several people deserve special mention. Herb Johnson not only provided me with the opportunity to write this book, but also shepherded the manuscript through some difficult times and is responsible for numerous significant improvements. My wife, Peggy, continues to put up with me, although there are many days when I am sure that she wonders why. Finally, David, Jonathan, and Elizabeth remind me of where my priorities should be.

The Chief Justiceship of
Warren Burger, 1969–1986

INTRODUCTION

The story of the chief justiceship of Warren E. Burger is in large measure the story of an effort to change the course of Supreme Court decision making. Implacably opposed to the liberal judicial activism of the Court under Earl Warren, President Richard M. Nixon was given the opportunity to appoint four justices in quick succession. He chose Burger, Harry A. Blackmun, Lewis F. Powell, Jr., and William H. Rehnquist with the avowed purpose of shifting the direction of the Court to a more conservative path.

In evaluating the success or failure of Nixon's efforts, the commentators have generally split into two camps. Some agree with the characterization of Herman Schwartz, who, while conceding that the Court's record was not entirely consistent in ideological terms, nonetheless describes the overall tenor of Burger-era jurisprudence as generally conservative. Others echo the sentiments of Francis Graham Lee, who characterizes the Burger Court as a centrist institution, "neither conservative nor liberal."[1]

Even those who share Lee's general view typically underestimate the extent of Nixon's failure. Far from being a conservative or centrist institution, on constitutional issues the Burger Court can plausibly be seen as having produced the most liberal jurisprudence in history—even more liberal than that generated by its predecessor. While not going as far as liberals might have hoped, the Burger Court advanced well beyond Warren Court jurisprudence on a variety of issues identified with liberal politics. Further, while cutting back at the margins, the Burger Court refused to overrule the core principles underlying Warren Court jurisprudence dealing with issues such as reapportionment and the Fourth and Fifth Amendments. However, given the makeup of the Court, what is perhaps most surprising is that its activism was almost *entirely* liberal-oriented; although there were a few notable exceptions, decisions invoking conservative values

---

1. Herman Schwartz, in *The Burger Years: Rights and Wrongs in the Supreme Court, 1969–1986*, ed. Herman Schwartz (New York: Penguin Books, 1987); Francis Graham Lee, *Neither Conservative nor Liberal: The Burger Court on Civil Rights and Liberties* (Malabar, Fla.: Robert E. Krieger, 1983).

to strike down liberal initiatives from other branches of government were extremely rare during the Burger era.

One explanation for this phenomenon is suggested by the work of commentators such as Ronald Kahn and Lee Epstein and Joseph F. Kobylka, who view the evolution of Burger Court jurisprudence as primarily the function of the application of distinctively legal principles. Kahn, for example, argues that, rather than ordinary policy judgments, "precedent, polity and rights principles, constitutional theory and the Court decisionmaking process [are the] key mediating factors in the development of the law." Kahn is no doubt correct in observing that many commentators have understated the significance of autonomous legal concepts in the evolution of constitutional doctrine; at the same time, however, his model also fails to convincingly account for many of the most important developments in late-twentieth-century constitutional law. Admittedly, distinctively legal reasoning dominated the Burger Court's treatment of some constitutional issues, particularly those which did not involve disputes over core political beliefs; where such beliefs were implicated, however, other factors were often of at least equal importance in the justices' analyses and conclusions.[2]

Of course, even in these cases, all of the justices of the Burger Court (with the possible exception of Justice Douglas) no doubt *believed* that they were consistently applying distinctively legal principles, rather than simply implementing their policy preferences. Moreover, some justices at times actually based their decisions on autonomous legal concepts; one can, for example, easily identify examples of Burger Court decisions that were influenced by the doctrine of stare decisis. However, the basic patterns of division among the justices on politically sensitive issues is flatly inconsistent with Kahn's argument.

If Kahn's theory was correct—that is, if ordinary political considerations were not a major determinant of constitutional decision making—then one would not expect there to be a correlation between the positions taken by the justices and their basic political orientations. As Harold Spaeth and Stuart H. Teger have convincingly demonstrated, even the most cursory review of the record of the Burger Court belies this conclusion. In cases which implicated the core issues dividing liberals and conservatives in the late twentieth century, the most committed conservatives on the Court—the chief justice himself and William H. Rehnquist—were also the most likely to oppose the liberal position. The records of the justices who most clearly embraced the liberal ideology—William O. Douglas, William Brennan, and Thurgood Marshall—are even more striking. While vociferously extolling the virtues of

2. Ronald Kahn, *The Supreme Court and Constitutional Theory, 1953–1993* (Lawrence: University Press of Kansas, 1994), 4; Lee Epstein and Joseph F. Kobylka, *The Supreme Court and Legal Change: Abortion and the Death Penalty* (Chapel Hill: University of North Carolina Press, 1992).

judicial activism when it favored liberal positions, they were almost *never* willing to find fundamental conservative positions enshrined in the Constitution. This pattern is hardly consistent with a jurisprudence based on distinctively legal principles.[3]

Faced with the record of the Burger Court and the descriptive inadequacy of a model based on distinctively legal principles, Vincent Blasi and Bernard Schwartz have concluded that the Burger Court's jurisprudence lacked any discernible focus—that it should be described as "rootless" or simply "pragmatic." Such formulations capture some of the flavor of the Burger era. Chief Justice Burger did not preside over a Court whose jurisprudence was defined by one or two schools of legal thought; instead, the Court was composed of nine independent contractors with widely differing political and jurisprudential agendas. Thus, it should not be surprising that the pattern of decisions emerging from the Court reflected the shifting coalitions among these independent contractors rather than a single, easily described intellectual theme. However, to concede that the patterns of decision making are not easily described does not imply that the patterns are nonexistent; instead, it simply suggests that the decisions are the product of the combination of the patterns of decision making of each of the individual justices, patterns which themselves reflect varying combinations of purely political and distinctively legal considerations.[4] This book is designed to give the reader a sense of the way in which the legal and political philosophies of thirteen quite disparate individuals interacted to produce the jurisprudence of the Burger Court.

---

3. Harold Spaeth and Stuart H. Teger, "Activism and Restraint: A Cloak for the Justices' Policy Preferences," in *Supreme Court Activism and Restraint,* ed. Stephen C. Halpern and Charles M. Lamb (Lexington, Mass.: D. C. Heath and Company, 1982). To the same effect, see Jeffrey A. Segal and Harold J. Spaeth, *The Supreme Court and the Attitudinal Model* (New York: Cambridge University Press, 1992).
4. Vincent Blasi, "The Rootless Activism of the Burger Court," in *The Burger Court: The Counter-Revolution That Wasn't,* ed. Vincent Blasi (New Haven, Conn.: Yale University Press, 1983); Bernard Schwartz, *The Ascent of Pragmatism: The Burger Court in Action* (New York: Addison-Wesley, 1990).

1

THE MOSAIC OF THE BURGER COURT

The seeds of the chief justiceship of Warren Burger were planted long before Burger's appointment, in the constitutional revolution of 1937. For roughly the first third of the twentieth century, the Supreme Court had been a bastion of conservatism, interposing the Constitution as a barrier to economic regulation by both the federal and state governments. The Court's attitude was epitomized by the decision in *Lochner v. New York*,[1] in which the Court struck down a New York law limiting the number of hours which bakers might work.

The Court's activism during the *Lochner* era drew criticism from a number of different quarters. Some of the criticism was couched in overtly ideological terms. For example, the American Federation of Labor asserted that "[w]hat confronts the workers of America . . . is . . . a series of adjudications of the highest tribunal of the land, successively destroying a basic right or cherished acquisition of organized labor, each forming a link in a fateful chain consciously designed to enslave the workers of America."[2]

More often, however, the critics of the Court during the *Lochner* era relied on institutional arguments. They contended that the Court was going beyond the proper bounds of the judicial function and usurping the powers of the legislature. The most famous of these institutional attacks was the dissent of Justice Oliver Wendell Holmes in *Lochner* itself:

This case is decided upon an economic theory which a large part of the country does not entertain. If it were a question whether I agreed with that theory, I should desire to study it further and long before making up my mind. But I do not conceive that to be my duty, because I strongly believe that my agreement or disagreement has nothing to do with the right of a majority to embody their opinions in law. . . . Some [economic

---

1. *Lochner v. New York*, 198 U.S. 45 (1905).
2. American Federation of Labor, Proceedings, 371, 372 (1922), quoted in Charles G. Haines, *The American Doctrine of Judicial Supremacy* (New York: Macmillan,1932), 450.

regulations] embody convictions or prejudices which judges are likely to share. Some may not. But a Constitution is not intended to embody a particular economic theory, whether of paternalism and the organic relation of the citizen to the state or of *laissez faire*. It is made for people of fundamentally differing views, and the accident of our finding certain opinions natural and familiar, or novel, and even shocking, ought not to conclude our judgment upon whether statutes embodying them conflict with the Constitution of the United States.[3]

The attacks on the Court's approach escalated sharply with the advent of the Great Depression and the election of Franklin Delano Roosevelt to the presidency.[4] Congress adopted a series of Roosevelt-inspired initiatives— the New Deal—which dramatically increased the role of the federal government in regulating the economy. The Supreme Court struck down a number of these initiatives.[5] Not surprisingly, Roosevelt and his adherents responded with strong criticisms of the Court, couched in both ideological and institutional terms.

The efforts of those who had opposed the jurisprudence of *Lochner* came to fruition in 1937. Abandoning the earlier positions of the Court, a majority of the justices began to consistently reject constitutional challenges to economic regulations adopted by both the state and federal legislatures.[6] Within five years the victory of the liberal forces was consolidated, as Roosevelt appointed a number of justices who were both ideologically committed to the New Deal and vigorously opposed to the judicial activism of the *Lochner* era.

While the 1937 revolution was largely a product of ideologically based objections to judicial intervention in support of conservative policies, institutional considerations drove the post-1937 Court to condemn liberal as well as conservative activism.[7] The vast majority of judges, lawyers, and law professors of that era had a strong ideological commitment to the concept of "neutral principles" or some variation thereof the idea that judicial decision making should be based on some principle or set of principles that tran-

---

3. *Lochner v. New York*, 198 U.S. 90 (Holmes, J., dissenting) (emphasis in original). For other examples of institutional criticism of the Court during the *Lochner* era, see Haines, *The American Doctrine of Judicial Supremacy*, chap. 17.

4. Laurence H. Tribe, *American Constitutional Law*, 2d ed. (Mineola, N.Y.: Foundation Press, 1988), 580–81, and sources cited therein.

5. E.g., *Carter v. Carter Coal Co.*, 298 U.S. 238 (1936); *Railroad Retirement Board v. Alton R.R. Co.*, 295 U.S. 330 (1935).

6. E.g., *NLRB v. Jones & Laughlin Steel Co.*, 301 U.S. 1 (1937); *West Coast Hotel v. Parrish*, 300 U.S. 379 (1937).

7. Tribe, *American Constitutional Law*, 582–83.

scends the specific issue presented to the court.[8] A constitutional jurisprudence based on the idea that (for example) the Court should always favor the liberal position would be entirely inconsistent with this ideological viewpoint. By contrast, a principle that the Court should defer generally to legislative judgments has no obvious political bias, and therefore fits comfortably within the basic framework of neutral principles. Moreover, such a principle also had great appeal on a purely institutional level to some who, like Justice Holmes, might not be deeply committed to the liberal political program. Thus it is not surprising that deference became the doctrinal basis for the Court's immediate post-1937 jurisprudence.

An emphasis on the institutional value of deference dominated academic commentary through the 1950s and 1960s.[9] On the Court itself, however, ideological forces began to undermine the commitment to deference. Given the acceptance of judicial review, the Court is inevitably the repository of considerable political power. The decision to defer is in essence a decision not to use that power—to instead allow other governmental actors final decision-making authority. From a purely instrumental perspective, such a decision is only defensible if judicial activism is viewed as likely to provoke an equally effective activist response from those holding opposing ideological views; otherwise, in conventional political terms, judicial activism is costless. Thus, liberal activism was likely to remain in check only so long as one of two related conditions prevailed—either liberals lacked a majority on the Court, or they were restrained by a fear that undue activism would generate a conservative backlash.

The electoral politics of the mid-twentieth century virtually guaranteed the rise of a liberal majority on the Court. From 1932 to 1968, Democrats held the presidency for all but the eight Eisenhower years and thus controlled appointments to the Court. While many of the early Democratic appointments—perhaps most notably Felix Frankfurter—were obviously haunted by the ghost of *Lochner* throughout their careers, as time passed the fear of a revival of conservative activism diminished, and with it one of the important factors restraining the Court. Further, the decision in *Brown v. Board of Education*[10] in 1954 demonstrated to many liberals that judicial activism need not be a negative influence in governmental affairs.

It is therefore not surprising that in the immediate post-*Brown* era, a new style of activism began to emerge on the Court. Ironically, two Eisenhower

---

8. See, for example, R. Kent Greenawalt, "The Enduring Significance of Neutral Principles," *Columbia Law Review* 78 (1978): 982–1021; Herbert Wechsler, "Toward Neutral Principles of Constitutional Law," *Harvard Law Review* 73 (1959): 1–35.

9. See, for example, Alexander M. Bickel, *The Least Dangerous Branch: The Supreme Court at the Bar of Politics* (Indianapolis: Bobbs and Merrill, 1962); Wechsler, "Toward Neutral Principles."

10. *Brown v. Board of Education*, 347 U.S. 483 (1954).

appointees—Earl Warren and William J. Brennan—became long-term pillars of liberal activism. From the mid 1950s onward they often joined with William O. Douglas, who had abandoned his early restrained posture to become the leading exponent of liberal activism on the Court, and Hugo Black, whose unswerving commitment to the imposition of the Bill of Rights on state action and absolutist view of the First Amendment often led him into the liberal camp. These four were often able to garner one or more additional votes, and thus were successful in constitutionalizing values associated with liberal ideology. With the appointment of Arthur Goldberg in 1962 a solidly liberal, activist majority was complete and remained intact through most of the 1960s. This majority was further strengthened by the addition of Thurgood Marshall to the Court in 1966. The result was that in the mid and late 1960s, a majority of the Court found increasingly often that liberal values were guaranteed by the Constitution on a wide variety of issues ranging from criminal procedure to voting rights and the right to use contraceptives.

The political tide began to turn against liberal activism in 1968. During his presidential campaign, Republican Richard M. Nixon strongly denounced the Court's approach to constitutional adjudication, focusing particularly on criminal-procedure issues. He did not, however, pledge to appoint justices committed to actively advancing conservative values; instead, he advocated "judicial conservatism"—a constitutional jurisprudence of restraint, which he associated with fidelity to the original understanding of the framers of the Constitution.[11]

This strategy was influenced by a variety of different factors. First, by emphasizing the institutional importance of restraint rather than the need for the advancement of conservative values, Nixon and his conservative allies could accuse their adversaries of politicizing the Court—a charge that had a strong emotive impact and drew substantial support from the dominant academics of the day. Further, in 1968, a conservative activism seemed unthinkable; fifteen years of Warren Court jurisprudence had created the strong impression that activism would inevitably be associated with liberal values. Finally, advocacy of conservative activism would have opened Nixon to the charge that he was urging a return to the *Lochner* era. Thus, in political context, Nixon's advocacy of judicial restraint had many advantages and few apparent drawbacks.

At the same time, Nixon's avowed constitutional theory was anathema to Earl Warren. Fearing a Nixon victory, Warren resigned well in advance of the election in order to allow President Lyndon Baines Johnson the opportunity to appoint his successor. Johnson nominated Associate Justice Abe Fortas—a close political associate who was one of the most liberal members of the Warren Court.

---

11. *New York Times*, May 22, 1969, p. 46, col. 1; May 23, 1969, p. 26, col. 4, p. 27, col. 2.

The Fortas nomination proved to be a disaster for those who supported the Warren Court approach to constitutional adjudication. Conservative opponents attacked not only Fortas's record on the Court but also improprieties in his personal and professional conduct. These factors combined to generate a successful filibuster that killed the nomination in the Senate. The charges against Fortas soon forced him to resign his seat as associate justice; thus, his nomination to be chief justice ultimately cost liberal activists two seats on the Court.

Given this context, the election of 1968 was crucial to the future direction of the Court. The Democratic candidate was Vice President Hubert H. Humphrey, who was leading a party that had been torn apart by controversy over the Vietnam War. Nixon won a narrow victory over Humphrey and gained the opportunity to immediately appoint a new chief justice and, ultimately, to substantially reshape the overall composition of the Court.

In this regard, the first order of business was, of course, to appoint a chief justice to replace Warren. Not surprisingly, a number of names were rumored to be under strong consideration. Among them were Chester Rhyne, a close personal friend of the president and a former leader of the American Bar Association; John Mitchell, Nixon's attorney general and most influential advisor; Thomas Dewey, former governor of New York and the Republican presidential nominee in 1948; Associate Justice Potter Stewart; and Herbert Brownell, who had served as attorney general under Dwight D. Eisenhower. According to Nixon, Rhyne and Mitchell were rejected because it was felt that, in the wake of the Fortas affair, the nominee should be free from the charge of cronyism. Dewey, Stewart, and Brownell all eliminated themselves from consideration—Dewey because of his advanced age, Stewart because he felt that it was unwise to elevate a sitting justice, and Brownell because he felt that some of his actions as attorney general would be used against him in the confirmation process.

Against this background, the choice of Warren Earl Burger to be chief justice was no great surprise to Washington insiders.[12] Burger was a classic American success story—a self-made man who rose to the pinnacle of his chosen profession. He was born to working-class parents on September 17, 1907. In high school Burger was something of a Renaissance man—a solid student, president of the student council, editor of the school newspaper, and four-sport letterman. While he was offered a scholarship to Princeton, it was not large enough to defray the costs of his college education. Thus,

12. Leon Friedman, "Warren E. Burger," in *The Justices of the Supreme Court: Their Lives and Major Opinions,* ed. Leon Friedman and Fred L. Israel (New York: Chelsea House Publishers, 1997), 5: 1465–96, provides detailed biographical information on Burger.

upon graduation, Burger took a job as an insurance salesman. For the next six years he attended college and law school at night, graduating magna cum laude in 1931 from St. Paul College of Law. He then joined the St. Paul law firm of Boyesen, Otis, and Farley, becoming a partner in five years on the basis of a substantial practice in corporate, trust, real estate, and probate law.

Burger soon became active in Republican politics, playing an important role in the successful gubernatorial campaign of Harold E. Stassen in 1948, as well as Stassen's unsuccessful presidential campaigns in 1948 and 1952. The 1952 convention was a turning point in Burger's career; there he won the admiration of Herbert Brownell, Eisenhower's campaign manager. Burger impressed Brownell with his advocacy in the dispute over delegate credentials, and also played a crucial role in delivering the Stassen delegation to the Eisenhower forces. After Brownell became attorney general, he brought Burger to Washington to take charge of what was to become the Civil Division of the Justice Department.

The most widely noted case that Burger handled in this role involved John F. Peters, a professor of medicine at Yale University who was discharged as a federal health consultant on loyalty grounds in 1953. Although the case was ultimately decided by the Supreme Court on other grounds, the central issue in the case was whether an employee who was denied a security clearance had the right to confront his accusers. Burger unsuccessfully argued the government's case before the Court after Solicitor General Simon E. Sobeloff refused to sign the Justice Department brief because he found the defense of "faceless accusers" personally unpalatable.

Burger was preparing to return to private practice when he was offered a position on the United States Court of Appeals for the District of Columbia Circuit in 1955. After hesitating, Burger accepted the nomination. Confirmation was delayed for nearly a year, as the Senate Judiciary Committee investigated charges of discrimination by three Civil Division employees. However, Burger was ultimately confirmed and was sworn in on April 13, 1956.

As a member of the court of appeals, Burger became a leading voice for conservative positions on a generally liberal court—particularly on matters relating to criminal procedure. Burger's opinions and speeches criticizing the expansion of the insanity defense, the *Mallory* and *Miranda* rules on confessions, and the Fourth Amendment exclusionary rule earned him the respect of more conservative members of Congress and often found their way into the *Congressional Record*. Thus, while he did not have a national reputation among the public at large, his positions were well known in government circles. Given Nixon's avowed determination to advance "law and order" by reversing the trend of liberal criminal-procedure opinions from the Supreme Court, Warren Burger became a logical choice for elevation to the chief justiceship.

The confirmation process presented no real difficulties for Burger. Conservatives were quite pleased with the nomination; liberals, by contrast, were demoralized by the Fortas affair and not disposed to attack a nominee whose only apparent vice was that he was relatively conservative. Thus Burger was confirmed by the Senate with only three dissenting votes and sworn in as the fourteenth chief justice of the United States on June 23, 1969. Burger served as chief justice until September 26, 1986, when he left the Court to oversee the celebration of the Bicentennial of the Constitution.

As one contemporary noted, Burger looked, acted, and sounded like a chief justice. He was a handsome, heavyset man with a dignified carriage; his most striking feature was a mane of flowing white hair. Even his voice—a deep baritone—fit the standard image of his office. In short, if his abilities had matched his appearance, Warren Burger would surely be remembered as one of the greatest of all chief justices.

Indeed, if one considered only the energy and skill with which he performed his administrative duties, this assessment might well be warranted. Burger did much to improve the physical conditions under which the justices worked, making improvements ranging from the introduction of copying machines to the redesign of the bench at which the justices sat to hear oral argument. No detail was too small for his attention; he even helped choose new glassware and china for the cafeteria.

Moreover, his administrative contributions went well beyond a simple concern for the proper operation of the Supreme Court itself. From the beginning of his term, Burger saw himself not only as the leader of the Court, but also as the titular head of the legal profession as a whole. He often spoke out on the need for lawyers to maintain the standards and dignity of the profession, focusing among other things on the desirability of maintaining civility in the judicial process. Early in his term, he created a furor by asserting that as many as half of the trial lawyers in the country were not competent to try cases, and suggesting that it might be desirable to require lawyers to be certified as litigators before appearing in court. Concomitant to this suggestion, he emphasized the need for better training of litigators, comparing the American system unfavorably to the English Inns of Court, where inexperienced barristers received training and advice from both judges and more experienced practitioners.[13]

Burger also put great effort into the administrative duties of the chief justiceship. He was a tireless campaigner on behalf of the federal judiciary, pressing hard for increased salary and pension benefits for federal judges and more support services for the federal courts, including additional manpower such as circuit executives and additional clerks and staff attorneys.

13. *New York Times*, November 27, 1973, p. 1.

Burger was also instrumental in the expansion of the Federal Judicial Center, which provides needed logistical support for the entire system; the establishment of the Institute for Court Management to train court managers; and the National Center for State Courts, a clearinghouse and information center for state judges. Well aware of the importance of maintaining good relations with Congress, Burger also established the Legislative Affairs Office of the Administrative Office of the United States Courts to systematically work with Congress and present the position of the Judicial Conference on legislation in which the judiciary had an interest. Burger also participated actively in shaping legislation that limited the jurisdiction of three-judge courts, split the old Fifth Circuit into two different circuits (the Fifth and the Eleventh), and established the Federal Circuit to hear a variety of specialized litigation.

In sharp contrast to these successes, Burger failed in his efforts to gain implementation of the most dramatic judicial reform that he favored. Disturbed by what he saw as the Supreme Court's increasingly unmanageable workload, he proposed the creation of a national court of appeals, to be staffed on a rotating basis by appeals court judges from the various circuits. Burger's concept was that this new court would handle the more mundane splits between the circuits, expanding the capacity of the federal judiciary to establish uniform rules of federal law while at the same time reserving the energies of the Supreme Court itself for the resolution of more significant issues. While the proposal was much discussed at the time and was supported by the American Bar Association, the idea never gained the kind of widespread support necessary for the implementation of such a dramatic alteration in the structure of the federal judicial system; indeed, some even argued that the creation of a national court of appeals separate from the Supreme Court was unconstitutional. Thus, Burger's most important policy initiative came to naught.

Nonetheless, it is difficult to fault Burger's overall record as an administrator; indeed, in this respect, one commentator rates Burger as the most efficient chief justice since Taft.[14] However, the historical reputation of chief justices typically does not rest primarily on their administrative accomplishments; instead, they are evaluated almost exclusively on their impact on American jurisprudence. Viewed from this perspective, Burger will clearly not be remembered as one of the most important or distinguished chief justices of the United States. Indeed, he was not even a central figure in the development of the law during his tenure as chief justice. Burger's views on a particular issue were rarely decisive; instead, he was a necessary but not sufficient member of any conservative majority. Moreover, Burger lacked the

---

14. Friedman, "Warren E. Burger," in *The Justices of the Supreme Court,* ed. Friedman and Israel, 1492.

mental capacity and rhetorical skill to adequately elaborate and defend an alternative approach to Warren Court activism; indeed, his efforts to assert intellectual leadership over the Court often degenerated into fiascoes. Thus, during Burger's tenure as chief justice, the task of articulating a plausible theory of conservative jurisprudence fell largely to William H. Rehnquist. In short, from a purely jurisprudential perspective, the Burger era bears its name only because he held the formal title of chief justice.[15]

Nonetheless, some of the criticisms that commentators have aimed at Burger have been overstated. As a leader, Burger is often compared unfavorably with his predecessor Earl Warren. Critics suggest that Burger's shortcomings as chief justice were largely responsible for lack of cohesion on the Court and its failure to produce majority opinions in many important cases. These critics often underestimate the complexity of the situation that Burger faced.

Admittedly, Burger's personal characteristics probably exacerbated the divisions among the justices. Despite his formal manner, he was by all accounts warm and generous on a purely interpersonal level. Nonetheless, Burger was an ineffective leader of the weekly conferences at which the Court's tentative decisions were made. In addition, he was overly concerned with the prerogatives of his office and at times could be heavy-handed in exercising those prerogatives.

Burger's appropriation of the Court's conference room typifies this problem. Initially, Burger determined that his own office was too small to adequately entertain visiting dignitaries on ceremonial occasions, and that the much grander conference room was far more suitable. Without consulting the other justices, he simply arranged to have a desk moved into the conference room and used that room to receive guests. Trivial incidents such as this annoyed a number of the other justices.

However, even a more able leader would have had great difficulty in uniting the Burger Court. Burger was forced to deal with a highly diverse Court, whose justices had opinions spanning every aspect of the American political and jurisprudential mainstream. During Burger's tenure, no particular viewpoint could command a consistent majority. The Warren Court, by contrast, had a clear liberal majority and lacked a true conservative voice; Potter Stewart, who with John Marshall Harlan marked the conservative extreme of the Warren Court, is generally viewed as a centrist figure on the Burger Court. Moreover, outside the area of school desegregation, Warren's vaunted persuasive powers were often insufficient to persuade even these centrists to join the Warren Court's activist forays. There is no good reason

---

15. A number of different aspects of Burger's jurisprudence are discussed in detail in "Symposium: The Jurisprudence of Warren Burger," *Oklahoma Law Review* 45 (1992): 1–168.

to believe that he would have been any more successful in persuading justices such as William Rehnquist and Sandra Day O'Connor to support his agenda. Conversely, Warren Burger can hardly be faulted for not finding common ground between these justices and men such as William Brennan and Thurgood Marshall. Against this background, it should not be surprising that the patterns of Burger Court decision making are more complex than those of the Warren Court and can only be understood by focusing on the individuals involved in the decision-making process.

THE WARREN COURT HOLDOVERS

Throughout the Burger era, members of the Warren Court continued to serve on the Supreme Court. Three of these justices—Abe Fortas, Hugo L. Black, and John Marshall Harlan—served only a short time under Burger. Five others, however—William O. Douglas, William J. Brennan, Jr., Thurgood Marshall, Potter Stewart, and Byron White—participated in a substantial number of the Burger Court decisions. Douglas, Brennan, and Marshall had been consistent supporters of Warren Court activism; by contrast, while sometimes taking activist positions during the Warren era, Stewart and White also at times criticized what they viewed as undue judicial interference with the prerogatives of other governmental actors.

The Liberal Activists

William Orville Douglas. William Orville Douglas was born on October 16, 1898, in Maine, Minnesota.[16] The work of his father, a missionary for the Presbyterian Church, brought the family to a town fifty miles from Yakima, Washington, in 1904. Douglas's father died in that year, and he moved with his mother to Yakima, where he spent a poverty-stricken childhood.

In 1916 Douglas entered Walla Walla College, graduating in 1920 after a brief interruption for military service in World War I. Hoping to save enough money to attend law school, Douglas worked as a schoolteacher in 1920 and 1921; however, realizing that a schoolteacher's salary would never provide sufficient funds, Douglas set off for Columbia Law School in September 1922. He crossed the country on freight trains, sometimes working, sometimes hitch-

---

16. A detailed account of Douglas's life and career is provided by his two-volume autobiography, William O. Douglas, *Go East Young Man: The Early Years* (New York: Random House, 1974), and *The Court Years, 1939–1975: The Autobiography of William O. Douglas* (New York: Random House, 1980); as well as James F. Simon, *Independent Journey: The Life of William O. Douglas* (New York: Harper & Row, 1980). A number of aspects of his jurisprudence are analyzed in detail in Stephen L. Wasby, ed., *"He Shall Not Pass This Way Again": The Legacy of William O. Douglas* (Pittsburgh: University of Pittsburgh Press, 1990).

hiking. Then, working his way through law school, he graduated second in his class in 1925. After graduation, he worked for two years in a major Wall Street law firm and spent a year in private practice in Yakima before returning to Columbia to teach in 1928. Douglas then moved to Yale, where he taught from 1929 to 1934, specializing in corporate law.

In 1934 Douglas left Yale to work at the newly formed Securities and Exchange Commission, becoming a commission member in 1936 and chairman in 1937. He became a member of the New Deal inner circle, and when Louis D. Brandeis resigned from the Court in 1939, Douglas was a logical choice to succeed him. Ironically, Douglas was named in part because he was viewed as more conservative than his main competition, Senator Lewis Schwellenbach of Washington. Moreover, the only opposition votes to Douglas's confirmation came from four senators who accused him of being a reactionary tool of Wall Street. After his confirmation, despite an offer to run for vice president with Harry Truman in 1948, Douglas served on the Court until ill health forced his resignation in 1975.

Douglas was brilliant but, to say the least, irascible. He was aptly described by one observer who, although generally sympathetic to Douglas's views on constitutional issues, characterized him as "the quintessential loner, a lover of humanity who did not like people," with virtually no regard for the feelings of his professional staff or, for that matter, the other justices. For example, he routinely "fired" for incompetence the recent law school graduates who served as his law clerks only to "rehire" them shortly thereafter.[17]

Even during the Warren era, Douglas was the most liberal member of the Court. Until his retirement, he occupied the same ideological niche on the Burger Court. Despite Douglas's undoubted talents as a legal analyst, many of his Burger-era opinions have an offhand, unfinished quality, displaying an almost open contempt for the niceties of doctrine.

William J. Brennan, Jr. On both the Warren and Burger Courts, William Joseph Brennan, Jr., played a different role than Douglas. Brennan was born on June 8, 1906, in Newark, New Jersey.[18] His father was a respected labor leader who was also active in city government. Brennan was an outstanding student, both in high school and at the University of Pennsylvania's Wharton School of Finance. In 1931 he graduated in the top 10 percent of his

---

17. Bernard Schwartz, *Swann's Way: The School Busing Case and the Supreme Court* (New York: Oxford University Press, 1986), 35.

18. Hunter C. Clark, *Mr. Justice Brennan, The Great Conciliator* (New York: Birch Lane Press, 1995), provides a detailed account of Brennan's life. Different aspects of his jurisprudence are described in Frank I. Michelman, "Super Liberal: Romance, Community, and Tradition in William J. Brennan, Jr.'s, Constitutional Thought," *Virginia Law Review* 77 (1991): 1261–332, and in "Justice Brennan: Foundation for the Future," *Pace Law Review* 11 (1991): 455–533.

class from Harvard Law School. The same year he joined an established Newark law firm, specializing in labor law.

After being an important figure in a successful drive for constitutional reform of the state courts, Brennan was appointed a state trial court judge in 1949. He was elevated to the state supreme court three years later. When Sherman Minton retired in 1956, President Eisenhower's political advisors saw an opportunity to reach out to the Catholic and labor voters of the Northeast in the upcoming presidential election. Brennan was the perfect choice to advance this political agenda.

On the Warren Court, Brennan was the legal technician who would often be called upon to fashion the doctrinal arguments necessary to attract and hold together liberal majorities. He was well suited, both intellectually and temperamentally, to perform this function. Brennan's gifts for analysis were complemented by a warm, vibrant personality and a willingness to compromise in order to reach his prime objective. However, the changes in the ideological composition of the Court worked against Brennan during the Burger era; thus, despite some notable successes, Brennan was often in the minority in cases where the Court was closely divided.

Thurgood Marshall. Even if he had never been appointed to the Supreme Court, Thurgood Marshall would have been one of the most important figures in twentieth-century legal history. Born Thorougood Marshall on July 2, 1908, Marshall was raised in a middle-class household in Baltimore, Maryland.[19] Throughout his early life, he attended segregated, all-black schools, graduating from Lincoln University and Howard University Law School, where he was a student of Dean Charles H. Houston. After graduation, Marshall first practiced law as a solo practitioner in Baltimore; however, after Houston established the NAACP Legal Defense Fund in 1933, he chose Marshall to head the organization in 1936. For the next twenty-five years Marshall was involved in much of the major civil rights litigation in the country, arguing *Brown v. Board of Education* before the Supreme Court in 1953 and 1954. John F. Kennedy named Marshall to the United States Court of Appeals for the Second Circuit in 1961. Marshall left the court of appeals in 1965 to become solicitor general of the United States under Lyndon Johnson; in 1967 Johnson appointed Marshall to be the first African American to serve on the Supreme Court. Despite opposition from some southern senators, Marshall was confirmed easily.

---

19. Marshall's life is chronicled in Michael D. Davis and Hunter R. Clark, *Thurgood Marshall, Warrior at the Bar, Rebel on the Bench* (New York: Birch Lane Press, 1992). His performance on the Court is discussed in detail in Mark V. Tushnet, *Making Constitutional Law: Thurgood Marshall and the Supreme Court, 1961–1991* (New York: Oxford University Press, 1997).

A large, plainspoken man with a gift for storytelling, Marshall was better suited to be a litigator than a justice. He had little interest in many of the technical issues of law that form a large part of the Supreme Court's docket, and often followed Brennan's lead in these cases. Further, more than any other justice, Marshall relied on his clerks for the actual mechanics of opinion writing. As one might expect, the major exception was in cases involving race-related issues; there, Marshall's published views resonate with the emotive force generated by his years of struggle in the civil rights movement. As such, they were an important complement to Brennan's more traditional legal rhetoric.

Other Warren Court Holdovers

Potter Stewart. Although each would be characterized as a swing justice on both the Warren and Burger Courts, Potter Stewart and Byron White differed substantially from one another in personal background, as well as jurisprudential philosophy. Stewart was born on January 23, 1915, the son of a politically active father who served as Republican mayor of Cincinnati and later on the Ohio Supreme Court.[20] He was educated in private schools and received his undergraduate degree from Yale University. Following a year of postgraduate study at Cambridge, Stewart returned to Yale for law school, graduating in 1941.

After a short stint at a Wall Street law firm, Stewart entered the navy after World War II broke out, serving as a deck officer on oil tankers in the Atlantic Ocean and Mediterranean Sea. Soon after the war ended, Stewart joined one of the leading law firms in his native Cincinnati. There he also entered politics and was a member of the city council when Eisenhower appointed him to the United States Court of Appeals for the Sixth Circuit in 1954. When Harold Burton retired from the Court in 1958, Stewart was a logical choice to fill his seat. He was nominated and confirmed without incident.

The friendly, witty Stewart was a competent craftsman, but not an innovator. When asked to characterize himself as either a liberal or a conservative, he replied simply, "I am a lawyer . . . and I find it impossible to know what [those terms] mean when they are carried over to judicial work." Stewart is perhaps best remembered for writing that, while he could not define

---

20. A detailed biographical sketch is provided in "Potter Stewart," in *The Justices of the Supreme Court,* ed. Friedman and Israel, 5: 1546–73. His jurisprudence is discussed in Gayle Binion, "Justice Potter Stewart: The Unpredictable Vote," *Journal of Supreme Court History* (1992): 99–108; and Ethel S. White, "The Protection of the Individual and the Free Exchange of Ideas: Justice Potter Stewart's Role in First and Fourth Amendment Cases," *University of Cincinnati Law Review* 54 (1985): 87–128.

hard-core pornography, "I know it when I see it." During the early Burger years, he could clearly be classified as a moderate conservative, closely allied with Lewis Powell. Beginning with the 1976 term, however, he moved discernibly leftward. Thus, by the time of his retirement after the 1980 term, Stewart was more accurately described as a centrist on the Court.[21]

Byron White. Even before his nomination to the Supreme Court, Byron White was well-known to much of the American public for reasons entirely unrelated to law or politics. He was born in Fort Collins, Colorado, on June 8, 1917, and grew up in Wellington, a small, impoverished northern Colorado agricultural community.[22] At the University of Colorado, "Whizzer" White was both an outstanding football player and valedictorian of the class of 1938. Before beginning his term as a Rhodes scholar at Oxford, White played one year for the Pittsburgh Steelers of the National Football League, leading the league in rushing yards. After spending nine months at Oxford, he enrolled in Yale Law School in September 1939, earning the highest academic average in his first-year class. He temporarily left Yale after his first year, playing professional football with the Detroit Lions until he was drafted after the attack on Pearl Harbor. White served throughout World War II as a lieutenant in Naval Intelligence in the South Pacific. There White renewed his acquaintance with John F. Kennedy, whom White had first met while both were in England.

After the end of the war, White returned to Yale Law School, graduating magna cum laude in 1946. After serving a year as a law clerk with Chief Justice Fred M. Vinson, White entered private practice in Denver. Beginning in 1959, he was extremely active in the Kennedy presidential campaign, impressing Robert Kennedy with his organizational abilities. After the election of John F. Kennedy, Robert Kennedy was appointed attorney general, and (at Robert's request) White was made deputy attorney general. In that position White was charged with evaluating the professional qualifications, experience, and fitness of candidates for judicial appointments. When Charles Whittaker retired the attorney general recommended that White be chosen to take his seat, and President Kennedy accepted the recommendation and appointed White. Less than two weeks later, he was confirmed without incident.

While he could be extremely charming in a purely social context, in conference White was intense, combative, and at times gruff to the point of

---

21. Bernard Schwartz, *The Ascent of Pragmatism*, 22–23; *Jacobellis v. Ohio*, 378 U.S. 184, 197 (1964).

22. White's life and jurisprudence are chronicled in Dennis J. Hutchinson, *The Man Who Once Was Whizzer White: A Portrait of Justice Byron R. White* (New York: Free Press, 1998). A detailed biographical sketch is provided in Friedman and Israel eds., *The Justices of the Supreme Court*, 5: 1574–1606. White's jurisprudence is examined in "Justice Byron R. White Tribute," *Brigham Young University Law Review* (1994): 206–368.

rudeness. Throughout his career on the Court, his opinions were generally terse and to the point. White also showed a greater respect for distinctively legal institutional concerns than many of the justices on the Burger Court. During the Burger era, he was a staunch nationalist who often adopted the liberal-activist position on race-related issues. However, on other issues, he more often supported the Court's conservatives—a tendency which became increasingly apparent during the late Burger era as his voting pattern moved ever closer to that of the chief justice and Justices Rehnquist and O'Connor.

The Nixon Appointees

In addition to Chief Justice Burger, Richard Nixon had the opportunity to appoint three associate justices to the Burger Court. Each played a quite different role in the dynamic that produced Burger Court jurisprudence.

Harry A. Blackmun. After the resignation of Abe Fortas, Richard Nixon consciously sought to replace him with a nominee from a southern state. His first choice—Clement Haynsworth of South Carolina—was a distinguished member of the United States Court of Appeals for the Fourth Circuit. Liberal members of the Senate, however, used the Haynsworth nomination as an opportunity to exact revenge for the defeat of Fortas. They painted Haynsworth as an enemy of civil rights and organized labor, and exaggerated minor incidents in an effort to demonstrate that Haynsworth lacked the requisite integrity for service on the Court. This campaign was successful, and Haynsworth was denied confirmation.

After the Haynsworth defeat, Nixon nominated G. Harrold Carswell of Georgia from the United States Court of Appeals for the Fifth Circuit. The basic problem with the Carswell nomination was not ideology or integrity, but rather competence; the high point of the debate over his nomination was the declaration by one supporter that mediocre people deserved representation on the Supreme Court. Against this background, Nixon's nominee was once again denied confirmation.

Publicly despairing of having a southerner confirmed to the Court, Nixon turned to Harry Andrew Blackmun. [23] Blackmun was a childhood friend of Chief Justice Burger and served as best man at his wedding. Born in Nashville, Illinois, on November 12, 1908, Blackmun grew up in a working-class neighborhood of St. Paul, Minnesota. He attended college and law

---

23. A detailed account of Blackmun's life and career can be found in Friedman and Israel, eds. *The Justices of the Supreme Court*, 5: 1607–28. A number of different aspects of his jurisprudence are examined in "Dedication to Justice Harry A. Blackmun," *Hamline Law Review* 8 (1985): 29–151.

school at Harvard, graduating from the law school in 1932. Joining a prominent Minneapolis law firm, he specialized in tax and estate planning until joining the Mayo Clinic as general counsel in 1950. In 1959 President Dwight D. Eisenhower appointed Blackmun to the United States Court of Appeals for the Eighth Circuit, where he served until his appointment to the Supreme Court.

In the wake of the protracted struggle over Haynsworth and Carswell, the quiet, mild-mannered Blackmun seemed to be a godsend. Generally perceived to be a moderate conservative, he was described by one popular news publication as "a judicial superblend of intelligence, industry, fairness, excellence and probity." Even the executive director of the liberal American Civil Liberties Union praised Blackmun effusively, declaring that the nominee possessed "a capacity for objectivity and fairness in the highest degree, combined with a high intellect and sharply-honed legal mind." Against this background, it should not be surprising that Blackmun was quickly and unanimously confirmed by the Senate.[24]

Unfortunately, Blackmun's performance did not vindicate the high expectations surrounding his appointment. He is normally described by such terms as diligent, hardworking, and dedicated. At the same time, however, he was also excruciatingly slow in producing opinions. Moreover, his arguments generally lack rhetorical power and in many cases fail to adequately come to grips with fundamental considerations presented by the cases before the Court. Thus, Blackmun's opinions often lack persuasive force.

Blackmun is no doubt most famous for his opinion for the Court in *Roe v. Wade,* which struck down all existing state abortion laws.[25] The opinion exemplifies Blackmun's work product. It is best described as ponderous—a fifty-page exegesis that is a veritable gold mine of information on the historical and moral dimensions of the abortion question. But its treatment of the legal issues is conclusory and generally unsatisfying, even to most of those who agree that the right to choose an abortion should be constitutionally protected. In the words of one commentator, "[A]s a matter of simple craft [the opinion in *Roe* was] dreadful."[26]

Whatever his ultimate place in the pantheon of jurists, Blackmun clearly played a key role in the evolution of Burger Court jurisprudence. Initially, he was firmly ensconced in the conservative camp; indeed, he and Burger were often referred to as the "Minnesota Twins," after their

---

24. *Newsweek,* April 27, 1970, 28; *U.S. News and World Report,* April 27, 1970, 22.

25. *Roe v. Wade,* 410 U.S. 113 (1973).

26. Mark V. Tushnet, "Following the Rules Laid Down," *Harvard Law Review* 96 (1984): 820.

local baseball team. However, in the 1977 term he suddenly made a dramatic shift to the center. Another equally dramatic shift in Blackmun's voting pattern took place in 1981, and he became closely aligned with Brennan and Marshall for most of the remainder of the Burger era.

William H. Rehnquist and Lewis F. Powell. In 1971 the Supreme Court lost two of its most distinguished members, Hugo L. Black and John Marshall Harlan. Nixon first considered Virginia congressman Richard Poff. In 1956, however, Poff had signed the Southern Manifesto, which had avowed unalterable opposition to the *Brown* decision. Unwilling to participate in what surely would have been a bruising confirmation battle, Poff withdrew his name from consideration. A number of other possibilities were then floated for public reaction. Senator Richard Byrd of West Virginia fell out of contention for the simple reason that he had never even passed a bar examination, let alone practiced law. The names of both Mildred L. Lillie, a state appeals court judge from California, and Herschel H. Friday, a municipal bond lawyer from Arkansas, were submitted to the American Bar Association (ABA) for its opinion. Lillie, however, was rated unqualified, and the ABA committee split evenly on Friday. Faced with mounting criticism over the quality of his appointments to the Supreme Court, Nixon turned to two men whose professional abilities were beyond question.

William Hobbes Rehnquist was born in 1924 outside of Milwaukee, Wisconsin.[27] After initially attending Kenyon College and serving in the army for three years during World War II, he received his undergraduate degree from Stanford University in 1948. Prior to attending law school, Rehnquist received an M.A. in political science from Stanford in 1949, followed by an M.A. in government from Harvard in 1950. In December 1952 he graduated first in his class from Stanford Law School. Rehnquist then served as a law clerk to Justice Robert Jackson, thereafter entering private practice in Phoenix, Arizona. During his years in Phoenix, Rehnquist was an outspoken, politically active conservative, criticizing the Warren Court for "extreme solicitude for the claims of Communists and other criminal defendants" and at one point opposing open-housing laws as an unjustifiable infringement on private property rights. When Nixon was elected president, he chose Rehnquist to head the Office of Legal Counsel in the Justice Department. In that position Rehnquist often served as the administration's spokesman on controversial legal issues.

---

27. Details of Rehnquist's early life can be found in Donald E. Boles, *Mr. Justice Rehnquist: Judicial Activist* (Ames: Iowa State University Press, 1987), 1–18; and Sue Davis, *Justice Rehnquist and the Constitution* (Princeton: Princeton University Press, 1988), 3–19.

Rehnquist's nomination set off a bitter struggle over confirmation in the Senate. No one questioned his intellectual capacity; however, Senate liberals were disturbed by his record on civil rights. In particular, they focused on two points. The first was a memorandum that Rehnquist had written to Justice Jackson in connection with *Brown v. Board of Education,* which argued that *Plessy v. Ferguson* "was right and should be reaffirmed." The second was Rehnquist's participation in a Republican poll-watching project that challenged voting credentials in predominantly African American and Hispanic neighborhoods in Phoenix. Rehnquist responded that Jackson himself had requested a defense of *Plessy,* and that he had engaged in no wrongdoing during the poll-watching project. Ultimately, Rehnquist was confirmed on a vote of sixty-eight to twenty-six.

Once confirmed, Rehnquist quickly emerged as an able champion of the conservative ideology that developed in reaction to Warren Court activism. Throughout the Burger era, he and the chief justice formed a kind of conservative odd couple. In sharp contrast to Burger's sometimes pompous style, Rehnquist was known for his friendliness, informality, and irreverent sense of humor. More importantly, Rehnquist had all of the intellectual firepower that the chief justice lacked. His opinions reflect a technical mastery of the law and are marked by a forceful writing style which at times employs colorful, emotionally charged imagery to underscore distaste for the positions of his more liberal colleagues. In responding to Brennan, Marshall, and (in the early Burger years) Douglas, he clearly articulated an originalist theory of judicial review, often modified by a preference for judicial restraint.

Lewis Franklin Powell, Jr., was born on September 19, 1907, in a suburb of Norfolk, Virginia.[28] After attending a series of public and private schools, he entered Washington and Lee University in 1925, graduating Phi Beta Kappa and president of his class in 1929. Powell also attended law school at Washington and Lee, completing the curriculum in only two years and graduating first in his class. After spending a year at Harvard, Powell began private practice with a small Richmond firm in 1932. Two years later he joined the most prestigious firm in Richmond as an associate, and he remained with that firm until his appointment to the Court.

Powell had an extremely distinguished career in private practice, serving at various times as president of the American Bar Association, the American College of Trial Lawyers, and the American Bar Foundation, as well as vice president of the National Legal Aid and Defender Society. He was also active

---

28. Powell's life and jurisprudence are explored in detail in John C. Jeffries, Jr., *Justice Lewis F. Powell, Jr.* (New York: Charles Scribner's Sons, 1994).

in local affairs, heading the Richmond Chamber of Commerce, the Family Service Society of Richmond, and, most notably, the Richmond School Board from 1952 to 1961—the tumultuous period immediately preceding and following the decision in *Brown.*

Powell had been Nixon's first choice for the Court after the Clement Haynsworth nomination had been defeated in the Senate; however, Powell had withdrawn his name from consideration at that time. In 1971, however, he agreed to accept a nomination. With Rehnquist drawing the fire of liberal activists, the Senate confirmed Powell with little controversy.

Powell was the quintessential southern aristocrat—soft-spoken, genteel, and polite to a fault. His judicial opinions vary greatly in quality. Powell's greatest strength lay in his ability to clearly articulate general principles—an ability reflected in cases such as *San Antonio Independent School District v. Rodriguez*[29] and *Warth v. Seldin.*[30] However, his efforts to explain the relationship of those principles to specific fact situations often appeared strained, particularly when Powell was attempting to apply the balancing tests that he favored, as in *Memphis Light, Gas, and Water Division v. Craft*[31] and *Moore v. City of East Cleveland.*[32]

However one evaluates Powell as a judicial craftsman, he played an absolutely pivotal role on the Court during the Burger era. Indeed, his jurisprudence largely defined that of the Court as a whole. Powell's importance was not a by-product of either the intellectual power of his arguments or an unusually strong ability to influence his brethren; indeed, there is no evidence that any of the other justices consistently changed his views in response to Powell's arguments. Instead, Powell's impact on the law reflected the simple fact that he was consistently the justice most likely to be in the majority during the Burger era. He was not, however, a true centrist in the sense that he was almost equally likely to favor the positions of the liberals or conservatives; throughout his judicial career, he showed a clear preference for the positions of the chief justice and Justice Rehnquist over those of Justices Brennan and Marshall. Instead, it is more accurate to note that, on most issues, the liberals could almost never form a majority *without* Powell's vote—particularly after the appointment of Sandra Day O'Connor and the rightward turn of Byron White in the late Burger era.

The overall shape of Powell's jurisprudence reflected a confluence

29. *San Antonio Independent School District v. Rodriguez,* 411 U.S. 1 (1973).
30. *Warth v. Seldin,* 422 U.S. 490 (1975).
31. *Memphis Light, Gas, and Water Division v. Craft,* 436 U.S. 1 (1978).
32. *Moore v. City of East Cleveland,* 431 U.S. 494 (1977).

of a variety of personal and professional influences. Before coming to the Court, he was the quintessential establishment lawyer; thus, it should not be surprising that his jurisprudence was modeled on that of Felix Frankfurter and John Marshall Harlan—two of the icons of the mainstream bar during Powell's long career in private practice. Thus, like Frankfurter and Harlan, he distrusted sharp-edged, categorical rules, preferring instead to rely on ad hoc balancing. Conversely, Powell's passionate attachment to federalism and local control reflected the views that one might expect from a privileged white southerner. Other influences were more personal; his service on the local school board both reflected and reinforced a strong belief in the importance of public education, as well as a particularly strong attachment to local control in this area—beliefs which are reflected consistently in his opinions.

The Post-Nixon Appointees

John Paul Stevens. After a long bout with failing health, William O. Douglas resigned from the Supreme Court in 1975. Although Republicans retained the presidency at that time, the political atmosphere was quite different from that which had produced the appointments of Burger, Blackmun, Powell, and Rehnquist. The Watergate scandal had driven Nixon from office, and he had been replaced by Gerald Ford, who in turn had assumed the office of vice president after Spiro B. Agnew had resigned after being indicted for criminal misconduct.

Whatever his personal views on the proper direction of constitutional law, Ford was hardly in a position to do political battle over the nomination of Douglas's replacement. The selection process reflected this reality. Ford made no effort to identify a candidate who would reinforce the conservative wing of the Court; indeed, Solicitor General Robert Bork was apparently eliminated from consideration because he was *too* conservative. Instead, Ford leaned heavily on the judgment of newly appointed attorney general Edward Levi, the former president of the University of Chicago and dean of the University of Chicago Law School. Following instructions from the president, Levi first prepared a list of potential candidates without regard to political considerations. He then methodically whittled down the list until John Paul Stevens emerged as Levi's choice and Ford's ultimate nominee.[33]

---

33. Stevens's career is discussed in detail in Robert J. Sickel, *John Paul Stevens and the Constitution: A Search for Balance* (University Park: Pennsylvania State University Press, 1988). His nomination and confirmation are explored in Victor H. Kramer, "The Case of Justice Stevens: How to Select, Nominate, and Confirm a Justice of the United States Supreme Court," *Constitutional Commentary* 7 (1990): 325–40.

Stevens was born into a prominent family in Chicago, Illinois, on April 20, 1920. He graduated Phi Beta Kappa from the University of Chicago in 1941 and then served as a naval officer in World War II. After the end of the war Stevens attended Northwestern University School of Law, graduating magna cum laude after two years in 1947 with the highest grade-point average in the history of the school.

Beginning in 1948 Stevens was in private practice with a major law firm in Chicago. In 1951 he journeyed to Washington, D.C., to serve as associate counsel to the House Antitrust Subcommittee, where he worked on the subcommittee's Study of Monopoly Power. Returning to private practice in Chicago in 1952, Stevens specialized in antitrust counseling and litigation until Richard Nixon appointed him to the United States Court of Appeals for the Seventh Circuit in 1970. His opinions as an appellate judge earned high marks for intelligence and clarity.

The diminutive Stevens is in some ways the most enigmatic of all the justices who served on the Burger Court. Personally exuberant and outgoing, he was also the Court iconoclast—an iconoclasm symbolized by his decision to appear at oral arguments wearing a bow tie instead of the traditional court garb. During the Burger era, only William Rehnquist could match his ability to turn a phrase; however, unlike Rehnquist's, Stevens's approach to legal analysis defied characterization as either liberal or conservative—particularly in his early years on the Court. Instead, Stevens's approach to constitutional adjudication is best described as idiosyncratic. While Stevens articulated a number of thought-provoking, unusual theories during his tenure, his jurisprudence is perhaps best symbolized by his approach to equal protection analysis. Rather than articulating different levels of scrutiny or a "sliding scale" analysis, Stevens instead declared that there is only one equal protection clause and forthrightly examined government actions for indications of prejudice and distortions of the lawmaking process. At times Stevens would convince his colleagues of the efficacy of his analysis; often, however, he would stand alone in his approach. Thus, he was in the minority far more often than other "centrist" justices such as Potter Stewart, Byron White, Harry Blackmun, and Lewis Powell.

Stevens's independence is perhaps best symbolized by his voting pattern in the 1978 term, in which he was almost equally likely to join seven of his eight colleagues. This pattern soon began to change, however, and from the 1982 term through the end of Burger's tenure as chief justice, Stevens became loosely associated with Justices Brennan and Marshall—a necessary but not sufficient vote in any majority coalition supporting liberal constitutionalism.

Sandra Day O'Connor. When Potter Stewart announced his retirement from the Court in 1981, Ronald Reagan had his first opportunity to appoint a justice to the Court. Reagan was ideologically predisposed to appointing a staunch, pro-life conservative to the Court. At the same time, however, during the presidential campaign Reagan had pledged to appoint a woman to the Court, and he still suffered from a "gender gap" in popularity that the appointment of a woman might ease somewhat.

Reconciling these two conflicting imperatives presented something of a problem for Reagan. Women had not begun entering law schools in large numbers until the early 1970s; thus, in 1981 the pool of women who had the requisite credentials and experience for appointment to the Court was relatively small. From Reagan's perspective, this pool was further reduced because (for obvious reasons) many of the women who had become lawyers prior to 1970 were strong supporters of the feminist movement, and thus politically antithetical to the administration. Faced with this problem, Reagan settled on Sandra Day O'Connor—in the words of one Justice Department official, "the most conservative woman we could find."[34]

O'Connor was born Sandra Day on March 26, 1930, and spent her childhood on a large ranch on the Arizona–New Mexico border.[35] After being educated at a private boarding school, she entered Stanford University at the age of sixteen and completed both her undergraduate and law school education there in only five years. There she compiled an outstanding academic record and graduated in the same law school class as William Rehnquist.

In 1952 no prestigious California law firm would hire women as lawyers; thus, O'Connor's first job was as a deputy county counsel in San Mateo, California. When her husband joined the army's Judge Advocate Corps and spent three years in Germany, O'Connor worked there as a civilian lawyer. In 1957 she settled in Phoenix, Arizona, spending the next eight years as a housewife before becoming an assistant attorney general of the state of Arizona. In 1969 O'Connor was appointed to a vacant seat in the state senate, and in three years she rose to the post of majority leader. She abandoned her seat and was elected a state trial judge in 1974; in 1979 Democratic governor Bruce Babbitt appointed her to the state intermediate appellate court, where she sat until appointed by Reagan to the Supreme Court.

After being confirmed unanimously, O'Connor in general proved an able defender of conservative jurisprudence. Known for her personal toughness and somewhat forbidding demeanor, she became William Rehnquist's

---

34. David G. Savage, *Turning Right: The Making of the Rehnquist Court* (New York: John Wiley & Sons, 1992), 114.

35. Nancy Maveety, *Justice Sandra Day O'Connor: Strategist on the Supreme Court* (London: Rowan & Littlefield, 1996), provides a detailed account of Justice O'Connor's life.

closest ally in the late Burger era. While O'Connor was not a doctrinal innovator, her opinions are generally coherent and well reasoned. Her most
notable efforts involved issues of federalism, where O'Connor emerged as a
passionate defender of states' rights.

At the margins, however, O'Connor's conservatism was less hard-edged
than that of Rehnquist or (for example) Antonin Scalia or Robert Bork—later
Reagan appointees to the Supreme Court. For example, her views on affirmative action were actually slightly to the left of those of Potter Stewart, whom she
replaced on the Court; O'Connor also showed some sympathy for claims
under the Establishment Clause of the First Amendment. Further, she ultimately refused to retreat completely from the notion that abortion rights were
protected by the Constitution. Nonetheless, in general, conservatives had
good reason to be well pleased with O'Connor's performance on the Court.

Competing Judicial Philosophies

The appointment of Justice O'Connor completed the mosaic that was the
Burger Court. Obviously, the men and women who served during the chief
justiceship of Warren Burger were extremely diverse in their political and
judicial philosophies. This diversity is well illustrated by an examination of
the justices' different approaches to the analyses of the issues that arose
under the Fifth and Fourteenth Amendments.

Despite the differences in their respective backgrounds, Justices Douglas,
Brennan, and Marshall shared a strong commitment to the jurisprudence of
liberal activism. One of the most striking aspects of their approach is an almost
militant ahistoricism. Thus, for example, disingenuously claiming to be the
intellectual heir of the dissent in *Lochner,* Justice Douglas declared:

> We agree, of course, with Mr. Justice Holmes that the Due Process
> Clause of the Fourteenth Amendment "does not enact Mr. Herbert
> Spencer's Social Statics." Likewise, the Equal Protection Clause is not
> shackled to the political theory of a particular era. In determining what
> lines are unconstitutionally discriminatory, we have never been con-
> fined to historic notions of equality, any more than we have restricted
> due process to a fixed catalogue of what was at a given time deemed to
> be the limits of fundamental rights.[36]

Similarly, toward the end of his career, Justice Brennan derided the
notion that the Constitution should be treated as "a stagnant, archaic, hide-
bound document steeped in the prejudices and superstitions of a time long

---

36. *Harper v. Virginia State Board of Elections,* 383 U.S. 663 (1966).

past," arguing instead that "[the terms] 'liberty' and 'property' [in the Due Process Clause] are broad and majestic terms. . . . They are among the great [constitutional] concepts purposefully left to gather meaning from experience. . . . They relate to the whole domain of social and economic fact, and the statesmen who founded this nation knew too well that only a stagnant society remains unchanged." Having dismissed history as a dispositive guide, he then argued that the touchstone of Fourteenth Amendment adjudication should be the principle that "we are not an assimilative, homogeneous [society], but a facilitative, pluralistic one, in which we must be willing to abide someone else's unfamiliar or even repellent practice because the same tolerant impulse protects our own idiosyncracies."[37]

Based on this description of their philosophy, Justices Douglas, Brennan, and Marshall are sometimes portrayed as the defenders of individual rights against intrusions by the government.[38] Such characterizations are dramatically oversimplified. Admittedly, these justices were far more likely to strike down government actions than were other members of the Burger Court; moreover, there was little of the communitarian in their approach. However, even a cursory review of their voting records reveals that their commitment to individual rights was selective. For example, none of these justices showed sustained interest in developing substantive protection for economic rights through the Takings Clause, the Due Process Clauses, or the Contracts Clause. Similarly, while vigorously defending the right of minority political groups to gain unfettered access to the political process, Brennan and Marshall were extremely sympathetic to government efforts to limit both campaign contributions and corporate political participation generally.

Against this background, it seems clear that the constitutional jurisprudence of Douglas, Brennan, and Marshall cannot be described as libertarian in any meaningful sense. Instead, they were driven by an overriding commitment to the ideology generally shared by liberal Democrats during the late 1970s and 1980s. Despite the Warren Court's liberal reputation, that Court's efforts to promote this ideology had actually been limited largely to a relatively small number of issues—rights of criminal defendants, discrimination against minority races and the poor, voting rights, and First Amendment questions. During the Burger era, by contrast, Douglas, Brennan, and Marshall sought to dramatically expand the use of constitutional adjudication as a vehicle for the implementation of the liberal agenda. They argued vigorously for abortion rights and enhanced scrutiny of laws limiting welfare benefits and access to

---

37. *Michael H. v. Gerald D.*, 491 U.S. 110, 138 [quoting *Board of Regents v. Roth*, 408 U.S. 564, 571 (1972)], 141 (1989).

38. See, for example, David E. Marion, *The Jurisprudence of Justice William J. Brennan, Jr.: The Law and Politics of "Libertarian Dignity"* (Lanham, Md.: Rowman & Littlefield Publishers, 1997).

education; in addition, they sought special constitutional protection for a wide variety of groups, including women, gay and lesbian people, the elderly, illegitimate children, aliens, and the mentally disabled.

As a corollary to its view of the judicial role, the Warren Court had also moved toward dismantling traditional legal principles which limited access to federal courts. During the Burger era, Douglas, Brennan, and Marshall sought to continue this trend. They generally advocated relaxation of the standing, mootness, and political-question doctrines, all of which were designed to circumscribe the nature of the controversies that came before the courts.

Finally, Douglas, Brennan, and Marshall were staunch nationalists. They saw federal power as limited only by individual rights (as defined by liberal Democratic ideology), and rejected the notion that states remained quasi-sovereign, largely self-governing communities. Instead, they saw the state governments as little more than administrative conduits for the development and implementation of national policy. The one notable exception emerged as the Burger Court proved relatively hostile to claims by criminal defendants; unfurling the banner of federalism, Brennan became one of the most prominent advocates of the use of state constitutions to provide defendants with greater protections than those recognized by the Burger Court under the federal Constitution.[39] This argument reflected perhaps the most important tenet of liberal judicial activism during the Burger era—virtually all principles were subordinate to the need to protect the liberal Democratic conception of individual rights. This principle was the most important unifying theme of the jurisprudence of Justices Douglas, Brennan, and Marshall during the Burger era.

Justice Rehnquist occupied the other end of the jurisprudential and ideological spectrum of the Burger Court. He argued that the historical understanding of the Constitution provided the *only* legitimate justification for judicial activism, asserting, "[T]o the extent that it makes possible an individual's persuading one or more appointed federal judges to impose on other individuals a rule of conduct that the popularly elected branches of government would not have enacted and the voters have not and would not have embodied in the Constitution, [nonoriginalist review] is genuinely corrosive of the fundamental values of our democratic society."[40]

Given this jurisprudential approach and his innate political conservatism, it is no surprise that, in cases where liberals sought to deploy the Constitution in support of their values, he was the most consistent and effective advocate

39. William J. Brennan, Jr., "State Constitutions and the Protection of Individual Rights," *Harvard Law Review* 90 (1977): 489.

40. William H. Rehnquist, "The Notion of a Living Constitution," *Texas Law Review* 54 (1976): 693–706, at 705. For different perspectives on Rehnquist's jurisprudence, see Sue Davis, *Justice Rehnquist and the Constitution*; and David L. Shapiro, "Mr. Justice Rehnquist: A Preliminary View," *Harvard Law Review* 90 (1976): 293–357.

of this judicial philosophy on the Burger Court. By contrast, in cases where litigants sought to deploy the Constitution *against* liberal government programs, Rehnquist's voting pattern clearly reflects the tensions inherent in the conservative political/judicial theory of the Burger era. Rehnquist was the Burger Court justice who was most likely to uphold constitutional challenges raised by conservatives against liberal political programs. Moreover, in some of these cases Rehnquist's positions cannot be explained in terms other than pure politics; for example, his rejection of all race-based affirmative-action plans is inexplicable in any other terms. In other cases, however, he embraced doctrines of judicial restraint in rejecting constitutional challenges raised by conservatives. For example, following his general theory that corporations are creatures of the state and thus can constitutionally be made subject to whatever restraints the state government wishes to impose, Rehnquist consistently voted to uphold restraints on corporate political activities— hardly a policy that most conservative politicians would embrace.[41] In short, despite his obvious gifts, Rehnquist never fully resolved the potential conflicts between Nixon's "judicial conservatism" and the political conservatism with which it was associated.[42]

Dissatisfied with both the open-ended activism of the liberal justices and Justice Rehnquist's (theoretically at least) strict originalism, both Justice Powell and Justice Stevens sought to find a jurisprudential middle ground. One of Powell's most articulate efforts involved this elaboration of the proper role of substantive due process in the Court's analysis:

Substantive due process has at times been a treacherous field for the Court. There *are* risks when the judicial branch gives enhanced protection to certain liberties without the guidance of the more specific provisions of the Bill of Rights. As the history of the *Lochner* era demonstrates, there is reason for concern lest the only limits to such intervention become the predilections of those who happen to be Members of this Court. That history counsels caution and restraint. But it does not counsel abandonment. . . .

. . . Appropriate limits on substantive due process come . . . from careful "respect for the teachings of history [and] solid recognition of the basic values that underlie our society."[43]

41. *First National Bank of Boston v. Bellotti,* 435 U.S. 765 (1978) (Rehnquist, J., dissenting).
42. See the analysis of Jeffrey A. Segal and Harold J. Spaeth, *The Supreme Court and the Attitudinal Model,* 326–27.
43. *Moore v. City of East Cleveland,* 431 U.S. 494 (1977), quoting *Griswold v. Connecticut,* 381 U.S. 479, 501 (1965) (Harlan, J., concurring in the judgment).

By contrast, Justice Stevens's most clearly articulated theoretical contributions to Fourteenth Amendment jurisprudence came in his equal-protection analysis, where he emphasized the importance of searching for prejudice in the decision-making process.

All of these different strands were important elements in the tapestry of Burger Court jurisprudence. The contributions of the remaining justices were equally significant, but none articulated clear jurisprudential principles of general application. The chief justice and Justice O'Connor were often allies of Justice Rehnquist; at the same time, they were more likely to stray from his hard-edged approach to join in liberal-activist decisions. By contrast, the pattern of decisions of Justices Stewart, White, and Blackmun simply defy any easy description. Taken together, the aggregate of these approaches defined the jurisprudence of the Burger era.

2

THE IDEA OF JUDICIAL RESTRAINT

The debate over the basic concept of judicial restraint was one of the major themes of the Burger era. This debate was a mirror image of the doctrinal struggle that culminated in the constitutional revolution of 1937. As we have seen, the liberal political forces that triumphed in 1937 advocated a jurisprudence which emphasized the principle that the federal courts should generally not interfere with state and federal legislative decisions on issues of social and economic policy. By 1969, however, a number of different developments had combined to undermine support for this principle among those who held liberal political views.

First, the nature of the economic and social issues presented to the Burger Court was often quite different from those that had come to the Court in the late 1930s and early 1940s. The immediate post-1937 cases were primarily concerned with regulation of business activities. While these issues continued to occupy a significant part of the docket during the Burger era, the Court was also confronted with a variety of challenges to limitations on the availability of government benefits.

These challenges came against the background of a renewed political commitment from liberal political groups to use the power of government—particularly the federal government—to ameliorate the condition of poor people in American society. This commitment, reflected in President Lyndon Johnson's "War on Poverty," resulted in a number of new federal programs which funneled benefits to lower-income Americans. Advocates for these groups sought to use the Court to provide protection for the right to receive many of these benefits, as well as to provide additional protection for poor people generally.

Doctrinal developments during the Warren era provided additional impetus to these efforts. The Court's aggressive deployment of the Constitution in support of liberal positions on issues such as school desegregation, rights of criminal defendants, and school prayer had reversed the psychology that produced Roosevelt-era jurisprudence; rather than being seen as an obstacle to the implementation of liberal social policies, judicial activism was now seen as a

31

potential bulwark of such policies. Against this background, it is not surprising that a number of late Warren Court decisions seemed to suggest that the Court was on the verge of substantially expanding its role in supervising social policy. For example, *Shapiro v. Thompson* could easily have been read to indicate that the right to receive welfare benefits had a special constitutional status.[1]

The appointment of the Nixon justices substantially changed the equation. Generally less sympathetic to the expansion of the welfare state than were the justices they had replaced, Chief Justice Burger and Justices Blackmun, Powell, and Rehnquist also professed to favor a renewed commitment to the idea of judicial restraint that had marked the revolution of 1937. Thus, the debate between the justices on the Court's role reflected doctrinal as well as ideological differences.

The differing conceptions of the function of the Court in the American political system were reflected in a number of different contexts. First, the justices engaged in a complex dispute over the technical legal rules that governed access to courts, with all members of the Court understanding that liberalization of access rules necessarily implied an aggrandizement of the judicial role. Second, the justices differed sharply on issues of immunity from judicial process; obviously, expansive grants of immunity limited the powers of the courts. Finally, and most frequently, the justices disagreed over the levels of scrutiny to be applied in constitutional cases.

The most important of the debates over court access involved the rules governing standing to sue.[2] Traditionally, the requirements for standing were those described in 1937 in *Tennessee Power Co. v. TVA,* where the Court concluded that a plaintiff lacked standing "unless the right invaded is a legal right—one of property, one arising out of contract, one protected against tortious invasion, or one founded on a statute which conveys a privilege."[3] In general, standing issues played little role in the development of Warren Court jurisprudence; nonetheless, the traditional doctrine showed some signs of erosion by the end of the Warren era. In *Flast v. Cohen*[4] the Court modified the venerable rule of *Frothingham v. Mellon,*[5] which had held that simple status as a taxpayer did not confer standing to challenge government expenditures. The *Flast* Court concluded that all taxpayers possessed standing to argue that government expenditures violated the Establishment Clause of the First Amendment. By its terms, however, the *Flast* exception was limited to cases in which

1. *Shapiro v. Thompson,* 394 U.S. 618 (1969).

2. The Burger Court's approach to standing issues is described in detail in C. Douglas Floyd, "Justiciability Decisions for the Burger Court," *Notre Dame Law Review* 60 (1985): 862–946; and Gene R. Nichol, Jr., "Rethinking Standing," *California Law Review* 72 (1984): 68–102.

3. *Tennessee Power Co. v. TVA,* 306 U.S. 118, 137–38 (1937).

4. *Flast v. Cohen,* 392 U.S. 83 (1968).

5. *Frothingham v. Mellon,* 262 U.S. 447 (1923).

the taxpayer was challenging an exercise of federal power under the Taxing and Spending Clause *and* was asserting a specific constitutional limitation on the taxing and spending power, rather than alleging generally that the expenditure was simply beyond the power conferred by the Taxing and Spending Clause itself. Thus, it was left to the Burger Court to fundamentally reshape the law of standing.

The process began in *Associated Data Processing Services, Inc. v. Camp*, where the Court rejected the legal interest test of *Tennessee Power*. There, interpreting a provision of the Administrative Procedure Act, which conferred standing to sue on all those "adversely affected or aggrieved" by agency action, the Court held that all parties within "the zone of interests to be protected or regulated by the statute or constitutional guarantee in question" had standing to bring suit in federal court.[6]

Adapso clearly signaled a relaxation of traditional standing requirements. The post-*Adapso* case law reflected sharp disagreements over the proper application of the new standards. Unlike *Adapso*, which was purely a case of statutory interpretation, most of the other important decisions involved constitutional issues. In *Sierra Club v. Morton*, with Justices Powell and Rehnquist not participating and Justices Douglas, Brennan, and Blackmun dissenting, the Court concluded that an allegation of general concerns about the quality of the environment was insufficient to confer standing to challenge the approval of a proposed development in a hitherto undeveloped area.[7] By contrast, in *United States v. SCRAP*, over the objections of the chief justice and Justices White and Rehnquist, the Court conferred standing on a group challenging the rate structure established for railroads by the Interstate Commerce Commission. The plaintiffs alleged that the rate structure favored raw materials over recyclable goods, which would increase the relative price of recyclable bottles, which would in turn cause the use of more nonrecyclable products, which would create more litter in parkland that the plaintiffs frequented.[8]

Ultimately, *Warth v. Seldin* redefined the basic parameters of standing jurisprudence in relatively conservative terms. *Warth* was a challenge to the zoning ordinance of the town of Penfield, New York, an ordinance which the plaintiffs alleged unconstitutionally excluded poor people from the town. The plaintiffs included a number of poor people who alleged that they wished to live in Penfield; residents of the town, who contended that they were being denied the benefits of living in a diverse community; residents of the neighboring city of Rochester, who argued that, because poor people were not able to find housing in Penfield, Rochester was forced to accommodate a dispro-

---

6. *Associated Data Processing Services, Inc. v. Camp*, 397 U.S. 150, 153 (1970).

7. *Sierra Club v. Morton*, 405 U.S. 727 (1972).

8. *United States v. SCRAP*, 412 U.S. 727 (1973).

portionate number of people with low and moderate incomes; and two associations of builders, who alleged that some of their members had been denied the opportunity to build projects in Penfield that would have provided more affordable housing.[9]

Over the dissents of Justices Douglas, Brennan, Marshall, and White, the Court concluded that none of these plaintiffs had standing to bring the lawsuit. Speaking for the majority, Justice Powell began by distinguishing between the constitutional limitations on standing, which he saw as implicit in the Article 3 requirement that federal courts hear only "cases or controversies," and what he described as "prudential" rules—"essentially matters of judicial self-governance." In his view, Article 3 required that the plaintiff allege facts from which it can be inferred that he has suffered a concrete injury, and that, if victorious on the merits, his injury will be redressed. In the absence of explicit statutory authorization, prudential concerns mitigated against invoking judicial authority to redress "generalized grievance[s] shared in substantially equal measure by all or a large class of citizens," and usually limited parties to the assertion of their own rights. Applying these standards in *Warth*, Powell concluded that the low-income plaintiffs lacked standing because they had not identified a potential project which would have provided housing they could have afforded if they won their lawsuit; the Penfield plaintiffs lacked standing because they were asserting only a generalized grievance; and the Rochester plaintiffs lacked standing because they were asserting the rights of third parties (low-income people who wished to live in Penfield). Finally, the associations of builders were held to lack standing to seek injunctive relief because there were no currently live applications to build low- and moderate-income housing in Penfield, and they were held to lack standing to seek damages because the damages would rightfully go to only a few of their members, rather than the membership as a whole.

Many Burger Court standing decisions followed the pattern of *Warth* in rejecting the broadest definitions of standing to sue. For example, in *Valley Forge Christian College v. Americans United for Separation of Church and State,* over the objections of Justices Brennan, Marshall, Blackmun, and Stevens, the Court essentially limited *Flast* to its facts. In *Valley Forge Christian College,* the plaintiffs asserted that they had standing as taxpayers to mount an Establishment Clause challenge to the decision of the secretary of education to transfer certain property without charge to a religiously affiliated college. Reaffirming the *Frothingham* rule, the majority distinguished *Flast* on two grounds: first, that the plaintiffs were challenging an executive decision, rather than legislative action itself; and second, that the statute granting the secretary the authority to make such transfers was

---

9. *Warth v. Seldin*, 422 U.S. 490 (1975).

passed pursuant to Article 4, section 3, clause 2, which grants Congress the power to "make all needful Rules and Regulations respecting the . . . Property belonging to the United States," rather than the taxing and spending power of Article 1, section 8, clause 1.[10]

While decisions such as *Valley Forge* were common in the late Burger era, the Court was by no means uniformly hostile to expansive views of standing during the post-*Warth* period. For example, in *Village of Arlington Heights v. Metropolitan Housing Development Corp.*, the Court unanimously concluded that a builder who had been denied a permit to construct a low-income housing project had standing to raise the substantive claims that the Court had declined to consider in *Warth* itself.[11] Similarly, in *Craig v. Boren*, only the chief justice and Justice Rehnquist dissented from the conclusion that the owner of a bar had standing to assert the rights of a young man who had been denied the right to purchase 3.2 percent beer from her because of his sex.[12]

The situation in *Duke Power Co. v. Carolina Environmental Study Group* was more complex. *Duke Power* was a challenge to the Price-Anderson Act, which limited the potential liability of the operators of nuclear power plants in the event of an accident. Plaintiffs argued that this limitation violated the Due Process Clause of the Fifth Amendment. Given the fact that no serious nuclear accident had ever occurred in the United States, the possibility that the plaintiffs would actually not be adequately compensated was too speculative to provide the injury in fact necessary to establish their standing. Instead, they alleged a *SCRAP*-type injury to the environmental and aesthetic qualities of areas that they frequented. The plaintiffs further contended that these injuries would be abated if they succeeded in their lawsuits because the defendants would not operate the power plants in the absence of Price-Anderson protection. Thus, while the plaintiffs were asserting their own rights—the rights to potential compensation—and had suffered injury in fact—the environmental damage—there was no nexus between the asserted rights and the injury.[13]

Given these facts, Justices Stewart, Rehnquist, and Stevens would have ordered the plaintiff's action dismissed for want of standing, with Stevens asserting that "the string of contingencies that supposedly holds this litigation together is too delicate for me."[14] In practical terms, however, such a resolution of *Duke Power* would have had a significant downside. The lower court had reached the merits and declared the Price-Anderson Act uncon-

10. *Valley Forge Christian College v. Americans United for Separation of Church and State*, 454 U.S. 464 (1982).
11. *Village of Arlington Heights v. Metropolitan Housing Development Corp.*, 429 U.S. 252 (1977).
12. *Craig v. Boren*, 429 U.S. 190 (1976).
13. *Duke Power Co. v. Carolina Environmental Study Group*, 438 U.S. 59 (1978).
14. Ibid., 102 (Stevens, J., concurring in the result).

stitutional. If the Supreme Court now dismissed the case on standing grounds, the act would have remained under a significant constitutional cloud. Against this background, it should not be surprising that Chief Justice Burger spoke for the remainder of the Court in concluding that the plaintiffs had standing but that, on the merits, the constitutional claim should be rejected.

The divisions over standing were replicated in many different contexts as the Court addressed a wide variety of substantive constitutional issues. In general, the more liberal members of the Court took an expansive view of the judicial role, while the conservative justices advocated a more restrained judicial posture. However, in *United States v. Nixon,* all of the justices would concur in one of the most dramatic assertions of judicial power of the Burger era.[15]

Nixon would bring the Court to the center of one of the gravest constitutional crises in American history. The crisis was generated by the Watergate scandal, which drew its name from the Watergate office complex, the headquarters of the Democratic National Committee (DNC) during the 1972 presidential election campaign. On June 17, 1972, five men were arrested during an attempted break-in at DNC headquarters; it soon became clear that the purpose of the break-in was the replacement of a faulty wiretap on the DNC telephone and the installation of an additional electronic listening device. One of the men—James W. McCord, Jr.—was the security coordinator for both the Republican National Committee and the Committee to Reelect the President. McCord was dismissed from his posts the day after his arrest; before the scandal would finally run its course, it would claim as its victims many higher ranking officials—including President Richard M. Nixon himself.[16]

In the wake of the initial break-in, persistent reports of large, illegal contributions to the Nixon campaign began to surface in the media. The reports did not play a major role in the election itself; Nixon was reelected in 1972 in a landslide of historic proportions. After the election, evidence of both illegal activity and a high-level White House cover-up continued to mount, and on February 7, 1973, a select committee was established in the Senate to investigate the Watergate affair and related matters. Nixon continued to deny any personal involvement in illegal activity or foreknowledge of such activity; however, on April 30, in an effort to reestablish White House credibility, three of Nixon's closest advisors resigned—Chief of Staff H. R. Haldeman, Chief Domestic Policy Advisor John D. Ehrlichman,

---

15. *United States v. Nixon,* 418 U.S. 683 (1974).
16. The events of the Watergate scandal are described in detail in J. Anthony Lucas, *Nightmare: The Underside of the Nixon Years* (New York: Viking Press, 1976).

and Attorney General Richard G. Kleindeinst. The same day, announcing that he would appoint Elliot Richardson to replace Kleindeinst, Nixon stated that Richardson would have the authority to appoint a "special supervising prosecutor" to oversee the investigation of Watergate-related issues. The following day, the Senate adopted a resolution calling for the appointment of just such a special prosecutor. Richardson responded by appointing as special prosecutor Archibald Cox, a professor at Harvard Law School and former solicitor general. In that capacity, Cox assumed responsibility for the ongoing prosecutions of a number of former Nixon administration officials who had already been indicted for crimes allegedly related to the Watergate incident.

It was not until July 16, however, that the matter which would ultimately involve the Supreme Court came to light. Testifying before the Senate Watergate Committee on that date, a Nixon aide disclosed that President Nixon had secretly created audiotapes of all of his private conversations with others since the spring of 1971. The contents of these tapes obviously had the potential to provide conclusive evidence that could either support or refute Nixon's claim that he had no knowledge of the illegal activity underlying Watergate. Thus, the Watergate Committee requested that the president provide the tapes for its scrutiny, and Cox sought and obtained a subpoena duces tecum ordering the production of the tapes for use in pending criminal prosecutions against former members of the administration who had become ensnared in the Watergate scandal. Nixon both denied the Senate committee request and resisted the enforcement of the subpoena, arguing that the tapes were privileged and that he was therefore not required to produce them.

Both the federal district court and the court of appeals rejected the claim of absolute privilege and ordered the tapes produced for inspection in camera by the district judge overseeing the Watergate prosecutions. Nonetheless determined to resist, President Nixon then ordered Cox to cease his pursuit of the tapes; when the special prosecutor refused, on October 20 Nixon ordered Attorney General Richardson to dismiss Cox. Richardson resigned rather than execute this order, as did his deputy, William D. Ruckelshaus. In order to preserve some continuity of leadership at the Justice Department, Solicitor General Robert Bork reluctantly agreed to execute Nixon's order, remove Cox, and assume the post of acting attorney general.

This sequence of events, which became known as the "Saturday Night Massacre," generated an immediate firestorm of criticism. Unable to resist the public pressure, Nixon released some of the tapes; moreover, he acquiesced in the appointment of a new special prosecutor—Leon Jaworski, a well-known litigator from Houston, Texas, and former president of the American Bar Association. Based largely on the information in the tapes that were released, impeachment proceedings began in the House of Representatives. In May 1974 Jaworski requested and received a subpoena that would require the production of additional tapes and documents. Once again Nixon asserted executive privilege as a defense. Once again the district court rejected this defense and ordered Nixon to comply with the subpoenas, and Nixon once again appealed to the court of appeals.[17]

At this stage, Jaworski took the dramatic step of petitioning the Supreme Court to bypass the court of appeals and review the judgment of the district court on an expedited schedule. Given the timing, such expedited consideration would require the Court to forego part of its traditional four-month summer recess. Nonetheless, over the objections of the chief justice and Justices White and Blackmun, Jaworski's petition was granted. Justice Rehnquist had recused himself because of his prior service in the Nixon Justice Department. Thus, it was an eight-person Court which heard the oral argument that took place on July 8, 1974.

Prior to *Nixon*, the leading case on executive privilege was the 1807 decision in *United States v. Burr*. There, sitting on circuit, Chief Justice John Marshall had issued a subpoena ordering President Thomas Jefferson to produce a letter requested by the defense in a criminal trial, declaring that "the propriety of introducing any paper into a case, as testimony, must depend on the character of the paper, not the person who holds it." Jefferson produced the letter, but insisted that he was doing so voluntarily. Thus, there was no occasion for the Supreme Court to define the parameters of executive privilege.[18]

By contrast, the *Nixon* Court was required to meet the problem head-on. At the conference which followed the oral argument, all of the justices agreed that the subpoena should be enforced.[19] Nonetheless, they disagreed sharply on a number of important issues which would necessarily be central to any opinion that would dispose of the case. In most situations, the justices could have simply agreed to disagree, with differing views being expressed in separate opinions. However, *Nixon* was not an ordinary case; not only would it effectively determine the fate of the president of the United States, but the president had suggested that he might refuse to obey any but the

---

17. Leon Jaworski, *The Right and the Power: The Prosecution of Watergate* (New York: Reader's Digest Press, 1976), relates the story of Watergate from the perspective of the special prosecutor.

18. *United States v. Burr*, 35 Fed. Cas. 30, 34 (C.C.D. Va. 1807).

19. Detailed accounts of the internal deliberations of the Court in *Nixon* can be found in John C. Jeffries, Jr., *Justice Lewis F. Powell, Jr.* (New York: Charles Scribner's Sons, 1994), chap. 12; Bernard Schwartz, *The Ascent of Pragmatism: The Burger Court in Action* (New York: Addison-Wesley, 1990), 81–87; and Bob Woodward and Scott Armstrong, *The Brethren: Inside the Supreme Court* (New York: Simon and Schuster, 1979), 287–347.

most definitive and explicit opinion of the Court. In short, all of the justices understood that unanimity was essential.

A period of maneuvering and bargaining followed; its intensity was no doubt exacerbated by the fact that the justices had disposed of all of the other cases in the term and could focus their energies entirely on *Nixon*. Justice White led a group of justices who sought to minimize recognition of special presidential prerogatives. Justice Powell, on the other hand, pressed hard for an opinion that would provide maximum protection for the powers of future presidents. The dispute focused on two related but analytically separate issues.

The first issue involved the threshold legal standard to be used by the trial judge in deciding whether to issue a subpoena to the president. In general, the Federal Rules of Criminal Procedure provided for the issuance of subpoenas for material that is relevant to criminal investigations. White argued that the applicable standard should be no different when the president was the target of the subpoenas. Powell, on the other hand, suggested that the courts should only issue subpoenas to the president upon a showing of necessity.

The other issue was whether the president could assert a claim of executive privilege to avoid compliance with an otherwise valid subpoena. Justices White, Douglas, Marshall, and Blackmun rejected the entire concept of executive privilege. Powell, however, insisted that the constitutional position of the president carried with it a qualified privilege for confidential communications.

The justices ultimately compromised in the interest of achieving consensus. Powell agreed to give way on the issue of the proper standard for the issuance of a subpoena, while the other justices acquiesced in the recognition of the basic concept of executive privilege. Thus, the basic parameters of a unanimous opinion were established.

The basic agreement on substance did not end the Court's internal difficulties in *Nixon*. Earlier, Justice Brennan had suggested that, given the gravity of the situation, a single opinion signed by all of the justices would be ideal. While such an opinion would have been highly unusual, it was not unprecedented; the Court had taken just such an approach in its dramatic reaffirmation of judicial supremacy in *Cooper v. Aaron*.[20] However, the chief justice rejected Brennan's proposal, choosing instead to assign the opinion to himself. Unfortunately, the draft that he produced was unacceptable to the other members of the Court.[21] Not only was the workmanship and analy-

---

20. *Cooper v. Aaron*, 358 U.S. 1 (1958).
21. Burger's initial draft is reproduced in Bernard Schwartz, *The Unpublished Opinions of the Burger Court* (New York: Oxford University Press, 1988), 202–28.

sis generally weak, but the draft defined the prerogatives of the executive very broadly, suggesting that the president might have an absolute privilege where the "core functions" of his office were implicated. Thus, while continuing to bear the name of the chief justice, the opinion that ultimately emerged was instead drafted almost entirely in pieces by the other members of the Court.

The opinion first confronted an issue of justiciability. President Nixon contended that the trial court lacked jurisdiction to issue the subpoena because the matter was simply an intrabranch dispute between the president and a subordinate cabinet officer. Rejecting this argument, Burger first observed that the regulation creating the office of special prosecutor gave Jaworski explicit authority to contest the invocation of executive privilege. While conceding that it was "theoretically possible" for the attorney general to amend or revoke the regulation, Burger also alluded to the unusual circumstances surrounding the appointment of the special prosecutor and concluded that, so long as the regulation remained in effect, the relationship between the parties was sufficiently adverse to provide an appropriate context for judicial action.[22]

Turning to the merits, the *Nixon* opinion began by reiterating Chief Justice John Marshall's famous assertion that "it is emphatically the province and duty of the judicial department to say what the law is." Chief Justice Burger conceded that the preservation of confidentiality in the communications between the president and his advisors was of great importance, and that "it is . . . necessary in the public interest to afford Presidential confidentiality the greatest protection consistent with the fair administration of justice." Moreover, Burger explicitly noted that the claim of privilege had constitutional underpinnings. Nonetheless, he rejected the view that either these considerations or general principles of separation of powers were sufficient to support the president's claim of absolute privilege, asserting that "the impediment that an absolute, unqualified privilege would place in the way of the primary constitutional duty of the Judicial Branch to do justice in criminal prosecutions would plainly conflict with the function of the courts under Art. III." Thus, although concluding that the subpoenaed material was presumptively privileged, the *Nixon* Court upheld the district court's finding that the special prosecutor had made a sufficient showing to rebut the presumption, and required the production of the material for inspection in camera by the lower court, expressing confidence that "the District Judge will at all times accord to Presidential records [a] high degree of deference."[23]

---

22. *United States v. Nixon*, 418 U.S. 692–96.

23. Ibid., 703 [quoting *Marbury v. Madison*, 5 U.S. (1 Cranch) 137 (1803)], 715 (footnote omitted), 707, 715.

Taken as a whole, the *Nixon* opinion is best understood as an emphatic assertion of the doctrine of judicial supremacy. Admittedly, the Court recognized the need to preserve confidentiality in presidential communications, and counseled the lower courts to give strong consideration to that need in making its final determinations on which tapes to release. However, in the event of a dispute between the district judge and the president over the appropriateness of releasing particular information, it was the judge who was to have ultimate decision-making authority. Thus, the judiciary was to be the final arbiter in this interbranch dispute.

The unanimity of the Court on this issue contributed substantially to defusing a looming constitutional crisis. By mid 1974 it appeared that Congress and the president might be headed toward a calamitous power struggle. Further, it was widely feared that President Nixon was prepared to resist anything less than a unanimous decision from the Court on the issue of whether he was required to produce the disputed tapes. The lack of dissent in *Nixon* clearly hastened the ultimate resolution of the crisis. On July 27 the House Judiciary Committee voted to recommend that the full House of Representatives impeach the president; on August 8 Richard Nixon became the first president to resign from office. He was soon pardoned for any criminal wrongdoing by his successor, Gerald Ford. However, in other contexts, the internal divisions that had been suppressed in the *Nixon* opinion soon emerged publicly.

Even before the *Nixon* decision, these divisions had been aired in *Bivens v. Six Unknown Named Agents*.[24] Focusing on the Fourth Amendment, *Bivens* established the general principle that the text of the Constitution could imply the right to maintain a cause of action for damages against at least low-level federal officials, notwithstanding the absence of statutory authorization. Chief Justice Burger and Justices Black and Blackmun had dissented from this holding, arguing that the Court was usurping a legislative function; thus, it was predictable that efforts to extend *Bivens* actions to alleged wrong doing by high executive officials would create sharp disagreements on the Court.

Despite the *Bivens* holding that some federal officials could be sued for damages directly under the Constitution, the applicability of this principle to officials in high office remained in doubt until the post-*Nixon* decision in *Butz v. Economou*. The plaintiff in *Butz* controlled a company that had at one time been licensed as a commodities futures commission merchant. The lawsuit was a reaction to an ultimately unsuccessful attempt by the Department of Agriculture to revoke or suspend the company's license. Seeking damages from the secretary of agriculture and a number of his subordinates, the

---

24. *Bivens v. Six Unknown Named Agents*, 403 U.S. 388 (1971).

plaintiff alleged that the institution of the administrative revocation procedure had violated a number of his constitutional rights. The defendants responded that they were entitled to absolute immunity from such suits for actions taken in their official capacities. With Chief Justice Burger and Justices Rehnquist, Stevens, and Stewart dissenting, the Court rejected this contention with respect to most of the defendants, holding that, in general, officials of the executive branch were entitled to only qualified immunity. The majority and dissent clashed sharply over the characterization of existing case law; however, differing policy judgments lay at the core of their disagreement. The dissenters argued that the fear of lawsuits might "dampen the ardor of all but the most resolute, or the most irresponsible, in the unflinching discharge of their duties," and that denying absolute immunity would lead to a flood of expensive and potentially disruptive litigation. By contrast, the majority suggested that a grant of absolute immunity would in effect place officials above the law, and expressed confidence that judges could act swiftly to weed out frivolous lawsuits, thus reducing any burden created by additional litigation.[25]

Neither the majority nor the dissent saw *Butz* as raising constitutional issues; instead, their differences reflected opposing perspectives on conflicting policy concerns, bolstered by divergent views of the import of relevant precedents. By contrast, arguments related to the separation of powers dominated *Davis v. Passman*. In *Passman,* a congressional staffer who had been dismissed because of her gender brought suit for damages in federal court. Unlike private employees and most federal government employees, as an employee of a member of Congress she could not claim the protection of Title 7 of the Civil Rights Act of 1964, which prohibited employment discrimination on the basis of sex. Thus, she made a *Bivens*-type claim, alleging that she was entitled to damages under the Due Process Clause of the Fifth Amendment.[26]

The Court's consideration of *Passman* was complicated by the language of Article 1, section 6, clause 1, which provides that "for any Speech or Debate in either House [Senators and Representatives] shall not be questioned in any Place." Thus, lawsuits against members of Congress raised two related but analytically separate issues: first, whether the lawsuit was barred by the specific language of the Speech and Debate Clause; and second, whether it ran afoul of more general principles of separation of powers. The *Passman* majority held that the second question was in fact subsumed in the first and that unless the decision to dismiss the employee was protected by the Speech and Debate Clause, the plaintiff could maintain her cause of action.

25. *Butz v. Economou,* 438 U.S. 478, 487–97, 519–24 (Rehnquist, J., concurring and dissenting), 523 [quoting *Gregoire v. Biddle,* 177 Fed. 579, 581 (2d Cir. 1949)] (1978).
26. *Davis v. Passman,* 442 U.S. 228 (1979).

As the dissenters observed, recognition of such a right of action would cut deeply into the traditional prerogatives of legislators, in essence establishing a judicial veto over congressional staffing decisions, based upon an independent determination that the decisions were founded upon inappropriate criteria. For Justice Powell, this consideration was sufficiently important to induce him to abandon his allies in *Butz* and vote to recognize congressional immunity in *Passman*. However, Powell's defection was counterbalanced by the decision of Justice Stevens against immunity, which created a five-justice majority which concluded that, unless inquiry into the staffing decision was barred by the Speech and Debate Clause, recognition of a private right of actions was appropriate. Speaking for the majority, Justice Brennan declared that, in the structure of the Constitution, "the judiciary is clearly discernible as the primary means through which . . . rights may be enforced" and that "if [the defendant's] actions are not shielded by the [Speech and Debate] Clause, we apply the principle that 'legislators ought . . . generally be bound by [the law] as are ordinary persons.'"[27]

Despite its reservation of the Speech and Debate Clause issue, the majority opinion in *Passman*—like that in *United States v. Nixon*—stands as an emphatic endorsement of the principle that the judiciary is supreme over other branches of government. However, in *Nixon v. Fitzgerald* a similarly narrow majority found that this supremacy was not absolute. In *Fitzgerald*, a government employee who had been dismissed during the Nixon regime sued Nixon himself as well as a number of other government officials, alleging that he was entitled to damages for wrongful termination under an implied right of action. Speaking for four of the five members of the *Butz* majority, Justice Byron White noted that, unlike members of Congress, the president had no express constitutional protection against lawsuits; moreover, he argued that recognition of absolute presidential immunity from such a suit would in effect place the president "above the law." A narrow majority of the Court disagreed, however; Justice Stevens joined the four *Passman* dissenters in concluding that, at least in the absence of a federal statute specifically authorizing such a suit, the president had absolute immunity from damage claims based upon actions taken in his official capacity. Speaking for the majority, Justice Powell noted the "unique position [of the president] in the constitutional scheme" and argued that "[b]ecause of the singular importance of the President's duties, diversion by concern with private lawsuits would raise unique risks to the effective functioning of government." Powell also relied on basic principles of separation of powers; distinguishing *United States v. Nixon* on the ground that it involved a criminal prosecution, he contended that the constitutional weight to be accorded to the right to maintain a private suit for

---

27. Ibid., 241 (Burger, C. J., dissenting), 241, 246 [quoting *Gravel v. United States*, 408 U.S. 606, 615 (1972)].

damages was insufficient to overcome "the dangers of intrusion on the authority and functions of the Executive Branch." Finally, rejecting the dissent's claim that he was in effect placing the president above the law, Powell noted that he would still be deterred from wrongdoing by the possibility of impeachment, as well as a variety of potential informal sanctions.[28]

By providing the president with immunity from damage actions, *Fitzgerald* plainly limited the scope of *Nixon*. Neither case, however, dealt with the judiciary's role in evaluating the substance of executive policy decisions. In some areas—most notably, those involving foreign policy and military affairs—the Court has historically been loathe to interfere with executive judgments. The Burger Court was confronted with this tradition in a variety of different contexts.

One of the most important decisions came in *New York Times v. United States*—more commonly known as the *Pentagon Papers* cases.[29] In *Pentagon Papers*, the Court was called upon to resolve major First Amendment issues against the background of the bitter political divisions engendered by the ongoing American military involvement in the struggle for control of the Asian nation of South Vietnam. While the origins of this involvement are complex, and historians differ over the allocation of responsibility for the depth of American involvement, one point is clear: the decision to commit large numbers of American ground combat troops in defense of the government of South Vietnam was made during the administration of Lyndon Johnson in the mid 1960s. By the end of 1965, two hundred thousand American ground troops were stationed in South Vietnam, and the United States was engaged in an intensive bombing campaign against the nation of North Vietnam, which was aiding rebel forces in the south. As the war dragged on and American involvement escalated, the political opposition to the war gained momentum and became increasingly strident. The antiwar movement became particularly powerful within the Democratic Party, creating divisions within the party that led Johnson to decide not to seek a second term and contributed to the election of Richard Nixon as president in 1968.

One of the legal difficulties related to the Vietnam conflict was that it was conducted without an express declaration of war by Congress. Thus, the entire enterprise was arguably unconstitutional. Not surprisingly, antiwar activists pressed the courts for a judgment to that effect. However, like the Warren Court

28. *Nixon v. Fitzgerald,* 457 U.S. 731, 764–97 (White, J., dissenting), 749, 751, 754, 757–58 (1982).

29. *New York Times Co. v. United States [Pentagon Papers],* 403 U.S. 713 (1971). All aspects of the *Pentagon Papers* case are discussed and analyzed in detail in David Rudenstine, *The Day the Presses Stopped: A History of the Pentagon Papers Case* (Berkeley: University of California Press, 1996). For much briefer accounts focusing on the internal deliberations of the Supreme Court, see Bernard Schwartz, *The Ascent of Pragmatism,* 158–62; and Woodward and Armstrong, *The Brethren,* 138–50.

before it, the Burger Court consistently refused to hear such constitutional challenges; only Justices Douglas and Stewart publicly dissented from denials of certiorari to lower court judgments which either upheld the presidential authority to prosecute the conflict or found the issue nonjusticiable.[30]

The *Pentagon Papers* case, however, presented quite different legal issues. While the publication of the Pentagon Papers and the legal dispute surrounding it would not occur until well into Nixon's term of office, the papers themselves were actually produced during the Johnson administration. In 1967, without the consent or knowledge of the president, Robert McNamara—the secretary of defense who oversaw the American military buildup in Vietnam—commissioned a historical study of the United States' involvement with that nation's affairs from 1940 to 1967. Completed only five days before Nixon took office, the study ultimately ran to forty-seven volumes, including four thousand pages of government documents and three thousand pages of historical studies based on those documents. Although some of the material in the forty-seven volumes was taken from the public record, the entire study was classified "top secret—sensitive" because the release of some of the material was deemed to be inimical to the interests of the United States.

Despite this top-secret classification, in early 1971 Daniel Ellsburg resolved to make the Pentagon Papers public. Ellsburg, an employee of a Washington, D.C., think tank, had been an early supporter of the Vietnam War but changed his views after spending over a year in South Vietnam in the mid 1960s. He had actually participated in drafting one section of the papers; however, he did not read the entire project until 1969, after briefing Nixon's transition team on his view of the appropriate position that the new administration should take on the war. Ellsburg hoped that the release of the papers would bolster the political forces that opposed further escalation of the war and pressed for withdrawal of all American military forces from South Vietnam. Ellsburg first approached two antiwar senators who had appropriate security clearances, hoping that they would agree to publicize the papers under the protection of the immunity provided by the Speech and Debate Clause. When they refused his request, Ellsburg furnished the complete text of the Pentagon Papers to the *New York Times,* which decided to publish a series of articles based on the study beginning on Sunday, June

---

30. *Mora v. McNamara*, 389 U.S. 934 (1967); *Orlando v. Laird,* 443 F. 2d 1039 (2d Cir. 1971), *cert. denied,* 404 U.S. 869 (1971); *Da Costa v. Laird,* 405 U.S. 979 (1972). Woodward and Armstrong allege that Harlan voted to grant certiorari in at least one case, and that Brennan would also have been willing to consider the constitutionality of continuing the Vietnam War if Congress explicitly opposed military action; see Woodward and Armstrong, *The Brethren,* 125–27. While their characterization of Brennan's position is consistent with his expressed views in other cases, Woodward and Armstrong offer no citations to support their conclusions on this point, and it is not independently verified by other secondary sources.

13, 1971. After three installments were published, the government obtained a temporary restraining order against further publications. Ellsburg then provided substantial parts of the Pentagon Papers to the *Washington Post*, which began to publish excerpts on Friday, June 18.

A flurry of litigation followed, as the government attempted to prevent the publication of any additional information from the classified study. By Wednesday, June 23, the United States Court of Appeals for the Second Circuit had issued an order temporarily preventing the *New York Times* from revealing important parts of the Pentagon Papers, but the United States Court of Appeals for the District of Columbia Circuit had refused to restrain the publication by the *Washington Post*. On Thursday, June 24, the *Times* appealed the Second Circuit decision to the Supreme Court, and the government also appealed the decision of the District of Columbia Circuit. Initially, Justices Black, Douglas, Brennan, and Marshall wished to immediately free both newspapers from legal restraints on publication, while the chief justice and Justices Harlan, White, and Blackmun favored restraining both newspapers until the fall, when the Court could consider the legal issues as part of its normal schedule. The balance of power was held by Justice Stewart, who threatened to vote with the Black group unless the Court gave the issues immediate consideration. Faced with this prospect, the remaining four justices agreed to Stewart's demands. Thus, all of the parties were ordered to submit briefs and supporting documents by 11 A.M. on Saturday, June 26, and an oral argument was scheduled for that time.

From a purely legal perspective the proper resolution of the *Pentagon Papers* case turned on an interpretation of the Court's classic 1931 decision in *Near v. Minnesota*.[31] In *Near*, the Court established the general rule that the First Amendment prohibited prior restraints on publication. At the same time, however, the majority opinion in *Near* also noted that "when a nation is at war, many things that might be said in time of peace are such a hindrance that their utterance will not be endured so long as men fight." By a six-to-three vote, the Court concluded that this admonition was inapposite to *Pentagon Papers*, and that the publication of the documents should not be restrained by the courts. Each of the justices wrote separately to express his views. For Justices Douglas, Black, and Brennan, *Pentagon Papers* was a straightforward First Amendment case. Speaking in typically absolute terms, Douglas and Black reiterated their oft-expressed view that "the First Amendment . . . leaves . . . no room for governmental restraint on the press." Brennan was only slightly less emphatic, declaring that "only governmental accusation and proof that publication must inevitably, directly and immediately cause the occurrence of an

---

31. *Near v. Minnesota*, 283 U.S. 697 (1931).

event kindred to imperiling the safety of a transport already at sea can support even the issuance of an interim restraining order."[32]

For at least five of the remaining justices, however, the fact that *Pentagon Papers* had national security implications weighed heavily in their analysis. For Chief Justice Burger and Justices Harlan and Blackmun, this factor was dispositive. After decrying the haste with which they were forced to decide the case, they conceded that "the judiciary must review the initial Executive determination to the point of satisfying itself that the subject matter of the dispute does lie within the proper compass of the President's foreign relations power,"[33] and could require that a determination that disclosure of the subject matter would irreparably damage the national interest be made by the head of the relevant department after due consideration. However, under their view, once this determination was made, the judiciary was required to respect it and issue an injunction if requested to do so.

Justices Stewart and White took a middle view. They ultimately concluded that the issuance of restraining orders or injunctions against publication violated the First Amendment; however, unlike Douglas, Black, and Brennan, they strongly intimated that those who published the Pentagon Papers could appropriately be subject to criminal prosecution. Stewart and White conceded that "under the Constitution the Executive must have the largely unshared duty to determine and preserve the degree of internal security necessary to exercise [the foreign affairs] power."[34] At the same time, however, they also concluded that it was the duty of the executive, rather than the judiciary, to enforce these judgments—particularly where Congress provided for criminal sanctions rather than injunctive relief as a means to deter inappropriate disclosure of sensitive documents. Justice Marshall also focused on this point, contending that it would violate the principle of separation of powers for the judiciary to construct a remedy that Congress had declined to provide.

Pentagon Papers was clearly a victory for those who valued unfettered freedom of speech over the need to respect executive decisions on matters related to national security. At the same time, however, the structure and tone of the Stewart and White opinions left the precise scope of that victory unclear, leaving open the possibility that if the context were different, a different balance might be struck as well. The replacement of Justices Black and Harlan by Justices Powell and Rehnquist tipped the balance further in favor of executive prerogatives. Thus, in 1980, the decision in *Snepp v. United States* implicitly limited the principles underlying *Pentagon Papers*.[35]

---

32. *New York Times Co. v. United States*, 403 U.S. at 726–27 (Brennen, J., concurring).
33. Ibid., 757 (Harlan, J., dissenting).
34. Ibid., 729 (Stewart, J., concurring).
35. *Snepp v. United States*, 444 U.S. 507 (1980).

In *Snepp,* a former agent of the Central Intelligence Agency published a book detailing CIA activities during the Vietnam War, notwithstanding the fact that in his contract of employment he had agreed not to publish any materials related to his CIA experiences without the express consent of the agency. Based on this agreement, the CIA sought to impose a constructive trust for the government's benefit on all profits from the book. The author argued that the agreement was unenforceable because it was an unconstitutional prior restraint on First Amendment freedoms. Justices Brennan, Marshall, and Stevens found this argument substantial; however, without even full briefing and argument, a majority of the Court disagreed, imposing the trust and declaring that "the Government has a compelling interest in protecting both the secrecy of information important to our national security and the appearance of confidentiality [and moreover] the agreement that Snepp signed is a reasonable means for protecting this vital interest."[36]

While *Pentagon Papers* and *Snepp* implicated executive power over issues related to national defense and foreign affairs, important elements of both cases also plausibly supported assertions of independent judgment by the Court. First, neither case involved an effort to have the judiciary interfere directly with the activities of the executive; instead, in each case, it was the executive that sought the aid of positive judicial action. Equally important was the nature of the constitutional issues presented by the two cases; the defendants were not simply claiming that the executive was exceeding its general authority, but rather that the executive was seeking to enlist the courts in a violation of First Amendment rights—rights that the more liberal members of the Burger Court in particular saw as being of great importance. When neither of these factors was present, support for deference to executive judgment was correspondingly greater. Even in these cases, however, some divisions remained.

Goldwater v. Carter illustrates this point.[37] *Goldwater* found its roots in the complexities which arose after Communists under the leadership of Mao Tse Tung seized control of the Chinese mainland from the Nationalist government in 1948. Representatives of the Nationalists fled to the offshore island of Taiwan, from which they continued to claim to be the legitimate government of all China. The Communist victory came at the beginning of the post–World War II struggle for world hegemony between the United States and the Soviet Union—a struggle that would continue until well after the chief justiceship of Warren Burger. Viewing the Maoist government of China as an ally of the Soviets, the government of the United States continued to recognize the Nationalists as the legitimate government of China and sought to

36. Ibid., 520–21 and n. 10 (Stevens, J., dissenting), 509 n. 3 (citation omitted).
37. *Goldwater v. Carter,* 444 U.S. 996 (1979).

diplomatically isolate the Maoists. At the same time, the Maoists claimed that Taiwan was part of China and periodically threatened to invade the island. Against this background, the United States and the Nationalist government executed a mutual defense treaty, which was duly ratified by the Senate.

United States policy toward the Maoist government began to change under Richard Nixon, who in 1972 became the first American president to visit mainland China since the defeat of the Nationalists. Jimmy Carter—Nixon's successor—sought to fully normalize diplomatic relations with the Maoist government; however, the Maoists demanded that the mutual defense treaty be abrogated as a precondition to normalization. Acceding to this demand, Carter unilaterally abrogated the treaty. This action was challenged by a number of staunchly anti-Communist senators and representatives, who sought a declaratory judgment holding that Carter had exceeded his authority by acting without the consent of Congress.

Each of the seven justices who reached the issue concluded that the plaintiffs were not entitled to the declaratory judgment; however, they differed sharply on the appropriate rationale for this conclusion. Chief Justice Burger and Justices Stewart, Rehnquist, and Stevens argued that the case presented a nonjusticiable political question, relying on the general need to defer to the executive on issues involving foreign affairs, together with the fact that the Constitution itself provided no clear guidance on the issue. Justices Powell and Brennan expressly rejected this argument. While concluding that the case was not ripe for review because Congress as an institution had not expressed its opposition to the abrogation of the treaty, Powell contended that none of the normal indicia of a political question was present in *Goldwater* and argued that "the specter of the Federal Government brought to a halt because of the mutual intransigence of the President and Congress would require this Court to pursue a resolution pursuant to our duty 'to say what the law is.'"[38] Brennan went even further, reaching the merits and holding that Carter had acted within his authority in abrogating the mutual defense treaty.

While the plurality opinion in *Goldwater* reflected the judiciary's traditional unwillingness to second-guess the president on issues related to foreign affairs, the Powell and Brennan opinions demonstrated that a number of the members of the Burger Court were willing to at least seriously consider a more activist posture. However, *Goldwater* itself did not involve a truly acute international crisis. When President Carter faced such a crisis, almost all members of the Court would show the same reluctance to intervene that had marked its treatment of direct challenges to the Vietnam War.

The crisis arose in the midst of the revolution that overthrew the United States–backed government of the nation of Iran. During the revolution, the

38. Ibid., 1001 (Powell, J., concurring in the judgment).

American Embassy in the capital of Iran was seized, and a number of American diplomatic personnel were taken hostage. In response, on November 14, 1979, President Carter took a number of actions, including ordering both the deportation of all Iranian nationals who were students at American universities and the seizure of all the economic assets of the Iranian government that were within the jurisdiction of the United States.

A judicial challenge to the deportation order forced the courts to confront a collision between two of the most basic premises of modern constitutional jurisprudence. On one hand, the courts have shown extreme reluctance to interfere with executive management of foreign crises; on the other hand, however, a distaste for classifications that overtly discriminated against unpopular races or national origins had become the cornerstone of late-twentieth-century constitutional analysis. Faced with this conflict, an en banc United States Court of Appeals for the District of Columbia Circuit split along political lines. A majority of the court, including all Republican appointees, voted to reject the constitutional challenge; conversely, all of the Democratic appointees except one seemed to believe that the deportation order was unconstitutional.[39] The Supreme Court, however, never reached the merits of the controversy; only the indefatigable Justice Brennan voted to grant a writ of certiorari to review the judgment of the District of Columbia Circuit.[40]

By contrast, the asset seizures set in motion a chain of events that led to a major decision on the scope of executive power over foreign affairs. *Dames and Moore v. Regan* arose from the interaction between the seizure order itself and the terms of the settlement between the United States and Iran that ended the hostage crisis.[41] After the Iranian assets had been seized, the plaintiff in *Dames and Moore* had filed an action against the government of Iran that was not directly related to the hostage crisis itself. As allowed by the seizure order, certain Iranian assets were attached to secure any judgment that might be obtained in that action.

Before a judgment was entered, on January 20, 1981, the governments of the United States and Iran entered into an agreement which provided that the hostages would be freed and that, prior to July 19, 1981, all the seized assets would be transferred to a bank account and used to satisfy the judgments of a special Claims Tribunal, which would arbitrate all claims between American nationals and the Iranian government. On January 27 the *Dames and Moore* plaintiff obtained summary judgment against the Iranian government. However, when the plaintiff attempted to levy on the previously attached assets, it was blocked by the hostage agreement, which also

---

39. *Narenji v. Civiletti*, 617 F.2d 745 (D.C. Cir. 1979).

40. *Narenji v. Civiletti*, 446 U.S. 957 (1980).

41. *Dames and Moore v. Regan*, 453 U.S. 654 (1981).

in effect transferred jurisdiction over the plaintiff's action to the Claims Tribunal. The plaintiff then challenged the executive orders effectuating the hostage agreement, contending that they went beyond the authority granted to the president by the Constitution.

The Court unanimously rejected this challenge. In his opinion for the Court, Justice Rehnquist first concluded that the transfer of the assets in general terms was specifically authorized by statute, and as such was "supported by the strongest of presumptions." By contrast, Rehnquist conceded that the transfer of jurisdiction over the plaintiff's specific claim lacked specific statutory authorization; nonetheless, the Court upheld the president's authority in this context as well, finding it to be within "the general tenor of Congress' legislation in this area." Thus, while disclaiming any intent to "lay down general 'guidelines' covering other situations," the *Dames and Moore* Court essentially reaffirmed the breadth of executive authority to act in times of national crisis.[42]

Despite the unanimity of the *Dames and Moore* Court, the overall pattern of decisions dealing with executive power demonstrated that the Burger Court was deeply divided over the proper relationship between the judiciary and the executive branches. These divisions were replicated in disputes over the constitutional standards governing the actions of other branches of government. For example, early in the Burger era, liberals vigorously urged the Court to impose substantial restrictions on government decisions that limited and allocated the welfare benefits provided to poor families. However, in *Dandridge v. Williams,* a majority of the Court rejected the view that such decisions merited special constitutional scrutiny. Speaking for the Court, Justice Stewart applied the traditional rational basis test in upholding a state regulation that limited payments under the Aid to Families with Dependent Children (AFDC) program to $250 per month per family. Dissenting, Justices Marshall and Brennan observed that "[the challengers] are not a [business organization]; they are needy children and families who are discriminated against by the State." They contended that because the AFDC program provided the basic necessities of life to its clients, a higher level of scrutiny was appropriate. Justice Douglas also dissented, arguing that the state regulation was inconsistent with the federal statute governing the AFDC program.[43]

Dandridge clearly established the rational basis test as the standard of review for cases involving the distribution of benefits by the government. *San Antonio Independent School District v. Rodriguez* took the same view of the sys-

---

42. Ibid., 674 [quoting *Youngstown Sheet and Tube Co. v. Sawyer,* 358 U.S. 534, 637 (1952)] (Jackson, J., concurring), 678, 661.
43. *Dandridge v. Williams,* 397 U.S. 471 (1970).

tem for financing public education. *Rodriguez* was a challenge to the approach taken by the state of Texas, which followed the widespread practice of financing education largely through local taxes on real property, with the taxes imposed by each school district used only to finance the schools of that district. This approach was challenged by residents of districts that had relatively low property tax bases, who argued that the system violated the Equal Protection Clause. Justice Potter Stewart joined the four Nixon appointees in rejecting this challenge.[44]

Speaking for the majority, Justice Lewis Powell first noted that the financing system did not discriminate against poor people per se, but rather against residents of districts with relatively low values of real property—a characteristic that does not necessarily correlate with low average personal income. Next, declaring that "it is not the province of the Court to create substantive constitutional rights in the name of guaranteeing equal protection of the laws," Powell concluded that the Texas approach need only satisfy the rational basis test. Emphasizing the Court's lack of expertise in matters involving fiscal educational policy, Powell concluded that the Texas system was free from constitutional infirmities.

The dissenters found a variety of different flaws in the majority's analysis. Justice Brennan contended that strict scrutiny was appropriate because "education is inextricably linked to the right to participate in the political process and [First Amendment rights]." Justices Douglas and Marshall took a similar view, emphasizing a perceived link between the challenged classification and discrimination on the basis of wealth itself.

In addition to being divided on the question of the proper standard of review to be applied, the members of the *Rodriguez* Court also differed sharply on the stringency of the rational basis test itself.[45] Thus, Justice White was joined by Justices Douglas and Brennan in concluding that reliance on local property taxes failed to pass even the rational basis standard. In *United States Railroad Retirement Board v. Fritz,* the justices more clearly articulated their differing visions of the role of the rational basis test in constitutional analysis.[46]

Fritz was a challenge to a federal statute designed to restructure the railroad retirement system in order to place it on sounder financial footing. As part of the restructuring, the statute decreed that certain employees who had retired prior to the effective date of the act would no longer be eligible to receive benefits from both the railroad retirement fund and the social security

44. *San Antonio Independent School District v. Rodriguez,* 411 U.S. 1 (1973).

45. The Burger Court's struggles with the rational basis test are described in detail in Edward L. Barrett, "The Rational Basis Standard for Equal Protection Review of Ordinary Legislative Classifications," *Kentucky Law Journal* 68 (1980): 845–78.

46. *United States Railroad Retirement Board v. Fritz,* 449 U.S. 166 (1980).

system—described as a "windfall" benefit in Justice Rehnquist's majority opinion and as an "earned dual benefit" in Justice Brennan's dissent. By a seven-to-two vote, the Court held that this provision was constitutional.

In a remarkably candid assessment of the state of the law, Justice Rehnquist observed that "[t]he most arrogant legal scholar would not claim that all of [the cases purporting to apply the rational basis test have] applied a uniform or consistent test under the Equal Protection Clause. And realistically speaking we can [not] be certain that this opinion will remain undisturbed." Citing *Dandridge* as the relevant authority, Rehnquist declared that "[w]here, as here, there are plausible reasons for Congress' action, our inquiry is at an end. It is . . . 'constitutionally irrelevant whether this reasoning in fact underlay the legislative decision.'"[47]

Concurring only in the result, Justice Stevens also disavowed any reliance on actual legislative purpose. However, he saw the rational basis test in quite different terms from Justice Rehnquist, arguing that the rational basis test required "a correlation between the classification and either the actual purpose of the statute or a legitimate purpose that we may reasonably presume to have motivated an impartial legislature." In voting to uphold the statute, Stevens concluded that the classification in *Fritz* was related to the purpose of providing stability in the retirement system while making plausible distinctions between beneficiaries.[48]

Speaking in dissent for himself and Justice Marshall, Justice Brennan took a far more expansive view of the proper scope of rational basis analysis:

[T]his Court [should not] sustain a challenged classification under the rational basis test merely because Government attorneys can suggest a "conceivable basis" upon which it might be thought rational. . . . [W]here Congress has articulated a legitimate government objective, and the challenged classification rationally furthers that objective, we must sustain the provision. In other cases, however, the courts must probe more deeply. Where Congress has expressly stated the purpose of a piece of legislation, but where the challenged classification is either irrelevant to or counter to that purpose, we must view any *post hoc* justifications proffered by Government attorneys with skepticism.[49]

Noting that at least some legislators had voted for the law based on the representation that no person's benefit would be reduced, Brennan concluded that the statute lacked a rational basis.

47. Ibid., 176 n. 10, 178–79.
48. Ibid., 181 (Stevens, J., concurring in the result).
49. Ibid., 188 (Brennan, J., dissenting).

Fritz provides a striking example of one of the major jurisprudential issues that divided the Burger Court. At one end of the spectrum, the majority opinion reflects the view that legislative decisions are generally to be respected simply because they are legislative, and not to be overturned unless forbidden by some specific constitutional imperative. By contrast, the dissent (and to a lesser extent Justice Stevens's concurrence) reflects the view that the Court should take an active role to ensure that legislative decisions reflect both substantive justice and appropriate consideration by the legislature itself.

In purely formal terms, the principles established by the majority in *Dandridge, Rodriguez,* and *Fritz* continued to be the "doctrine of the Court" throughout the Burger era. Nonetheless, even after the departure of Justice Douglas, Justices Brennan and Marshall were occasionally able to attract enough allies to vindicate the claims of groups that were denied access to welfare benefits or education. *United States Department of Agriculture v. Moreno* and *Plyler v. Doe* provide classic examples.[50]

Moreno was a challenge to a provision of the Food Stamp Act of 1971 that denied food stamps to any household containing an individual who was unrelated to any other member of the household. With only the chief justice and Justice Rehnquist dissenting, the Court held the exclusion unconstitutional under the equal protection principles that applied to the federal government. Both the majority and the dissent purported to be applying the rational basis test from *Dandridge.* However, Justice Brennan's majority opinion had a strikingly different tone from that of *Dandridge.* In *Dandridge,* Justice Stewart suggested that any correlation between the challenged classification and a legitimate goal would satisfy the rational basis test; he contended that "if [a] classification has some 'reasonable basis,' it does not offend the Constitution simply because the classification 'is not made with mathematical nicety or because in practice it results in some inequality'" and that "a statutory discrimination will not be set aside if any state of facts reasonably may be conceived to justify it." By contrast, Justice Brennan seemed to reject the theory that a simple correlation was sufficient; even conceding that fraud was more likely in households containing unrelated individuals, Brennan concluded that "the denial of federal food assistance to *all* otherwise eligible households containing unrelated members [does not constitute] a rational effort to deal with [potential fraud]."[51]

Plyler, on the other hand, involved a Texas statute that withheld state funds for the education of any child not legally admitted into the United States. In addition, the statute permitted local school districts to deny

50. *United States Department of Agriculture v. Moreno,* 413 U.S. 523 (1973); *Plyler v. Doe,* 457 U.S. 202 (1982).

51. *United States Department of Agriculture v. Moreno,* 413 U.S. 528, 535–36 (emphasis in original).

enrollment to such children. All members of the Court agreed that the unlawfully present children were "persons" for purposes of equal protection analysis; however, they disagreed sharply on the import of this conclusion. Four justices (including Justice White, who had dissented in *Rodriguez*) argued that the rational basis test provided the applicable level of scrutiny, and that the statute should be held constitutional. Justices Brennan, Marshall, Stevens, Blackmun, and Powell took the opposing view, concluding that the exclusion of the illegal aliens should be struck down; however, it was only after complex negotiations that a majority opinion ultimately emerged.

At the conference on *Plyler*, Justice Blackmun argued that the Court should rely on the theory that the Texas statute ran afoul of the exclusive federal authority to regulate immigration and naturalization. By contrast, the remaining members of the majority preferred to rely on equal protection theory, and Blackmun demurred on this point.[52] As the senior justice in the majority, Brennan assigned the case to himself and set out to craft an opinion that would command the support of the five justices who found the Texas statute objectionable.

Initially, Brennan produced a sweeping draft which not only indicated that discrimination against illegal aliens should in general be subject to strict judicial scrutiny, but also would have essentially limited *Rodriguez* to its facts. The draft reiterated the view of the *Rodriguez* dissenters that the right to receive a public education was an essential prerequisite to the effective vindication of First Amendment rights, and included a long historical discussion designed to illustrate that the drafters of the Fourteenth Amendment themselves saw access to public education as a matter of paramount importance in the Reconstruction process. The application of the rational basis test in *Rodriguez* was characterized as a function of the inappropriateness of judicial intervention with issues of school finance particularly, rather than state decisions on education generally.[53]

Brennan's draft brought a quick response from Justice Powell, who objected both to the characterization of illegal aliens as a suspect class and the effort to circumscribe or limit the implications of *Rodriguez*. Powell then circulated a draft opinion which would have concurred only in the result, arguing that the Texas classification should be held unconstitutional under intermediate scrutiny. The opinion seemed to base its rejection of the rational basis test on a combination of the characteristics of the excluded children and the fact that they were being denied all access to public education.[54]

52. Conference notes, *Plyler v. Doe*, William J. Brennan Papers, Library of Congress; Blackmun to Brennan, March 10, 1982, Brennan Papers.
53. Draft opinion on *Plyler v. Doe*, Brennan Papers.
54. Powell to Brennan, January 30, 1982, Brennan Papers; draft concurrence, *Plyler v. Doe*, Brennan Papers.

Powell's defection would have deprived any opinion of majority status; thus, it is not surprising that other members of the majority put forth ideas designed to obviate his objections to the Brennan draft. Justice Blackmun suggested that the complete denial of public education to any identifiable class should be subject to strict scrutiny—a suggestion that Powell firmly rejected. Powell was more receptive to Justice Stevens's suggestion that the Texas classification should be declared unconstitutional under the rational basis test.[55]

Ultimately, however, Brennan was able to gain Powell's concurrence in an opinion that incorporated many elements of the draft concurrence. Brennan initially focused his attention on the nature of the class being denied access to education. Brennan conceded that "[p]ersuasive arguments support the view that a State may withhold its beneficence from those whose very presence within the United States is the product of their own unlawful conduct," and that "those who enter our territory by stealth and in violation of our law should be prepared to bear the consequence." However, Justice Brennan argued that illegally present children stand in a different posture because their entrance was typically the product of their parents' decisions, rather than their own, and contended that "[i]t is . . . difficult to conceive of a rational justification for penalizing those children for their presence within the United States."[56]

Brennan then turned to the nature of the interest at stake. He omitted any effort to link the right to public education to the original understanding, and also scrupulously avoided any suggestion that the implications of Powell's opinion in *Rodriguez* were limited. At the same time, however, he declared that education "is [not] merely some governmental 'benefit' indistinguishable from other forms of social welfare legislation. Both the importance of education in maintaining our basic institutions, and the lasting impact of its deprivation on the life of the child, mark the distinction." Combining these observations with his assessment of the constitutional status of undocumented children, Brennan argued that the burden was on the state to demonstrate that its classification furthered a substantial state interest. Concluding that the state had failed to satisfy this burden, the majority concluded that the Texas statute was unconstitutional.

On one level, *Plyler*'s significance was quite limited. The case was doctrinally stillborn, limited to its facts by the internal structure of the majority opinion itself. Concurring, Justices Powell and Blackmun—the two defectors from the *Rodriguez* majority—made this point explicitly, emphasizing the

---

55. Blackmun to Brennan, March 10, 1982; Powell to Brennan, March 12, 1982; Stevens to Brennan, March 12, 1982, all in Brennan Papers.
56. *Plyler v. Doe*, 457 U.S. at 219–20.

uniqueness of the fact pattern in *Plyler* and specifically reaffirming their allegiance to the basic principles announced in *Rodriguez*.

On another level, however, the juxtaposition of *Rodriguez* and *Plyler* provides a classic example of the basic structure of Burger Court jurisprudence, a jurisprudence marked by shifting alliances among the justices that produced an extraordinarily complex pattern of decisions. In particular, the liberal victory in *Plyler* reflects two of the most important themes of the Burger era—the gradual leftward drift of Justice Blackmun and the absolutely pivotal role played by Justice Powell in cases where the Court was deeply divided. Moreover, Powell's votes in both cases can be seen as products of his lifelong belief in the significance of public education to American society. While his opinion in *Rodriguez* emphasized the importance of local control over the process of public education, his vote in *Plyler* demonstrates an unwillingness to countenance a complete denial of public education to any member of American society—even one who has no legal right to a continuing presence in this country.

In the entire line of cases from *Dandridge* through *Plyler*, restraint was generally advocated by the more politically conservative members of the Court, while the liberal justices supported a more expansive judicial role. This was the most common pattern during the Burger era; there were, however, important exceptions—situations in which the more conservative members of the Court were more likely to embrace judicial activism. This pattern is reflected in some aspects of the Burger Court's treatment of federalism-related issues.

Table 2.1: Voting Patterns

	Bur	Dou	Bre	Mar	Whi	Stew	Bla	Reh	Pow	Stev	Oco
Standing											
Adapso v. Camp 397 U.S. 150 (1970) (zone of interest)	S	S	S	S	S	S	S	NP	NP	NP	NP
Sierra Club v. Morton 405 U.S. 727 (1972) (concern for environment)	NS	S	S	NS	NS	NS	S	NP	NP	NP	NP
United States v. SCRAP 412 U.S. 669 (1973) (noneconomic harm)	NS	S	S	S	NS	S	S	NS	NP	NP	NP
Warth v. Seldin 422 U.S. 490 (1975) (failure to provide low-income housing)	NS	S	S	S	S	NS	NS	NS	NS	NP	NP
Valley Forge Christian College v. Americans United 454 U.S. 464 (1982) (government property to secular institution)	NS	NP	S	S	NS	NP	S	NS	NS	S	NS
Craig v. Boren 429 U.S. 190 (1976) (bartender raising rights of customer)	NS	NP	S	S	S	S	S	S	S	S	NP
Duke Power Co. v. Carolina 438 U.S. 59 (1978) (construction of nuclear power plant)	S	NP	S	S	S	S	NS	NS	S	NS	NP

	Bur	Dou	Bre	Mar	Whi	Stew	Bla	Reh	Pow	Stev	Oco
Executive Power											
United States v. Nixon 416 U.S. 683 (1974) (presidential immunity)	NI	NI	NI	NI	NI	NI	NI	NP	NI	NP	NP
Butz v. Economou 438 U.S. 478 (1978) (executive immunity)	I	NP	NI	NI	NI	I	NI	I	NI	I	NP
Davis v. Passman 442 U.S. 228 (1979) (legislative immunity)	I	NP	NI	NI	NI	I	NI	I	I	NI	NP
Nixon v. Fitzgerald 457 U.S. 731 (1982) (presidential immunity)	I	NP	NI	NI	NI	NP	NI	I	I	I	I
Goldwater v. Carter 444 U.S. 996 (1979) (termination of treaty)	NJ	NP	J	NJ	?	NJ	?	NJ	J	NJ	NP
Dames and Moore v. Regan 453 U.S. 654 (1981) (settlement of claims)	C	NP	C	C	C	C	C	C	C	C	NP
New York Times Co. v. United States 403 U.S. 713 (1971) (injunction against publication)	C	U	U	U	U	U	C	NP	NP	NP	NP
Snepp v. United States 444 U.S. 507 (1980) (enforcement of nonpublication agreement)	C	NP	IL	IL	C	C	C	C	IL	NP	NP

	Bur	Dou	Bre	Mar	Whi	Stew	Bla	Reh	Pow	Stev	Oco
Rational Basis											
Dandridge v. Williams 397 U.S. 471 (1970) (limitation on AFDC benefits)	C	L	U	U	C	C	C	NP	NP	NP	NP
San Antonio v. Rodriguez 411 U.S. 1 (1973) (school finance)	C	U	U	U	U	C	C	C	C	NP	NP
United States R.R. Retirement Board v. Fritz 449 U.S. 166 (1980) (reallocation of retirement benefits)	C	NP	U	U	C	C	C	C	C	C	NP
Plyler v. Doe 457 U.S. 202 (1982) (denial of education to illegal immigrants)	C	NP	U	U	C	NP	U	C	U	U	NP
U.S. Dept. of Agriculture v. Moreno 413 U.S. 523 (1973) (limitation on access to food stamps)	C	U	U	U	U	U	U	C	U	NP	NP

Key

S	= plaintiff has standing	J	= justiciable	NP	= not participating
NS	= plaintiff lacks standing	NJ	= nonjusticiable	?	= position unclear
I	= defendant has immunity	C	= constitutional		
NI	= defendant does not have immunity	U	= unconstitutional		
		IL	= illegal under statute		

3

THE BURGER COURT AND FEDERALISM

Disputes over federal-state relations forced the Burger Court to directly confront some of the most basic tenets of post-1937 jurisprudence. The New Deal Court's approach to federalism-related issues had emerged in a series of cases dealing with the scope of congressional power to regulate economic activity under the Commerce Clause. The Commerce Clause does not explicitly provide Congress with authority over all of the economic affairs of the nation; instead, it grants power only to regulate "Commerce with foreign Nations, and among the several States, and with the Indian tribes." Prior to 1937, the Court held that congressional power was limited to those activities that had a direct effect on interstate or foreign commerce. However, in decisions such as *NLRB v. Jones and Laughlin Steel Corp.,*[1] *Wickard v. Filburn,*[2] and *United States v. Darby,*[3] the Roosevelt Court vastly expanded the scope of permissible federal action, concluding that the Constitution allowed Congress to regulate any activity that had an effect on interstate commerce. In practical terms, this new approach left Congress with unfettered authority to control all economic activity.

This dramatic aggrandizement of federal power challenged the most basic premises of state autonomy. Implicitly, judicial deference to congressional decision making in cases such as *Jones and Laughlin, Wickard,* and *Darby* reflected the view that the United States is a national economy, whose affairs ought to be governed for the benefit of the citizenry as a whole. This view is in considerable tension with the traditional idea that, subject only to a limited, well-defined set of constitutional constraints, state governments should be allowed to regulate their territory with a view to advancing the unique interests of their own citizenry.

The diminished importance of states as quasi-sovereign entities was reflected in the basic structure of the Court's constitutional jurisprudence from 1937 to 1969. Prior to 1937, issues of federal-state relations were central to constitutional analysis; however, in the wake of the expansion of the commerce

---

1. *NLRB v. Jones and Laughlin Steel Corp.,* 301 U.S. 37 (1937).
2. *Wickard v. Filburn,* 317 U.S. 111 (1942).
3. *United States v. Darby,* 312 U.S. 100 (1941).

power, issues of federalism played a greatly diminished role. Instead, the Court focused its attention almost entirely on the relationship between the judiciary and the legislature—an emphasis reflected perhaps most clearly in the famous *United States v. Carolene Products Co.* footnote.[4]

The justices of the Warren Court almost uniformly embraced this aspect of Roosevelt Court jurisprudence; however, the question of the extent to which state autonomy should be considered a significant element in constitutional jurisprudence became an important issue dividing the liberal and conservative justices of the Burger Court. Respect for states' rights had little place in the jurisprudence of Justices Douglas, Brennan, and Marshall; indeed, they consistently emphasized the broad scope of federal authority, and typically viewed constitutional adjudication not in terms of its impact on state autonomy, but rather as a clash between judicial and legislative authority. By contrast, the rhetoric of state autonomy was a consistent feature of the opinions of Justices Powell, Rehnquist, and O'Connor.

Despite their rhetoric, even the most conservative members of the Burger Court acquiesced in the view that Congress had virtually unlimited power to regulate private economic activity. For example, in *Hodel v. Virginia Surface Mining and Reclamation Ass'n.*, the conservative justices agreed unanimously that the Commerce Clause granted Congress authority to pass the Surface Mining Act, notwithstanding Justice Powell's comment that the statute "mandates an extraordinarily intrusive program of federal regulation and control of land use and land reclamation, activities normally left to state and local governments."[5] By contrast, the conservative commitment to state autonomy emerged clearly in efforts to protect the operations of the state governments themselves from undue interference and, to a lesser extent, to protect state government authority over the political process.

Oregon v. Mitchell provided the earliest example of the conservative solicitude for state autonomy.[6] *Mitchell* tested the limits of the doctrine articulated by the Warren Court in *Katzenbach v. Morgan.*[7] In *Morgan,* over the dissents of Justices Harlan and Stewart, the Court held that Congress could rely on its authority to enforce the Fourteenth Amendment to bar the use of literacy tests as a qualification for suffrage, even though the Court itself had held that the use of such tests per se did not violate the Fourteenth Amendment.

Mitchell itself was a challenge to a federal statute requiring states to lower the minimum voting age to eighteen. Justices Douglas, Brennan, White, and Marshall argued that the statute was constitutional, reasoning

---

4. *United States v. Carolene Products Co.*, 308 U.S. 144, 152 n. 4 (1938).

5. *Hodel v. Virginia Surface Mining and Reclamation Ass'n.*, 452 U.S. 264, 305 (Burger, C. J., concurring), 305–7 (Powell, J., concurring), 307–13 (Rehnquist, J., concurring in the judgment) (1981).

6. *Oregon v. Mitchell*, 400 U.S. 112 (1970).

7. *Katzenbach v. Morgan*, 384 U.S. 641 (1966).

that Congress could have concluded that the denial of the right to vote to persons between the ages of eighteen and twenty-one was irrational, and thus violated the Equal Protection Clause. By contrast, Chief Justice Burger and Justice Blackmun joined Harlan and Stewart in concluding that the statute was unconstitutional, contending that the *Morgan* rationale should be limited to cases in which Congress had found that a particular practice was in fact used to discriminate against a class that was entitled to special protection under the Fourteenth Amendment. Hugo Black cast the deciding vote; he agreed that in general *Morgan* should be limited to racial discrimination, but argued that Congress had plenary power to set the voting age for federal elections. Thus, he took the view that the statute was unconstitutional with respect to state elections, but constitutional with respect to federal elections.

The practical impact of *Mitchell* was short-lived. The decision created a situation in which some states would be required to maintain separate voting lists for state and federal elections. This situation was obviously intolerable. Thus, in 1971 the Twenty-Sixth Amendment to the Constitution was quickly adopted, explicitly providing that persons over the age of eighteen should be allowed to vote in all elections.

Although somewhat more arcane, the Burger Court's interpretations of the Eleventh Amendment had more staying power.[8] Adopted in 1798 in response to the Court's decision in *Chisolm v. Georgia*,[9] the Eleventh Amendment provides that "the Judicial power of the United States shall not be construed to extend to any suit . . . prosecuted against one of the United States by Citizens of another State, or by Citizens or Subjects of a Foreign State." On its face, the language of the amendment does not preclude the exercise of jurisdiction over a lawsuit brought against a state by one of its own citizens; nonetheless, the 1890 decision in *Hans v. Louisiana*[10] held that these suits were barred by the amendment as well. On the other hand, in 1908, the Court held in *Ex parte Young*[11] that suits could be maintained against state officials for allegedly violating the Constitution while acting in their official capacity, and that they could be ordered to cease such violations.

Until 1973, it was generally assumed that the principle of *Ex parte Young* permitted federal courts to order state officials to pay damages from the state

8. Detailed studies of the Court's Eleventh Amendment jurisprudence include Vicki C. Jackson, "The Supreme Court, the Eleventh Amendment, and State Sovereign Immunity," *Yale Law Journal* 98 (1988): 1–126; and Erwin Chemerinsky, "State Sovereign and Federal Court Power: The Eleventh Amendment after *Pennhurst v. Halderman*," *Hastings Constitutional Law Quarterly* 12 (1985): 643–68.

9. *Chisolm v. Georgia*, 2 U.S. (2 Dal.) 419 (1793).

10. *Hans v. Louisiana*, 134 U.S. 1 (1890).

11. *Ex parte Young*, 209 U.S. 123 (1908).

treasury to indemnify those whose federal rights had been violated; moreover, the Court had summarily affirmed a number of lower court decisions
ordering just such relief. However, in *Edelman v. Jordan,* a majority of the
justices concluded that these awards were in effect judgments against the
state itself, and thus barred by the Eleventh Amendment. Dissenting, Justices Douglas, Marshall, and Blackmun insisted that the award of damages
fell within the purview of *Ex parte Young;* Justice Brennan went even further, arguing that the Eleventh Amendment should be interpreted according to its plain meaning, and held not to bar suits brought against states by
their own citizens.[12]

For four of the members of the *Edelman* majority, the decision reflected
a commitment to the preservation of a substantial degree of state autonomy
within the federal system—a commitment that was reflected in other areas
of Burger Court jurisprudence as well. However, they were able to prevail in
Edelman only because they gained the support of Justice White—more often,
one of the stronger nationalists on the Court. As the Burger era progressed,
the same majority (with Justice O'Connor having replaced Justice Stewart)
continued to expand the reach of Eleventh Amendment protections. In
Pennhurst State School and Hospital v. Halderman, the five justices concluded
that the Eleventh Amendment prevented federal courts from ordering state
officials to conform their behavior to state law—even when the federal court
had pendent jurisdiction over the state law claim. Dissenting, Justice Stevens
argued that *Ex parte Young* was premised on the view that illegal actions by
state officials were ultra vires, and that this rationale applied equally to ille-
gality under state and federal law. By contrast, the majority reasoned that *Ex
parte Young* reflected the need to vindicate the supreme authority of federal
law, and that this need was absent where the only claim was that the state official was acting in a manner inconsistent with state law.[13]

The *Edelman* majority's treatment of the impact of federal statutes on
Eleventh Amendment questions was even more significant. Even before
Edelman, it had been firmly established that Congress could require states to
waive their Eleventh Amendment immunity as a precondition for participation in federal programs. Subsequently, in *Fitzpatrick v. Bitzer,* reasoning that
the Fourteenth Amendment had modified the Eleventh, the Court unanimously held that Congress could abrogate a state's immunity when acting
under its authority to enforce the Fourteenth Amendment.[14] However, in
Atascadero State Hospital v. Scanlon, the *Edelman* majority held that courts
should conclude that Congress intended to subject states to suits in federal

12. *Edelman v. Jordan,* 415 U.S. 651 (1973).

13. *Pennhurst State School and Hospital v. Halderman,* 465 U.S. 89 (1984).

14. *Fitzpatrick v. Bitzer,* 427 U.S. 445 (1976).

court only if the legislative intent was expressed "in unmistakable language in the [relevant] statute itself."[15]

Notwithstanding decisions such as *Edelman* and *Atascadero,* it would be a mistake to suggest that the Burger Court was uniformly receptive to claims of immunity by state and local governments. For example, in *Hutto v. Finney,*[16] only Justices White and Rehnquist dissented from the conclusion that the federal courts could order payments that were ancillary to prospective injunctive relief. Moreover, in *Monell v. New York City Dept. of Social Services*[17] Justices Powell and White joined the *Pennhurst* and *Atascadero* dissenters to overrule the Warren Court's decision in *Monroe v. Pape*[18] and hold that local governments were subject to suit under 42 U.S.C., section 1983—the primary statutory vehicle for lawsuits alleging violations of federal constitutional rights. Nonetheless, the overall tenor of the Burger Court's treatment of immunity issues reflected far more concern for state autonomy than had the jurisprudence of the Warren Court.

By contrast, the conservative justices were ultimately unsuccessful in their efforts to protect state governments from commercial legislation adopted by Congress. The decision in *National League of Cities v. Usery*[19] was the high-water mark for these efforts. *Usery* was a challenge to the application of the provisions of the federal Fair Labor Standards Act to state and municipal employees. A five-justice majority overruled the Warren Court's decision in *Maryland v. Wirtz*[20] and found that this application was unconstitutional. Speaking for the majority, Justice Rehnquist conceded that regulation of wages and hours generally was within the scope of congressional power to regulate interstate commerce. Nonetheless, he argued that the exercise of this power was limited by the principle that certain aspects of state sovereignty were themselves constitutionally protected—a principle that Rehnquist found to be explicitly embodied in the Tenth Amendment. He concluded that the statute at issue in *Usery* ran afoul of this principle because it interfered with the integral governmental functions of state and local government.

Dissenting, Justices Brennan, White, Marshall, and Stevens took the view that principles of state sovereignty imposed no significant constraints on Congressional exercises of the commerce power. Brennan's dissent was phrased in almost apocalyptic terms, analogizing the arguments of the majority to the approach taken by those justices who sought to strike down

15. *Atascadero State Hospital v. Scanlon,* 473 U.S. 234 (1985).
16. *Hutto v. Finney,* 437 U.S. 678 (1978).
17. *Monell v. New York City Dept. of Social Services,* 436 U.S. 658 (1978).
18. *Monroe v. Pape,* 365 U.S. 167 (1961).
19. *National League of Cities v. Usery,* 426 U.S. 833 (1976).
20. *Maryland v. Wirtz,* 392 U.S. 183 (1968).

New Deal legislation in the 1930s.[21] In fact, the implications of *Usery* were far more limited than Brennan suggested. All of the members of the *Usery* majority saw the principles of the case as limited to regulation of government entities; as already noted, during the Burger era, none was willing to impose meaningful restraints on congressional authority to regulate private economic activity under the commerce power.

Federal Energy Regulatory Commission [FERC] v. Mississippi brought the conservative position into sharp perspective. *FERC* was a challenge to a federal statute that focused on the energy-use policies of local public utilities. The statute allowed FERC to exempt local utilities from certain types of state and local regulations. In addition, the statute required the state agencies regulating these utilities to consider certain other types of regulations. Three of the five members of the *Usery* majority dissented from the judgment upholding the mandatory consideration provision; they were joined by Justice Sandra Day O'Connor, who had replaced Potter Stewart and would become one of the Court's most passionate defenders of states' rights. In *FERC*, O'Connor complained that the statute "conscript[s] state utility commissions into the national bureaucratic army." At the same time, however, O'Connor and all members of the *Usery* majority joined the portion of the *FERC* opinion that reaffirmed federal power to directly overturn state regulations of even the intrastate activities of the utilities, notwithstanding the fact that regulation of the operation of public utilities has historically been a matter left to the states. According to Justice O'Connor, the difference was that the direct federal regulation "merely pre-empts state control of private conduct, rather than regulating the 'States as States.'" Thus, *FERC* clearly reflected the limitations of the holding in *Usery*.[22]

FERC also exemplified another crucial factor in the *Usery* line of cases— the central position occupied by Justice Blackmun on this issue. In *Usery*, Blackmun had provided the critical fifth vote for the majority opinion; however, he had also filed a brief concurring opinion reflecting some reservations and suggesting that he might oppose any extension of the holding. In subsequent cases, he consistently joined the *Usery* dissenters, thereby creating five-justice majorities that gave the *Usery* principles their narrowest possible scope. Finally, in *Garcia v. San Antonio Metropolitan Transit Authority*, Blackmun wrote for this group in overruling *Usery*, arguing that judicial oversight was unnecessary because the Constitution provided sufficient structural protections for state sovereignty, and that, in any event, it had proved

21. *National League of Cities v. Usery*, 426 U.S. at 856–60, 868 (Brennan, J., dissenting), 880–81 (Stevens, J., dissenting).

22. *Federal Energy Regulatory Commission [FERC] v. Mississippi*, 456 U.S. 742, 775–76 and n. 1 (O'Connor, J., dissenting in part) (1982). To the same effect, see ibid., 771–75 (Powell, J., dissenting in part).

impossible to devise a principled line that divided permissible federal regulations of the states from unconstitutional intrusions on state autonomy.[23] Thus, the Burger Court ultimately left the scope of federal power to regulate economic activity basically where the Court had found it—essentially unchecked, except by specific constitutional prohibitions.

By contrast, the Burger Court made important changes in the principles governing so-called "dormant" Commerce Clause jurisprudence. While the Commerce Clause by its terms is only a grant of power to Congress, it has traditionally been held to constrain the authority of the states to regulate interstate commerce as well. Disputes over the extent of these constraints have occupied the Supreme Court since the era of John Marshall. During the chief justiceship of Warren Burger, dormant Commerce Clause analysis took a markedly nationalistic turn.[24]

Historically, the demarcation of the line between permissible and impermissible state regulation under dormant Commerce Clause analysis has reflected two different types of arguments—functional arguments, which rest on the observation that the national economy as a whole will function more smoothly if, in the absence of explicit federal action, certain activities remain subject to state regulation, and essentialist arguments, which take the view that states retain inherent authority to regulate certain types of activity. Under the pre-1937 regime, the essentialist component of dormant Commerce Clause analysis was the flip side of the jurisprudence of federal power. Under that regime, the federal government lacked authority to regulate economic activities that had only an indirect effect on interstate commerce. Thus, states perforce retained authority to regulate such activities. The law relating to direct state regulations of interstate commerce was more complex. While such statutes were often held unconstitutional, states were allowed to adopt regulations which were deemed intrinsic to their sovereign prerogatives.[25] In addition, states were allowed to regulate matters which, for functional reasons, were best left to local control.[26]

---

23. *Garcia v. San Antonio Metropolitan Area Transit Authority,* 469 U.S. 528 (1985). The line of cases from *Usery* to *Garcia* is discussed in detail in Martha A. Field, *"Garcia v. San Antonio Metropolitan Transit Authority:* Demise of a Misguided Doctrine," *Harvard Law Review* 99 (1985): 84–118; and William W. Van Alstyne, "The Second Death of Federalism," *Michigan Law Review* (1985): 1709–33.

24. The argument which follows is made in greater detail in Earl M. Maltz, "The Impact of the Constitutional Revolution of 1937 on the Dormant Commerce Clause—A Case Study in the Decline of State Autonomy," *Harvard Journal of Law and Public Policy* 19 (1995): 121–45.

25. See, for example, *Baltimore and Ohio Railroad Co. v. Maryland,* 88 U.S. (21 Wall.) 456 (1874); *Reid v. Colorado,* 187 U.S. 137 (1902); *Geer v. Connecticut,* 161 U.S. 519 (1896).

26. The classic statement of this position is *Cooley v. Board of Wardens,* 53 U.S. (12 How.) 299 (1851).

The sea change in constitutional law that took place in 1937 was not directly related to dormant Commerce Clause analysis. Nonetheless, the revolution of 1937 indirectly threatened preexisting dormant Commerce Clause doctrine on a number of different levels. First, the essentialist elements of pre-1937 law were based on a formalistic approach to constitutional adjudication generally. By contrast, reflecting the influence of the Legal Realist movement, post-1937 constitutional jurisprudence was based primarily on functional principles.

Moreover, the cornerstone of the pre-1937 regime was the view that states possessed unique responsibilities in the federal system. In the wake of *Jones and Laughlin* and its progeny, however, this view lost much of its descriptive force. Once it is assumed that the federal government has unbridled authority to regulate all aspects of the national economy, the idea that states should retain plenary authority over intrastate activities potentially becomes an anachronism. Thus, in some respects, the jurisprudential changes of the mid-twentieth century suggested that states should be subject to greater constraints under dormant Commerce Clause analysis.

Other elements of post-1937 constitutional jurisprudence pointed in different directions in dormant Commerce Clause cases. One of the central themes of the revolution of 1937—the importance of deference to legislative judgments—clearly suggested that the Court should defer to the state legislatures, even in the face of claims that the actions of the legislatures interfered with interstate commerce. This theme was a critical element of the analysis of Justice Hugo Black, one of the central figures in the development of post–New Deal jurisprudence.

However, post-1937 analysis clearly did not require judicial deference to legislative judgment in all cases. In a footnote to his 1938 opinion in *United States v. Carolene Products Co.*, Chief Justice Harlan Fiske Stone suggested that legislative enactments might be subject to more intense scrutiny if they either corrupted the legislative process itself or had a disproportionate effect on groups whose interests were inadequately represented in the legislature.[27] Combined with the pervasive nationalism of the post-1937 federal power cases, this theory potentially suggested a foundation for increased judicial activism under the rubric of the dormant Commerce Clause.

Against this background, the Stone and Vinson Courts developed a new approach to dormant Commerce Clause analysis. This approach distinguished sharply between discriminatory and nondiscriminatory state regulations. Statutes which discriminated between interstate and

---

27. *United States v. Carolene Products Co.*, 308 U.S. 144, 152 n. 4.

intrastate commerce were generally subjected to stringent judicial scrutiny. By contrast, evenhanded state regulations were measured against a balancing test which purported to compare the burden on commerce with the state's interest in maintaining its regulation. Finally, the Court showed great deference to state laws which implicated matters of uniquely local concern.[28]

Unlike many areas of constitutional law, dormant Commerce Clause analysis escaped the Warren era largely unscathed; indeed, the Warren Court showed little interest at all in the dormant Commerce Clause. By contrast, dormant Commerce Clause cases figured prominently on the docket of the Burger Court, and the Court made substantial refinements to existing doctrine. The refinements ultimately created a regime which made significant new inroads on state autonomy.[29]

Some of the most important decisions involved the constitutionality of laws that discriminated against interstate commerce. A majority of the Burger Court justices enthusiastically supported the view that such laws were almost invariably unconstitutional. Moreover, they were generally willing to enforce this principle even at the cost of substantially devaluing the traditional notion that the polity of each state forms a distinct, quasi-independent society.

Admittedly, there was one exception to this trend—the recognition of the so-called "market participant" exception. *Hughes v. Alexandria Scrap Corp.*[30] and *Reeves, Inc. v. Stake*[31] are the seminal cases. In *Alexandria Scrap,* the state of Maryland paid bounties to junkyards that reprocessed abandoned cars found on state highways. To qualify for the bounties, out-of-state junkyards had to file more extensive title documentation than that required of processors located within Maryland. A Virginia processor argued that the statute unconstitutionally discriminated against out-of-state concerns by interfering with the flow of abandoned vehicles to non-Maryland processors. In *Reeves,* the Commerce Clause challenge was more straightforward. There, the state of South Dakota operated a cement manufacturing plant, and state residents were given first priority to purchase the plant's products. A Wyoming customer argued that this policy unconstitutionally discriminated against out-of-state residents.

---

28. See, for example, *Dean Milk Co. v. City of Madison,* 340 U.S. 349 (1951); *Southern Pacific Co. v. Arizona,* 325 U.S. 761 (1945); *South Carolina State Highway Dept. v. Barnwell Bros.,* 303 U.S. 177 (1938).

29. Donald H. Regan, "The Supreme Court and State Protectionism: Making Sense of the Dormant Clause," *Michigan Law Review* 86 (1986): 1091–287, provides a comprehensive survey and analysis of the Burger Court's approach to this area of the law.

30. *Hughes v. Alexandria Scrap Corp.,* 426 U.S. 794 (1976).

31. *Reeves, Inc. v. Stake,* 447 U.S. 429 (1980).

In each case, a majority of the Court refused to strike down the statute at issue. The two majority opinions declared that where a state acts as a market *participant*, rather than a market *regulator*, its actions were immune from Commerce Clause scrutiny. In both cases, the majority relied on essentialist arguments to support its position. Thus, in *Alexandria Scrap*, Justice Powell declared that "[n]othing in the purposes animating the Commerce Clause prohibits a State . . . from participating in the market and exercising the right to favor its own citizens over others"; and in *Reeves*, Justice Blackmun asserted that "[r]estraint in this area is . . . counseled by considerations of state sovereignty, the role of each state "as guardian and trustee for its people" and "the long recognized right of trader or manufacturer, engaged in an entirely private business, freely to exercise its own independent discretion as to parties with whom he will deal."[32]

Not surprisingly, both decisions were far from unanimous. Justices Brennan, White, and Marshall dissented in *Alexandria Scrap*, while Justices Powell and Stevens joined Brennan and White in dissent in *Reeves*. In responding to the arguments of the majority, the dissenters relied in part on purely formal arguments, noting that the free flow of interstate commerce was inhibited in both cases, and that neither fell into exceptions that had been explicitly established by pre-*Alexandria Scrap* jurisprudence. Underlying their arguments, however, was a rejection of essentialism, either in whole or in part. Thus, arguing that the approach which he himself had taken in *Alexandria Scrap* should be limited to cases involving the "'integral operatio[n] in areas of traditional governmental functions,'" Powell contended in *Reeves* that "[i]f . . . the State enters the private market and operates a commercial enterprise for the advantage of its private citizens, it may not evade the constitutional policy against economic Balkanization." In essence, Powell's argument was that a state could not rely on a special relationship with its own citizens to limit the distribution of governmentally created benefits to those citizens.[33]

Despite these dissents, defenders of state autonomy obviously scored important victories in the market participation cases. The extent of this victory, however, should not be overstated. *Alexandria Scrap* and *Reeves* challenged one of the most widely shared tenets of the essentialist view of state autonomy—the idea that a state government may limit its largesse to those who owe allegiance to that government. Nonetheless, in both cases the statutes escaped invalidation only by narrow margins. Indeed, in *Reeves*, the statute was upheld only because of the inexplicable support of Justice

---

32. *Hughes v. Alexandria Scrap Corp.*, 426 U.S. at 810; *Reeves, Inc. v. Stake*, 447 U.S. at 438–39 (citation omitted).

33. *Hughes v. Alexandria Scrap Corp.*, 426 U.S. at 817–32 (Brennan, J., dissenting); *Reeves, Inc. v. Stake*, 447 U.S. at 447–54 (Powell, J., dissenting), 449–50.

Thurgood Marshall—a dissenter in *Alexandria Scrap,* who was normally one of the most thoroughgoing anti-essentialist nationalists on the Court. Thus, in a certain sense, *Alexandria Scrap* and *Reeves* actually reflected the weakness of the influence of the concept of state autonomy on the dormant Commerce Clause jurisprudence of the Burger Court.

This weakness was underscored by the subsequent decision in *South-Central Timber Development Corp. v. Wunnicke.* In *Wunnicke,* the state of Alaska sold a substantial amount of timber owned by the state. Each of the contracts for sale required that the purchaser partially process the timber prior to shipping it outside the state. The purchasers argued that this restriction ran afoul of the dormant Commerce Clause. Responding to this argument, Justices Rehnquist and O'Connor contended that the restriction fell within the market participant exception of *Alexandria Scrap* and *Reeves.* They reasoned that the state, if it had so chosen, could have processed the timber itself prior to sale, and argued that it would be "unduly formalistic" to treat the contractual provision any differently. By contrast, Justice Blackmun joined *Reeves* dissenters Brennan, White, and Stevens in arguing that the market participant exception did not apply, and that the restriction was unconstitutional. In addition to focusing on the intuitive distinction between the earlier market participation cases and *Wunnicke,* they relied on analogies to both the common-law distaste for restraints on alienation and the prohibition on vertical restraints of trade, a prohibition that is central to antitrust law. The balance of power was held by Chief Justice Burger and Justices Marshall and Powell; they, however, declined to express an opinion on the issue, preferring instead to remand the decision to the lower courts for initial determination.[34]

Wunnicke aptly reflects the deep divisions on the Burger Court on dormant Commerce Clause issues. While the strong advocates of state autonomy were able to gain enough support to prevail in *Alexandria Scrap* and *Reeves,* more often they met defeat in cases involving claims of discrimination against interstate commerce. The decision in *Philadelphia v. New Jersey* is a particularly clear example.[35]

In *New Jersey,* the state of New Jersey prohibited the importation of liquid or solid waste except for certain defined purposes. Over the objection of Chief Justice Burger and Justice Rehnquist, the Court concluded that this prohibition ran afoul of the dormant Commerce Clause. Speaking for the majority, Justice Stewart observed that the legislation "overtly block[ed] the flow of interstate commerce at a State's border," and concluded that the statute fell within a "virtually *per se* rule of invalidity." In

---

34. *South-Central Timber Development Corp., Inc. v. Wunnicke,* 467 U.S. 82 (1984).
35. *Philadelphia v. New Jersey,* 437 U.S. 617 (1978).

defending this conclusion, Stewart was forced to distinguish earlier cases which had allowed a state to prohibit the importation of things such as diseased cattle that posed a danger to the state. Stewart characterized the earlier cases as dealing with items whose "very movement risked contagion." By contrast, he asserted, in *New Jersey* the state considered only the *disposal* of waste—not its transportation—to be a problem.[36]

Considered in isolation, this contention is implausible on its face. The dangers against which the state was attempting to protect itself were entirely noncommercial. New Jersey was simply trying to limit the exposure of its citizenry to unhealthy conditions. Indeed, the New Jersey regulatory scheme included specific exceptions covering the importation of waste for commercial uses, in which out-of-state entrepreneurs presumably would compete with New Jersey waste producers.

Apparently aware of this problem, Justice Stewart sought to bolster his argument by characterizing the relevant commodity as New Jersey landfill space. According to the majority, the state legislature intended to preserve a local resource—landfill space—for its own residents. This analysis has some superficial appeal; however, it ignores the connection between waste and landfills. The presence of neither is desirable from a state's perspective. When faced with a waste problem, the state must choose between (1) allowing the waste to lie around randomly, (2) providing landfills, or (3) providing some other means of disposal. Thus, New Jersey provided for landfills not because they are intrinsically desirable, but because they are the lesser among evils. In short, the real issue was the waste itself—a commodity from which a state should have the right to protect itself and its citizenry under essentialist theory. Indeed, this point is implicit in the clearest statement of the underlying rationale of the majority opinion:

> Today, cities in Pennsylvania and New York find it expedient or necessary to send their waste into New Jersey for disposal, and New Jersey claims the right to close its borders to such traffic. Tomorrow, cities in New Jersey may find it expedient or necessary to send their waste into Pennsylvania or New York for disposal, and those States might then claim the right to close their borders. The Commerce Clause will protect New Jersey in the future, just as it protects her neighbors now, from efforts by one State to isolate itself in the stream of interstate commerce from a problem shared by all.[37]

---

36. *Philadelphia v. New Jersey,* 437 U.S. at 624, 626–29.
37. Ibid., 626–28, 629.

In evaluating this formulation of the principles underlying dormant Commerce Clause analysis, it is important to recognize that the problem which produced the New Jersey statute was "shared by all" only in a limited sense. The problem is only shared to the extent that all states must find some means to dispose of their own, locally produced waste. In theory, each state could be required to resolve this problem within its own borders; that is, there is no reason why Philadelphia's waste disposal problems should necessarily affect the quality of life in New Jersey, or vice versa.

Thus, *New Jersey* is fundamentally inconsistent with any strong theory of state autonomy. The decision rests on a vision of federalism that requires all states to participate in the solution to problems that many states suffer—even where such participation would place burdens on a state which are disproportionate to the problems faced by the state itself. Thus, the majority opinion implicitly rejects the view that each state is primarily responsible to its own citizenry; instead, it essentially conceptualizes the state governments as administrative units of the federal government, whose mission is to further the interests of the general populace of the nation.

The Burger Court's treatment of evenhanded regulations suggests a similar vision. Early in the tenure of Warren Burger, in *Pike v. Bruce Church, Inc.,* the Court committed itself to the balancing test that had become the dominant mode of dormant Commerce Clause analysis in the post-1937 era:

> Although the criteria for determining the validity of state statutes affecting interstate commerce have been variously stated, the general rule that emerges can be phrased as follows: Where the statute regulates evenhandedly to effectuate a legitimate local public interest and its effects on interstate commerce is only incidental, it will be upheld unless the burden on such commerce is clearly excessive in relation to the putative local benefits. If a legitimate local purpose is found, then the question is one of degree. And the extent of the burden that will be tolerated will of course depend on the nature of the local interest involved, and on whether it could be promoted as well with a lesser impact on interstate activities.[38]

Even in the post-1937 era, this test was traditionally qualified by the proviso that, where a matter was of sufficiently local concern, evenhanded state regulation would be subject only to a rational basis test. This principle suffered significant erosion during the Burger era—particularly in the area of highway regulation.

---

38. *Pike v. Bruce Church, Inc.,* 397 U.S. 137 (1970) (citation omitted).

Any effort to assess the Burger Court's treatment of state highway regulations must begin with the 1938 decision in *South Carolina State Highway Department v. Barnwell Brothers, Inc. Barnwell* was a challenge to a South Carolina statute that limited the weight and width of the trucks allowed on state highways. Eighty-five to 90 percent of the trucks used in interstate commerce failed to satisfy the statutory requirements. Nonetheless, the Court unanimously rejected a constitutional challenge to the regulation, holding, inter alia, that the statute was not inconsistent with the strictures of the dormant Commerce Clause.[39]

Justice Stone's opinion for the Court drew heavily on essentialist analysis. He asserted that "few subjects of state regulation are so peculiarly of local concern as is the use of state highways" and noted that "local highways are built, owned and maintained by the state or its municipal subdivisions [and] the state has a primary and immediate concern in their safe and economical administration." Moreover, he reaffirmed the principle that "a state can, if it sees fit, build and maintain its own highways, canals and railroads and . . . in the absence of Congressional action their regulation is peculiarly within its competence." In addition, however, Stone also made functional arguments, emphasizing the superior fact-finding ability of legislatures, and suggested in a footnote that the judicial condemnation of discriminatory state action is based upon the view that, in those situations, state legislative action "is not likely to be subjected to those political restraints which are normally exerted on legislation where it affects adversely some interests within the state."[40]

Despite this reference to themes that would soon be elaborated in *Carolene Products, Barnwell* is best viewed as a reaffirmation of state authority to adopt nondiscriminatory state highway regulations. The erosion of this authority began in *Bibb v. Navajo Freight Lines, Inc.*, where the Warren Court relied on the dormant Commerce Clause to strike down an Illinois regulation that required trucks traveling on state highways to use contoured mudguards. Distinguishing *Barnwell*, the Court focused its attention on the fact that at least forty-five other states allowed the use of straight mudguards, and that one state required the use of straight guards. Under these circumstances, the Court held the Illinois regulation invalid because of the conceded expense and disruptive effect of requiring trucks to change mudguards at the Illinois border and the state's failure to demonstrate that contoured mudguards had any advantage over their straight counterparts.[41]

---

39. *South Carolina State Highway Department v. Barnwell Bros.*, 303 U.S. 177.
40. Ibid., 187, 190–92, 185 n. 2.
41. *Bibb v. Navajo Freight Lines, Inc.*, 354 U.S. 520, 523, 527–28, 529–30 (1959).

The reasoning of the *Bibb* Court was antithetical to the state-autonomy-based analysis of *Barnwell*. Under Stone's *Barnwell* analysis, the fact that other states may have preferred straight mudguards would have been irrelevant, since only Illinois (and the federal government) have authority to regulate Illinois highways. However, the case makes perfect sense when viewed against the background of the functional, post-1937 vision of a national economy, regulated for national purposes. From that perspective, since the Illinois regulation created major inconveniences for the national economy, it would be invalid absent a showing of some countervailing benefit.

In any event, the *Bibb* Court itself was careful to limit the scope of its analysis. The majority opinion repeatedly emphasized that state highway regulations would rarely be invalidated under the dormant Commerce Clause, and explicitly limited the import of its argument to cases where state regulations imposed inconsistent requirements on the interstate transportation of goods. The Burger Court, however, would greatly expand the scope of the *Bibb* analysis.

This expansion began with the decision in *Raymond Motor Transportation, Inc. v. Rice*. In *Rice*, the Court dealt with Wisconsin regulations prohibiting the use of most trucks longer than fifty-five feet in length. By contrast, the states bordering Wisconsin allowed the use of sixty-five-foot double trailers on interstate highways. Against this background, a trucking company contended that the Wisconsin regulation ran afoul of the dormant Commerce Clause. The challenger demonstrated that the state law raised its costs by requiring that some cargo be unloaded and reloaded at the Wisconsin border and that other cargo be rerouted around Wisconsin. The challenger also introduced evidence which supported its contention that sixty-five-foot double trailers were no more unsafe than fifty-five-foot single trailers when operated on interstate highways. The state, by contrast, introduced no safety evidence, choosing instead to argue that the length regulation was immune from dormant Commerce Clause scrutiny under *Barnwell*.[42]

Although the chief justice and Justice Rehnquist were initially inclined to accept this argument,[43] they ultimately joined a unanimous Court which struck down the regulation. Speaking for the Court, Justice Lewis Powell concluded that the *Bibb* analysis was not limited to cases involving irreconcilable state regulations; instead, he applied the *Bruce Church* balancing test. Given the record before the Court, Powell deter-

42. *Raymond Motor Transportation, Inc. v. Rice*, 434 U.S. 429, 436–43 (1978).
43. Bernard Schwartz, *The Ascent of Pragmatism: The Burger Court in Action* (New York: Addison-Wesley, 1990), 113.

mined that the Wisconsin regulation failed to satisfy this test. He bolstered this conclusion by arguing that exemptions which favored local interests in *Rice* weakened the internal political check, although he conceded that this factor was "not decisive." Admittedly, Powell took care to reemphasize the strong presumption of validity for state highway regulations; however, the theory that a state had inherent authority to regulate the highways that it constructed and maintained was mentioned only in a single sentence in a footnote that also referred to the *Barnwell* footnote's discussion of the internal political check.[44]

Viewed in isolation, despite its reference to the *Bruce Church* test, *Rice* might have been viewed as one of the rare examples of a plaintiff carrying its stringent burden of proof under the rational basis test that is generally applicable to all legislation. Indeed, speaking for himself, Chief Justice Burger, and Justices Stewart and Rehnquist, Justice Blackmun emphasized the "narrow scope of the decision," noting that *Rice* was a case in which "safety interests have not been shown to exist as a matter of law," and asserting that "if safety justifications are not illusory, the Court will not second-guess legislative judgment about their importance in comparison with relative burdens on interstate commerce."[45] However, the decision in *Kassel v. Consolidated Freightways Corp.* would soon belie any such limited interpretation.[46]

Kassel presented the Court with the issue that had been left open in *Rice*. Like the state of Wisconsin in *Rice*, the state of Iowa in *Kassel* limited the length of trucks allowed on the state's highways, banning the use of single trailers longer than fifty-five feet and double trailers longer than sixty feet. However, unlike Wisconsin, when faced with a dormant Commerce Clause challenge, the state of Iowa introduced evidence to support the view that the limitation was a rational safety measure. For the chief justice and Justices Stewart and Rehnquist, the existence of such evidence was dispositive; they concluded that so long as the state introduced *any* safety evidence to support a nondiscriminatory highway regulation, then that regulation should survive a dormant Commerce Clause challenge. Six justices disagreed, however, and the Iowa statute was held unconstitutional.[47]

Given his professed concern for state autonomy, one might have expected Justice Powell to have had considerable sympathy for the state's argument in *Kassel*. However, the lure of the balancing methodology proved too strong; Powell authored an opinion joined by Justices White, Blackmun,

44. Ibid., 442–47 and nn. 18 and 23.
45. Ibid., 448–50 (Blackmun, J., concurring).
46. *Kassel v. Consolidated Freightways Corp.*, 450 U.S. 662 (1981).
47. Ibid., 687–706 (Rehnquist, J., dissenting), 664–79 (opinion of Powell, J.), 679–87 (Brennan, J., concurring in the result).

and Stevens extending the *Rice* analysis and concluding that the Iowa limitation was unconstitutional. He argued that, notwithstanding the evidence introduced by the state, the federal district court could properly weigh the evidence and make an independent determination that the longer trucks were in fact no safer than those which the state allowed on its highways. Further, Powell rejected the state's claim that its judgment was entitled to special deference. Focusing on the importance of the internal political check, he noted that in *Kassel* the state had granted exemptions for both agricultural vehicles and trucks entering cities which bordered on states that allowed use of the longer vehicles and contended that these exemptions weakened the internal political check. Finally, citing evidence which suggested that the state simply wished to preserve its highways from the damage caused by increased through traffic, Powell declared that "a State cannot constitutionally promote its own parochial interests by requiring safe vehicles to detour around it."[48]

The latter theme was emphasized by Justice Brennan, who wrote for himself and Justice Marshall. Brennan first turned his attention to the fact that, in vetoing a bill that would have eased the length restrictions, the governor of Iowa had noted that the change "would benefit only a few Iowa-based corporations while providing a great advantage for out-of-state trucking firms and competitors at the expense of our Iowa citizens." Brennan also quoted from the testimony of the director of the Iowa Department of Transportation, who had conceded that the imposition of the Iowa restriction would raise the total number of traffic fatalities in the nation at large, and had stated that "[o]ur primary concern is the citizens of Iowa and our own highway system we operate in this state." Noting that the existence of the Iowa restrictions had in fact caused trucks to travel more overall miles, creating more fatalities and more wear on highways in the nation as a whole (apparently because longer trucks were forced to detour around Iowa), Brennan concluded that

> Iowa may not shunt off its fair share of the burden of maintaining interstate truck routes, nor may it create increased hazards on the highways of neighboring states in order to decrease the hazards on Iowa highways. . . . Just as a State's attempt to avoid interstate competition in economic goods may damage the prosperity of the Nation as a whole, so Iowa's attempt to deflect interstate truck traffic has been found to make the Nation's highways as a whole more hazardous. This attempt should therefore be subject to "a virtually *per se* rule of invalidity."[49]

---

48. Ibid., 669–78 (opinion of Powell, J.) (citation omitted).
49. Ibid., 685–86 (Brennan, J., concurring in the judgment).

This analysis strikes at the core of the essentialist justification for state regulation of interstate commerce. The essentialist justification rests on the view that state governments have a special relationship with and responsibility to their own citizens and may consider the interest of those citizens paramount in making policy determinations (subject only, of course, to the caveat that, in general, the same rules should apply to both citizens and noncitizens). Brennan's opinion, by contrast, suggests that state governments are required to consider the interests of *the nation as a whole* in making commerce-related policy judgments, and when the evidence indicates that the state has elevated its local welfare over that of the nation, the state policy should be rejected. Under this view, the only justification for state regulation would be the presumption that state legislation on matters of local concern in fact advanced the shared national interest in issues such as highway safety. Such a conclusion is entirely inconsistent with the idea that states are self-governing societies that may legitimately pursue their own interests.

Kassel is an apt reflection of the deep divisions on the Burger Court on the issue of state autonomy. Like *Rice* and *New Jersey*, it also reflects one of the profound ironies of the dormant Commerce Clause cases. Generally, it is the Burger Court conservatives who are viewed as having been hostile to economic regulation. Nonetheless, driven by an intense nationalism, it was often the liberal justices—particularly Justice Brennan—who would deploy the dormant Commerce Clause against such regulations. Conversely, Justice Rehnquist—the most conservative member of the Court—consistently defended economic regulations against dormant Commerce Clause attacks.

This pattern in turn reflects one of the most important features of the federalism cases. Neither liberals nor conservatives saw the substantive *content* of the challenged government actions as constitutionally objectionable. Thus, for example, Justice Rehnquist certainly saw no barrier to state governments making an independent decision to pay a certain wage rate to their employees, and Justices Powell and Brennan would similarly have not objected to a federal statute that restricted the length of trucks engaged in interstate commerce. Thus, in a very real sense, the debate in the Commerce Clause cases turned on the question of whether the process by which the laws were adopted was appropriate—a point that was implicit in the repeated references to *Carolene Products*-type principles in the dormant Commerce Clause. By contrast, substantive values were more directly implicated in the Court's treatment of federal regulatory statutes and state statutes dealing with internal economic issues.

Table 3.1: Voting Patterns

	Bur	Dou	Bre	Mar	Whi	Stew	Bla	Reh	Pow	Stev	Oco
Federal Power											
Hodel v. Virginia Surface Mining 452 U.S. 264 (1981) (strip mining regulation)	C	NP	C	C	C	C	C	C	C	C	NP
Oregon v. Mitchell 400 U.S. 112 (1970) (regulation of voting age)	U	C	C	C	C	U	U	NP	NP	NP	NP
National League of Cities v. Usery 426 U.S. 833 (1976) (application of FLSA to state government)	U	NP	C	C	C	U	U	U	U	C	NP
FERC v. Mississippi 456 U.S. 742 (1982) (requirement that states consider regulations)	U	NP	C	C	C	NP	C	U	U	C	U
Garcia v. SAMTA 469 U.S. 528 (1985) (application of FLSA to state government)	U	NP	C	C	C	NP	C	U	U	C	U
Immunity of States and Subdivisions											
Edelman v. Jordan 415 U.S. 651 (1973) (damage awards against state officials)	U	C	C	C	U	U	C	U	U	NP	NP
Fitzpatrick v. Bitzer 427 U.S. 445 (1976) (federal statute abrogating state immunity)	C	NP	C	C	C	C	C	C	C	C	NP
Atascadero State Hospital v. Scanlon 473 U.S. 234 (1985) (unmistakable language rule)	I	NP	NI	NI	I	NP	NI	I	I	NI	I

	Bur	Dou	Bre	Mar	Whi	Stew	Bla	Reh	Pow	Stev	Oco
Hutto v. Finney 437 U.S. 678 (1978) (payments ancillary to injunctive relief)	NI	NP	NI	NI	I	NI	NI	I	NI	NI	NP
Monell v. New York City 436 U.S. 658 (1978) (municipal immunity)	I	NP	NI	NI	I	NI	NI	I	NI	NI	NP

Dormant Commerce Clause

	Bur	Dou	Bre	Mar	Whi	Stew	Bla	Reh	Pow	Stev	Oco
Hughes v. Alexandria Scrap 426 U.S. 794 (1976) (market participant exception)	C	NP	U	U	U	C	C	C	C	C	NP
Reeves v. Stake 447 U.S. 429 (1980) (market participant exception)	C	NP	U	U	U	C	C	C	U	C	NP
South Central Timber v. Wunnicke 467 U.S. 82 (1984) (market participant exception)	?	NP	U	U	U	NP	U	C	?	U	C
Philadelphia v. New Jersey 437 U.S. 617 (1978) (prohibition on importation of waste)	C	NP	U	U	U	U	U	C	U	U	NP
Raymond Motor Transportation v. Rice 434 U.S. 429 (1978) (truck length limitation)	U	NP	U	U	U	U	U	U	U	U	NP
Kassel v. Consol. Freightways 450 U.S. 662 (1981) (truck length limitation)	C	NP	U	U	U	C	U	C	U	U	NP

Key

C	= Constitutional	NI	= Not Immune	I	= Immune
U	= Unconstitutional	NP	= Not Participating	?	= Unclear Position

4

The Burger Court and
Economic Regulations

During the Burger era, the Court was confronted with many issues related to economic regulations. While the nature of these issues varied greatly in detail, in general terms they were divided into two categories. One group of cases involved the interpretation of federal regulatory statutes; the other raised constitutional issues.

The statutory problems included a vast array of issues dealing with the relationship between labor unions and corporate management. The political dynamic that generated the decisions in these cases differed substantially from that which governed the interpretation of other business-related statutes. Justice Douglas, for example, often opposed the position of the unions, notwithstanding the fact that such positions were typically associated (at least loosely) with liberal ideology. Moreover, while in general terms the decisions at times reflected the typical liberal-conservative divisions between the justices, at other times the issues created alliances which crossed standard ideological categories. Against this background, it should not be surprising that both labor unions and management won important victories. Nonetheless, by the end of the Burger era, the overall state of the law had shifted somewhat in favor of management.[1]

One area in which the Burger Court's jurisprudence did reflect a classic liberal-conservative split involved employers' claims that particular groups of employees were not covered by the National Labor Relations Act (NLRA). The seminal case was *National Labor Relations Board [NLRB] v. Bell Aerospace Co.* In *Bell Aerospace,* a union petitioned the NLRB to hold an election to determine if the union should be certified as the bargaining agent for a group of buyers in the purchasing and procurement department of a major manufac-

---

1. William B. Gould IV, "The Burger Court and Labor Law: The Beat Goes On—Marcato," *San Diego Law Review* 24 (1987): 51–76, provides a comprehensive overview of the Burger Court's approach to labor-management relations.

turing company. The company resisted the petition, contending that the buyers were managerial employees, and thus outside the protections of the NLRA. Nonetheless, the board ordered the election to be held. After the union won the election, the company refused to bargain with the union, leading to a board finding that the company had committed an unfair labor practice.[2]

The Supreme Court considered the legality of this finding against the background of a long history of statutory, administrative, and judicial efforts to deal with the relationship between the NLRA and managerial employees. The Wagner Act, which in 1935 established the basic structure of labor-management relations law in the United States, did not contain any specific exceptions for either managers or supervisory employees; thus, in 1947, the Supreme Court in *Packard Co. v. NLRB* held that foremen were entitled to unionize under the statute. The same year, Congress responded in the Taft-Hartley Act by overruling *Packard* and excluding "supervisors" from the protections of the NLRA. From 1947 until 1970, the NLRB itself took the position that managerial employees who did not meet the definition of supervisors were nonetheless excluded from coverage. However, in a case decided shortly before the decision in *Bell Aerospace* itself, the board reversed its position and announced that it would henceforth treat nonsupervisor managers like all other employers.[3]

Speaking for himself and Justices Brennan, Stewart, and Marshall, Justice White concluded that the board's new position should be upheld. White's opinion noted that the statute by its terms covered all employees other than those specifically excluded; that in providing an exception for supervisors, Congress had explicitly limited the exception to a specific, narrowly defined class of individuals; and that other language in the statute implicitly suggested an understanding that managerial employees generally were covered.

However, the chief justice and Justices Douglas, Blackmun, Powell, and Rehnquist disagreed. Speaking for the majority, Justice Powell relied heavily on Justice Douglas's dissent in *Packard*, where Douglas had argued that allowing managers the right to unionize "tends to obliterate the line between management and labor" and is thus inconsistent with the basic philosophy underlying the NLRA. Powell bolstered his argument with references to the legislative history of the Taft-Hartley Act exclusion and the board's consistent pre-1970 position that managers could not avail themselves of the protection of the NLRA.[4]

---

2. *National Labor Relations Board [NLRB] v. Bell Aerospace Co.*, 416 U.S. 267 (1974).

3. *Packard Co. v. NLRB*, 330 U.S. 485 (1947).

4. *National Labor Relations Board [NLRB] v. Bell Aerospace Co.*, 416 U.S. 279 (quoting *Packard Co. v. NLRB*, 330 U.S. at 493) (Douglas, J., dissenting) (1974).

With the replacement of Justice Douglas by Justice Stevens, the Court's treatment of coverage issues under the NLRA took on an even more clearly ideological cast. Thus, in *NLRB v. Yeshiva University,* with Justices Stewart and Blackmun switching sides, Stevens joined the remaining members of the *Bell Aerospace* majority in concluding that members of a university faculty were managerial employees and therefore could not claim the protections of the NLRA.[5] Similarly, in *NLRB v. Catholic Bishop of Chicago,* the same majority concluded that the board could not exercise jurisdiction over lay teachers employed at high schools operated by the Catholic church. Speaking for the majority, the chief justice first noted that an assertion of jurisdiction by the board would raise serious constitutional questions under the Religion Clauses of the First Amendment. Thus, given that in his view the statutory language did not contain a "clear expression of an affirmative intention of Congress that teachers in church-operated schools should be covered by the Act," Burger concluded that the statute should be interpreted to exclude the lay teachers from its coverage.[6] By contrast, speaking for the four *Bell Aerospace* dissenters, Justice Brennan argued that the statutory language and the legislative history led inescapably to the conclusion that the lay teachers were entitled to the protection of the NLRA.

Bell Aerospace, Yeshiva, and *Catholic Bishop* exemplify the Burger Court's general movement toward a jurisprudence that was less favorable to union interests. However, a number of important Burger-era decisions did not follow this trend. Moreover, the political dynamic that generated these decisions was at times much less clear than that which was so apparent in the *Bell Aerospace* line of cases. The Court's treatment of efforts to enjoin work stoppages which were in violation of contractual no-strike clauses exemplifies both of these points.

Typically, these clauses were included in conjunction with provisions that required all disputes arising from the contract to be resolved through the grievance and arbitration procedures described in the contract itself. Nonetheless, in *Boys Markets, Inc. v. Retail Clerks Union,* the union chose to press its grievances through a work stoppage. Management in turn sought an injunction against the work stoppage in state court; however, the union removed the suit to federal court and sought to have the action dismissed under the Norris-LaGuardia Act of 1934, which barred federal courts from issuing injunctions "in any case involving or growing out of any labor dispute." Management, by contrast, argued that the Norris-LaGuardia Act had been superseded by section 301(a) of the Taft-Hartley Act of 1947, which

---

5. *NLRB v. Yeshiva University,* 444 U.S. 672 (1980).
6. *NLRB v. Catholic Bishop of Chicago,* 440 U.S. 490, 504 (1979).

authorized suits in federal court "for violations of contracts between an employer and a labor organization."[7]

In *Sinclair Refining Co. v. Atkinson,* the Warren Court had held that section 301 did not supersede the Norris-LaGuardia prohibition and that the federal courts lacked authority to enjoin even those strikes which were forbidden by collective bargaining agreements.[8] By contrast, in *Boys Markets,* the Burger Court overruled *Sinclair Refining,* with the majority concluding that the strikes could be enjoined and the union forced to pursue the procedures outlined in the contract to resolve its grievances. Like the decisions that limited the coverage of the NLRA, *Boys Markets* clearly favored management over labor unions; however, unlike *Bell Aerospace* and related cases, the *Boys Markets* Court did not split along traditional liberal-conservative lines, with only Justices White and Black dissenting from the Court's decision and Justice Marshall not participating.

In any event, the subsequent decisions in *Buffalo Forge Co. v. United Steelworkers*[9] and *Jacksonville Bulk Terminals, Inc. v. International Longshoreman's Association*[10] limited the scope of the *Boys Markets* doctrine, holding that injunctions could not be issued against sympathy strikes and strikes over political issues, respectively. Taken together, *Buffalo Forge* and *Jacksonville Bulk Terminals* clearly reflect the doctrinal and political complexity of the forces that produced the Burger Court's labor law jurisprudence. The pro-union decision in *Buffalo Forge* featured a five-justice majority that would more typically be associated with conservative political doctrine—the chief justice and Justices Stewart, White, Blackmun, and Rehnquist. In *Jacksonville Bulk Terminals,* however, the chief justice joined Justices Powell and Stevens in dissent, arguing that a political strike was not a "labor dispute" within the meaning of the Norris-LaGuardia Act; moreover, while concurring in the result, Justice O'Connor (who had replaced Justice Stewart) implied that she was accepting the judgment only because the majority was unwilling to overrule *Buffalo Forge.* The majority opinion itself found the two most liberal dissenters from *Buffalo Forge*—Justices Brennan and Marshall—allied with the three remaining members of the *Buffalo Forge* majority (including Justice Rehnquist, the most conservative justice on the Court).

The development of the case law from *Boys Markets* to *Jacksonville Bulk Terminals* is representative of the general tenor of Burger-era decision making in cases related to labor unions. Certainly, the Burger Court may appropriately be viewed as more sympathetic to management positions than its

7. *Boys Markets, Inc. v. Retail Clerks Union,* 398 U.S. 235 (1970).

8. *Sinclair Refining Co. v. Atkinson,* 370 U.S. 496 (1962).

9. *Buffalo Forge Co. v. United Steelworkers,* 428 U.S. 397 (1976).

10. *Jacksonville Bulk Terminals, Inc. v. International Longshoreman's Association,* 457 U.S. 702 (1982).

predecessor; however, the Court's record in this regard was far from consistent. Moreover, decisions lacked the clear, consistent ideological divisions so apparent in other areas of Burger Court jurisprudence.

The latter point no doubt reflects the change in the relationship between organized labor and the political process generally in the late twentieth century. To be sure, liberals during this period were generally sympathetic to union interests; conversely, conservatives typically supported management prerogatives. However, by the 1970s, other issues had assumed greater importance in defining the differences between liberal and conservative ideology. Thus, the justices of the Burger Court were more likely to be influenced by distinctively legal arguments in deciding cases under the NLRA and related statutes.

Other issues deriving from business-related statutes found the Court more clearly divided along ideological lines. One of the most important ongoing disputes in this area involved questions of the availability of private rights of action to recover damages for violations of the federal securities laws.[11] In 1933 and 1934 Congress passed the Securities Act of 1933 and the Securities Exchange Act of 1934, which together comprehensively regulated the issuance of securities and the markets in which the trading of securities took place. At the same time, Congress also established the Securities and Exchange Commission and armed the commission with the authority to enforce both statutes. Subsequent legislation expanded both the web of federal securities regulation in general and the scope of administrative enforcement authority in particular. However, Congress often did not specifically address the issue of whether private parties could also bring actions based on violations of specific provisions of the statutes—that is, whether the simple presence of these provisions also implied the existence of a judicially enforceable right of action for damages.

The methodology for addressing such questions underwent considerable refinement during the Burger era. The traditional rule, established in 1916 in *Texas and Pacific Railroad Co. v. Rigsby*,[12] was that if a statute was enacted for the benefit of a special class, the judiciary ordinarily allowed members of that class to maintain a private right of action. However, in 1975, the Court modified this analysis in *Cort v. Ash,* concluding that the judiciary should consider not only the issue of whether the statute was designed to benefit a particular class, but also indicia of legislative intent—whether implication of a private right of action was consistent with the underlying

---

11. For a comprehensive survey of the Burger Court's treatment of issues related to securities regulation, see Alfred F. Conrad, "Securities Regulation in the Burger Court," *University of Colorado Law Review* 56 (1985): 193–225.

12. *Texas and Pacific Railroad Co. v. Rigsby*, 241 U.S. 33 (1916).

purpose of the statute and whether the cause of action was in an area traditionally relegated to state law.[13] Later cases, by contrast, simply focused directly on the question of whether Congress had intended to create a private right of action.[14]

In any event, the implied right-of-action issues were in many ways analogous to standing questions; indeed, at times the Court conflated the two inquiries.[15] Thus, it should not be surprising that the liberal justices on the Court were, on the whole, more sympathetic to claims that particular statutory provisions implied the existence of private rights of action[16]—just as they were also more likely to find that particular transactions involved "securities," and were thus subject to federal regulation. However, the ideological divisions between the justices emerged much more sharply in cases involving the interpretation of the antitrust laws.[17]

In large measure, these disputes reflected an underlying disagreement over the purposes of antitrust law generally. The more conservative justices saw the antitrust laws as a device to ensure that the market operated efficiently, contending that "an antitrust policy divorced from market considerations would lack any objective benchmarks." By contrast, Justice White, for example, saw the preservation of the autonomy of individual businesses as a value which included but transcended simple economic benefits.[18] In practical terms, those who favored the purely economic approach were more likely to countenance both mergers and restraints on trade generally.

United States v. Topco Associates provided an early indication of the divisions on the Court.[19] *Topco* was a challenge to the activities of an association of small- and medium-sized regional supermarket chains, which, acting on behalf of those chains, procured and distributed to its members a variety of products that were sold under the Topco brand name. The association assigned members territories in which they had the exclusive right to sell Topco products. This agreement among the association members was challenged under the Sherman Act, which prohibited "every contract, combination . . . or conspiracy, in restraint of trade." The trial judge found that, while limiting competition in the Topco products themselves, the overall effect of

---

13. *Cort v. Ash,* 422 U.S. 66, 78 (1975).

14. See, for example, *Merrill, Lynch, Pierce, Fenner, and Smith v. Curran,* 456 U.S. 353 (1982); *Touche Ross and Co. v. Redington,* 442 U.S. 560 (1979).

15. *Piper v. Chris-Craft Industries, Inc.,* 430 U.S. 1 (1977).

16. See, for example, *Merrill, Lynch, Pierce, Fenner, and Smith v. Curran,* 456 U.S. 353 (1982).

17. Edward Brunet, "Streamlining Litigation by 'Facial Examination' of Restraints: The Burger Court and the Per Se–Rule of Reason Distinction," *Washington Law Review* 60 (1984): 1–32, surveys the major antitrust decisions of the Burger era.

18. *Continental T.V., Inc. v. G.T.E. Sylvania,* 430 U.S. 36, 53 n. 21 (citation omitted), 66–68 (White, J., concurring in the result) (1977).

19. *United States v. Topco Associates,* 405 U.S. 596 (1972).

the policy was actually procompetitive because it enhanced the ability of the Topco members to compete in the marketplace with larger, national chains. On this basis, the judge concluded that the restriction was not illegal because it was reasonable.

In the Supreme Court, only the chief justice agreed with this analysis. Speaking for all of the other sitting justices except Justice Blackmun, Justice Marshall seemed to be willing to concede that the overall effect of the territorial restrictions was procompetitive. Nonetheless, he concluded that the restraint was subject to a per se rule of invalidity, contending that "implicit in [the Sherman Act] is the notion that [competition] cannot be foreclosed with respect to one sector of the economy because certain private citizens or groups believe that such foreclosure might promote greater competition in a more important segment of the economy" and that "courts are of limited utility in examining difficult economic problems. Our inability to weigh, in any meaningful sense, destruction of competition in one sector of the economy against promotion of competition in another sector is one important reason we have formulated *per se* rules."[20]

Despite the near unanimity of the *Topco* Court, the jurisprudence of the Burger era soon began to move toward a loosening of the restrictions of the antitrust laws. In *Topco* itself, Justice Blackmun indicated that he agreed with much of the chief justice's analysis, and concurred in the result only because he felt compelled to do so by the doctrine of stare decisis. Justice Stewart's vote in *Topco* also proved to be something of an aberration. Personnel changes provided additional support for Burger's view; Justices Powell and Rehnquist, who would soon take their seats, would prove hostile to Marshall's position, and later, Justice Stevens would be less absolute in his opposition to restraints of trade than his predecessor Justice Douglas.

Continental T.V., Inc. v. G.T.E. Sylvania exemplifies the decision-making dynamic in antitrust cases during the middle and late Burger era.[21] *G.T.E. Sylvania* was also a challenge to a territorial restriction on the sale of a certain brand of goods—in this case a type of television set. However, unlike *Topco*, where the Court struck down a "horizontal" agreement between competitors, *G.T.E. Sylvania* involved a "vertical" restraint imposed upon franchisers by a manufacturer of the product being sold. In *United States v. Arnold Schwinn and Co.*, the Warren Court had concluded that such restrictions were per se illegal under the Sherman Act.[22] However, over the objections of Justices Brennan, White, and Marshall, a majority of the Court concluded that *Schwinn* should be overruled and the agreement subjected to the rule of reason. Speaking for the majority, Justice

---

20. Ibid., 610 (citation omitted), 609–10 (footnote omitted).
21. *Continental T.V., Inc. v. G.T.E. Sylvania*, 430 U.S. 36 (1970).
22. *United States v. Arnold Schwinn and Co.*, 388 U.S. 365 (1967).

Powell emphasized not only the pure economic theory of antitrust analysis, but also the very point that had been rejected in *Topco*—the possibility that improvement in *interbrand* competition might more than counterbalance any harm that the territorial restriction caused to *intrabrand* competition.[23]

The same basic coalition which formed the *G.T.E. Sylvania* majority also worked to loosen antitrust restrictions in other contexts. For example, over the objections of Justices Douglas, Brennan, White, and Marshall, the Court in *United States v. Marine Bancorporation, Inc.*[24] and *United States v. General Dynamics*[25] also took a probusiness view of section 7 of the Clayton Act, which prohibited business mergers whose effect "may be substantially to lessen competition, or to tend to create a monopoly." In short, taken together, the Burger Court's antitrust decisions clearly moved the political orientation of the law substantially to the right. By contrast, conservatives on the Court were far less successful in deploying *constitutional* doctrine to advance business interests.

In part, this lack of success no doubt reflected the continuing influence of the constitutional revolution of 1937 on the jurisprudential outlook of many members of the Court. One of the cardinal rules of post-1937 analysis was that the Court should generally defer to legislative judgment on issues of economic regulation. In many cases decided under the Equal Protection and Due Process Clauses, this argument dominated the reasoning of the Burger Court. For example, in *New Orleans v. Dukes* the Court unanimously overruled the only Warren Court decision that had struck down an economic regulation on equal protection grounds.[26] However, the more conservative members of the Court sought to reinvigorate the Contract Clause and the Takings Clause as limits on the power of government to regulate economic affairs. While generally opposing these efforts, liberal members of the Court sought to impose other, more novel restraints on government. These restraints also had the effect of limiting economic regulations (if only as a by-product of other ideological considerations).

The constitutional prohibition on state impairments of the obligation of contract had been one of the major casualties of the constitutional revolution of 1937. In the nineteenth century, the Contract Clause was an important weapon against state economic regulation. In 1934 the Court had seemingly eviscerated the clause in *Home Building and Loan Association v.*

---

23. *Continental T.V., Inc. v. G.T.E . Sylvania*, 430 U.S. at 53 n. 21, 51–52. Justice White did concur in the result in *G.T.E. Sylvania*; however, he would have distinguished *Schwinn* and, more importantly, argued that noneconomic factors should influence antitrust analysis. Ibid., 66–68 (White, J., concurring in the result).

24. *United States v. Marine Bancorporation, Inc.*, 418 U.S. 602 (1974).

25. *United States v. General Dynamics*, 415 U.S. 486 (1974).

26. *New Orleans v. Dukes*, 427 U.S. 297 (1976) (per curiam).

Blaisdell;[27] however, in 1977 it was revived in *United States Trust Co. of New York v. New Jersey.*[28]

The plaintiffs in *United States Trust* were bondholders of the New York and New Jersey Port Authority, an agency created by an interstate compact between the states of New York and New Jersey. Their suit was based on a "statutory covenant," enacted by the legislatures of both states, which provided that "the 2 States covenant and agree with each other and with the [bondholders]" not to finance the future deficits of other mass transit systems with the revenue pledged to retire the bonds—that is, revenue derived from bridges and tunnels operated by the authority. Twelve years later, both states repealed this covenant, seeking to gain more flexibility to use the Port Authority revenue to subsidize mass transit. The bondholders argued that the repeal of the covenant effectively impaired the contractual obligations of New York and New Jersey and was thus unconstitutional.

With Justices Stewart and Powell not participating, a four-justice majority reinstated the covenant. Speaking for the majority, Justice Blackmun conceded that the Contract Clause was not an absolute bar to modification of a state's financial obligations; however, he argued that such a modification could survive only if it were both reasonable and necessary to serve an important public purpose. While agreeing that financing mass transit was a sufficiently important governmental interest, Blackmun concluded that abrogation of the covenant was not necessary to serve this interest, contending that the state could have adopted other means to deal with the persistent deficits of its transit system.

The following year, the reach of the Contract Clause was extended to regulations of private contracts in *Allied Structural Steel Co. v. Spannaus.* The plaintiff in *Spannaus* was a corporation that had maintained an office in the state of Minnesota and provided a pension plan for certain classes of employees in that office. Under the terms of the plan, the corporation retained virtually unrestricted authority to amend or terminate the plan for any reason. When the corporation closed its Minnesota office, state law subjected it to a "pension funding charge," sufficient to cover full pensions for all employees who had worked in the office for at least ten years, notwithstanding the fact that under the rules of the plan itself the benefits of many of these employees had not yet vested.[29]

In *Spannaus,* the participating members of the *United States Trust* majority joined the two justices who had been absent in that case to hold that the Minnesota law was unconstitutional. Speaking for the majority, Justice Stew-

---

27. *Home Building and Loan Association. v. Blaisdell,* 290 U.S. 398 (1934).
28. *United States Trust Co. of New York v. New Jersey,* 431 U.S. 1 (1977).
29. *Allied Structural Steel Co. v. Spannaus,* 438 U.S. 234 (1978).

art asserted that the strictures of the Contract Clause applied to state laws which increased the duties of an obligor as well as those which diminished those duties. Emphasizing the retroactive application of the statutory standards, he distinguished *Blaisdell* on a number of grounds, noting that the *Spannaus* statute was not aimed at a widespread social or economic problem, did not operate in an area already subject to state regulation at the time the contract was made, effectuated a "severe, permanent and immediate change in the relationships [between the parties]," and was aimed at only a small class of employers.

Like *Fritz, United States Trust* and *Spannaus* highlight the differences in the jurisprudential perspectives of the various Burger Court justices. For Justices Brennan and Marshall (now joined by Byron White) the commitment to functional analysis that had led them to condemn the classification in *Fritz* counseled deference in *United States Trust* and *Spannaus*. For the dissenters, the fact that the Constitution *specifically* protected contractual obligations was of little moment; thus, in *Spannaus*, Brennan contended that "there is nothing sacrosanct about expectations rooted in contract that justify according them a constitutional immunity denied other property rights." He further observed that "the only difference between the present case and [others in which economic regulations have been upheld] is that there was a prior contractual relationship between the members of the benefitted and burdened classes" and declared, "I simply cannot accept that this difference should possess constitutional significance." Conversely, in *United States Trust*, Brennan saw no need for judicial intervention because, in his view, the interests of bondholders were adequately protected by the legislative process and the realities of the financial markets.

By contrast, the influence of formal, textual considerations was clearly reflected in the views of the majority. The fear of effectively reading a provision out of the Constitution was particularly apparent. For example, in *United States Trust*, Justice Blackmun observed that "if a State could reduce its financial obligations whenever it wanted to spend the money for what it regarded as an important public purpose, the Contract Clause would provide no protection at all"; and in *Spannaus*, Justice Stewart asserted that "if the Contract Clause means anything at all, it means Minnesota could not constitutionally do what it tried to do . . . in this case." At the same time, similar textual considerations provided important limitations on the scope of the majority's analysis; because the Contract Clause by its terms applies only to the states, none of the justices was willing to conclude that the level of scrutiny applied in *United States Trust* and *Spannaus* should also apply to analogous federal action.

Moreover, even the revival of the Contracts Clause as a constraint on state action proved to be a matter of largely theoretical interest. The Burger

Court declined all further invitations to expand the scope of its Contracts Clause jurisprudence; indeed, *United States Trust* and *Spannaus* proved to be the only cases in which the Court relied on this constitutional provision to invalidate state action. Thus, while the Burger-era treatment of the Contract Clause undoubtedly reflected a conservative shift in the Court's jurisprudence, the shift was of little practical significance.

The Court's treatment of takings issues reflected a similar dynamic. In 1922 Justice Oliver Wendell Holmes accurately described the basic problem in takings cases, noting that "while property may be regulated to a certain extent, if regulation goes too far it will be recognized as a taking," thus triggering the Fifth Amendment's requirement of "just compensation" for the property owner.[30] The difficulty, of course, lies in drawing the line between permissible regulations and takings.

In addressing this problem, the Burger Court inherited a constitutional jurisprudence that eschewed bright line rules in favor of ad hoc, factual determinations based on factors such as the character of the government action, the economic impact of the action, and the degree of its interference with reasonable investment-backed expectations. While formally adhering to this approach, in practice the Warren Court almost invariably ruled against takings claims. The Burger Court was slightly more sympathetic to takings claims; however, the significance of this shift should not be overstated.

First, the willingness of even the most conservative justices to constitutionalize economic rights was circumscribed by their professed commitment to the concept of judicial deference and concerns for states' rights. The limitations on the conservative view of the Takings Clause emerged clearly in *Pruneyard Shopping Center v. Robins*.[31] *Pruneyard* was the final skirmish in a long-running dispute over the right of shopping-center owners to limit political speech within the confines of the shopping center. In the waning days of the Warren era, the Court held, in *Food Employees Union Local 590 v. Logan Valley Plaza, Inc.*,[32] that shopping centers were the functional equivalent of company towns and that attempts by a shopping-center owner to limit political speech were therefore state action and subject to First Amendment constraints. However, over the protests of the remaining members of the *Logan Valley* majority, the Burger Court first limited *Logan Valley* to its facts in *Lloyd v. Tanner*[33] and then overruled the decision entirely in *Hudgens v. NLRB*.[34] In the wake of *Hudgens*, the *federal*

---

30. *Pennsylvania Coal Co. v. Mahon*, 260 U.S. 393, 415 (1922).

31. *Pruneyard Shopping Center v. Robins*, 447 U.S. 74 (1980).

32. *Food Employees Union Local 590 v. Logan Valley Plaza, Inc.*, 391 U.S. 308 (1968).

33. *Lloyd v. Tanner*, 407 U.S. 551 (1972).

34. *Hudgens v. NLRB*, 424 U.S. 507 (1976).

Constitution imposed no limitations on the ability of shopping-center owners to limit speech on their premises.

By its terms, however, *Hudgens* did not speak to the status of shopping centers under *state* law. Subsequently, the California Supreme Court held that under the state constitution, shopping-center owners were required to allow solicitations of signatures on a political issue. The owners then appealed to the Supreme Court, alleging (among other things) that the California state rule effected a taking of their property by depriving them of the right to exclude others from the property. Speaking for a unanimous Court in rejecting this claim, Justice Rehnquist observed that "States [possess] residual authority . . . to define 'property' in the first instance" and that "[the owners] have failed to demonstrate that the 'right to exclude others' is so essential to the use or economic value of their property that the state-authorized limitation of it amounted to a 'taking.'"[35]

In other contexts, the Court was more divided on takings claims. Chief Justice Burger and Justices Rehnquist and Stevens were the most sympathetic to arguments based on the Takings Clause; by contrast, Justices Brennan and Blackmun almost uniformly rejected such arguments. As with many Burger Court doctrines, the balance of power was held by four swing justices—in this case, Justices Stewart, White, Marshall, and Powell—each of whose position depended on the precise nature of the issue before the Court.

The most important victories for the defenders of property rights came in cases involving actual physical invasions of property. The issue first came before the Burger Court in *Kaiser Aetna v. United States*. In *Kaiser Aetna*, a developer had improved a natural pond, creating a marina. As part of the improvements, the developer had dredged a channel connecting the pond to an adjacent bay and the Pacific Ocean in order to create an entrance and exit for boats using the marina. The Army Corps of Engineers argued that because the improvements had created a navigable waterway, the pond had become subject to an overriding federal navigational servitude, and the developer was required to allow members of the public to have access to the facilities that it had created.[36]

Over the dissents of Justices Brennan, Marshall, and Blackmun, the Court concluded that the creation of the servitude was a taking that could not be accomplished without compensation. Speaking for the majority, Justice Rehnquist noted repeatedly that, absent the owner's improvement, the pond would not have constituted navigable waters. Against this background, he concluded that "the 'right to exclude,' so universally held to be a funda-

35. *Shopping Center v. Robins Pruneyard*, 447 U.S. at 84.
36. *Kaiser Aetna v. United States*, 444 U.S. 164 (1979).

mental element of the property right, falls within [the] category of interests that the Government cannot take without compensation."[37]

This principle was reaffirmed and expanded in *Loretto v. Teleprompter Manhattan CATV Corp.* There, with Justices Brennan, White, and Blackmun dissenting, the Court held that a state law requiring landlords to allow installation of the small cables that carried cable television signals was a taking of the landlord's property and therefore triggered the requirement of just compensation. Speaking for the majority, Justice Marshall concluded that *any* permanent, physical invasion of private property—no matter how minor—constituted a taking for constitutional purposes; *Pruneyard* was distinguished on the ground that the relevant state constitutional principle permitted only a *temporary* physical invasion.[38]

However, in other contexts, a majority of the Burger Court justices showed little sympathy for takings claims. *Penn Central Transportation Co. v. City of New York* is a prime example. In *Penn Central,* the owners of the Grand Central Terminal building in New York City sought to construct a fifty-story addition above the existing building. The addition would have been consistent with the generally applicable zoning ordinance governing the building; however, because the terminal had been designated a historic landmark, the owners were also required to obtain permission from the Landmark Preservation Commission. The owners' lawsuit alleged that the denial of this permission worked a taking of their property.[39]

With only the chief justice and Justices Rehnquist and Stevens dissenting, the Court rejected this contention. Speaking for the majority, Justice Brennan argued that the limitation on the development of historic landmarks was for constitutional purposes no different from an ordinary zoning regulation. The dissenters, by contrast, noted that only four hundred out of over a million buildings in the city had been designated landmarks. They argued further that the owners of the terminal received no "reciprocal benefits" from the additional restrictions imposed upon them, and contended that the city was in effect imposing the costs for the public purpose of landmark preservation solely on the owners of the property.

Against the background of cases such as *Pruneyard* and *Penn Central,* decisions such as *Kaiser Aetna* and *Teleprompter* emerge as relatively minor expansions of constitutional protection for economic rights. Like the Burger Court's Contract Clause jurisprudence, the changes in takings analysis were of considerable theoretical import; nonetheless, in practical terms, the takings decisions left governments with broad authority to regulate and restrict

---

37. Ibid., 179–80 (footnote omitted).
38. *Loretto v. Teleprompter Manhattan CATV Corp.*, 458 U.S. 419 (1982).
39. *Penn Central Transportation Co. v. City of New York*, 438 U.S. 104 (1978).

property rights. In other contexts, by contrast, the Burger Court did impose important practical limitations on governmental authority to regulate economic interests. Ironically, however, the most important of these decisions were victories for the liberal wing of the Court. As we have already seen, the dormant Commerce Clause cases provide one such example; the Burger Court's First Amendment jurisprudence provides another.

Table 4.1: Voting Patterns

	Bur	Dou	Bre	Mar	Whi	Stew	Bla	Reh	Pow	Stev	Oco
Labor Law											
NLRB v. Bell Aerospace 416 U.S. 267 (1974) (coverage of managerial employees)	PM	PM	PL	PL	PL	PL	PM	PM	PM	NP	NP
NLRB v. Yeshiva University 444 U.S. 672 (1980) (coverage of university faculty)	PM	NP	PL	PL	PL	PM	PL	PM	PM	PM	NP
NLRB v. Catholic Bishop 440 U.S. 490 (1979) (coverage of lay faculty)	PM	NP	PL	PL	PL	PM	PL	PM	PM	PM	NP
Boys Markets v. Retail Clerks 398 U.S. 235 (1970) (injunction against strike)	PM	PM	PM	NP	PL	PM	NP	NP	NP	NP	NP
Buffalo Forge v. United Steelworkers 428 U.S. 397 (1976) (injunction against sympathy strike)	PL	NP	PM	PM	PL	PL	PL	PL	PM	PM	NP
Jacksonville Bulk Terminals v. Int'l Longshoremen 457 U.S. 702 (1982) (injunction against sympathy strike)	PM	NP	PL	PL	PL	NP	PL	PL	PM	PM	PL
Antitrust											
United States v. Topco Assoc. 405 U.S. 596 (1972) (rights to exclusive distribution)	RR	PS	PS	PS	PS	PS	PS	NP	NP	NP	NP

	Bur	Dou	Bre	Mar	Whi	Stew	Bla	Reh	Pow	Stev	Oco
Continental T.V. v. G.T.E. Sylvania 430 U.S. 36 (1977) (vertical territorial restriction)	RR	NP	PS	PS	RR	RR	RR	RR	RR	RR	NP

Constitutional Cases

	Bur	Dou	Bre	Mar	Whi	Stew	Bla	Reh	Pow	Stev	Oco
New Orleans v. Dukes 427 U.S. 297 (1976) (equal protection)	C	NP	C	C	C	C	C	C	C	C	NP
United States Trust Co. of New York v. New Jersey 431 U.S. 1 (1977) (contracts clause)	U	NP	C	C	C	NP	U	U	U	U	NP
Allied Structural Steel v. Spannaus 438 U.S. 234 (1978) (contracts clause)	U	NP	C	C	C	U	NP	U	U	U	NP
Pruneyard Shopping Center v. Robins 447 U.S. 74 (1980) (regulatory taking)	C	NP	C	C	C	C	C	C	C	C	NP
Penn Central Trans. Co. v. City of New York 438 U.S. 104 (1978) (regulatory taking)	U	NP	C	C	C	C	C	U	C	U	NP
Kaiser Aetna v. United States 444 U.S. 164 (1979) (physical taking)	U	NP	C	C	U	U	C	U	U	U	NP
Loretto v. Teleprompter 458 U.S. 419 (1982) (physical taking)	U	NP	C	U	C	NP	C	U	U	U	U

Key

PM	= Promanagement	C	= Constitutional	NP	= Not Participating
PL	= Prolabor	PS	= Per se Invalid		
RR	= Rule of Reason	U	= Unconstitutional		

5

FREEDOM OF SPEECH

The Burger era produced important developments on a wide variety of issues related to freedom of speech. These developments took place against the background of a Warren Court jurisprudence that had developed an increasingly libertarian vision of free-speech rights—a vision that had become an important aspect of the liberal political canon. During both the Warren and Burger eras, some of the most significant of these developments related to categorical exceptions to the basic principle that the government cannot abridge freedom of expression—types of speech that have historically been denied First Amendment protection. The Burger Court dealt with such problems in a number of different contexts.

The most politically charged of these issues involved the regulation of sexually explicit material. The Warren Court had invested a substantial amount of time and energy in dealing with the question of when such material loses its First Amendment protection. Beginning with the decision in *Roth v. United States*[1] the Court had struggled to unite around a formulation that would adequately distinguish obscene materials, which lacked First Amendment protection, from other sexually explicit materials, which merited strong constitutional protection. Late in the Warren era, the most commonly cited standard was derived from the plurality opinion in *Memoirs v. Massachusetts*. There, Justice Brennan declared that, in order for a publication to be deemed obscene, and thus outside the protections of the First Amendment, "three factors must coalesce: it must be established that a) the dominant theme of the material taken as a whole appeals to a prurient interest in sex; b) the material is patently offensive because it affronts contemporary community standards relating to the description or representation of sexual matters; and c) the material is utterly without redeeming social value."[2]

Even if the *Memoirs* standard had commanded majority support on the Court, it would likely have required the justices to engage in a laborious, indi-

---

1. *Roth v. United States*, 354 U.S. 476 (1957).
2. *Memoirs v. Massachusetts*, 383 U.S. 413, 418 (opinion of Brennan, J.) (1966).

vidualized analysis of each piece of literature that was alleged to be obscene under constitutional standards. This problem was exacerbated by the fact that the other justices advocated a wide variety of different approaches to the problem, ranging from the view that all sexually explicit literature was entitled to full First Amendment protection—a position most prominently associated with Justices Black and Douglas—to Justice Stewart's position that "under the First and Fourteenth Amendments criminal laws in this area are constitutionally limited to hard core pornography [and] I know it when I see it."[3] The result was an administrative nightmare, with the Court flooded with obscenity-related cases that were generally resolved through per curiam opinions.

One possible solution to this problem would have been for the Court to simply adopt the Black-Douglas position, thereby obviating the need to define obscenity for constitutional purposes. By 1973 Justices Brennan, Stewart, and Marshall were willing to join Douglas in embracing this position; however, in *Miller v. California* the five remaining justices rallied around a quite different approach. Chief Justice Burger's majority opinion in *Miller* concluded that sexually explicit speech could be proscribed so long as the finder of fact found that "'the average person, applying contemporary community standards' would find that the work, taken as a whole, appeals to the prurient interest . . . the work depicts or describes, in a patently offensive way, sexual conduct specifically defined by the applicable state law; and . . . the work, taken as a whole, lacks serious literary, artistic, political, or scientific value."[4]

The tone of the *Miller* standards was clearly more favorable to state regulation than the *Memoirs* approach; moreover, in emphasizing the role of the finder of fact, the *Miller* majority plainly envisioned a regime where jury determinations of obscenity would receive great deference from reviewing courts. At the same time, however, the majority averred that "no one will be subject to prosecution for the sale or exposure of obscene materials unless these materials depict or describe patently offensive 'hard core' sexual conduct."[5] The significance of this limitation became clear the following year in *Jenkins v. Georgia*, as a unanimous Court reversed the conviction of the owner of a movie theater for showing the film *Carnal Knowledge*—a sexually explicit work which was produced by an important mainstream Hollywood studio and was widely praised by critics. Speaking for the majority, Justice Rehnquist concluded that "the film . . . could not be found under the *Miller* standards to depict sexual conduct in a patently offensive way."[6]

---

3. *Jacobellis v. Ohio*, 378 U.S. 184, 197 (1964).
4. *Miller v. California*, 413 U.S. 15, 24 (1973). The internal struggle that ultimately led to Burger's victory is described in Bob Woodward and Scott Armstrong, *The Brethren: Inside the Supreme Court* (New York: Simon and Schuster, 1979), 192–204, 244–53.
5. Ibid., 27.
6. *Jenkins v. Georgia*, 418 U.S. 153, 161 (1974).

Even given the result in *Jenkins,* the Burger Court plainly broadened the relatively narrow definition of obscenity that had dominated late Warren Court jurisprudence. Moreover, during the mid and late Burger years, a majority of the justices also endorsed the view that the government possessed substantial authority to regulate sexually explicit speech and expressive conduct that was not obscene under the *Miller* standards.

In 1975 *Erznoznik v. City of Jacksonville* seemed to point in the opposite direction. There, over the objections of Chief Justice Burger and Justices White and Rehnquist, the Court struck down a city ordinance that prohibited the display of nudity on drive-in theater screens that were visible from outside the theater. Speaking for the majority, Justice Powell concluded that "the limited privacy interest of persons on the public streets cannot justify the censorship of otherwise protected speech on the basis of its content."[7]

Soon after the decision in *Erznoznik,* however, the tide began to turn in favor of government regulation of sexually oriented speech. One important factor was the replacement of Justice Douglas by Justice Stevens; while Douglas had been a passionate proponent of an absolutist view of the First Amendment, Stevens joined Chief Justice Burger and Justice Rehnquist as a strong supporter of government power in this area. Moreover, Justice Powell's opinion in *Erznoznik* proved to be something of a chimera; in subsequent cases, he would generally join in voting to uphold regulations of offensive speech, although his reasoning at times differed from that of the chief justice and Justices Rehnquist and Stevens. In the key cases, this group of four was able to obtain the concurrence of either Justice White or Justice Blackmun to form a majority in favor of their positions.

The strength of the new coalition first emerged in *Young v. American Mini-Theatres, Inc.* In *Young,* over the dissent of Justices Brennan, Marshall, Stewart, and Blackmun, the Court upheld a city ordinance that placed significant limitations on the location of theaters displaying sexually explicit motion pictures—even if the pictures would not be considered obscene under the *Miller/Jenkins* standards. Despite these restrictions, however, the ordinance left enough sites to accommodate all those who wished to view the sexually explicit movies. Speaking for all members of the majority except Justice Powell, Justice Stevens argued that the speech being regulated was deserving of lesser First Amendment protection than core political speech. After noting that the ordinance did not discriminate on the basis of political viewpoint, Stevens observed that "few of us would march our sons and daughters off to war to preserve the citizen's right to see 'Specified Sexual Activities' exhibited in the theatres of our choice."

---

7. *Erznoznik v. City of Jacksonville,* 422 U.S. 205, 212 (1975) (footnote omitted).

Against this background, the Court found the government interest sufficiently weighty to justify the location restrictions.[8]

However, Stevens failed to rally a majority behind his view that sexually explicit speech was entitled to only a relatively low level of First Amendment protection. Providing the critical fifth vote to uphold the ordinance, Justice Powell explicitly refused to embrace this position. Instead, he argued that, rather than a time, place, or manner restriction based on content, "we have here merely a decision by the city to treat certain movie theatres differently because they have markedly different effects upon their surroundings." Against this background, describing the interests of the city as "both important and substantial," Powell agreed with the ultimate conclusion of the plurality without endorsing its reasoning.[9]

The Court's treatment of *Federal Communications Commission v. Pacifica Foundation* followed much the same pattern. *Pacifica* was a challenge to a declaratory ruling of the FCC. The ruling concluded that a radio station could have been sanctioned for broadcasting a satiric, humorous monologue that focused on the use of seven words, a number of which referred crudely to either scatological or sexual matters. Over the objections of Justices Brennan, Marshall, Stewart, and White, the Court concluded that the FCC order did not violate the First Amendment and was within the agency's statutory authority to regulate "indecent" programming. Speaking for himself, the chief justice, and Justice Rehnquist, Justice Stevens argued that the order was constitutional under both the *Young* rationale and the principle that the government had greater leeway to regulate broadcast speech than other forms of expression. By contrast, while concurring in the judgment, Justices Blackmun and Powell relied only on the latter theory.[10]

Strengthened by the addition of Justice O'Connor, the members of the majority coalition in *Young* finally united around a single opinion in *City of Renton v. Playtime Theatres, Inc.* In *Renton*, with only Justices Brennan and Marshall dissenting, the Court upheld a zoning ordinance that imposed restrictions much like those in *Young*. Speaking for the majority, Justice Rehnquist essentially adopted Justice Powell's approach, which emphasized the strength of the state's interest, as well as the fact that the ordinance did not discriminate on the basis of the political content of the message. Thus, he was able to reject the constitutional challenge without relying on Justice Stevens's theory that the communication at issue was entitled to something less than full First Amendment protection.[11]

---

8. *Young v. American Mini-Theatres, Inc.*, 427 U.S. 50, 70 (1976).

9. Ibid., 82 n. 6, 80.

10. *Federal Communications Commission v. Pacifica Foundation*, 438 U.S. 726 (1978).

11. *City of Renton v. Playtime Theatres, Inc.*, 475 U.S. 41 (1986).

The Burger Court's treatment of commercial speech issues took a quite different path.[12] At the time Warren Burger was appointed chief justice, *Valentine v. Chrestensen*[13] was generally viewed as having established the rule that the First Amendment did not impose any significant restrictions on government regulation of purely commercial speech. Indeed, constitutional challenges to such restrictions were often not conceptualized in First Amendment terms at all. *Williamson v. Lee Optical of Oklahoma, Inc.* is a classic example from the Warren era.[14] *Williamson* was a constitutional challenge to a state prohibition on the advertisement of eyeglass frames. Viewing the claim in substantive due process terms, the Court unanimously rejected the challenge, applying the most lenient version of the rational basis test.

By the mid 1970s, however, two quite different developments combined to undermine the continued vitality of the *Valentine* principles. The first was the general movement of left/center political thought toward the libertarian vision of free speech; the second was a change in the political climate surrounding limitations on commercial speech specifically. At the time they were adopted, regulations such as those challenged in *Williamson* were seen as serving the public interest by enhancing professionalism and preventing inappropriate competition. By contrast, as the twentieth century progressed, *Williamson*-like regulations were increasingly viewed as devices by which special interests shielded themselves from the rigors of the marketplace, thereby depriving the public generally of the benefits of competition.

These themes came together in the watershed decision in *Virginia State Board of Pharmacy v. Virginia Citizens Consumer Council, Inc.* In that case, with only Justice Rehnquist dissenting, the Court invalidated a state statute that prohibited pharmacists from advertising the prices that they would charge for prescription drugs. Speaking for the Court, Justice Blackmun first observed that the mere fact that the pharmacists were operating a business did not deprive them of free speech rights, noting that, in other contexts, the First Amendment had been held to protect speech that is sold for profit. The only question remaining, therefore, was whether *purely* commercial speech was entitled to First Amendment protection. In concluding that the First Amendment did protect the advertising in *Virginia Pharmacy*, Blackmun focused primarily on the interest of the consumer in receiving product information, declaring that "so long as we preserve a predominantly free enterprise economy, the allocation of our resources in large

---

12. Robert E. Riggs, "The Burger Court and Individual Rights: Commercial Speech as a Case Study," *Santa Clara Law Review* 21 (1981): 957–94, surveys the major commercial speech decisions of the Burger Court.

13. *Valentine v. Chrestensen*, 316 U.S. 52 (1942).

14. *Williamson v. Lee Optical of Oklahoma, Inc.*, 348 U.S. 483 (1955).

measure will be made through numerous private economic decisions. It is a matter of public interest that those decisions, in the aggregate, be intelligent and well informed. To this end, the free flow of commercial information is indispensable." He sounded a similar theme in rejecting the claim that the prohibition was necessary to preserve the professionalism of pharmacists and to protect the public from those who would offer inferior service at low prices:

> There is . . . an alternative to this highly paternalistic approach. That alternative is to assume that this information is not in itself harmful, that people will perceive their best interest if only they are well enough informed, and that the best means to that end is to open channels of communication rather than to close them. . . . The choice among these approaches is not ours to make or the Virginia Assembly's. It is precisely this kind of choice, between the dangers of suppressing information, and the danger of its misuse, that the First Amendment makes for us.[15]

Virginia Pharmacy clearly sounded the death knell for the theory that commercial speech lacked all First Amendment protection. However, the majority also suggested that the state might have wider latitude to regulate commercial speech than other types of communication, specifically noting that the state could take steps to suppress false or misleading commercial advertising. In *Central Hudson Gas and Electric Corp. v. Public Service Corp.*, the Court established a four-step standard of review for regulations of commercial speech:

> For commercial speech to come within th[e] protection [of the First Amendment], it at least must concern lawful activity and not be misleading. Next, we ask whether the asserted governmental interest is substantial. If both inquiries yield positive answers, we must determine whether the regulation directly advances the governmental interest served, and whether it is not more extensive than is necessary to serve that interest.[16]

While only Justice Rehnquist refused to embrace this standard, the remaining justices differed sharply on its proper application. Justices Brennan, Marshall, Stevens, and Blackmun consistently argued that the First Amendment afforded broad protection to commercial speech; indeed, Brennan and Marshall showed more enthusiasm for protecting corporate

15. *Virginia State Board of Pharmacy v. Virginia Citizens Consumer Council, Inc.*, 425 U.S. 748 (1976).

16. *Central Hudson Gas and Electric Corp. v. Public Service Corp.*, 447 U.S. 557 (1980).

commercial speech than corporate *political* speech. By contrast, Chief Justice Burger and Justices Powell and Stewart took a more expansive view of government authority to regulate commercial speech; after replacing Justice Stewart, Justice O'Connor took a similar position. Against this background, Justice White became the swing vote, and his position generally determined the outcome of commercial speech cases.

The Court's treatment of regulations of attorney advertising clearly reflects this pattern. Traditionally, state regulatory bodies had banned virtually all advertising by attorneys. Moreover, concurring in *Virginia Pharmacy,* Chief Justice Burger specifically suggested that the states could continue to regulate or even prohibit advertising by the "traditional learned professions of medicine or law." However, in *Bates v. State Bar of Arizona* Justice White joined Justices Brennan, Marshall, Blackmun, and Stevens in concluding that the states could not prevent attorneys from advertising the price for "routine legal services."[17] Subsequently, the same majority would require states to allow a wide range of attorney advertising, balking only at the prospect of overly aggressive, in-person solicitation of clients.[18]

Conversely, in *Posadas de Puerto Rico Associates v. Tourism Company of Puerto Rico*[19] and *Dun and Bradstreet, Inc. v. Greenmoss Builders, Inc.,*[20] White's vote was critical to decisions that limited the constitutional protections for commercial speech. *Posadas* was a relatively straightforward dispute over the application of the *Central Hudson* test to a Puerto Rican statute which prohibited local casinos from advertising their facilities to residents of Puerto Rico. Analogizing the regulation to limits on the advertising of tobacco and alcohol, the five-justice majority saw the regulation as vindicating the governmental interest in limiting the demand of its citizenry for a harmful activity; by contrast, the dissenters contended that there was no evidence to show that the Puerto Rican legislature considered gambling per se harmful, or that the challenged statute would be an effective means of controlling the potentially harmful ancillary by-products of the casino industry.

The doctrinal background of *Dun and Bradstreet* was somewhat more complex. The case stood at the intersection of two different lines of First Amendment jurisprudence, dealing with commercial speech and defamation, respectively. *Dun and Bradstreet* began as a libel action, based upon a report that was sent to five subscribers by a credit reporting company. The report grossly misrepresented the assets and liabilities of a company in

---

17. *Bates v. State Bar of Arizona,* 433 U.S. 350 (1977).

18. Compare *In re Primus,* 436 U.S. 412 (1978), with *Ohralik v. Ohio State Bar Association,* 436 U.S. 447 (1978).

19. *Posadas de Puerto Rico Associates v. Tourism Company of Puerto Rico,* 478 U.S. 328 (1986).

20. *Dun and Bradstreet, Inc. v. Greenmoss Builders, Inc.,* 472 U.S. 749 (1985).

unflattering terms. Without a showing of actual malice, the jury returned a verdict awarding both presumed and punitive damages against the defendant. The reporting company argued that enforcement of this judgment would violate the First Amendment.

The line of cases culminating in *Dun and Bradstreet* began with the Warren Court's unanimous decision in *New York Times Co. v. Sullivan*.[21] Prior to the decision in that case, libelous statements had been generally thought to be totally outside the protection of the First Amendment. In *Sullivan*, however, the Court held that a finding of actual malice—either knowledge of falsity or a reckless disregard of the truth—was necessary for a public official to prevail in a libel action against critics of his official conduct. By its terms, *Sullivan* dramatically changed the preexisting law of defamation in many states; it also left open the possibility that evolving First Amendment doctrine would require other changes as well.

Initially, the Burger Court was in complete disarray on this issue.[22] For example, when *Rosenbloom v. Metromedia* posed the question of whether the *Sullivan* standards were applicable to defamation actions by private individuals in which matters of public interest were implicated, the Court produced five different opinions, none of which commanded the adherence of more than three justices.[23] A decade after *Sullivan*, the Burger Court provided clear guidance on this question in *Gertz v. Robert Welch, Inc.* In *Gertz*, an unusual coalition of five justices concluded that "so long as they do not impose liability without fault, the States may define for themselves the appropriate standard of liability for a . . . defamatory falsehood injurious to a private individual." At the same time, however, the majority concluded that the states could not permit the award of presumed or punitive damages in the absence of a showing of actual malice.[24]

Gertz produced dissents not only from Justices Douglas and Brennan, who argued that the majority standard provided insufficient protection for free speech, but also from the chief justice and Justice White, who contended that the decision intruded unduly on the power of the states to protect their citizens from defamation. Moreover, even some members of the majority embraced the decision with something less than total enthusiasm; Justice Blackmun announced that he was abandoning his personal views in

---

21. *New York Times Co. v. Sullivan*, 376 U.S. 254 (1964).

22. William F. Couzzi and Lee Sporn, "Private Lives and Public Concerns: The Decade since *Gertz v. Robert Welch*," *Brooklyn Law Review* 51 (1985): 425–78, describes the development of the law of defamation during the Burger era.

23. *Rosenbloom v. Metromedia*, 403 U.S. 29 (1971).

24. *Gertz v. Robert Welch, Inc.*, 418 U.S. 323 (1974). *Gertz* is discussed in detail from the perspective of one of the parties in Elmer Gertz, Gertz v. Robert Welch, Inc.: *The Story of a Landmark Libel Case* (Carbondale: Southern Illinois University Press, 1992).

order to produce a definitive opinion, and one can infer that Justice Rehnquist's adherence to the majority was based on similar considerations. Thus, it should not be surprising that the Court would be deeply divided when called upon to consider the applicability of the *Gertz* standards to commercial defamation in *Dun and Bradstreet*.

Although clearly implicating problems relating to commercial speech, from a strictly political perspective, *Dun and Bradstreet* presented issues quite unlike *Virginia Pharmacy* and its progeny. Restrictions on commercial advertising might well be characterized as efforts by business interests to preserve monopoly profits at the expense of consumer welfare; thus, efforts to overturn such restrictions fit comfortably into prevailing liberal ideology. By contrast, a restriction on damage awards in *Dun and Bradstreet* could not be characterized as pro-consumer in any sense; as Justice Brennan noted, it is consumers who are often most at risk from inaccurate credit reports and would therefore potentially benefit most from presumed or punitive damages.

Nonetheless, the division in *Dun and Bradstreet* was much the same as in the other commercial speech cases. By a five-to-four vote, the Court concluded that the damage award survived constitutional scrutiny. Chief Justice Burger and Justice White reiterated their view that *Gertz* itself placed undue limitations on state defamation law. However, Justices Powell, Rehnquist, and O'Connor chose instead to distinguish *Gertz*, concluding that the standards of that case applied only to speech on matters of public concern and that, as commercial speech, the credit report did not involve a matter of public concern. Speaking for the four dissenters, Justice Brennan recognized that consumers faced some danger from inaccurate credit reporting; nonetheless, he concluded that the credit report in *Dun and Bradstreet* fell outside the realm of the commercial speech exception and that the *Gertz* standards should apply

Dun and Bradstreet provides an excellent illustration of the complexity of the political and doctrinal forces that generated the overall pattern of Burger Court jurisprudence. In the most narrowly political terms, one would have expected the more liberal justices on the Court—William Brennan and Thurgood Marshall—to favor the consumers in a case such as *Dun and Bradstreet*. However, enthralled with the libertarian vision of free speech, they instead voted to hold that the First Amendment protected business interests from the consequences of making a damaging, inaccurate credit report. Conversely, Justice Rehnquist and his allies—normally characterized as pro-business—were driven by the basic concept of judicial deference and underlying concerns of federalism to support the consumer. A similarly complex interaction between doctrine and politics would be reflected in the justices' treatment of what was arguably the most significant speech-related problem of the Burger era—the issue of campaign finance reform.

In the wake of the Watergate scandal, both the federal and state governments adopted measures designed to reduce what was perceived as the corrupting influence of large campaign contributions on the political process. Opponents of these measures argued that they constituted unwarranted restrictions on First Amendment rights. Warren Court precedents did not clearly answer the question of whether these arguments had merit; thus, it should not be surprising that the Burger Court would be deeply divided on the proper scope of government authority to regulate campaign finances.

Buckley v. Valeo was the seminal case. *Buckley* was a challenge to the 1974 amendments to the Federal Election Campaign Act. Adopted in the midst of the Watergate scandal, these amendments sought to limit the influence of large contributors by *(a)* limiting to one thousand dollars the amount which any individual could contribute to any candidate for federal elective office, and to five thousand dollars the amount which any political committee could contribute to such a candidate; *(b)* limiting to one thousand dollars the amount which any person might spend to advance the candidacy of a person to whom he had no relation, and also imposing limits on the amounts which the candidate and his family might contribute to the campaign; *(c)* imposing limits on the total amounts which could be spent by the candidate on his campaign; *(d)* requiring the reporting of campaign contributions in excess of one hundred dollars; and *(e)* establishing a system whereby the candidates of the two major parties would automatically receive federal funding in presidential elections, funding that matched the amount of private contributions, but allowing others access to matching funds only in narrowly defined circumstances. The statute also established a Federal Election Commission (FEC) to administer the statute; the FEC was to be composed of two members appointed by the president, two members appointed by the Speaker of the House of Representatives, and two members appointed by the president pro tempore of the Senate.[25]

Opponents of the 1974 amendments raised a variety of constitutional challenges. They argued that the disclosure requirements and the limits on contributions and expenditures violated First Amendment rights of speech and association, as did the entire concept of public funding of elections. In addition, the challengers contended that the decision to fund only the major parties unconstitutionally discriminated against minor parties. Finally, they asserted that the procedure for staffing the FEC violated the Appointments Clause, which vests the president with the authority to appoint "all . . . Officers of the United States."

---

25. *Buckley v. Valeo*, 424 U.S. 1 (1976).

In the Supreme Court, the consideration of these challenges was marked by the denouement of the sad drama that led to the departure of Justice Douglas. The event which precipitated Douglas's decision to resign was a massive stroke which he suffered on December 31, 1974. The stroke left Douglas physically incapacitated and mentally impaired, completely incapable of performing his duties on the Court. Nonetheless, for a time he was determined to remain. Faced with such intransigence and constitutionally unable to remove Douglas, the remaining justices agreed privately that no case would be decided by a five-to-four vote with Douglas in the majority.[26] Finally, after ten months, even Douglas was forced to concede that he could no longer continue; on November 12, 1975, Douglas retired from the Court.

Difficulties arose, however, because *Buckley* had been argued on November 10—two days *before* Douglas's resignation. Even after his retirement, Douglas made repeated efforts to participate in the disposition of the case. At one point, he circulated a memorandum which not only discussed the merits of the *Buckley* case, but also complained of his treatment since retirement; later, he sought to have the memorandum published as an opinion dissenting from the Court's disposition of the case. Not surprisingly, the active justices rebuffed these efforts at every turn. The entire episode was a rather pathetic ending to an otherwise noteworthy career on the Court.[27]

In any event, *Buckley* presented the remaining eight justices with constitutional issues that had enormous practical implications. Moreover, the issues generated complex doctrinal and ideological problems for members of both wings of the Court. For Justices Brennan and Marshall, the cases presented conflicts between the libertarian approach to freedom of expression, an approach which dominated the other aspects of their First Amendment philosophy, and the egalitarian theory of government reflected in cases such as *Reynolds v. Sims,*[28] *Kramer v. Union Free School District,*[29] and their progeny. Conversely, while in other contexts the conservatives on the Court had generally been less supportive of expansive notions of First Amendment rights, it was conservative political forces that generally opposed restrictions on campaign contributions and expenditures. The situation was further complicated by the fact that the Court was under severe time pressure; the 1976 presidential election campaign was already

---

26. John C. Jeffries, Jr., *Justice Lewis F. Powell, Jr.* (New York: Charles Scribner's Sons, 1994), 417–18.
27. This incident is described in detail in Woodward and Armstrong, *The Brethren,* 394–99.
28. *Reynolds v. Sims,* 377 U.S. 533 (1964).
29. *Kramer v. Union Free School District,* 395 U.S. 621 (1969).

well under way, and at least one candidate had already applied for matching funds.

Against this background, only the reporting and disclosure sections of the statute were uncontroversial at the initial conference; all of the justices agreed that these provisions were constitutional. By contrast, they were deeply divided on the constitutionality of the structure of the Federal Elections Commission. Justices Brennan, White, Marshall, and Powell all indicated that they believed the process by which the commissioners were selected was constitutional, the chief justice and Justices Blackmun and Rehnquist took the opposing view, and Justice Stewart was not yet ready to express an opinion.[30] Ultimately, however, all were willing to concur in the conclusion that, because the members of the FEC were "Officers of the United States," the Constitution required that they be appointed by the president. This holding, however, was only a minor inconvenience to those who supported the basic thrust of the 1974 amendments; the FEC was quickly reconstituted as a body appointed by the president, and performed functions indistinguishable from the original commission. By contrast, the First Amendment and equal-protection attacks on the contribution and expenditure limits threatened the core principles of the campaign finance statute.

Although the justices were again deeply divided, Justices Brennan, Powell, and Stewart were able to quickly produce a massive per curiam opinion that had the support of a majority of the justices on all points. The opinion distinguished sharply between limitations on contributions and limitations on expenditures. Noting that "a primary effect of [the] expenditure limitations is to restrict the quantity of campaign speech by individuals, groups and candidates," the majority found the government interests insufficient to justify these limitations. By contrast, while conceding that the contribution limitations "operate in an area of the most fundamental First Amendment activities," the per curiam opinion nonetheless found that "Congress was surely entitled to conclude that . . . contribution ceilings were . . . necessary . . . to deal with the reality or appearance of corruption inherent in a system permitting unlimited financial contributions," observing that the limitation left potential contributors free to express their speech and associational rights in other contexts. The majority also upheld the system of providing matching funds for major party presidential candidates, and conditioning the eligibility for such funds on the acceptance of spending limits. Once again, the Court relied on the significant governmental interest in eliminating the "improper influence of large private contributions" and concluded that Congress could constitu-

---

30. Bernard Schwartz, *The Ascent of Pragmatism: The Burger Court in Action* (New York: Addison-Wesley, 1990), 88–89.

tionally take into account the differences between major parties and minor parties in establishing the criteria for eligibility for matching funds.[31]

All of these conclusions drew dissents. Among the dissenters, only the position of Justice White was explicable in purely doctrinal terms; rarely a proponent of expansive views of the First Amendment, White concluded that the limitations on both contributions and expenditures were constitutional. Rehnquist's explicit support for the limits on contributions was also consistent with his general approach to First Amendment issues. However, his conclusion that the statute unconstitutionally discriminated between candidates from major parties and those from minor parties was a significant departure from his generally restrained view of the concept of equal protection—a departure which can most plausibly be explained as a by-product of his political preconceptions. Similar preconceptions were even more apparent in the position of the chief justice and Justice Blackmun, neither of whom was generally a strong supporter of an expansive view of the First Amendment, but both of whom concluded that both the contribution and expenditure limitations were unconstitutional. Conversely, Justice Marshall— in other contexts a champion of free expression—was the only other justice who ultimately argued for less judicial activism in *Buckley,* dissenting from the majority's conclusion that the government could not constitutionally limit the contributions made by a candidate and his own family.[32]

As other campaign finance cases came before the Court, many of the justices continued to reiterate the same themes that were inherent in their views in *Buckley;* for example, Justice White consistently voted to uphold regulations on campaign finance, while Chief Justice Burger was almost equally

---

31. Ibid., 39, 28, 85–108. Bernard Schwartz suggests that at the initial conference, Justice Powell took the position that both the contribution and expenditure limitations were unconstitutional, while Justice Brennan argued that the statute was entirely free from constitutional infirmities (Bernard Schwartz, *The Ascent of Pragmatism,* 143–45). If this were in fact the case, their ultimate concurrence in the per curiam opinion could perhaps best be explained as the embodiment of an arrangement in which both agreed to compromise in order to produce a clear, definitive result.

Schwartz does not identify the sources that he relied on for his account of *Buckley.* Moreover, based on internal documents, my impression is that, although Powell had some misgivings about the limitation on contributions, both he and Brennan independently came to the conclusions embodied in the per curiam opinion even prior to the conference on *Buckley.*

Powell's initial thoughts can be found in his preconference memorandum, case file on *Buckley v. Valeo,* Lewis Powell Papers, Washington and Lee Law Library, Lexington, Va.; while Brennan's preconference memorandum can be found in the case file on *Buckley v. Valeo,* William J. Brennan Papers, Manuscripts Division, Library of Congress. Steven J. Wermeil, author of a forthcoming biography on Justice Brennan, also generously shared his thoughts on Brennan's thought processes.

32. *Buckley v. Valeo,* 424 U.S., at 257–66 (opinion of Marshall, J.).

consistent in his opposition. Similarly, while Justices Stewart, Powell, and Stevens continued to hold to the distinction between contributions and expenditures, Justice Blackmun continually reiterated his view that the distinction was illogical. By contrast, the subsequent decisions in *First National Bank of Boston v. Bellotti*[33] and *Federal Election Commission v. National Conservative Political Action Committee [NCPAC]*[34] reflected both the efforts of Justice Rehnquist to reconcile his jurisprudential theories with his political philosophy and the continuing strong influence of liberal egalitarian theory on the jurisprudence of Justices Brennan and Marshall.

Bellotti was a challenge to a Massachusetts statute that prohibited corporations from making expenditures to affect the outcome of referenda that did not materially affect their business, property, or assets; *NCPAC,* on the other hand, prohibited independent political committees from spending more than one thousand dollars to promote the presidential candidacy of any person who chose to accept federal matching funds. Only Justice Rehnquist found the two cases distinguishable; while concluding that the *NCPAC* statute violated the First Amendment, in *Bellotti* he retreated to his basic formalistic, positivist approach to law, arguing that since corporations were by their nature creatures of state law, states could constitutionally limit the powers that were appurtenant to the corporate form. Not surprisingly, Justices Brennan and Marshall saw the cases quite differently; in *NCPAC,* Marshall abandoned his previously expressed view that expenditure limitations generally violated the First Amendment, and Brennan saw *Bellotti* and *NCPAC* as distinguishable from *Buckley,* joining Justice White in asserting that governments could constitutionally "avoid the deleterious influences on federal elections resulting from the use of money by those who exercise control over large aggregations of capital."[35]

However, the support of Justices Brennan and Marshall was insufficient to save the *Bellotti* and *NCPAC* statutes. The remaining members of the *Buckley* plurality joined the chief justice and Justice Blackmun to form a majority that found both expenditure limitations unconstitutional. Thus, the campaign finance decisions provide a sharp contrast to the Court's other speech-related decisions, providing a clear example of Burger Court activism in support of conservative positions. By contrast, the Court's treatment of other issues related to the electoral process reflected a quite different dynamic.

---

33. *First National Bank of Boston v. Bellotti,* 435 U.S. 765 (1978).

34. *Federal Election Commission v. National Conservative Political Action Committee [NCPAC],* 470 U.S. 480 (1985).

35. *Federal Election Commission v. National Conservative Political Action Committee [NCPAC],* 470 U.S. at 521 (Marshall, J., dissenting); *First National Bank of Boston v. Bellotti,* 435 U.S. at 804–22 (White, J., dissenting).

Table 5.1: Voting Patterns

	Bur	Dou	Bre	Mar	Whi	Stew	Bla	Reh	Pow	Stev	Oco
Sexually Oriented Speech											
Miller v. California 413 U.S. 15 (1973) (local standards for obscenity)	C	U	U	U	C	U	C	C	C	NP	NP
Jenkins v. Georgia 418 U.S. 153 (1974) (suppression of *Carnal Knowledge*)	U	U	U	U	U	U	U	U	U	NP	NP
Erznoznik v. City of Jacksonville 422 U.S. 205 (1975) (prohibition on nudity in drive-in theatres)	C	U	U	U	C	U	U	C	U	NP	NP
Young v. American Mini-Theatres 427 U.S. 50 (1976) (zoning restrictions on sexually oriented movies)	C	NP	U	U	C	U	U	C	C	C	NP
FCC v. Pacifica 438 U.S. 726 (1978) (prohibition on broadcast of "Seven Dirty Words")	C	NP	U	U	U	U	C	C	C	C	NP
City of Renton v. Playtime Theatres 475 U.S. 41 (1986) (zoning restrictions on sexually oriented movies)	C	NP	U	U	C	NP	C	C	C	C	C
Commercial Speech											
Virginia St. Bd. of Pharmacy v. Virginia Citizens 425 U.S. 748 (1976) (prohibition on drug advertising)	U	NP	U	U	U	U	U	C	U	NP	NP

	Bur	Dou	Bre	Mar	Whi	Stew	Bla	Reh	Pow	Stev	Oco
Bates v. State Bar of Arizona 433 U.S. 350 (1977) (prohibition on lawyer advertising)	C	NP	U	U	U	C	U	C	C	U	NP
Posadas de Puerto Rico v. Tourism Co. 478 U.S. 328 (1986) (prohibition on domestic gambling advertisements)	C	NP	U	U	C	NP	U	C	C	U	C

Defamation

	Bur	Dou	Bre	Mar	Whi	Stew	Bla	Reh	Pow	Stev	Oco
Gertz v. Robert Welch, Inc. 418 U.S. 323 (1974) (liability based on negligence)	C	U	U	C	C	C	C	C	C	NP	NP
Gertz v. Robert Welch, Inc. 418 U.S. 323 (1974) (punitive damages without malice)	C	U	U	C	U	U	U	U	U	NP	NP
Dun and Bradstreet v. Greenmoss 472 U.S. 749 (1985) (punitive damages without malice in commercial defamation)	C	NP	U	U	C	NP	U	C	C	U	C

Campaign Financing

	Bur	Dou	Bre	Mar	Whi	Stew	Bla	Reh	Pow	Stev	Oco
Buckley v. Valeo 424 U.S. 1 (1976) (contribution limitations)	U	NP	C	C	C	C	U	C	C	NP	NP
Buckley v. Valeo 424 U.S. 1 (1976) (expenditure limitations)	U	NP	U	U	C	U	U	U	U	NP	NP
First National Bank of Boston v. Bellotti 435 U.S. 765 (1978) (limit on corporate expenditures)	U	NP	C	C	C	U	U	C	U	U	NP

	Bur	Dou	Bre	Mar	Whi	Stew	Bla	Reh	Pow	Stev	Oco
FEC v. NCPAC 470 U.S. 480 (1985) (limit on committee expenditures)	U	NP	C	C	C	NP	U	U	U	U	U

Key

C   = Constitutional   U   = Unconstitutional   NP   = Not Participating

6

THE STRUCTURE OF GOVERNMENT

At the time that Warren Burger was chosen to be chief justice, the Court was already deeply involved in supervising the process by which government officials were chosen. This involvement was almost entirely a product of Warren Court innovations. Prior to the Warren era, with the exception of race-related cases, the Court had been generally unwilling to intervene in disputes over the structure of other branches of government. However, beginning with *Baker v. Carr*,[1] which held disputes over legislative apportionment to be justiciable, the Warren Court had aggressively supervised the electoral process. In *Reynolds v. Sims*[2] and *Lucas v. Forty-fourth General Assembly*[3] the Court held that all state legislatures must be apportioned in accordance with the principle of one person, one vote. In *Wesberry v. Sanders*,[4] the Court applied the same principle to elections for the House of Representatives. In addition, decisions such as *Harper v. Virginia State Board of Elections*[5] and *Kramer v. Union Free School District*[6] established the principle that restrictions on the right to vote would generally be subject to strict scrutiny.

These decisions not only broke new doctrinal ground, but also had wide-ranging practical implications. The reapportionment cases in particular forced dramatic changes in the way in which both state legislators and members of Congress were chosen. However, little of the political controversy that surrounded the Warren Court focused on cases such as *Reynolds* and *Kramer*—in part, no doubt, because any opposition to the principles expressed in those decisions might be characterized as opposition to the basic concept of democracy itself. Nonetheless, the apportionment and voting cases clearly ran afoul of the theory of judicial restraint that had become part and parcel of conservative political ideology.

---

1. *Baker v. Carr*, 369 U.S. 186 (1962).
2. *Reynolds v. Sims*, 377 U.S. 533 (1964).
3. *Lucas v. Forty-fourth General Assembly*, 377 U.S. 713 (1964).
4. *Wesberry v. Sanders*, 376 U.S. 1 (1964).
5. *Harper v. Virginia State Board of Elections*, 383 U.S. 663 (1966).
6. *Kramer v. Union Free School District*, 395 U.S. 621 (1969).

Against this background, it should not be surprising that the more conservative justices on the Burger Court would seek to modify the strict application of the principle of one person, one vote.[7] They had some success in providing state and local governments with a degree of flexibility on issues relating to apportionment and voting rights. For example, over the dissents of Justices Douglas, Brennan, and Marshall, the Court in *Mahan v. Howell*,[8] *Gaffney v. Cummings*,[9] and *Brown v. Thompson*[10] held that deviations of as much as 16.4 percent from "ideal" district size were acceptable measures to preserve the integrity of lines between political subdivisions and that 10 percent deviations were permissible in any event. Further, the same basic majority concluded in *Salyer Land Co. v. Tulare Lake Basin Water Storage Dist.*[11] and *Ball v. James*[12] that, in elections for officials with limited powers, the states could restrict the right to vote to those whose interests would be strongly affected by the exercise of those powers.

Even in the state and local context, however, it would be a mistake to overstate the degree to which the Burger Court retreated from Warren Court precedents on apportionment and voting rights. *Mahan* and its progeny allowed only very limited deviations from the concept of one person, one vote; similarly, despite cases such as *Salyer*, decisions such as *Dunn v. Blumstein*[13] and *Hill v. Stone*[14] emphatically reaffirmed the Court's commitment to the basic doctrine enunciated in *Harper* and *Kramer*. In short, while the Court showed marginally greater tolerance than its predecessor for deviations from an idealized form of democracy in state and local elections, the basic structure of Warren Court jurisprudence in this area remained intact.

Moreover, in the context of federal elections, the Burger Court did not tolerate even small deviations from the principle of one person, one vote. In *White v. Weiser*,[15] the Court unanimously concluded that even minor variations from population equality were impermissible in elections for the federal House of Representatives. For a majority of the Court, the distinction between apportionment for state legislatures and apportionment for Congress was more a matter of precedent than of principle. In *Kirkpatrick v. Preisler*[16] and

---

7. The Burger Court's treatment of issues related to legislative apportionment is described in detail in Nancy Maveety, *Representation Rights and the Burger Years* (Ann Arbor: University of Michigan Press, 1991).

8. *Mahan v. Howell*, 410 U.S. 315 (1973).

9. *Gaffney v. Cummings*, 412 U.S. 735 (1973).

10. *Brown v. Thompson*, 462 U.S. 535 (1983).

11. *Salyer Land Co. v. Tulare Lake Basin Water Storage Dist.*, 410 U.S. 719 (1973).

12. *Ball v. James*, 451 U.S. 355 (1981).

13. *Dunn v. Blumstein*, 405 U.S. 330 (1972).

14. *Hill v. Stone*, 421 U.S. 289 (1975).

15. *White v. Weiser*, 412 U.S. 783 (1973).

16. *Kirkpatrick v. Preisler*, 394 U.S. 526 (1969).

Wells v. Rockefeller[17] the Warren Court had established the rule that the Burger Court applied in *Weiser.* Justices Stewart and White had dissented in *Preisler* and *Wells;* therefore, their silent concurrence in *Weiser* is only explicable in terms of respect for precedent. Moreover, Chief Justice Burger and Justices Powell and Rehnquist *explicitly* stated that they would have voted to reject the constitutional challenge in *Weiser* if the case had been one of first impression.[18] Thus, *Weiser* stands as one of the clearest examples of the impact of the doctrine of stare decisis on Burger Court decision making.

In any event, even *Weiser* did not exhaust the commitment of many of the Burger Court justices to an idealized vision of democracy; in *Davis v. Bandemer,* a majority of the Court was willing to extend judicial control of both state and federal electoral processes even beyond that established by the Warren Court. *Bandemer* was a challenge to the apportionment plan adopted for elections to the Indiana state legislature. The apportionment plan satisfied the one person, one vote standard of *Reynolds* and its progeny; however, Indiana Democrats alleged that the plan violated the Equal Protection Clause because districts had been gerrymandered in an effort to minimize the number of Democrats elected to the legislature. Chief Justice Burger and Justices Rehnquist and O'Connor insisted that the case presented a political question, resolution of which would require courts to make policy judgments without guidance from judicially manageable standards. The remaining justices disagreed, concluding that the matter was justiciable; however, they were sharply divided on both the appropriate standard to be applied and the merits of *Bandemer* itself.[19]

Speaking for himself and Justices Brennan, Marshall, and Blackmun, Justice White analogized political gerrymandering to racial gerrymandering (which will be discussed in detail in a later chapter) and contended that the challengers were required to show both a discriminatory intent and a discriminatory effect. Under White's analysis, a simple showing of a lack of proportional representation was insufficient to demonstrate the requisite effect; instead, he contended that "unconstitutional discrimination occurs only when the electoral system is arranged in a manner that will consistently degrade a voter's or a group of voters' influence on the political process as a whole." Finding that the plaintiffs in *Bandemer* had failed to make the requisite demonstration of discriminatory effect, White concluded that the Indiana apportionment plan passed constitutional muster.

In an opinion joined by Justice Stevens, Justice Powell took a quite different view of the merits. He argued that a districting plan violates the Equal

17. *Wells v. Rockefeller,* 394 U.S. 542 (1969).

18. *White v. Weiser,* 412 U.S. at 798 (Powell, J., concurring in the result).

19. *Davis v. Bandemer,* 478 U.S. 109 (1986).

Protection Clause only when it "serves no purpose other than to favor one segment—whether racial, ethnic, religious, economic, or political—that may occupy a position of strength at a particular time, or to disadvantage a politically weak segment of the community"—a question to be determined by reference to "the configurations of the districts, the observance of political subdivision lines, and other criteria that have independent relevance." Powell concluded that the districting plan in *Bandemer* presented a "paradigm example of unconstitutional discrimination against the members of a political party" and should be struck down.

In purely doctrinal terms, *Bandemer* obviously reflected the willingness of a majority of the Burger Court to move beyond the simple one person, one vote requirement of Warren Court jurisprudence. However, despite their decision to reach the merits, even those justices who joined the White and Stevens opinions were clearly unwilling to engage in the kind of aggressive judicial intervention against partisan gerrymandering that had characterized the assault on malapportioned legislatures in the immediate post-*Reynolds* era. The stringency of the burden of proof imposed by Justice White's opinion was apparent in his disposition of *Bandemer* itself. Moreover, even Justices Powell and Stevens—the only two who voted to overturn the apportionment plan—took care to emphasize the deference ordinarily due to state legislatures on apportionment issues. Thus, so long as the mandate of one person, one vote was satisfied, state legislatures remained generally free to engage in partisan gerrymandering without fear of having their decisions overturned by the post-*Bandemer* federal courts.

In short, in cases where race was not directly involved, the Burger Court made only marginal changes in the constitutional standards governing apportionment and voting rights. By contrast, it substantially altered the basic constitutional principles governing the appointment of low-level government officials. The Warren Court had laid the groundwork for the new approach. Prior to the Warren era, constitutional scrutiny of decisions to hire, discipline, or dismiss such officials had been limited by the legal distinction between rights stemming from constitutional or common-law sources, and mere privileges, which the government could confer or deny at will. Government employment clearly fell into the latter class; thus, in the words of Oliver Wendell Holmes, under pre–Warren Court law "[a person] may have [had] a constitutional right to talk politics but he [had] no constitutional right to be a policeman." Under Warren Court jurisprudence, by contrast, the distinction between rights and privileges lost much of its constitutional significance. Thus, for example, in *Keyishian v. Board of Regents*,[20]

_____

20. *Keyishian v. Board of Regents*, 385 U.S. 589 (1967).

the Court held that an applicant could not be denied employment as a teacher solely because he or she was a member of a "subversive" organization. However, the Warren Court had no occasion to comprehensively examine the full implications of the new doctrinal developments for the selection of government employees who were not directly involved in policy making.

The Burger Court's approach to this issue was presaged by its assault on the exclusion of aliens from civil service positions. The assault began in *Sugarman v. Dougall*. *Sugarman* was a challenge to a New York law that excluded noncitizens from the state civil service. With only Justice Rehnquist dissenting, the Court found the exclusion unconstitutional. Speaking for the Court, Justice Blackmun emphasized that the case involved a "flat statutory prohibition against the employment of aliens in the competitive classified civil service," rather than "a legislative scheme that bars some or all aliens from closely defined and limited classes of public employment." Thus, the Court rejected the state's argument that the discrimination "rests on the fundamental concept of identity between a government and the members, or citizens of the state" and that because the civil servant "participates directly in the formulation and execution of governmental policy," he must be free of "compelling obligations to another power." Justice Blackmun argued that, for this purpose, the classification was both overinclusive and underinclusive because it would apply to positions which did not involve the formulation of policy, while at the same time not applying to some policy-making jobs. Thus, with respect to this justification, the statute was not drawn with sufficient precision to pass constitutional muster.[21]

Sugarman did not break any new doctrinal ground; in *Graham v. Richardson*,[22] the Court had already concluded that state classifications based on alienage would generally be subject to strict scrutiny. The decision is more interesting, however, for its ideological underpinnings. In striking down the New York statute, the *Sugarman* Court necessarily rejected the idea that political association with a government—the essence of citizenship—was an important qualification for a representative of that government. Instead, a majority of the Court implicitly treated the holders of non-policy-making positions as simple technocrats, best chosen through merit selection. This point emerged even more clearly in *Hampton v. Mow Sun Wong*.[23]

In *Hampton*, the Court was once again faced with a regulation which barred resident aliens from competitive civil service positions. However, unlike *Sugarman*, which dealt with a state rule, *Hampton* was a challenge to a

21. *Sugarman v. Dougall*, 413 U.S. 634, 638–39, 641, 642 (1973).
22. *Graham v. Richardson*, 403 U.S. 365 (1971).
23. *Hampton v. Mow Sun Wong*, 426 U.S. 88 (1976).

regulation that had been adopted by the *federal* Civil Service Commission. From a doctrinal perspective, this distinction was critical; historically, the Court had been loathe to question federal treatment of aliens, conceptualizing the issue as an aspect of the conduct of foreign affairs. Moreover, in *Mathews v. Diaz*—decided the same day as *Hampton*—the Court had unanimously reaffirmed its commitment to judicial deference in this area.[24]

Nonetheless, over the objections of the chief justice and Justices White, Blackmun, and Rehnquist, the Court found the *Hampton* regulation unconstitutional. Speaking for the majority, Justice Stevens was ambivalent about the appropriate standard of review. He asserted that when a federal action was applicable to the District of Columbia or an insular possession, and when there was no "special national interest" implicated, the Due Process Clause would have the same significance as the Equal Protection Clause. Nonetheless, Stevens recognized that there may be overriding national interests which justify selected federal legislation that would be unacceptable for an individual state, particularly where, as in *Hampton,* the challenged discrimination was nationwide in application.[25]

Ultimately, Stevens did not resolve the case on equal-protection grounds. Instead, he relied on a concept of structural due process that would become an important theme in his jurisprudence during the Burger era. Stevens argued that when the federal government asserts an "overriding national interest" to justify a rule which would violate the Equal Protection Clause if adopted by a state, "due process requires that there be a legitimate basis for presuming that the rule was actually intended to serve that interest." He observed that where Congress or the president adopts such a rule, the Court "might presume that any interest which might rationally be served by the rule did in fact give rise to its adoption." By contrast, where the challenged enactment was promulgated by an administrative agency, he contended that the presumption of validity applied only to agency enactments where the enacting agency "has direct responsibility for fostering or protecting [the asserted] interest." In such a case, the presumption could be fortified by "an appropriate statement of reasons identifying the relevant interest."

In *Hampton,* a number of potential justifications for the challenged regulations were put forward; however, the majority only recognized one of these—the promotion of an efficient federal service—as an appropriate concern of the Civil Service Commission. While recognizing that citizenship might be an "appropriate and legitimate requirement for some important and sensitive positions" and that "administrative convenience might provide

---

24. *Mathews v. Diaz,* 426 U.S. 67 (1976).
25. *Hampton v. Mow Sung Wong,* 426 U.S. at 100–101.

a rational basis for the general rule," Stevens nonetheless rejected the adequacy of such a justification in the case before the Court. He noted that "[t]he Civil Service Commission, like other administrative agencies, has an obligation to perform its responsibilities with some degree of expertise and to make known the reasons for its important decisions." The majority found nothing in the record to indicate that the commission had made a reasoned evaluation of the relative merits of a blanket exclusionary rule as compared to selective exclusion. Nor was the Court willing to infer that the administrative burden of establishing which classifications should exclude aliens would be a particularly onerous task for a personnel specialist. Thus, Stevens concluded, "Any fair balancing of the public interest in avoiding the wholesale deprivation of employment opportunities caused by the Commission's indiscriminate policy, as opposed to what may be nothing more than a hypothetical justification, requires rejection of the argument of administrative convenience in this case."[26]

Even more clearly than *Sugarman*, *Hampton* suggested a preference for merit selection in civil service positions. This preference became even more evident in a constitutional assault on the patronage system, which allows elected officials to fill jobs on the public payroll with political supporters. The attack began in *Elrod v. Burns*. *Elrod* was a suit by a number of non–civil service employees of the Sheriff's Office of Cook County, Illinois; they alleged that they had been dismissed by the newly elected Democratic sheriff solely on the ground that they were members of the Republican Party. By a five-to-three vote, the Court held that such a dismissal would violate the First Amendment.[27] Four years later, in *Branti v. Finkel*, a similarly divided Court concluded that the dismissal of an assistant public defender on the basis of his political affiliation was also constitutionally infirm.[28]

In part, the division on the Court reflected differing assessments of the state interests reflected in the patronage system. Thus, in *Elrod*, dissenting for himself, the chief justice, and Justice Rehnquist, Justice Powell argued that the patronage system encouraged stable political parties and helped avoid excessive political fragmentation. By contrast, in his plurality opinion, Justice Brennan contended that the patronage system actually undermined the freedom of the electoral process, and that for employees without policy-making responsibilities, none of the asserted interests was sufficient to justify what he described as severe encroachments on First Amendment freedoms.[29]

---

26. Ibid., 103–4, 115–16.
27. *Elrod v. Burns*, 427 U.S. 347 (1976).
28. *Branti v. Finkel*, 445 U.S. 507 (1980).
29. *Elrod v. Burns*, 427 U.S. at 374 (Powell, J., dissenting), 356 (opinion of Brennan, J.).

More generally, the opinions in *Elrod* reflected sharply different perspectives on the role of history in constitutional adjudication. The historical pedigree of patronage hiring was virtually irrelevant to Justice Brennan's analysis; for him, current doctrine (which, of course, reflected prevailing liberal orthodoxy) was paramount. Thus, Brennan's historical discussion was extremely brief and concerned largely with the decline of the patronage system. By contrast, Justice Powell depended on "[h]istory and long-prevailing practice" to support his view that the use of patronage hiring passed constitutional muster.[30]

The patronage cases also reflected the deep divisions among the justices on the significance of federalism to constitutional analysis. Justice Brennan's opinion made no reference to federalism-related concerns; for him, the fact that he was imposing a national standard on a matter hitherto governed by local authority was apparently irrelevant. By contrast, the dissenters were acutely aware of the issues of federal-state relations implicit in *Elrod* and *Branti*. Thus, Chief Justice Burger complained of the "[c]onstant inroads on the powers of the States to manage their own affairs," and Justice Powell declared, "My conviction . . . is that we should not foreclose local options in the name of a constitutional right perceived to be applicable for the first time after nearly two centuries."[31]

Powell's criticism implicitly suggested the strong analogy between the *Elrod/Branti* doctrine and the reapportionment cases. In each case, the Court was faced with decisions regarding the proper makeup of state governments. In each case, the practice under attack had been widespread for much of the nation's history and had been generally believed to be free of constitutional infirmity. And in each case, the Court forged new constitutional doctrine to invalidate the challenged practice (although the analysis of the majority in *Elrod* and *Branti* was admittedly less novel than that in *Baker, Reynolds,* and their progeny).[32]

Indeed, for Justices Brennan, Marshall, Stevens, and, to a lesser extent, Stewart, the alienage and patronage cases are perhaps best viewed as a continuation of the project begun by the Warren Court in *Baker* and *Reynolds*—the constitutionalization of a structure of government that had appealed to many liberal intellectuals since the Progressive era. This structure was divided into two parts. The first was a set of policy makers chosen under principles of one person, one vote, and designed to make decisions reflecting

---

30. Ibid., 353–55 (opinion of Brennan, J.; Powell, J., dissenting).

31. Ibid., 374–76 (Burger, C. J., dissenting), n. 12 (Powell, J., dissenting).

32. The implications of *Elrod* and *Branti* are discussed in detail in Bryan A. Schneider, "Do Not Go Gentle into That Good Night: The Unquiet Death of Political Patronage," *Wisconsin Law Review* (1992): 511–46.

the will of a majority of the populace. The second was an apolitical arm, chosen by merit selection, designed to ensure that policy decisions are carried out without regard to political considerations.

Admittedly, the results in *Hampton, Elrod,* and *Branti* cannot be fully explained in such simple terms. The performance of the swing voters—in these cases, Justices White, Blackmun, and Powell—clearly reflects a more complicated agenda. Nonetheless, the decisions of the Burger Court clearly reflect the confidence of a number of justices in both the model itself and the ability of the judiciary to safeguard the model.

The same justices would exhibit similar confidence in other, related contexts. Supervision of the processes of government did not end with oversight over the selection of the officials themselves; instead, in the view of Brennan and his allies, it required extensive intervention in the decision-making process in individual cases—civil, administrative, and criminal. Much of the Burger Court's docket involved challenges to the constitutionality of such processes.

Table 6.1: Voting Patterns

	Bur	Dou	Bre	Mar	Whi	Stew	Bla	Reh	Pow	Stev	Oco
Mahan v. Howell 410 U.S. 315 (1973) (deviation from one person, one vote in state elections)	C	U	U	U	C	C	C	C	NP	NP	NP
Ball v. James 451 U.S. 355 (1981) (deviation from one person, one vote in water district election)	C	NP	U	U	U	C	U	C	C	C	NP
Hill v. Stone 421 U.S. 289 (1975) (property required to vote in bond election)	C	NP	U	U	U	C	U	C	U	NP	NP
White v. Weiser 412 U.S. 783 (1973) (deviation from one person, one vote in congressional election)	U	U	U	U	U	U	U	U	U	NP	NP
Davis v. Bandemer 478 U.S. 109 (1986) (partisan gerrymander)	NJ	NP	C	C	C	NP	C	NJ	U	U	NJ
Sugarman v. Dougall 413 U.S. 634 (1973) (exclusion of aliens from state employment)	U	U	U	U	U	U	U	C	U	NP	NP
Hampton v. Mow Sun Wong 426 U.S. 88 (1976) (exclusion of aliens from federal employment)	C	NP	U	U	C	U	C	C	U	U	NP

	Bur	Dou	Bre	Mar	Whi	Stew	Bla	Reh	Pow	Stev	Oco
Elrod v. Burns 427 U.S. 347 (1976) (loss of government job because of party affiliation)	C	NP	U	U	U	U	U	C	C	C	NP
Branti v. Finkel 445 U.S. 507 (1980) (public defender dismissed because of party affiliation)	U	NP	U	U	U	C	U	C	C	U	NP

Key

C = Constitutional   NJ = Nonjusticiable   NP = Not Participating
U = Unconstitutional

Chief Justice Warren Burger
From the collection of the Supreme Court Historical Society. Photograph by
Robert S. Oakes, National Geographic Society.

Justice William O. Douglas
From the collection of the
Yakima Valley Museum,
Yakima, Washington.

Justice William J. Brennan, Jr.
From the collection of the
Supreme Court Historical
Society. Photograph by Ken
Heinen.

Justice Potter Stewart
Courtesy of Mayhew & Peper,
Photographers.

Justice Byron R. White
Courtesy of the Supreme
Court of the United States.

Justice Thurgood Marshall
Courtesy of the Supreme Court
of the United States.

Justice Harry A. Blackmun
Courtesy of the Supreme Court
of the United States.

Justice Lewis F. Powell, Jr.
Courtesy of the Supreme
Court of the United States.

Justice William H. Rehnquist
Courtesy of the Supreme
Court of the United States.

Justice John Paul Stevens
Courtesy of the Supreme Court
of the United States.

Justice Sandra Day O'Connor
Courtesy of the Supreme Court
of the United States.

7

LAWYER'S LAW

CHOICE OF LAW AND PERSONAL JURISDICTION
IN THE BURGER ERA

While the public generally notes only those Supreme Court cases that deal with high-profile political issues, other decisions can have equally important practical implications. In particular, the Court's elaboration of what might be described as "lawyer's law"—the technical rules governing the conduct of civil law suits—can profoundly influence the outcome of a wide variety of litigation, both public and private. Moreover, the justices' treatment of these issues at times reflects and illuminates the broader themes that mark their jurisprudence generally. During the Burger era, the Court was actively involved in the elaboration of lawyer's law, particularly on issues involving choice of law and personal jurisdiction.

The Court was confronted with two related but different kinds of choice of law issues. One type of issue involved the question of whether federal or state law should govern disputes in federal courts where subject-matter jurisdiction was based on diversity of citizenship. The other issue was the extent to which the Constitution constrained choice of law decisions by state courts.

On the first issue, the most important decision was *Day and Zimmerman, Inc. v. Challoner.*[1] In *Challoner*, Court was asked to reconsider or modify the rule of *Klaxon v. Stentor Electric Manufacturing Co.*[2] The *Klaxon* rule required a federal district court sitting in diversity to apply the choice of law rules of the state in which it sits. *Klaxon* in turn was a gloss on the landmark 1938 decision in *Erie Railroad Co. v. Tompkins,* where the Court overruled a long line of decisions and held that diversity actions should generally be governed by state law rather than federal common law.[3] The rule of *Erie* was never

---

1. *Day and Zimmerman, Inc. v. Challoner,* 423 U.S. 3 (1975) (per curiam).
2. *Klaxon v. Stentor Electric Manufacturing Co.,* 313 U.S. 487 (1941).
3. *Erie Railroad Co. v. Tompkins,* 304 U.S. 64 (1938).

absolute, however; in the post-*Erie* world, the federal courts remained free to craft their own procedural rules.

When *Klaxon* was decided in 1941, its practical significance was limited. American courts unanimously adhered to the approach of the First Restatement of Conflicts, which mandates that substantive choice of law issues be resolved by a series of territorialist rules. At the time, it would have been unthinkable for the federal courts to adopt any other approach as a matter of federal common law. Thus, the question of which jurisdiction's choice of law rules would apply was important only at the margins, where the First Restatement was itself unclear, or in the rare case in which a state had adopted a specific rule that deviated from First Restatement analysis.

The situation was quite different when *Challoner* came to the Burger Court in 1975. Beginning in the mid 1950s, a number of state courts began to reject the First Restatement in favor of a variety of other approaches to choice of law issues. Scholarly commentators loudly applauded this trend and unanimously encouraged the courts to adopt some alternative to First Restatement analysis. Nonetheless, many state courts refused to abandon the traditional approach.

Challoner was a products liability claim that was brought in a federal district court in the state of Texas—one of those states which continued to adhere to the First Restatement. The case arose from the Vietnam War; the plaintiff sought to recover for injuries that he suffered in the nation of Cambodia when a 105-millimeter howitzer shell allegedly exploded prematurely. Although both the plaintiff and defendant were American, under First Restatement rules, the courts were required to apply the substantive law of Cambodia—the place where the injury occurred. By contrast, virtually all modern theorists rejected this conclusion because, in their view, Cambodia was a disinterested jurisdiction. Against this background, the court of appeals held that the federal courts could decline to apply Cambodian law. In a brief per curiam opinion, the Supreme Court unanimously disagreed, rejecting the invitation to reconsider *Klaxon* and declaring that "a federal court in a diversity case is not free to engraft upon . . . state [conflicts] rules exceptions which may commend themselves to the federal court, but which have not commended themselves to the State in which the federal court sits."[4]

Challoner emphatically reaffirmed the basic principle that state law should generally govern the substantive aspects of diversity litigation in the federal courts. Thus, the justices declined an opportunity to reallocate power from state institutions to federal institutions—an opportunity which might well have seemed attractive on some level to the more nationalistic justices of the Burger Court. At the same time, however, *Challoner* also presented a situation

---

4. *Day and Zimmerman, Inc. v. Challoner*, 423 at U.S. 4.

in which the force of the appeal to distinctively legal principles was particularly strong—a case involving judicial procedure with no obvious political overtones. In this context, it should not be surprising that none of the justices was willing to abandon a clearly applicable precedent.

In any event, *Challoner* ensured that the federal courts would not increase the pressure on state courts to abandon traditional choice of law methodology. Equally important were the Burger Court decisions that effectively left states free to adopt truly radical approaches to choice of law issues. To be sure, in *Phillips Petroleum Co. v. Shutts,* all members of the Court except Justice Stevens agreed that a state could not constitutionally apply its own law to a case with which it had absolutely no connection except as the situs of the litigation.[5] Nonetheless, the remaining justices also agreed that the state choice of law decisions should rarely be held unconstitutional. At the margins, however, they were split, with the conservative justices on the Court arguing for the more aggressive interpretation of constitutional norms. In large part this division reflected more general disagreements about the place of state governments in the American constitutional system.

Allstate Insurance Co. v. Hague exemplifies this point.[6] *Hague* arose from a fatal accident between a motorcycle and an automobile that took place in the state of Wisconsin. The decedent (who was riding on the back of the motorcycle) was a Wisconsin resident, as were the drivers of both vehicles. While neither driver was insured, the decedent carried an automobile insurance policy on three vehicles, a policy which provided for recovery in the event that he was involved in an accident in which an uninsured motorist was liable. Subsequently, the decedent's wife moved to Minnesota and brought suit on this policy in Minnesota state court.

The key question in the case was whether Minnesota or Wisconsin law governed the amount which the plaintiff could recover under the policy. Under Minnesota law, the plaintiff was entitled to recover the policy limits for each of the decedent's three vehicles. Under Wisconsin law, by contrast, the plaintiff was only allowed to receive the amount provided by the policy for one vehicle. Applying what they viewed as the better law, the Minnesota courts held that their own state's law should apply on this issue. The question before the Supreme Court in *Hague* was whether this decision was constitutional.

While five of the eight participating justices agreed that the Minnesota judgment was constitutional, they could not agree on the proper rationale for this conclusion. Justice Stevens argued that Minnesota could apply its own law because the rule was not substantively unfair to the defendant and

---

5. *Phillips Petroleum Co. v. Shutts,* 472 U.S. 797 (1985).
6. *Allstate Insurance Co. v. Hague,* 449 U.S. 302 (1981).

the application of the rule would not pose a threat to Wisconsin's sovereignty. The remaining seven justices took a different view, concluding that the proper test was whether the forum state had "a significant contact or significant aggregation of contacts creating interests, such that choice of its law is neither arbitrary nor fundamentally unfair." Nonetheless they were divided on the ultimate question of whether the Minnesota courts' decision passed constitutional muster. Speaking for himself and Justices Marshall, White, and Blackmun, Justice Brennan relied on three factors to argue for affirmance: the current residence of the plaintiff in Minnesota, the decedent's employment in Minnesota, and the fact that the insurance company did business in Minnesota. On the other hand, speaking for himself, the chief justice, and Justice Rehnquist, Justice Powell contended that these contacts were insufficient to support the application of Minnesota law.

Even the dissenters in *Hague* clearly indicated that they envisioned only "modest" constitutional restraints on the state choice of law process, to be applied with "restraint." Thus, on one level, the plurality and the dissent simply disagreed narrowly over the significance to be given the specific facts in the case. Viewed from a broader perspective, however, the dispute reflected wider areas of disagreement among the justices.

The dissenters viewed *Hague* as a threat to the quasi-sovereign status of the state of Wisconsin. In essence, they argued that the prerogatives of state governments enjoyed constitutional protection not only from infringement by the federal government, but also from the predations of other states. Thus, Powell's opinion was based on the view that limitations on state choice of law decisions "ensure that the States do not 'reach out beyond the limits imposed on them by their status of coequal sovereigns in a federal system.'" Against this background, it should not be surprising that *Hague* split the justices along classic liberal-conservative lines. Indeed, the five justices in the *Hague* majority were precisely the same as those who would ultimately reject the conservatives' efforts to insulate the structures of state government from undue interference by the federal authorities.

In any event, *Hague* clearly indicated that the Constitution would not significantly constrain state courts that chose to apply their own law to cases over which they possessed jurisdiction. It was in essence an open invitation for plaintiffs' attorneys to shop for a forum whose laws were favorable to the cause of their clients. The major constraint on this choice was the law of personal jurisdiction, which limited the range of cases that a court would consider.

Like the principles governing choice of law analysis, the law of personal jurisdiction had undergone a major transformation in the mid twentieth century, shifting from a purely formal analysis to a more open-ended approach that focused on practical considerations. However, unlike the revolution in choice of law theory, which dealt almost entirely with the common law, constitutional questions were central to the resolution of personal jurisdiction issues. The traditional rule was established in 1877 by the decision in *Pennoyer v. Neff*, where the Court held that a state court might exercise jurisdiction over an absent nondomiciliary defendant if and only if the defendant either had property in the forum state or had been served with process in that state.[7] In 1945 *Pennoyer* was at least partially overruled in *International Shoe Co. v. Washington*, which established the principle that a state may assert jurisdiction only over those defendants who "have certain minimum contacts with [the forum state] such that the maintenance of the suit does not offend 'traditional notions of fair play and substantial justice.'"[8]

The minimum contacts standard obviously expanded the permissible range of state court jurisdiction; at the same time, the parameters of the new analysis were far from clear. While the Warren Court at times grappled with personal jurisdiction issues, its decisions did not meaningfully refine the concept of minimum contacts. By contrast, the decisions of the Burger Court provided much clearer guidelines for the resolution of disputes over personal jurisdiction.[9]

The personal jurisdiction issue first came to the Burger Court in *The Bremen v. Zapata Offshore Oil Co.*[10] *The Bremen* dealt with the status of forum selection clauses—devices which were commonly used to provide certainty in an era of expanded personal jurisdiction and widely divergent approaches to choice of law. The case arose from an agreement under which a German corporation agreed to tow an oceangoing oil-drilling rig from Louisiana to Italy. During the process of towing the rig in international waters, the tug that was owned by the German corporation encountered a severe storm in the Gulf of Mexico. The storm damaged the oil rig, and its American owners ordered the tug to tow the rig to Tampa, Florida—the nearest port of refuge. The contract provided that "any dispute arising must be treated before the London Court of Justice"; nonetheless, the owners of the oil-drilling rig sued the German corporation in the federal district court in Tampa, alleging negligent towing and breach of contract.

Traditionally, courts had been reluctant to enforce forum selection clauses, often finding them contrary to public policy because their effect was to "oust the court of jurisdiction." Nonetheless, with only Justice Douglas dis-

---

7. *Pennoyer v. Neff*, 95 U.S. 714 (1877).

8. *International Shoe Co. v. Washington*, 326 U.S. 310, 316 (1945).

9. The Burger Court's approach to personal jurisdiction issues is described in detail and analyzed from a variety of different perspectives in "Symposium: *Asahi Metal Industry Co. v. Superior Court* and the Future of Personal Jurisdiction," *South Carolina Law Review* 39 (1988): 729–896.

10. *The Bremen v. Zapata Offshore Oil Co.*, 407 U.S. 1 (1972).

senting, the Supreme Court held that the federal courts should generally enforce such provisions and dismiss the lawsuit. Speaking for the Court, Chief Justice Burger declared that "the correct approach [is] to enforce the forum selection clause specifically unless . . . enforcement would be unreasonable and unjust, or . . . the clause was invalid for such reasons as fraud or overreaching."[11]

The Bremen was not by its terms a constitutional decision; instead, the Court was deciding only the content of the federal common law applicable to admiralty cases. Nonetheless, some of the important themes of the decision would resonate through the Court's treatment of related constitutional issues as well. For example, one of the most important premises of the majority opinion is that choice of law issues should not drive jurisdictional analysis. In dissent, Justice Douglas noted that the substantive law of England would be far more favorable than American law to the German defendant, and that an American court would not enforce an explicit choice of law provision on this point. Douglas relied heavily on this factor to support his conclusion that an American plaintiff should be allowed to bring his lawsuit in an American court. By contrast, the majority implicitly dismissed this argument, suggesting that it was quite reasonable for parties to a multinational transaction to use a forum selection clause to guarantee a favorable choice of law decision.

Analogous disputes over the relationship between issues of jurisdiction and choice of law also marked the justices' treatment of the cases raising constitutional challenges to the assertion of personal jurisdiction. Generally, the same commitment to antiformalist analysis that marked *The Bremen* was also reflected in other personal jurisdiction cases—most notably, the landmark decision in *Shaffer v. Heitner*.[12] *Shaffer* was a derivative action initiated in Delaware state court by a shareholder of the Greyhound Corporation, a Delaware corporation. The complaint stated that a number of present and former officers of the corporation and one of its subsidiaries had violated their respective duties to the corporation with the result that it had been held liable for penalties and damages under the antitrust laws. Personal jurisdiction over the defendants was based on a *quasi in rem* theory derived from *Pennoyer;* the plaintiffs sought to bring the defendants into court by attaching their stock in the corporation which, under Delaware law, was deemed to be "located" within that state.

The *International Shoe* Court had not directly addressed the question of the constitutionality of *quasi in rem* jurisdiction; nonetheless, with Justice Rehnquist not participating, the Court unanimously concluded that all

11. Ibid., 15.
12. *Shaffer v. Heitner,* 433 U.S. 186 (1977).

efforts to exercise personal jurisdiction would henceforth be subject to the minimum contacts analysis. Speaking for all of the participating justices except Justice Stevens, Justice Marshall began by noting that any *in rem* action is essentially an adjudication of individual rights in the res. Given this fact, he then argued that there is no reason to apply a standard different than that applied to other adjudications of individual rights, such as those typically at issue in in personam cases.[13]

Marshall then turned to the impact of the location of property on the problem of assessing minimum contacts. He conceded that "when claims to the property itself are the source of the underlying controversy between the plaintiff and the defendant, it would be unusual for the State where the property is located not to have jurisdiction." Marshall also noted a number of other situations in which the presence of property might be relevant. But in *Shaffer*, "the property which now serves as the basis for state court jurisdiction [is] completely unrelated to the plaintiff's cause of action . . . the only role played by the property is to provide the basis for bringing the defendant into court." In such a case, the opinion concluded, the mere presence of property in a state does not provide the requisite minimum contacts to support even *quasi in rem* jurisdiction.[14]

Despite the consensus on the basic principle that *Shaffer* was governed by the *International Shoe* standards, the justices were somewhat divided on the proper scope of the holding. Concurring only in the result, Justice Stevens argued that the real problem with the assertion of jurisdiction in *Shaffer* was that simple ownership of stock did not give the defendants adequate notice that they might be amenable to suit in Delaware. Making a related argument, Justice Powell suggested that he would have taken a different view of the case if jurisdiction had been premised on the seizure of real property. Finally, the justices had diverging views of the proper disposition of the case under the *International Shoe* test. Analogizing the jurisdictional inquiry to choice of law analysis, Justice Brennan argued that the state of Delaware had cognizable

---

13. Ibid., 207.

14. Ibid., 207 (footnote omitted), 208, 209 (footnote omitted). In *Shaffer* itself, Marshall identified three distinct categories of property-based actions: pure *in rem*, type I *quasi in rem*, and type II *quasi in rem*. A pure *in rem* action purports to settle all potential claims to a particular piece of property. In a type I *quasi in rem* action, a plaintiff seeks to establish the priority of his claim to the property over that of particular persons. In a type II *quasi in rem* action, the plaintiff seeks to establish his claim to the property based on an unrelated cause of action. Ibid, 199 n. 17 [quoting *Hanson v. Denckla*, 357 U.S. 235, 246 n.12 (1958)]. Except for problems of notice, for purposes of analyzing personal jurisdiction issues, a pure *in rem* case is virtually indistinguishable from a type I *quasi in rem* action. Thus for the sake of simplicity, in the remainder of this discussion, both of those categories will be subsumed under the label pure *in rem*, while the label *quasi in rem* will refer to type II situations.

interests in regulating the activities of the officers and directors of its corporations, and that these interests justified the assertion of personal jurisdiction by the Delaware courts. Speaking for all of the remaining justices except Justice Stevens, Justice Marshall took a different view. He conceded that Delaware arguably had important interests at stake in *Shaffer,* and that those interests would have been sufficient to justify the application of Delaware law. Nonetheless, Marshall concluded that the Delaware courts could not constitutionally exercise jurisdiction because the defendants had not "purposefully avail[ed] themselves of the privilege of conducting activities within the forum state." The centrality of the purposeful availment test—drawn from the Warren Court's decision in *Hanson v. Denckla*—was established even more clearly three years later in *World-Wide Volkswagen Corp. v. Woodson.*[15]

In *World-Wide Volkswagen,* the plaintiffs (then New York residents) had purchased an automobile from the defendants in Massena, New York. The following year the plaintiffs decided to move to Arizona. En route to their new home, they had an accident in Oklahoma and one of the plaintiffs suffered severe injuries. They sued the defendants on a products liability theory in Oklahoma state court.

The plaintiffs based their jurisdictional argument on the theory of actual foreseeability. They reasoned that because of the nature of the product, the defendants should have foreseen the possibility that it would be used in another state and cause injury there. Thus, notwithstanding the fact that the relevant defendants had no other contacts with the forum state, the plaintiffs contended that the assumption of jurisdiction in *World-Wide Volkswagen* was consistent with constitutional norms.

Speaking for a six-member majority, Justice White disagreed. While conceding that "foreseeability is [not] wholly irrelevant," White's opinion distinguished between *legal* foreseeability and *actual* foreseeability. "[T]he foreseeability that is critical to due process analysis is not the mere likelihood that a product will find its way into the forum state. Rather, it is that the defendant's conduct and connection with the forum state are such that he should reasonably anticipate being haled into court there." In turn, this type of foreseeability was to be determined by reference to the judicial interpretations of the *International Shoe* standards—most notably, by the question of whether a defendant "purposefully avails itself of the privilege of conducting activity within the state." Finding a "total absence of those affiliating circumstances that are a necessary predicate to any exercise of state court jurisdiction," White concluded that these standards had not been met in *World-Wide Volkswagen.*[16]

---

15. *Hanson v. Denckla,* 357 U.S. 235 (1958)]; *World-Wide Volkswagen Corp. v. Woodson,* 444 U.S. 286 (1980).

16. Ibid., 295–98.

Speaking for himself and Justice Blackmun, Justice Marshall took a different view. He contended that "jurisdiction [can be] premised on the deliberate and purposeful actions of the defendants . . . in choosing to become a part of a nationwide . . . network for marketing and servicing automobiles" and that each defendant was chargeable with knowledge that "the probability that some of the cars it sells will be driven in every one of the contiguous States must amount to a virtual certainty." In *Keeton v. Hustler Magazine, Inc.,*[17] however, it became clear that the differences between Marshall and Blackmun and the members of the *World-Wide Volkswagen* majority were relatively minor.

Keeton was a libel action in the federal district court for the state of New Hampshire. The defendant was an Ohio corporation whose principal place of business was in California; its only connection with New Hampshire was that a small proportion of the total number of magazines which it produced (some of which contained the allegedly libelous statements) were sold in that state. The plaintiff was a New York resident; her only connection with the forum was that her name appeared on the masthead of several magazines which were distributed in New Hampshire. Only a small portion of the damages which the plaintiff claimed to have suffered were allegedly connected to the forum state; moreover, the forum was rather clearly chosen because its statute of limitations was favorable to the plaintiff. Nonetheless, the Court unanimously held that the Fourteenth Amendment did not prevent the New Hampshire courts from asserting jurisdiction over the defendant, arguing that "[w]here, as in this case, [the defendant] has continuously and deliberately exploited the New Hampshire market, it must reasonably anticipate being haled into court there in a libel action based on the contents of its magazine."[18]

Taken together, *World-Wide Volkswagen* and *Keeton* clearly established the primacy of the concept of "purposeful availment" in personal jurisdiction analysis. In *World-Wide Volkswagen,* jurisdiction was barred because the only contact was that created by "unilateral activity of those who claim some relationship with [the] nonresident defendant." By contrast, where, as in *Keeton,* the defendant itself created the relationship, the assertion of jurisdiction was held constitutional. Moreover, *Keeton* also made clear that, at least for most of the justices, the personal jurisdiction inquiry would be based on qualitative rather than quantitative analysis of the defendant's contacts. To be sure, in *Burger King v. Rudcewicz,* seven justices suggested that, in rare instances, purposeful availment would not conclusively establish the propriety of personal jurisdiction;[19] however, even *Burger King* recognized that purposeful availment

17. *Keeton v. Hustler Magazine, Inc.,* 465 U.S. 770 (1984).
18. Ibid., 781 (citation omitted).
19. *Burger King Corp. v. Rudcewicz,* 471 U.S. 462 (1984).

was an indispensable prerequisite to the constitutional exercise of the forum state's authority to adjudicate.

Only Justice Brennan took a dramatically different approach. Brennan dissented in five of the six personal jurisdiction cases in which the Court was divided, and he concurred only in the result in *Keeton*. The most complete statement of Brennan's approach came in his *World-Wide Volkswagen* dissent, where he insisted that an interested state could constitutionally exercise jurisdiction over an absent defendant unless the defendant could show actual inconvenience of a constitutional magnitude. In practice, Brennan *never* held that the Fourteenth Amendment barred the exercise of personal jurisdiction by a state court. Thus, once again, it was the liberal activist who was the most likely to sustain the exercise of state power.

As in the choice of law area, this pattern can most plausibly be viewed as a reflection of Brennan's view of the role of states in the federal system. If the United States is appropriately viewed as a single, largely undifferentiated entity, then the place at which litigation is conducted should make little difference (except in the rare instance in which the defendant would suffer truly massive inconvenience by being forced to litigate in a particular state). Conversely, the members of the *World-Wide Volkswagen* majority also initially characterized the jurisdictional inquiry in terms of the theory of federalism:

> [W]e have never accepted the proposition that state lines are irrelevant for jurisdictional purposes, nor could we and remain faithful to the principles of interstate federalism embodied in the Constitution . . . the Framers . . . intended that the States retain many essential attributes of sovereignty, including, in particular, the sovereign power to try causes in their courts. The sovereignty of each State, in turn, implied a limitation on the sovereignty of all of its sister States—a limitation express or implicit in both the original scheme of the Constitution and the Fourteenth Amendment.
>
> . . . Even if the defendant would suffer minimal or no inconvenience from being forced to litigate before the tribunals of another State; even if the forum State has a strong interest in applying its law to the controversy; even if the forum State is the most convenient for litigation, the Due Process Clause, acting as an instrument of interstate federalism, may sometimes act to divest the State of its power to render a valid judgment.[20]

However, in *Insurance Corporation of Ireland v. Compagnie des Bauxites de Guinee,* all of the justices except Justice Powell abandoned their allegiance to this theory. In *Bauxites,* the plaintiff sought to have the defendant produce

---

20. *World-Wide Volkswagen Corp. v. Woodson,* 444 U.S. at 293–94.

documents in order to establish the facts that were prerequisite to the assertion of personal jurisdiction. The defendant refused to produce the documents. By its terms, the case turned on the question of whether, under those
circumstances, the Federal Rules of Civil Procedure allowed the federal
courts to subject the defendant to its jurisdiction. All of the justices agreed
that the court could assert jurisdiction in *Bauxites;* however, over Powell's
lone, vehement objection, Justice White's majority opinion also declared
that "the personal jurisdiction requirement . . . represents a restriction on
judicial power not as a matter of sovereignty, but as a matter of individual liberty," and in response to Powell's complaint asserted that

> the restriction on state sovereign power described in *World-Wide Volks-*
> *wagen Corp.* . . . must be seen ultimately as a function of the individual
> liberty interest preserved by the Due Process Clause. That clause is the
> only source of the personal jurisdiction requirement, and the clause
> itself makes no mention of federalism concerns. Furthermore, if the fed-
> eralism concept operated as an independent restriction on the sover
> eign power of the court, it would not be possible to waive the personal
> jurisdiction requirement: Individual actions cannot change the powers
> of sovereignty, although the individual can subject himself to powers
> from which he may otherwise be protected.[21]

Against this background, it should not be surprising that (with the
exception of Justice Brennan) the patterns of concurrence and dissent in
the Burger Court's personal jurisdiction decisions have an almost random
quality. Admittedly, Chief Justice Burger and Justice Rehnquist, the two most
conservative justices on the Court, joined Justice Stewart as the only members of the Court who joined the majority in every personal jurisdiction case
in which they participated; however, post–Burger Court developments
strongly suggest that Rehnquist would have dissented in *Shaffer.* Moreover,
other than Brennan, none of the justices showed a clear pattern of either
favoring or opposing jurisdiction in the cases which divided the Court.

The juxtaposition between the positions of Marshall and Brennan is particularly striking. Marshall wrote the majority opinion in three of the five
cases in which his normally close ally dissented; the only one of the five cases
in which they agreed was *World-Wide Volkswagen.* This pattern undoubtedly
reflects the fact that Marshall—like all of the other justices except Brennan
and Powell—did not view the personal jurisdiction cases as implicating fundamental notions of federalism, but rather as the kind of technical issue on

---

21. *Insurance Corporation of Ireland v. Compagnie des Bauxites de Guinee,* 456 U.S. 694, 702–3
n.10 (1982).

which pure lawyerlike analysis was appropriate. Against this background, it should not be surprising that standard ideological lines would not explain the patterns of concurrence and dissent. At times, the Court's treatment of decisions by administrative agencies reflected a similar dynamic; in other such cases, however, the more standard ideological divisions emerged clearly.

Table 7.1: Voting Patterns

	Bur	Dou	Bre	Mar	Whi	Stew	Bla	Reh	Pow	Stev	Oco
Day and Zimmerman v. Challoner 423 U.S. 3 (1975) (choice of law in diversity case)	SL	SL	SL	SL	SL	SL	SL	SL	SL	NP	NP
Allstate Ins. Co. v. Hague 449 U.S. 302 (1981) (application of forum law)	U	NP	C	C	C	NP	C	U	U	C	NP
Phillips Petroleum Co. v. Shutts 472 U.S. 797 (1985) (application of forum law)	U	NP	U	U	U	NP	U	U	NP	C	U
The Bremen v. Zapata Oil Co. 407 U.S. 1 (1972) (forum selection clause)	D	DD	D	D	D	D	D	D	D	NP	NP
Shaffer v. Heitner 433 U.S. 186 (1977) (*quasi in rem* jurisdiction)	U	NP	U	U	U	U	U	NP	U	U	NP
Shaffer v. Heitner 433 U.S. 186 (1977) (assertion of personal jurisdiction)	U	NP	C	U	U	U	U	NP	U	U	NP
World-Wide Volkswagen v. Woodson 444 U.S. 286 (1980) (assertion of personal jurisdiction)	U	NP	C	C	U	U	C	U	U	U	NP
Keeton v. Hustler Magazine 465 U.S. 770 (1984) (assertion of personal jurisdiction)	C	NP	C	C	C	NP	C	C	C	C	C

Key

C	= Constitutional	SL	= State Law	DD	= Do Not Dismiss Lawsuit
U	= Unconstitutional	D	= Dismiss Lawsuit	NP	= Not Participating

8

THE BURGER COURT AND
THE ADMINISTRATIVE STATE

The expansion of the role of administrative agencies in the modern era has presented the courts with a variety of novel legal problems. Such agencies often combine legislative, judicial, and executive functions, and as such do not fit neatly into the categories envisioned by the Constitution itself. While the struggle to define the appropriate relationship between the administrative agencies and other branches of government began long before the Burger era, the Burger Court made a number of significant doctrinal innovations in this area.[1]

One important set of cases involved congressional efforts to retain influence over the administrative process, either by vesting decision making in officials who were subject to the control of Congress or by providing for direct congressional review of specific administrative decisions. The Burger Court was faced with constitutional challenges to both devices. In each case, the Court imposed stringent limitations on congressional power.[2]

As we have already seen, in *Buckley v. Valeo,*[3] the Court unanimously rebuffed efforts to have members of the Federal Election Commission appointed by the Speaker of the House of Representatives and the president pro tempore of the Senate. In *Bowsher v. Synar,*[4] one of the provisions of the Gramm-Rudman-Hollings Act met a similar fate. Gramm-Rudman-Hollings was an effort to impose fiscal discipline on the federal government. In essence, the statute provided that, if the federal deficit was projected to

---

1. Bernard Schwartz, "Administrative Law and the Burger Court," *Hofstra Law Review* 8 (1980): 325–401, chronicles developments in administrative law during the early and middle years of the Burger era.
2. The Burger Court's treatment of these and related issues is discussed in Erwin C. Chemerinsky, "A Paradox without Principle: A Comment on the Burger Court's Jurisprudence of Separation of Powers," *Southern California Law Review* 60 (1987): 1083–111.
3. *Buckley v. Valeo,* 424 U.S. 1 (1976).
4. *Bowsher v. Synar,* 478 U.S. 714 (1986).

exceed a specified amount in the upcoming fiscal year, cuts in spending would automatically take place in order to reduce the deficit.

Reliable projections for upcoming revenues and expenditures were obviously crucial to the proper operation of Gramm-Rudman-Hollings. One potential difficulty was that both the legislative and executive branches of government might skew the estimates for political purposes. In order to avoid this problem, the statute required the director of the Office of Management and Budget and the Congressional Budget Office to independently estimate the upcoming budget deficit and the spending cuts that would be required, and to report their estimates to the comptroller general of the United States. Based on these reports, the comptroller general would then make his own calculation of the deficit and necessary spending cuts and report his conclusions to the president. The president was in turn required to implement the comptroller general's conclusions. With only Justices White and Blackmun dissenting, the Court concluded that the comptroller general could not constitutionally perform the functions required of him by the statute.

For the majority, the constitutional difficulty arose from the power of Congress to remove the comptroller general. After being selected by the president from a list of three names submitted by the Speaker of the House and the president pro tempore of the Senate, the comptroller general was subject to removal for cause by a joint resolution of the Senate and House of Representatives. Speaking for five justices, the chief justice concluded that the terms under which he served made the comptroller general a member of the legislative branch, and that the provisions of Gramm-Rudman-Hollings vested him with executive authority in contravention of the principle of separation of powers. Concurring only in the result, Justices Stevens and Marshall characterized the grant of power as legislative, but concluded that Congress could not constitutionally delegate legislative power to one of its own agents. Dissenting, Justice White questioned whether the comptroller general was in fact under the control of Congress, concluding that in any event the relevant provision of Gramm-Rudman-Hollings presented no real threat to the separation of powers. Finally, Justice Blackmun argued that if the existence of congressional removal power rendered Gramm-Rudman-Hollings unconstitutional, the proper remedy was to strike the removal power rather than the budget-balancing statute.[5]

Although of considerable doctrinal significance, *Bowsher* proved to be of little practical import. Congress responded by simply transferring the duties

---

5. Ibid., 721–34, 736–59 (Stevens, J., concurring in the result), 759–76 (White, J., dissenting), 776–83 (Blackmun, J., dissenting). The internal maneuverings that produced the final *Bowsher* opinion are described in detail in Bernard Schwartz, *The Ascent of Pragmatism: The Burger Court in Action* (New York: Addison-Wesley, 1990), 65–73.

of the comptroller general to the Office of Management and Budget, which was clearly part of the executive branch. By contrast, the decision in *Immigration and Naturalization Service v. Chadha*[6] imposed significant limitations on the powers of Congress.[7]

Chadha dealt with the constitutionality of "legislative vetoes," which were often appended to statutory grants of administrative rule-making authority. Designed to ensure that agencies did not abuse rule-making authority, these provisions automatically suspended rules adopted by administrative agencies if one or both Houses of Congress voted for such a suspension within a specified period of time. By 1983, fifty-five different statutes provided for a legislative veto in one form or another. However, in that year, the *Chadha* Court found the use of these devices unconstitutional.

Chadha itself revolved around a provision of the Immigration and Naturalization Act, which vested the attorney general with discretion, in the case of "extreme hardship," to suspend the deportation of an alien who was deportable by law and to change the alien's immigration status to that of permanent resident. At the same time, the statute provided that the decision of the attorney general could be reversed by majority vote in either the Senate or House of Representatives during a specified time frame. Justice Powell argued that, because the provision focused on the status of individual aliens, the statute unconstitutionally delegated a judicial function to the legislature; however, since such questions have historically been viewed as within the purview of the legislature, a large majority of the justices chose to address the more general issue of the constitutionality of the legislative veto.

Citing functional considerations, Byron White would have upheld the legislative veto. However, speaking for all of the remaining justices except William Rehnquist, Chief Justice Burger took a quite different view. Burger essentially argued that a congressional decision to overturn agency action was a species of legislation, functionally no different than other legislation. Thus, it could only have binding legal effect if adopted by both Houses of Congress and signed into law by the president.

The decision in *Chadha* left intact the formal authority of Congress to alter administrative regulations. Nonetheless, in practical terms, the elimination of the legislative veto made that authority much more difficult to exercise. Thus, the judicial role in supervising agency action—always important—assumed even greater relative significance during the Burger era.

Some of the most important issues involved questions of statutory interpretation. In 1946 Congress had provided the basic framework for judicial

---

6. *Immigration and Naturalization Service v. Chadha*, 462 U.S. 919 (1983).

7. The background and implications of *Chadha* are discussed in detail in Barbara H. Craig, *Chadha: The Story of an Epic Constitutional Struggle* (New York: Oxford University Press, 1988).

review of federal administrative decisions in the Administrative Procedure Act (APA). However, in some cases, the appropriate scope of judicial review under the APA was not entirely clear. Three major decisions of the Burger Court substantially limited the judicial function under the APA.

The first of these decisions, *Citizens to Preserve Overton Park v. Volpe,* revolved around a long-running dispute over the construction of a highway through a public park in Memphis, Tennessee. The relevant statutes prohibited the use of federal funds for such construction if a "feasible and prudent" alternative route could be found, and stated that in any event the funds could be expended only after "all possible planning to minimize harm" to the park. The secretary of transportation nonetheless approved the construction, concluding that the statutory criteria had been satisfied. Opponents of the highway charged that the decision of the secretary to proceed with the construction was wrong on the merits and, in any event, was invalid because he failed to make formal findings of fact supporting his conclusion.[8]

While the Court unanimously reaffirmed the strong presumption of reviewability of administrative action and concluded that the secretary's decision was reviewable, it also imposed restrictions on the scope of that review. In his opinion for the Court, Justice Marshall held that the decision was reviewable only for "abuse of discretion," rejecting the argument that the courts should engage in either de novo review or an inquiry into whether the decision was supported by substantial evidence. Marshall emphasized that the appropriate standard of review "is a narrow one," and that the court was to consider only "whether the decision was based on a consideration of relevant factors and whether there has been a clear error of judgment," and not "substitute its judgment for that of the agency." Moreover, the Court rejected the contention that formal findings of fact were required.[9]

A commitment to judicial deference was even more evident in *Chevron, U.S.A., Inc. v. Natural Resources Defense Council.*[10] In *Overton Park,* the appropriate substantive standard to be applied had not been in dispute; the only question in the case was whether the agency's conclusions of fact could withstand judicial scrutiny. In *Chevron,* by contrast, the agency was challenged on a purely legal question of statutory interpretation involving the Clean Air Act Amendments of 1977. Emphasizing the technical, complex nature of the statutory scheme, the Court once again rejected the notion of de novo review, declaring that, unless Congress had directly spoken to the precise question at issue, "the court does not simply impose its own construction on

---

8. *Citizens to Preserve Overton Park v. Volpe,* 401 U.S. 402 (1971).
9. Ibid., 416.
10. *Chevron, U.S.A., Inc. v. Natural Resources Defense Council,* 467 U.S. 837 (1984).

the statute, as would be necessary in the absence of an administrative interpretation. Rather, if the statute is silent or ambiguous with respect to the particular issue, the question for the court is whether the agency's answer is based on a permissible construction of the statute." Thus, "the court need not conclude that the agency construction was . . . the reading the court would have reached if the question initially had arisen in a judicial proceeding," but rather whether the agency view was "reasonable." The same basic theme was reflected in *Vermont Yankee Nuclear Power v. Natural Resources Defense Council,* as the Court emphatically rejected the view that courts in general possessed authority to require agencies to adopt procedures more stringent than those provided in the APA, declaring that, except in "extremely rare" circumstances, "the formulation of procedures [is] basically to be left within the discretion of the agencies to which Congress has confided the responsibility for substantive judgments."[11]

Overton Park, Chevron, and *Vermont Yankee* are remarkable not only for the consistency of the Court's commitment to judicial deference, but also for the unanimity of opinion in all three cases—itself an "extremely rare" circumstance on potentially controversial issues during the Burger era. However, none of these decisions envisioned a system in which the judiciary would have no role to play in supervising agency actions; indeed, both *Overton Park* and *Chevron* explicitly contemplated judicial intervention in some circumstances. The limits of judicial deference emerged more clearly in *Motor Vehicle Manufacturers Association of the United States, Inc. v. State Farm Mutual Automobile Insurance Co.*[12]

State Farm was a by-product of the sea change in federal government policies that occurred with the ascension of Ronald Reagan to the presidency in 1980. Many of the appointees of Democratic president Jimmy Carter, who preceded Reagan, had moved aggressively to regulate business and industry in order to protect what they saw as critical public interests in safety and the environment. By contrast, as a staunchly conservative Republican, Reagan was deeply suspicious of government regulation of business, and he staffed administrative agencies with appointees who generally shared that philosophy. At times, these appointees moved quickly to overturn what they viewed as unduly onerous regulations imposed during the Carter administration.

The specific regulation at issue in *State Farm* was a requirement that all motor vehicles produced after a certain date be equipped with passive restraints that protected vehicle occupants in the event of collisions. The regulation, issued during the Carter presidency by the National Highway

11. *Vermont Yankee Nuclear Power v. Natural Resources Defense Council,* 435 U.S. 519 (1978).
12. *Motor Vehicle Manufacturers Association v. State Farm Mutual Automobile Insurance Co.,* 463 U.S. 29 (1983).

Traffic Safety Administration (NHTSA), could be satisfied by providing either automatic seat belts or air bags. Subsequently, however, Reagan appointees to NHTSA sought to rescind the regulation, arguing that changes in circumstances suggested that there was no longer a basis for predicting that the passive restraint mandate would significantly improve the safety of vehicle occupants.

The Court unanimously found that the agency had acted arbitrarily and capriciously in rescinding the regulation. All of the justices agreed that the decision to rescind the regulation was subject to the same standard of review as the initial decision to adopt the regulation, and that the Reagan NHTSA had failed to provide a sufficiently reasoned justification for its action. At the same time, in an exchange reminiscent of the debate over the patronage system in *Elrod* and *Branti,* the justices suggested differing views on the appropriate role of politics in administrative decision making. Speaking for himself and Justices Brennan, Marshall, Blackmun, and Stevens, Justice White emphasized the importance of abstract "reason" in the formulation of agency policy. The remaining justices, by contrast, joined Justice Rehnquist, who asserted that "a change in administration brought about by the people casting their votes is a perfectly reasonable basis for an executive agency's reappraisal of the costs and benefits of its programs and regulations."[13]

The divisions in *State Farm* were by no means unique. Despite their agreement on basic principles, the Burger justices would occasionally divide along political lines in APA cases. However, the differences among the justices emerged more sharply in connection with the constitutional issues associated with administrative law.

In sharp contrast to the deference it showed to administrative agencies in APA actions, the Burger Court expanded the scope of the Due Process Clauses of the Fifth and Fourteenth Amendments as substantial constraints on administrative action. Historically, due process protections had been limited to cases involving deprivations of either traditional liberties or private property. However, as a corollary to the demise of the right/privilege distinction, the Court extended due process protection to termination of a variety of government benefits.[14]

Goldberg v. Kelly is the seminal case. *Goldberg* was a challenge to the sufficiency of the procedural safeguards surrounding the termination of benefits

---

13. Ibid., 51–57 (majority opinion), 59 (Rehnquist, J., concurring in part and dissenting in part).

14. The procedural due process decisions of the Burger Court are described in detail in Carol R. Goforth, "A Jurisprudential Reflection upon the Burger Court's Approach to Procedural Due Process," *Arkansas Law Review* 42 (1989): 837–85; and Susan N. Herman, "The New Liberty: The Procedural Due Process Rights of Prisoners and Others under the Burger Court," *New York University Law Review* 59 (1984): 482–575.

under the Aid for Dependent Children (AFDC) program. In *Goldberg*, AFDC recipients argued that they were entitled to formal hearings prior to having their benefits terminated. The chief justice and Justices Black and Stewart found their arguments unpersuasive. Justice Black was particularly scornful, analogizing the argument to *Lochner*-era jurisprudence and asserting that "it . . . strains credulity to say that the government's promise of charity to an individual is property belonging to that individual when the government denies that the individual is honestly entitled to receive such a payment."[15]

By contrast, speaking for the majority, Justice Brennan took a quite different view of the relevant considerations. Emphasizing that eligible persons had a statutory entitlement to AFDC benefits, Brennan found that "the extent to which procedural due process must be afforded . . . depends upon whether the recipient's interest in avoiding that loss outweighs the governmental interest in summary adjudication." While conceding that the government had an interest in conserving fiscal and administrative resources, he concluded that this interest was outweighed by the importance of AFDC benefits to recipients and the government's own interest in ensuring that eligible persons continued to receive an uninterrupted flow of benefits. Thus, Brennan determined that beneficiaries were constitutionally entitled to pretermination hearings marked by adequate written notice of the reasons for a proposed determination; an effective opportunity to defend by confronting adverse witnesses and presenting their own arguments; a right to have counsel present; a right to have the decision-maker's conclusion based solely on the legal rules and the evidence adduced at the hearing; and a right to a written statement of the reasons for the decision.[16]

Goldberg clearly established the principle that due process constraints did not apply only to deprivations of traditional liberty and property rights. Throughout the Burger era, a majority of the Court remained committed to this basic principle; however, the justices often split over the precise reach of the *Goldberg* analysis. Further, once an interest was found to be within the scope of Fourteenth Amendment protections, the justices also disagreed often on the nature of the process that was due.

Wisconsin v. Constantineau[17] and *Paul v. Davis*[18] exemplify the divisions over the nature of the property rights protected by the Fourteenth Amendment. In *Constantineau*, over the dissents of the chief justice and Justices Black and Blackmun, the Court struck down a state statute that allowed local law enforcement officials to post public notices forbidding the sale of alco-

---

15. *Goldberg v. Kelly*, 397 U.S. 254, 275 (Black, J., dissenting) (1970).
16. Ibid., 262–63.
17. *Wisconsin v. Constantineau*, 400 U.S. 433 (1971).
18. *Paul v. Davis*, 424 U.S. 693 (1976).

holic beverages to people whom the officials determined were subject to specified undesirable behavior caused by excessive consumption of such beverages. Speaking for the majority, Justice Douglas concluded that the posting deprived the designated person of a property interest in his reputation by imposing a stigma upon him. By contrast, five years later, the newly appointed Justices Powell and Rehnquist joined the remaining *Constantineau* dissenters and Justice Stewart in holding that the inclusion of a person's name on a list of known shoplifters did not deprive that person of any liberty or property right guaranteed by the Fourteenth Amendment. Speaking for the *Paul* majority, Justice Rehnquist argued that the result in *Constantineau* turned on the fact that the aggrieved person was denied a tangible right—the right to purchase alcoholic beverages—notwithstanding the language of Justice Douglas's opinion, which had focused solely on the damage to the plaintiff's reputation.

The Court's approach to the termination of public employment reflected an even more complex dynamic. The evolutionary process began in *Board of Regents v. Roth*, where the Court rejected the due process claim of a person who had been hired to teach at a public university for a fixed period of one year and was then informed without explanation that he would not be rehired the following year. Speaking for himself, the chief justice, and Justices White, Blackmun, and Rehnquist, Justice Stewart concluded that the disappointed job seeker had no cognizable property interest because he had a mere "unilateral expectation" that he would be rehired, rather than a "legitimate claim of entitlement" to renewal of his contract. By contrast, in dissent, Justice Douglas contended that the nonrenewal of the contract triggered the protections of the Due Process Clause. Justice Marshall went even further, arguing that "every person who applies for a government job is entitled to it unless the government can establish some reason for denying the employment."[19]

Two years later, *Arnett v. Kennedy* demonstrated that even the members of the *Roth* majority were split on the scope of property interests entitled to constitutional protection under the Due Process Clause. *Arnett* was a challenge to the dismissal of a nonprobationary employee in the competitive federal civil service. Under the provisions of the Lloyd-LaFollette Act, the employee could only be dismissed for cause; in addition, the act specified a detailed set of procedures to be followed before an employee could be dismissed, as well as providing for a posttermination trial-type proceeding in which the employee could challenge the dismissal. The dismissed employee argued that the Due Process Clause mandated even greater procedural protections.[20]

---

19. *Board of Regents v. Roth*, 408 U.S. 564, 577, 584 (Douglas, J., dissenting), 588 (Marshall, J., dissenting) (1972).
20. *Arnett v. Kennedy*, 416 U.S. 134 (1974).

Speaking for himself, Chief Justice Burger, and Justice Stewart, Justice Rehnquist argued that any potential due process claim was vitiated by the structure of the Lloyd-LaFollette Act. Rehnquist argued that "where the grant of a substantive right is inextricably intertwined with the limitations on the procedures which are to be employed in determining that right, [the dismissed employee] must take the bitter with the sweet," and that since "the property interest which [the employee] had in his employment was itself conditioned by the procedural limitations which accompanied the grant of that interest, [under *Roth* the government may] constitutionally deal with [the employee's] claims as it proposed to do here." If accepted by a majority of the Court, this analysis would have in effect resurrected the right/privilege distinction in the analysis of procedural due process issues.[21]

Although some of the six remaining justices agreed that the specific constitutional challenge in *Arnett* should be rejected, none accepted the view that a legislature could limit the constitutional status of an employee's interest simply by specifying the procedures by which that interest could be divested. Justice Powell summarized the position of a majority of the justices on this point, contending that "[Rehnquist's] approach is incompatible with the principles laid down in *Roth*. . . . While the legislature may elect not to confer a property interest in federal employment, it may not authorize the deprivation of such an interest, once conferred, without appropriate procedural safeguards." Thus, a majority of the Court clearly rejected the analysis of the *Arnett* plurality.[22]

Nonetheless, the content of positive law remained critical to the determination of whether a particular employee had a constitutionally cognizable property interest in retaining his position. Thus, in *Bishop v. Wood,* the newly appointed Justice Stevens spoke for himself, Justice Powell, and the members of the *Arnett* plurality in holding that a North Carolina police officer had no constitutional right to any kind of hearing in connection with his dismissal.[23] Stevens concluded that, notwithstanding a contract which described the officer as a "permanent" employee and a city ordinance which stated that such an employee could be dismissed for specified reasons, under state law the officer was an employee at will, and thus lacked the legitimate claim of entitlement that would have triggered due process protections. Speaking for the dissenters, Byron White argued that the majority had reinstated the rejected analysis of the *Arnett* plurality; however, any suggestion that the majority in fact took this view was vitiated by the subsequent decision in *Cleveland Board of Education v. Loudermill,*[24] in which only Justice Rehnquist

---

21. Ibid., 153–55 (opinion of Rehnquist, J.).
22. Ibid., 156–57 (opinion of Powell, J.) (footnote omitted).
23. *Bishop v. Wood,* 426 U.S. 341 (1976).
24. *Cleveland Board of Education v. Loudermill,* 470 U.S. 532 (1985).

dissented from a majority opinion which once again emphatically rejected the concept of "the bitter with the sweet" as a basis for procedural due process jurisprudence.

The central message of the decisions from *Roth* to *Loudermill* is that the Court was deeply divided on the role of nonconstitutional principles in defining the rights entitled to due process protections. None of the opinions in *Arnett* dealing with this issue garnered more than three votes. When these opinions are considered in conjunction with the dissents in *Roth* and the majority in *Bishop*, the typical Burger Court pattern emerges: two relatively extreme positions, each held by two or three justices, with the balance of power held by a group of swing voters—in this case, Justices White, Blackmun, Powell, and (later) Stevens.

Similar divisions were apparent in the assessments of what process was due in cases where constitutionally protected interests *were* implicated. In purely formal terms, all of the justices agreed on the standard to be applied; it was an ad hoc balancing test first clearly articulated by Justice Powell in *Mathews v. Eldridge*, which required the courts to consider

first, the private interest that will be affected by the official action; second, the risk of an erroneous deprivation of such interests through the procedures used, and the probable value, if any, of additional safeguards; and finally, the Government's interest, including the fiscal and administrative burdens that the additional or substitute procedural requirement would entail.[25]

By its nature, the *Eldridge* test required a highly impressionistic weighing of burdens and benefits; this almost inevitably split the Court along standard ideological lines.

The elaborate calculations that the balancing test required are perhaps best symbolized by the majority opinion in *Memphis Light, Gas, and Water Division v. Craft*, where the Court considered the procedures required for the termination of utility service by a government-owned private utility. Over the objection of the chief justice and Justices Rehnquist and Stevens, the majority concluded that the availability of common-law judicial remedies such as a pretermination injunction and a posttermination suit for damages or a refund provided insufficient protection for the customer's interest in continuing service. Speaking for the Court, Justice Powell characterized utility service as "a necessity of modern life" and emphasized what he saw as a substantial risk of erroneous deprivation because of computer errors. Against this background, he argued that the Constitution required that a

---

25. *Mathews v. Eldridge*, 424 U.S. 319, 335 (1976) (citation omitted).

pretermination remedy be available, and contended that a proceeding for injunctive relief is "likely to be too bounded by procedural constraints and too susceptible of delay to provide an effective safeguard against an erroneous deprivation." Thus, the majority concluded that the utility was also required to provide the customer with "notice reasonably calculated to apprize respondents of the availability of an administrative procedure to consider their complaint of erroneous billing and . . . to afford them an opportunity to present their complaint to a designated employee empowered to review disputed bills and rectify error."[26]

Craft dramatically illustrates the willingness of a majority of the Burger Court to reject the adequacy of traditional concepts and provide aggrieved persons with additional protections against the abuses of the administrative state. Admittedly, claimants were far from universally successful in their efforts to obtain additional procedural safeguards; in *Eldridge* itself, for example, only Justices Brennan and Marshall were willing to accept the view that recipients of disability payments under the Social Security program were entitled to a hearing prior to the termination of their benefits. Nonetheless, taken as a whole, the procedural due process jurisprudence of the Burger Court expanded such safeguards well beyond the parameters that existed prior to the Burger era.

Of course, challenges to administrative actions were not the only arena in which litigants attempted to maximize their procedural rights. Criminal defendants also sought a wide variety of constitutional protections. The differing views of the justices on the issues raised by these claims generated some of the sharpest exchanges of the Burger era.

---

26. *Memphis Light, Gas, and Water Division v. Craft*, 436 U.S. 1, 18, 20, 22 (1978) (footnote omitted).

Table 8.1: Voting Patterns

	Bur	Dou	Bre	Mar	Whi	Stew	Bla	Reh	Pow	Stev	Oco
Separation of Powers											
Buckley v. Valeo 424 U.S. 1 (1976) (Federal Elections Commission)	U	NP	U	U	U	U	U	U	U	NP	NP
Bowsher v. Synar 478 U.S. 714 (1986) (Gramm-Rudman-Hollings)	U	NP	U	U	C	NP	C	U	U	U	U
INS v. Chadha 462 U.S. 919 (1983) (legislative veto)	U	NP	U	U	C	NP	U	?	U	U	U
Administrative Procedure Act											
Citizens to Preserve Overton Park v. Volpe 401 U.S. 402 (1971) (standard of review)	D	NP	D	D	D	D	D	NP	NP	NP	NP
Chevron v. Natural Resources Defense Council 467 U.S. 837 (1984) (statutory interpretation)	D	NP	D	NP	D	NP	D	NP	D	D	NP
Vermont Yankee Nuclear Power v. Natural Resources Defense Council 435 U.S. 519 (1978) (agency procedures)	D	NP	D	D	D	D	NP	D	NP	D	NP
Motor Vehicle Manufacturers v. State Farm Mutual 463 U.S. 29 (1983) (recision of regulation)	O	NP	O	O	O	NP	O	O	O	O	O

	Bur	Dou	Bre	Mar	Whi	Stew	Bla	Reh	Pow	Stev	Oco
Procedural Due Process											
Goldberg v. Kelly 397 U.S. 254 (1970) (termination of welfare benefits)	C	U	U	U	U	C	NP	NP	NP	NP	NP
Wisconsin v. Constantineau 400 U.S. 433 (1971) (designation as alcohol abuser)	C	U	U	U	U	U	C	NP	NP	NP	NP
Paul v. Davis 424 U.S. 693 (1976) (designation as known shoplifter)	C	NP	U	U	U	C	C	C	NP	NP	NP
Board of Regents v. Roth 408 U.S. 564 (1972) (refusal to renew contract)	C	U	U	U	C	C	C	C	NP	NP	NP
Arnett v. Kennedy 416 U.S. 134 (1974) (termination of government employment)	C	U	U	U	U	C	C	C	C	NP	NP
Bishop v. Wood 426 U.S. 341 (1976) (termination of government employment)	C	NP	U	U	U	C	U	C	C	C	NP
Cleveland Bd. of Education v. Loudermill 470 U.S. 532 (1985) (termination of government employment)	U	NP	U	U	U	NP	U	C	U	U	U
Memphis Light, Gas, and Water v. Craft 436 U.S. 1 (1978) (termination of utilities)	C	NP	U	U	U	U	U	C	U	C	NP

Key

D	= Defer to Agency	C	= Constitutional	U	= Unconstitutional
O	= Overturn Agency	?	= Unclear Position	NP	= Not Participating

9

THE RIGHTS OF CRIMINAL DEFENDANTS

Criminal procedure was another area in which the Burger Court confronted a landscape that had been dramatically altered during the Warren era. The Warren Court had expanded the rights of criminal defendants in a variety of different contexts. This trend became one of the major sources of conservative dissatisfaction with the Court in the late 1950s and 1960s. It was therefore not surprising that Richard Nixon made criticism of the Warren Court's criminal procedure decisions an important theme in his 1968 presidential campaign and sought out appointees whom he believed would be less receptive to the claims of defendants.[1] Ironically, however, the most visible and dramatic change in criminal law during the Burger era—the constitutionalization of the law of capital punishment—actually *favored* defendants.

While a variety of applications of the death penalty had been held constitutional prior to the Burger era, the Court had never explicitly addressed the question of whether the use of the death penalty per se was cruel and unusual punishment under the Eighth Amendment. Indeed, given the prevalence of the death penalty in the United States, the argument would have been considered frivolous during most of American history. However, although states generally retained the possibility of imposing the death penalty for some offenses, the actual number of executions diminished almost to the vanishing point by the mid twentieth century. This trend not only heartened death-penalty opponents, but also added force to the contention that the use of the death penalty was inconsistent with the "evolving standards of decency" that had long been the touchstone of Eighth Amendment jurisprudence.

The impact of this development began to make its mark on the Court's jurisprudence near the end of the Warren era; in *Witherspoon v. Illinois*,[2] the Court struck down the practice of "death qualifying" juries in cap-

---

1. *New York Times*, May 22, 1969, p. 46 col. 1; May 23, 1969, p. 26 col. 4, p. 27 col. 2.
2. *Witherspoon v. Illinois*, 391 U.S. 510 (1968).

ital cases—the practice of eliminating those jurors who believed that imposition of the death penalty was immoral. However, a majority of the Burger
Court justices initially seemed disinclined to move far beyond *Witherspoon;* in
McGautha v. California, only Justices Douglas, Brennan, and Marshall were
willing to conclude that allowing jurors standardless discretion to impose the
death penalty violated the Constitution.[3]

However, only one year after *McGautha,* opponents of the death
penalty achieved a stunning victory in *Furman v. Georgia.*[4] With all of the
Nixon appointees dissenting, the Court held that the imposition of the
death penalty under currently existing statutes violated the Eighth Amendment. Each of the justices wrote separately; nonetheless, the opinions of
the four dissenters shared a number of common themes. First, they noted
that the text of the Fifth Amendment seemed to implicitly sanction the use
of the death penalty. Second, they relied on stare decisis, arguing that
McGautha and other cases were inconsistent with the view that the application of the death penalty was unconstitutional. Finally, they asserted that
the continued, widespread provision for capital punishment in state
statutes obviated any claim that the use of the death penalty offended
evolving standards of decency in the United States.

By contrast, the five-justice majority was deeply divided over the appropriate rationale for the decision. Justices Brennan and Marshall concluded
that evolving standards of decency had made all impositions of the death
penalty unconstitutional; Justice Douglas, on the other hand, relied on the
disproportionate application of capital punishment to members of minority races. However, Justices Stewart and White—both of whom had concurred in *McGautha*—relied on far more limited arguments in joining the
Furman judgment. In concluding that the imposition of the death penalty
under then-existing laws was unconstitutional, they focused on the infrequency with which the death penalty was actually imposed and the lack of
standards for distinguishing between cases in which the death penalty was
appropriate and those in which only a term of imprisonment should be
served. Thus, Stewart analogized the imposition of the death penalty to
being struck by lightning, and White complained that there was "no meaningful basis for distinguishing the few cases in which [the death penalty]
was imposed from the many cases in which it [was] not."[5]

Furman generated a flurry of legislative activity, as many state governments
sought to recast their death penalty statutes to meet the objections posed by

3. *McGautha v. California,* 402 U.S. 183 (1971).

4. *Furman v. Georgia,* 408 U.S. 238 (1972).

5. Ibid., 257–306 (Brennan, J., concurring in the judgment), 314–74 (Marshall, J., concurring in the judgment), 240–57 (Douglas, J., concurring in the judgment), 306–10 (Stewart,
J., concurring in the judgment), 310–14 (White, J., concurring in the judgment).

Justices Stewart and White. Post-*Furman* death penalty statutes fell into two basic categories. One group of statutes simply made the imposition of the death penalty mandatory for particular crimes. The other group followed the pattern established by the Model Penal Code adopted by the American Law Institute. The ALI proposal had two distinguishing features. First, it listed a set of aggravating circumstances that could justify imposition of the death penalty in the absence of mitigating circumstances. Second, it provided for bifurcated jury consideration of guilt and sentencing, thus allowing defendants to save their pleas for leniency until after their guilt had been determined.

In 1976 the Court considered a set of five statutes that presented variations on one or both of these themes.[6] The statutes from Georgia and Florida followed the basic pattern of the Model Penal Code, with the additional proviso that jury recommendations of capital punishment were subject to judicial review. At the other extreme, North Carolina law required the death penalty in all cases of premeditated murder. Louisiana provided for mandatory capital punishment in a much smaller set of cases, and also allowed juries to evade the death penalty by convicting the defendant only of a lesser included offense such as manslaughter or second-degree murder. Finally, Texas allowed juries to impose the death penalty not only where aggravating circumstances were present, but also for a separate, narrowly defined set of crimes.

The mandatory death penalty statutes created something of a dilemma for those justices who did not share the views of Justices Douglas, Brennan, and Marshall. In purely formal terms, the mandatory death penalty statutes seemed to meet the doctrinal objections raised by Stewart and White; under those statutes, imposition of the death penalty would not be a rare, freakish, or arbitrary occurrence, but would rather be the consistent, inevitable result of conviction for particular crimes. From a practical perspective, however, upholding these state laws would in essence have turned *Furman* on its head. Those who voted to strike down the statutes in *Furman* sought to limit the application of the death penalty; however, if the mandatory death penalty statutes were upheld, the decision would have set in motion a chain of events that would ultimately have led to a vastly expanded application of capital punishment.

Stewart was unwilling to accept this result. He had cast his vote in *Furman* in the hope that capital punishment would disappear through subsequent legislative inaction, and he had been surprised and dismayed when state legislatures moved quickly to reinstate the death penalty. Like the

6. The description of the Court's internal deliberations in the 1976 cases is taken from John C. Jeffries, Jr., *Justice Lewis F. Powell, Jr.* (New York: Charles Scribner's Sons, 1994), 416–30; and Bob Woodward and Scott Armstrong, *The Brethren: Inside the Supreme Court* (New York: Simon and Schuster, 1979), 430–40.

recently appointed Justice Stevens, Stewart was willing to countenance the revised Florida and Georgia laws; however, both justices had strong reservations about the constitutionality of the Texas statute and were firmly opposed to the mandatory punishment provisions from the Louisiana and North Carolina schemes.

White, however, saw the issue differently. He voted to approve the mandatory statutes, arguing that they did not lend themselves to the arbitrary, freakish application of the death penalty that had marked pre-*Furman* law.[7] If all of the Burger appointees had remained committed to their position that the Constitution placed no special restraints on the use of the death penalty, White's vote would have been sufficient to create a narrow majority upholding the statutes—notwithstanding the continuing opposition of Justices Brennan and Marshall.

At the initial conference, this result seemed possible. All of the Nixon appointees joined Justice White in expressing at least tentative approval for the statutes from Florida, Georgia, Louisiana, and Texas; the initial count on the North Carolina scheme was four to three against, with Justices Powell and Blackmun passing. Convinced that total victory was at hand, the chief justice assigned all five opinions to Justice White. However, uneasy about the specter of mass executions and accepting *Furman* as precedent, Powell ultimately abandoned his allies from *Furman* and joined Justices Stewart and Stevens in condemning both the Louisiana and North Carolina approaches; in return, Stewart and Stevens agreed to suppress their misgivings about the Texas statute. The result was that while the Florida, Georgia, and Texas laws were upheld over the dissents of Justices Brennan and Marshall, the Louisiana and North Carolina statutes were struck down by votes of five to four.[8]

Justice Stewart wrote the key plurality opinions in *Roberts v. Louisiana*[9] and *Woodson v. North Carolina*.[10] In concluding that the statutes were unconstitutional, Stewart contended that mandatory death penalties *(a)* were incompatible with "evolving standards of decency"; *(b)* left juries free to act arbitrarily by declining to enter verdicts of first degree murder in appropriate cases; and *(c)* failed to allow juries to engage in a "particularized consideration of relevant aspects of the character and record of [the] convicted defendant"—in the plurality's view, a constitutionally mandated requirement for the imposition of the death penalty.[11]

---

7. *Roberts v. Louisiana*, 428 U.S. 337–63 (White, J., dissenting) (1976).

8. *Jurek v. Texas*, 428 U.S. 262 (1976); *Gregg v. Georgia*, 428 U.S. 153 (1976); *Profitt v. Florida*, 428 U.S. 242 (1976); *Woodson v. North Carolina*, 428 U.S. 280 (1976); *Roberts v. Louisiana*, 428 U.S. 325.

9. *Roberts v. Louisiana*, 428 U.S.

10. *Woodson v. North Carolina*, 428 U.S.

11. Ibid., 303 (opinion of Stewart, Powell, and Stevens, JJ.).

For the remaining decade of Chief Justice Burger's tenure, the members of the Court struggled over the necessary prerequisites for the imposition of capital punishment, splitting along fairly predictable ideological lines in most of the cases.[12] By the end of the period, the parameters of the constitutional requirements had become fairly clear, and executions had once again resumed. Thus, liberal opponents of capital punishment did not obtain all that they wished from the Court. Nonetheless, on this issue, constitutional doctrine had clearly moved in a liberal direction during the Burger era. Beginning from a position in which the Constitution imposed almost no special restraints on the imposition of the death penalty, the Court ended with a regime in which capital punishment could only be imposed under relatively narrowly defined circumstances.

By contrast, in other areas the Burger Court clearly moved the law of criminal procedure in the opposite direction.[13] One prime example is the Court's treatment of the exclusionary rule, which barred the use of illegally obtained evidence in criminal proceedings. The Warren Court did not invent the exclusionary rule; even before Earl Warren became chief justice, all courts were required to exclude coerced or involuntary confessions, and the *federal* courts excluded evidence that had been obtained in violation of the Fourth Amendment. However, Warren Court jurisprudence greatly expanded the range of potentially probative evidence that was required to be excluded in criminal proceedings. First, in *Mapp v. Ohio*, the Court held for the first time that the Fourth Amendment exclusionary rule applied to *state* courts, as well as their federal counterparts.[14] Second, in a series of decisions, the Court significantly broadened the restrictions imposed by the Fourth Amendment. Third, in *Miranda v. Arizona*, the Court held that confessions in general must be excluded under the Fifth Amendment unless the suspect had been specifically warned that he had a right to remain silent and a right to an attorney.[15] Finally, in *Massiah v. United States*, the Court concluded that in some circumstances, a suspect's Sixth Amendment right to an attorney might independently require the exclusion of evidence obtained outside the attorney's presence.[16]

---

12. The case law is discussed in detail in Lee Epstein and Joseph F. Kobylka, *The Supreme Court and Legal Change: Abortion and the Death Penalty* (Chapel Hill: University of North Carolina Press, 1992).

13. The criminal procedure jurisprudence of the Burger Court is described in detail in John F. Decker, *Revolution to the Right: Criminal Procedure Jurisprudence during the Burger-Rehnquist Era* (New York: Garland Publishing, 1992); Stephen A. Saltzburg, "Foreword: The Flow and Ebb of Constitutional Criminal Procedure in the Warren and Burger Courts," *Georgetown Law Journal* 69 (1980): 151–209; and Peter Aranella, "Foreword: Rethinking the Functions of Criminal Procedure: The Warren and Burger Courts' Competing Ideologies," *Georgetown Law Journal* 72 (1983): 185–248.

14. *Mapp v. Ohio*, 367 U.S. 643 (1961).

15. *Miranda v. Arizona*, 384 U.S. 436 (1966).

16. *Massiah v. United States*, 377 U.S. 201 (1964).

To many conservatives, the Warren Court's expansion of the exclusionary rule came to symbolize much of what was wrong with the Court's jurisprudence. Indeed, Warren Burger's outspoken opposition to the Fourth Amendment exclusionary rule was an important factor in his appointment. Thus, it should not be surprising that he would attempt to move the Court in a different direction on criminal procedure issues.

His efforts in this regard met with only partial success. With the support of Byron White, Burger and his conservative allies were able to restrict the applicability of the exclusionary rule at the margins; however, Burger was never able to muster a majority to overturn the core principles of *Mapp, Miranda,* and *Massiah,* and these principles remained basically intact. A comprehensive analysis of the Court's jurisprudence in this area is beyond the scope of this book. However, the basic structure of the decision-making process is well illustrated by the examination of a relatively small number of decisions.

Even before the appointment of Justices Powell and Rehnquist, a new tone in the Court's criminal procedure decisions was reflected in *Harris v. New York.* In *Harris,* the question was whether a statement that had been obtained without following the rules laid down in *Miranda* could be used to impeach a defendant who took the stand in his own defense. The chief justice and Justice Blackmun joined Warren Court holdovers John Marshall Harlan, Potter Stewart, and Byron White—all of whom had dissented in *Miranda* itself—in concluding that the use of the statement for impeachment purposes did not violate the Fifth Amendment. Chief Justice Burger's majority opinion focused on two points. First, he argued that "assuming that the exclusionary rule has a deterrent effect on proscribed police conduct, sufficient deterrence flows when the evidence in question is made unavailable to the prosecution in its case in chief." Second, he adverted to the potential costs of excluding the statement, concluding that "the shield provided by *Miranda* cannot be perverted into a license to use perjury by way of a defense, free from the risk of confrontation with prior inconsistent utterances."[17]

Dissenting, Justice Brennan took a quite different view of the costs and benefits involved. Brennan was more willing to subordinate the search for truth to what he viewed as the legitimate interests of the defendant; moreover, he saw the exclusionary rule as a device to preserve the integrity of the judicial process itself.

"The constitutional foundation underlying the privilege [against self-incrimination] is the respect a government . . . must accord to the dignity and integrity of its citizens" . . . it is monstrous that courts should aid

---

17. *Harris v. New York,* 401 U.S. 222, 225, 226 (1971).

or abet the law-breaking officer. It is abiding truth that "[n]othing can destroy a government more quickly than its failure to observe its own laws, or worse, its disregard of the charter of its own existence."[18]

The same themes came to the fore even more pointedly in *United States v. Leon.* In *Leon,* police officers obtained a search warrant based on information provided by a confidential informant of unproven reliability. Armed with this warrant, they seized substantial quantities of cocaine, which the prosecution sought to introduce into evidence in a trial revolving around a conspiracy to possess and distribute cocaine. The lower courts concluded that the magistrate who issued the warrant had erred in determining that the police had demonstrated probable cause and held that the evidence should be suppressed—notwithstanding the fact that the police acted on the warrant in good faith. Over the dissents of Justices Brennan, Marshall, and Stevens, the Supreme Court concluded that the Fourth Amendment does not mandate exclusion of evidence seized when the police act in reasonable reliance on a search warrant later found to be invalid for want of probable cause.[19]

Speaking for the Court, Justice White argued that a focus on the deterrent effect of the exclusionary rule was particularly appropriate in the context of Fourth Amendment claims. He rejected the contention that the Fourth Amendment by its terms mandated the application of the exclusionary rule; instead, he contended that any damage to the defendants' Fourth Amendment rights was "fully accomplished" by the unlawful search itself and that the application of the exclusionary rule cannot remedy that intrusion. Thus, White asserted that the Fourth Amendment exclusionary rule can be justified *only* by its deterrent effect. Emphasizing the social costs incurred when a guilty person goes free because illegally seized evidence is excluded, he argued that the potential deterrent effect of exclusion must be balanced against these costs in determining whether the exclusionary rule should apply in any particular context. Finding little need to deter judges and magistrates from issuing search warrants founded on inadequate cause and no evidence that the exclusionary rule would have such an effect, White concluded that the exclusionary rule should not apply when police officers act in reasonable reliance on a search warrant issued by a magistrate or judge.[20]

Harris and *Leon* are prime examples of decisions where (depending on one's point of view) the Burger Court either failed to give the exclusionary rule the full scope suggested by Warren Court decisions or declined to expand the applicability of the rule. However, as with most controversial

18. Ibid., 233 (Brennan, quoting *Miranda,* 384 U.S. at 460; and *Mapp,* 367 U.S. at 659).
19. *United States v. Leon,* 468 U.S. 897 (1984).
20. Ibid., 906 [quoting *United States v. Calandra,* 414 U.S. 338, 354 (1974)].

issues, the majority in favor of a conservative approach to criminal procedure was somewhat unstable. Only the chief justice and Justices White and
Rehnquist consistently supported admissibility of a wide range of evidence;
occasionally, the more liberal members of the Court were able to score
notable victories by gaining two adherents from the group of Justices Stewart, Blackmun, and Powell. *Brewer v. Williams* provides a classic example. In
Brewer, the defendant was arrested in Davenport, Iowa, and charged with
abducting a girl in Des Moines, Iowa. The defendant—a deeply religious former mental patient—was given his *Miranda* warnings and then telephoned
an attorney in Des Moines; the Des Moines attorney agreed that two Des
Moines police officers would drive to Davenport and pick up the defendant,
on condition that they not interrogate the defendant until he had arrived in
Des Moines and consulted the attorney. The defendant also conferred with
a Davenport attorney, who also counseled him not to make any statements
until he had consulted with the Des Moines attorney. When the Des Moines
police officers arrived in Davenport, the Davenport attorney reiterated that
the defendant was not to be questioned on the trip to Davenport. During
that trip, the defendant repeatedly stated, "[W]hen I get to Des Moines and
see [my attorney] I am going to tell you the whole story."[21]

During the trip from Davenport to Des Moines, one of the detectives, who
had knowledge of the defendant's religious convictions and history of mental
illness, opined, "I feel that we should stop and locate the body, that the parents of [the kidnapping victim] should be entitled to a Christian burial for the
little girl who was snatched away from them on Christmas Eve and murdered."
The detective later conceded that the purpose of the statement was to elicit
information from the defendant. Without further prompting, the defendant
first led the detectives to the victim's shoes and then to her body. The question in *Brewer* was whether the fact that the defendant knew the location of the
shoes and the body should have been admitted into evidence at his trial.[22]

Over the dissents of the chief justice and Justices White, Blackmun, and
Rehnquist, the Court held that the evidence should have been excluded
under the rationale of *Massiah.* In purely doctrinal terms, the Court was
divided on two major issues: whether the "Christian burial" speech in fact
constituted "interrogation" and whether the defendant had waived his right
to have counsel present by choosing to lead the police to the incriminating
evidence. However, *Brewer* is perhaps most notable for its sharp exchanges
over the competing values implicated by the Court's decisions on criminal
procedure issues. The dissenters emphasized that the result of the decision
was that a guilty person would be freed; for example, noting the strength and

21. *Brewer v. Williams,* 430 U.S. 387 (1977).
22. Ibid., 392–93.

reliability of the evidence against the defendant, Justice Blackmun noted that "[t]his was a brutal, tragic crime inflicted upon a young girl on the afternoon of the day before Christmas" and that, given the lapse of time, a new trial was probably not an option. The chief justice was harsher, declaring with palpable outrage that "[t]he result in this case ought to be intolerable in any society which purports to call itself an organized society." Conversely, speaking for the majority, Justice Stewart observed: "The pressures on state executive and judicial officers charged with the administration of the criminal law are great, especially when the crime is murder and the victim a small child. But it is precisely those pressures that makes imperative a resolute loyalty to the guarantees that the Constitution extends to us all." Similarly, concurring, Justice Marshall's passion was no less apparent than that of Chief Justice Burger:

> The dissenters have, I believe, lost sight of the fundamental constitutional backbone of our criminal law. They seem to think that [the detective's] actions were perfectly proper, indeed laudable examples of "good police work." In my view, good police work is something far different from catching the criminal at any price. It is equally important that the police, as guardians of the law, fulfill their responsibility to obey its commands scrupulously. For "in the end life and liberty can be as much endangered from illegal methods used to convict those thought to be criminals as from the actual criminals themselves."[23]

Ultimately, the *Brewer* decision was of little practical benefit to the defendant. On retrial, he was once again convicted, with the shoes and body being admitted into evidence on the theory that they ultimately would have been found in any event. When the second conviction reached the Supreme Court, only Justices Brennan and Marshall were willing to reverse the judgment.[24]

Nonetheless, the initial decision in *Brewer* demonstrated that a number of justices on the Burger Court remained committed to a fairly strong vision of defendants' rights. Moreover, the decision was by no means an isolated phenomenon during the Burger era. Even after the appointment of Sandra Day O'Connor to replace Potter Stewart—an appointment which clearly moved the Court to the right on criminal procedure issues—liberals still won occasional victories by persuading both Justices Blackmun and Powell to accept their arguments.[25] Moreover, despite strenuous attacks from the chief justice, the basic principles of *Mapp, Miranda,* and *Massiah* remained

23. Ibid., 441 (Blackmun, J., dissenting), 416 (Burger, C. J., dissenting), 406, 407 [Marshall, J., concurring, quoting *Spano v. New York,* 360 U.S. 315, 320–31 (1959)].
24. *Nix v. Williams,* 467 U.S. 431 (1984).
25. See, for example, *Maine v. Moulton,* 474 U.S. 109 (1985).

intact. Nonetheless, decisions such as *Harris* and *Leon* clearly made some inroads into the principles established by the Warren Court.

Conservatives on the Burger Court were even more successful in rolling back the Warren Court's decisions which expanded the jurisdiction of the federal courts to entertain collateral attacks on state court convictions through the use of the writ of habeas corpus. In purely formal terms, these decisions generally did not involve constitutional issues; instead, they were interpretations of the federal statute governing the availability of the writ. Nonetheless, expansion of the availability of federal habeas corpus was crucial to the Warren Court's effort to subject state criminal proceedings to stringent federal constitutional standards. Given the practical limitations on the number of state court judgments that the Supreme Court is able to review on direct appeals, habeas corpus proceedings often presented state court defendants with their only opportunity to have their claims heard in a federal forum. Thus, an expansive view of habeas corpus jurisdiction was crucial to aggressive enforcement of the Court's newly fashioned rules of criminal procedure.

Against this background, the decision in *Stone v. Powell* was perhaps the most significant of all the Burger Court decisions limiting the scope of the Fourth Amendment exclusionary rule. In *Stone,* a six-justice majority concluded that, so long as a defendant had a full and fair opportunity to litigate a Fourth Amendment claim at trial, the defendant could not raise the issue in a subsequent habeas corpus proceeding. The arguments of Justice Powell's majority opinion and Justice Brennan's dissent presaged the debate which would culminate in the decision in *Leon.* Powell saw the exclusionary rule primarily as a device to deter Fourth Amendment violations, and argued that the possibility that a conviction would be overturned on collateral attack added little to the deterrent effect of the rule and simply magnified the possibility that a guilty defendant would go free. Dissenting, Justice White was even more sharply critical of the exclusionary rule but concluded that there was no justification for treating direct appeals differently from collateral attacks. Justice Brennan, by contrast, saw the right to have illegally seized evidence excluded as an interest of constitutional magnitude and (like White) contended that it was anomalous to deny federal courts the right to consider Fourth Amendment arguments in habeas corpus actions.[26]

Stone is best viewed as an important skirmish in the ongoing substantive dispute over the Fourth Amendment exclusionary rule; by contrast, *Wainwright v. Sykes* reflected divisions over the core function of federal habeas corpus in the system of criminal justice. In *Wainwright,* a defendant was convicted of murder in state court after admission of inculpatory statements

---

26. *Stone v. Powell,* 428 U.S. 465 (1976).

that he had made to the police. The defendant's attorney did not challenge the admissibility of these statements, either at trial or on appeal; however, the defendant later sought to argue in a federal habeas corpus proceeding that the statements had been obtained in violation of his Fifth and Sixth Amendment rights. The question in *Wainwright* was whether the defendant's failure to object at trial deprived him of the opportunity to have his claim considered in habeas corpus.[27]

A majority of the Court concluded that the federal courts could not consider the defendant's claim, and, in so holding, essentially limited the Warren Court's decision in *Fay v. Noia* to its facts. In *Fay*, the Court had held that a criminal defendant's failure to file a direct appeal from his conviction in state court did not bar collateral reconsideration of the judgment in habeas corpus. Speaking for the *Fay* majority, Justice Brennan conceded that such a procedural default would be an independent and adequate state ground that would have barred consideration of the judgment by the Supreme Court on direct appeal. However, he contended that, since a petition for habeas corpus was collateral rather than appellate, the same considerations did not apply. Emphasizing the importance of affording a federal remedy for violations of federal constitutional rights, Brennan concluded that a state procedural default would bar consideration of a habeas corpus petition only if the defendant had "deliberately by-passed the orderly procedure of the state courts and in so doing ha[d] forfeited his state court remedies," and that the question was whether there had been "an intentional relinquishment or abandonment of a known right or privilege."[28]

Speaking for the majority in *Wainwright*, Justice Rehnquist declined to hold that *Fay* was wrongly decided on its facts; at the same time, however, he rejected the knowing and deliberate waiver standard in favor of a rule that procedural defaults barred subsequent review on habeas corpus in the absence of a showing of cause for the default and actual prejudice resulting from the alleged constitutional violation. In support of his conclusions, Rehnquist focused on three considerations: the need to respect state courts, the desirability of finality in criminal proceedings, and the danger of defendants "sandbagging" by first taking their chances on the verdict and then raising their constitutional claims in federal habeas corpus if convicted. Dissenting for himself and Justice Marshall, Justice Brennan once again emphasized the importance of providing a federal forum for the adjudication of federal claims.

Ironically, the same respect for the concept of independent and adequate state grounds that underlaid *Wainwright* would undermine the Court's

---

27. *Wainwright v. Sykes*, 433 U.S. 72 (1977).

28. *Fay v. Noia*, 372 U.S. 391, 438, 439 [quoting *Johnson v. Zerbst*, 304 U.S. 458, 464 (1938)] (1963).

ability to ensure that its newly conservative approach to the exclusionary rule would have truly nationwide effect. In *Wainwright,* the doctrine was invoked to prevent federal review of state criminal decisions that rejected claims of federal right. In other contexts, however, the independent and adequate state grounds doctrine also began to be used as a device to shield state court judgments that upheld constitutional claims.

This development was largely a by-product of the general substantive course of Burger Court decision making—particularly in the area of criminal procedure. A number of state supreme courts clearly preferred a more liberal constitutional jurisprudence to that adopted by the Burger Court. These courts faced a problem, however. If they justified their decisions solely in terms of federal constitutional law, the decisions would be reviewable by the Burger Court itself—the very court whose methodology the state courts sought to reject. The solution to this problem—publicly encouraged by Justice Brennan—was for the state courts to rely on state constitutional grounds in reaching their decisions to strike down state statutes or craft rules of criminal procedure. Thus, even if the court also concluded that its conclusions were justified by federal constitutional principles, the independent and adequate state grounds doctrine would prevent the Supreme Court from reviewing the decision.[29]

From a purely formal perspective, the use of this technique was entirely unobjectionable. Each state court clearly possesses independent, plenary authority to interpret its own constitution, and the Supreme Court has no right to revise that interpretation. Nonetheless, some found this new trend profoundly disturbing—particularly where the state court relied entirely on federal precedents in reaching its decision, and the state constitutional ground was clearly added only as an afterthought to protect the decision from review. It was against this background that *Michigan v. Long* was decided.[30]

In *Long,* the Michigan Supreme Court had suppressed evidence used to convict a criminal defendant on the ground that it had been obtained through an illegal search of the defendant's automobile. The state court purported to rest its decision on both the state and federal constitutions; however, the court discussed only federal precedents in its analysis. Under these circumstances, only Justice Stevens concluded that the Court should not review the judgment; however, Stevens did not base his opinion on the independent and adequate state grounds doctrine, but rather on his view that the Court should never review a claim that a state court gave an overly

29. William J. Brennan, Jr., "State Constitutions and the Protection of Individual Rights," *Harvard Law Review* 90 (1977): 489.

30. *Michigan v. Long,* 463 U.S. 1032 (1983).

broad reading to a federal constitutional provision. Observing that "the State of Michigan has arrested one of its citizens and the Michigan Supreme Court has decided to turn him loose," Stevens argued that "since there is no claim that [anyone] has been mistreated by the State of Michigan, the final outcome of state processes offended no federal interest whatever."

Speaking for all of the other justices who addressed the jurisdictional issue, Justice O'Connor took a quite different view. She concluded that "where a state court decision fairly appears to rest primarily on federal law, or to be interwoven with federal law," absent a plain statement to the contrary in the state court opinion, the Supreme Court would assume that the judgment was based on the state court's understanding of federal law, and was thus reviewable. Finding that the Michigan judgment in *Long* fell into this category, the majority took jurisdiction and reversed the judgment. At the same time, however, Justice O'Connor also observed that "[i]f the state court decision indicates clearly and expressly that it is alternatively based on bona fide separate, adequate, and independent grounds, we of course, will not undertake to review the decision." Thus, the majority clearly signaled that, so long as state courts satisfied appropriate formal criteria, they were free to shield their expansive constitutional judgments from review by the Supreme Court.

Taken together with cases such as *Harris* and *Leon*, *Long* reflects the dual aspect of the conservative opposition to the Warren Court's innovations in criminal procedure. On one hand, conservatives objected to the substance of the rules established by *Miranda, Mapp,* and *Massiah* and like-minded decisions; by its terms, *Long* virtually guaranteed that any Burger Court actions that cut back on these rules would have only an uneven effect on the actual conduct of criminal trials nationwide. In addition, however, conservatives objected to the fact that the Warren Court had subordinated state rules of criminal procedure to national standards. From this perspective, *Long* complemented decisions such as those which limited the effect of the exclusionary rule. In short, with the notable exception of the capital punishment cases, Burger Court conservatives could at least claim to have slowed (if not reversed) the trend toward nationalization of criminal procedure.

Dissatisfaction with developments in criminal procedure was, however, only one source of conservative distaste for Warren Court jurisprudence. Attacks on the Court's treatment of religion and race-related issues also figured prominently in the political criticism of the Supreme Court in the 1960s. In these areas, Burger Court conservatives were less successful in changing the direction of the Court's jurisprudence.

Table 9.1: Voting Patterns

	Bur	Dou	Bre	Mar	Whi	Stew	Bla	Reh	Pow	Stev	Oco
Death Penalty											
McGautha v. California 402 U.S. 183 (1971) (standardless discretion)	C	U	U	U	C	C	C	NP	NP	NP	NP
Furman v. Georgia 408 U.S. 238 (1972) (existing death penalty statutes)	C	U	U	U	U	U	C	C	C	NP	NP
Roberts v. Louisiana 428 U.S. 325 (1976) (mandatory death penalty)	C	NP	U	U	C	U	C	C	U	U	NP
Jurek v. Texas 428 U.S. 262 (1976) (reconfigured death penalty)	C	NP	U	U	C	C	C	C	C	C	NP
Constitutional Criminal Procedure											
Harris v. New York 401 U.S. 222 (1971) (confession used for impeachment)	C	U	U	U	C	C	C	NP	NP	NP	NP
United States v. Leon 468 U.S. 897 (1984) (good faith exception to exclusionary rule)	C	NP	U	U	C	NP	C	C	C	U	C
Brewer v. Williams 430 U.S. 387 (1977) (Christian burial speech)	C	NP	U	U	C	U	C	C	U	U	NP
Nix v. Williams 467 U.S. 431 (1984) (inevitable discovery of evidence)	C	NP	U	U	C	NP	C	C	C	C	C

	Bur	Dou	Bre	Mar	Whi	Stew	Bla	Reh	Pow	Stev	Oco

Habeas Corpus

	Bur	Dou	Bre	Mar	Whi	Stew	Bla	Reh	Pow	Stev	Oco
Stone v. Powell 428 U.S. 465 (1976) (Fourth Amendment exclusionary rule)	AD	NP	PD	PD	PD	AD	AD	AD	AD	AD	NP
Wainwright v. Sykes 433 U.S. 72 (1977) (effect of procedural default)	AD	NP	PD	PD	AD	AD	AD	AD	AD	AD	NP

Key

C	= Constitutional	NP	= Not Participating	PD	= Prodefendant
AD	= Antidefendant	U	= Unconstitutional		

10

THE RELIGION CLAUSES

As in many other areas, much of the Burger Court's agenda on the relationship between religion and government derived from doctrinal innovations of
the Warren Court.[1] The most important of the issues faced by the Court fell
into three categories. One group of cases focused on claims that the Free
Exercise Clause required the government to grant religious exemptions from
generally applicable laws. A second dealt with Establishment Clause challenges to the grant of financial benefits to organizations affiliated with religious groups. The third involved Establishment Clause challenges to explicit
government endorsement of religion or religious activities.

All of these questions found the Court deeply divided along ideological
lines. Unlike other issues, however, the religion cases found the Court pulled
between not two but three doctrinal extremes. Not surprisingly, Justices Douglas, Brennan, and Marshall advocated the separationist position, which in turn
reflected dominant liberal orthodoxy; they were deeply suspicious of even
indirect government support for religion or religious organizations, but vigorously endorsed individual claims for exemptions from generally applicable
laws based upon religious scruples. Justice Rehnquist was at the other extreme
jurisprudentially; he generally favored deferring to government decisions on
most issues connected to religion. The third position—accommodationism—
clearly influenced the jurisprudence of Justice White; he argued that the government could constitutionally choose to accommodate religious beliefs and
was in some cases required to do so. The positions of the remaining members
of the Court were more difficult to characterize. The interaction among these
groups produced a familiar pattern—a jurisprudence that, while not fully
embracing prevailing liberal ideology, moved existing doctrine substantially to
the left on the political spectrum.

While less widely discussed than some of the Court's Establishment
Clause cases, Warren Court innovations in free exercise jurisprudence were

---

1. Leo Pfeffer, *Religion, State, and the Burger Court* (New York: Prometheus Books, 1984), provides a comprehensive discussion of the Burger Court's treatment of the religion clauses.

166

no less doctrinally important. The potential implications of *Sherbert v. Verner* were particularly significant. In *Sherbert*, the majority concluded that a state could not constitutionally deny workers' compensation benefits to a person who was discharged for refusing Saturday work on religious grounds, notwithstanding the fact that the relevant statute generally required the denial of benefits to those who refused "suitable work" without "good cause." Speaking for the majority, Justice Brennan concluded that the denial of benefits could be upheld only if justified by a compelling governmental interest.[2]

On this issue, most members of the Burger Court embraced the basic principles of Brennan's analysis; thus, in *Thomas v. Review Board of the Indiana Employment Security Division,* only Justice Rehnquist dissented from a specific reaffirmation of the *Sherbert* holding.[3] Indeed, almost a decade earlier, the Burger Court itself had adopted the *Sherbert* approach in *Wisconsin v. Yoder.* In *Yoder,* parents of a group of fourteen- and fifteen-year-old Amish students sought an exemption from a state law requiring that their children attend school at least until the age of sixteen, arguing that their religious beliefs required that the children leave school after the eighth grade. With Justice Rehnquist not participating, Chief Justice Burger spoke for a unanimous Court in declaring that "only those interests of the highest order and those not otherwise served can overbalance legitimate claims to the free exercise of religion." Burger concluded, first, that the requirement of further compulsory education for the children would "gravely endanger if not destroy the free exercise of [the Amish's] religious beliefs" and, second, that given the agricultural lifestyle of the Amish and the Amish community's program of informal vocational education, the state's interest in making certain that the students would be prepared for adult life was substantially diminished. Thus, the Court held that the Free Exercise Clause required the state to grant the exemption.[4]

Yoder demonstrated the strength of the Burger Court's commitment to an expansive reading of the Free Exercise Clause. There were, however, limits to this commitment. For example, in *United States v. Lee,* the Court unanimously rejected the free exercise argument of an Amish man who sought to interpose religious objections to the payment of social security taxes. Speaking for all members of the Court except Justice Stevens, the chief justice concluded that there was no principled distinction between social security taxes and other taxes and that, "because the broad public interest in maintaining a sound tax system is of such a high order, religious belief in conflict with the payment of taxes affords no basis for resisting the tax."[5]

---

2. *Sherbert v. Verner,* 374 U.S. 398 (1963).

3. *Thomas v. Review Board of the Indiana Employment Security Division,* 450 U.S. 707 (1981).

4. *Wisconsin v. Yoder,* 406 U.S. 205 (1972).

5. *United States v. Lee,* 455 U.S. 252, 260 (1982).

Goldman v. Weinberger more clearly reflected the divisions on the Court regarding free exercise issues. Speaking through Justice Rehnquist, the *Goldman* Court rejected the argument that the U.S. Air Force was required to grant an exemption to its dress code for an orthodox Jew who wished to wear a yarmulke on duty, as required by his religion. Unlike *Yoder* and *Lee*, however, in *Goldman* the Court was deeply divided, with Justices Brennan, Marshall, Blackmun, and O'Connor dissenting. Moreover, even the majority opinion itself was careful to note the limits of its analysis; Justice Rehnquist repeatedly emphasized that this was a case involving military decision making and stressed the traditional reluctance of the Supreme Court to overturn military regulations. Thus, while doctrinally important, *Goldman* by its terms had little precedential significance for nonmilitary decisions.[6]

By contrast, the Court's interpretation of a statutorily mandated accommodation of religious practices had far-reaching practical implications. Title VII of the Civil Rights Act of 1964 prohibited discrimination on the basis of religion; the 1972 amendments provided that "the term religion includes all aspects of religious observance and practice . . . unless an employer demonstrates that he is unable to reasonably accommodate to [a] religious observance or practice without undue hardship." In *TWA v. Hardison,* the Court was faced with the task of defining the scope of an employer's duty under this section.[7]

In *Hardison,* an employee who was required under a collective bargaining agreement to work on Saturdays requested an exemption from this requirement in order to observe the Sabbath, as required by his religion. He suggested a number of alternative scenarios under which he could avoid Saturday work, but all were rejected by either the employer or the union. With only Justices Brennan and Marshall dissenting, the Court held that the refusal to accommodate the employee's religious practice was lawful. Speaking for the majority, Justice White concluded that a proposed accommodation that required employers to bear more than *de minimis* cost would subject an employer to undue hardship, and thus the failure to provide such an accommodation did not subject an employer to liability under Title VII.

While disagreeing with the majority's interpretation of Title VII, the dissenters suggested that an unduly broad interpretation of the requirement of reasonable accommodation might create Establishment Clause difficulties. This possibility became reality in *Estate of Thornton v. Caldor.* In *Caldor,* with only Justice Rehnquist dissenting, the Court held that the Establishment Clause prohibited a state from granting employees an absolute right to refuse to work on Saturday for religious reasons. Speaking for the Court, the chief justice

6. *Goldman v. Weinberger,* 475 U.S. 503 (1986).
7. *TWA v. Hardison,* 432 U.S. 63 (1977).

emphasized the "absolute and unqualified nature" of the required accommodation, declaring that the statute contravened "a fundamental principle of the Religion Clauses" by giving employees "the right to insist that in pursuit of their own interests others must conform their conduct to [the employees'] own religious necessities."[8]

The juxtaposition of *Caldor* with cases such as *Yoder* and *Thomas* reflects the tension that most of the Burger Court justices saw between the two Religion Clauses of the First Amendment. On one hand, the Free Exercise Clause was viewed as a general prohibition on government actions that impeded religious belief or practice—a value that was reflected in *Yoder* and *Thomas*. By contrast, the Establishment Clause was seen as embodying the belief that the government should be sharply limited in its ability to aid religion or religious organizations—the essence of *Caldor*. The latter value would predominate as the Court wrestled with the constitutional issues posed by state aid to church-related schools and the students that chose to attend those schools.

Prior to the Burger era, the leading cases were *Everson v. Board of Education*[9] and the Warren Court's decision in *Board of Education v. Allen*.[10] In each case the Court concluded that state aid to parochial-school students was constitutional; the test articulated by the *Allen* majority was whether the state aid had the purpose or primary effect of aiding religion. However, both *Everson* and *Allen* were decided over vigorous dissents which urged the Court to be more vigilant in policing what Justice Wiley B. Rutledge described as "the complete division between religion and civil authority which our forefathers made." The concerns of the *Everson* and *Allen* dissenters dominated Burger Court jurisprudence in this area; while not banning all government aid to parochial schools and their students, the Court closely circumscribed both the nature of the aid that was permissible and the conditions under which it could be offered.

Beginning with the decision in *Lemon v. Kurtzman*, majority opinions invariably embraced a three-pronged test, concluding that state statutes violated the Establishment Clause if either their purpose or their primary effect was to advance religion, and were also unconstitutional if they fostered "excessive entanglement" between the government and religion.[11] Under this rubric, Justices Douglas, Brennan, and Marshall showed implacable hostility to state programs that either directly or indirectly provided state aid to

---

8. *Estate of Thornton v. Caldor*, 472 U.S. 703, 709, 710 [quoting *Otten v. Baltimore and Ohio R. Co.*, 205 F.2d 58, 61 (2d Cir. 1953)] (1985).

9. *Everson v. Board of Education*, 330 U.S. 1 (1947).

10. *Board of Education v. Allen*, 392 U.S. 236 (1968).

11. *Lemon v. Kurtzman*, 403 U.S. 602 (1971).

parochial schools; Justices Stevens was almost equally skeptical of the constitutionality of such programs, as was Justice Blackmun—at least with respect
to elementary and secondary schools. By contrast, Justice White consistently
supported the constitutionality of state aid, and he was often joined by the
chief justice and Justice Rehnquist. Thus, aid to parochial schools survived
constitutional challenges only if Justice Powell and either Justice Stewart or
O'Connor were willing to find it unexceptionable.

Against this background, state programs which provided state support
directly to parochial schools were almost universally invalidated during the
Burger era. This point was dramatically illustrated in two cases decided the
same day in 1985—*Grand Rapids v. Ball*[12] and *Aguilar v. Felton.*[13] In both cases,
the government provided instructors to teach purely secular courses to private-
school students on the premises of private schools, almost all of which were
church related. While a small percentage of the teachers in *Ball* had formerly
been teachers in the parochial schools, all of the teachers in both programs
were hired by the government itself, under neutral criteria established by the
government. In *Ball*, no attempt was made to monitor the secular courses for
religious content; in *Aguilar*, by contrast, the teachers were specifically instructed to avoid religious references in their teaching, and to minimize contact with the teachers who had been hired by the parochial schools themselves.
Moreover, the teachers were supervised by city-government personnel who
paid at least one unannounced visit to the classroom each month in order to
assure that the guidelines were followed. Over the dissents of Chief Justice
Burger and Justices White, Rehnquist, and O'Connor, Justice Brennan spoke
for a majority of the Court in concluding that neither program met the
requirements of the Establishment Clause. In *Ball*, Brennan emphasized the
lack of safeguards against the use of the program for religious indoctrination,
arguing that "teachers in [the atmosphere of a religious school] may well . . .
conform their message to the environment in which they teach, while students
will perceive the instruction in the context of the dominantly religious message of the institution, thus reinforcing the indoctrinating effect." Conversely,
in *Aguilar* he contended that the "pervasive monitoring" of the program by
government employees created the excessive entanglement that was banned
under *Lemon*. Taken together, the two decisions made it almost impossible for
the government to funnel aid directly to church-related elementary and secondary schools, even if that aid was used solely for secular instruction.

By contrast, the Burger Court did allow the government to provide some
financial relief for parents of children who attended such schools. In this context, however, the precise form of the aid provided took on special signifi-

---

12. *Grand Rapids School District v. Ball,* 473 U.S. 373 (1985).
13. *Aguilar v. Felton,* 473 U.S. 402 (1985).

cance. Thus, while the Court struck down a state program providing tax *credits* for children attending nonpublic schools in *Committee for Public Education and Religious Liberty v. Nyquist*,[14] in *Mueller v. Allen*[15] the Court upheld tax deductions for educational expenses in part because the deductions were available to students of both public and private schools. The chief justice and Justices White and Rehnquist would have found that both programs survived constitutional scrutiny; in *Mueller*, they were joined by Justice Powell—the only member of the Court to be in the majority in both cases—and Justice O'Connor, who had replaced Justice Stewart after the *Nyquist* decision

At the same time, government aid to church-related institutions of higher education fared far better during the Burger era—primarily because Justices Powell and Blackmun viewed the dangers attendant to such aid as less significant than in the context of other private and parochial schools. Thus, for example, in *Roemer v. Board of Public Works* they joined with the *Nyquist* dissenters in allowing annual noncategorical grants to religiously affiliated private colleges, subject only to the restriction that the grants not be used for "sectarian purposes."[16]

Obviously, the aid to education cases had significant practical consequences for a substantial portion of American society. By greatly restricting the aid which could be funneled to church-related schools, the decisions, in some circumstances, substantially increased the financial burden borne by those who chose to have their children educated in a religious context. However, other issues generated by Establishment Clause jurisprudence generated even stronger emotional responses.

During the Warren era, most of the public's interest in the Religion Clauses was focused on the Court's treatment of a single issue—the constitutionality of religious practices in public schools. A storm of protest followed the decisions in *Engel v. Vitale*[17] and *School District of Abington Township v. Schempp*,[18] in which the Court held that the widespread practice of beginning the public school day with the reading of a prayer or readings from the Bible violated the constitutional prohibition against the establishment of religion. Not surprisingly, some government bodies sought to craft policies that would avoid the strictures of *Engel* and *Schempp*, while at the same time allowing students the opportunity to pray in school. One of the most popular devices was a requirement that students observe a moment of silence at the beginning of the school day, during which they could pray if they wished.

---

14. *Committee for Public Education and Religious Liberty v. Nyquist*, 413 U.S. 756 (1973).
15. *Mueller v. Allen*, 463 U.S. 388 (1983).
16. *Roemer v. Board of Public Works*, 426 U.S. 736 (1976).
17. *Engel v. Vitale*, 370 U.S. 421 (1962).
18. *School District of Abington Township v. Schempp*, 374 U.S. 203 (1963).

Wallace v. Jaffree first brought the issue of the constitutionality of such requirements before the Court. In 1978 the Alabama state legislature adopted a statute which authorized a one-minute moment of silence for "meditation." Three years later the legislature passed a new statute which authorized a one-minute period of silence "for meditation or voluntary prayer." Over the objections of the chief justice and Justices White and Rehnquist, the *Wallace* Court held that the 1981 statute violated the Establishment Clause. Speaking for the Court, Justice Stevens examined the legislative history and concluded that the statute was unconstitutional because it had no secular purpose, but instead was rather clearly an effort to return prayer to the public schools. Thus, he found that the statute failed the first prong of the *Lemon* test.[19]

In other contexts, however, a majority of the Burger Court was more willing to countenance government action that appeared to endorse religion. For example, in *Marsh v. Chambers,* only Justices Brennan and Marshall dissented from the view that state legislatures could constitutionally begin each day's session with a prayer delivered by a state-paid chaplain. Speaking for the Court, Chief Justice Burger eschewed the direct application of the *Lemon* test in favor of reliance on the deep historical roots of the practice being challenged.[20]

Lynch v. Donnelly was of potentially broader significance. There, the members of the *Mueller* majority concluded that a city could constitutionally display a nativity scene in its annual Christmas display. Speaking for the majority, the chief justice emphasized the long history of government acknowledgment of religious holidays and suggested that the *Lemon* test might not be universally applicable to Establishment Clause analysis. Nonetheless, he concluded that the city's decision to display the nativity scene passed muster under the *Lemon* standards themselves. Burger found a secular purpose in "tak[ing] note of a significant historical religious event long celebrated in the Western World." While apparently conceding that the display provided marginal benefits to religion in general and Christianity in particular, he observed that these benefits were less substantial than those which the Court had found acceptable in cases such as *Roemer* and *Marsh.* Finally, the majority rejected the claim that the display fostered excessive entanglement between the government and religion, noting that the nativity scene did not require the government to engage in the kind of ongoing supervision that a majority of the Court had found troubling in *Aguilar,* and that there was no evidence that the display had generated any significant political divisiveness along religious lines.[21]

---

19. *Wallace v. Jaffree,* 472 U.S. 38 (1985).
20. *Marsh v. Chambers,* 463 U.S. 783 (1983).
21. *Lynch v. Donnelly,* 465 U.S. 668 (1984).

Lynch was obviously a defeat for the separationists on the Burger Court. Nonetheless, taken as a whole, the jurisprudence of the Burger era substantially advanced separationist values. Not only were the principles of decisions such as *Sherbert, Engel,* and *Schempp* reaffirmed and marginally expanded, but the Court imposed major new obstacles in the path of efforts to provide aid to parochial schools and their students. *Aguilar* in particular demonstrated the impact of the Burger Court's addition of the entanglement element to Establishment Clause analysis. Thus, the religion cases fit comfortably into the basic pattern of the constitutional jurisprudence of the Burger Court— a jurisprudence which moved the corpus of constitutional law significantly to the left. The same pattern emerged in the Court's treatment of the explosive issue of race relations.

Table 10.1: Voting Patterns

	Bur	Dou	Bre	Mar	Whi	Stew	Bla	Reh	Pow	Stev	Oco
Free Exercise											
Denial of Religious Exemptions											
Wisconsin v. Yoder 406 U.S. 205 (1972) (mandatory formal schooling)	U	U	U	U	U	U	U	NP	NP	NP	NP
Thomas v. Review Board 450 U.S. 707 (1981) (denial of benefits)	U	NP	U	U	U	U	U	C	U	C	NP
United States v. Lee 455 U.S. 252 (1982) (social security tax)	C	NP	C	NP	C	C	C	C	C	C	C
Goldman v. Weinberger 475 U.S. 503 (1986) (military dress)	C	NP	U	U	C	NP	U	C	C	C	U
TWA v. Hardison 432 U.S. 63 (1977) (scope of Title VII)	N	NP	B	N	N	B	N	N	N	N	NP
Establishment Clause											
In General											
Estate of Thornton v. Caldor 472 U.S. 703 (1985) (required religious accommodation)	U	NP	U	NP	U	U	U	U	C	U	U
Aid to Religious Schools											
Nyquist v. Committee for Public Education 413 U.S. 756 (1973) (tax credits)	C	U	U	U	C	U	U	C	U	NP	NP
Mueller v. Allen 463 U.S. 388 (1983) (tax deduction)	C	NP	U	U	C	NP	U	C	C	U	C

	Bur	Dou	Bre	Mar	Whi	Stew	Bla	Reh	Pow	Stev	Oco
Grand Rapids School District v. Ball 473 U.S. 373 (1985) (teaching of secular courses at parochial school)	C	NP	U	U	C	NP	U	C	U	U	C
Aguilar v. Felton 473 U.S. 402 (1985) (teaching of secular courses at parochial school)	C	NP	U	U	C	NP	U	C	U	U	C
Roemer v. Board of Public Works 426 U.S. 736 (1976) (higher education)	C	NP	U	U	C	U	C	C	C	U	NP

Religious Activities

	Bur	Dou	Bre	Mar	Whi	Stew	Bla	Reh	Pow	Stev	Oco
Wallace v. Jaffree 472 U.S. 38 (1985) (moment of silence in schools)	C	NP	U	U	C	NP	U	C	U	U	U
Marsh v. Chambers 463 U.S. 783 (1983) (prayer in Congress)	C	NP	U	U	C	NP	C	C	C	U	C
Lynch v. Donnelly 465 U.S. 668 (1984) (display of nativity scene)	C	NP	U	U	C	NP	U	C	C	U	C

Key

C	= Constitutional	N	= Narrow Interpretation of Statute	B	= Broad Interpretation of Statute
U	= Unconstitutional				
NP	= Not Participating				

11

THE BURGER COURT AND RACE

One of the most striking aspects of the Warren Court was its aggressiveness in attacking state-imposed racial segregation. The Warren era was the first in which the Court had been willing to consistently use its power to attempt to improve the situation of African Americans in United States society. By the time that Warren Burger became chief justice, it had become clear that overt discrimination against minority races would no longer receive legal sanction. It was left to the Burger Court, however, to deal with many of the more complex issues of race relations in American society.

Some of these issues revolved around the persistence of racial imbalance in many American schools. Racial segregation in schools had been the institution which triggered the Warren Court's assault on the American system of apartheid. Beginning with the decision in *Brown v. Board of Education*,[1] the Court had conducted a long-running campaign aimed at dismantling the rigid dual school systems that had characterized the southern states prior to 1954. During the Warren era, however, the Court never clearly stated whether students had a right to attend racially balanced schools, or simply a right to be free from officially imposed segregation. This ambiguity in turn cast doubt on the appropriate scope of the remedies to be imposed on dual school systems.

Nonetheless, by the end of Warren's tenure, the Court was clearly impatient with the slow pace of desegregation and the continued resistance of local authorities. In the second *Brown* case, the Court had instructed district courts to proceed with "all deliberate speed."[2] Ten years later, in *Griffin v. County School Board,* the Court declared that "[t]here has been entirely too much deliberation and not enough speed."[3] Rejecting a freedom of choice plan in 1968, the language of *Green v. County School Board* was even more emphatic. There the Court called upon the local school

---

1. *Brown v. Board of Education,* 347 U.S. 483 (1954).
2. *Brown v. Board of Education,* 349 U.S. 294, 301 (1955).
3. *Griffin v. County School Board,* 377 U.S. 218, 229 (1964).

board "to come forward with a plan that promises realistically to work, and realistically to work *now*."[4]

Soon after Burger took office, the Court unanimously reaffirmed the principles underlying *Green* in *Alexander v. Holmes County Board of Education*. In *Alexander*, the Court emphatically rejected even a slight delay in the implementation of a desegregation order, despite the fact that the delay had been requested by both the Justice Department and the Department of Health, Education, and Welfare. Despite the lack of public dissent, the apparent unanimity of the Court was something of a mirage; the chief justice and Justices Harlan, Stewart, and White would have preferred an order that would have left some flexibility in the timing of desegregation. They reluctantly agreed to concur in a more stringent order only because they believed that it was important to preserve the unbroken tradition of unanimity in the post-*Brown* desegregation decisions.[5]

Despite the concessions made in *Alexander*, cracks began to appear in the facade of judicial unity even before the end of Burger's first term. *Alexander* was handed down on October 9, 1969; in a consolidated group of cases decided on December 1 of that year, the United States Court of Appeals for the Fifth Circuit ordered that all aspects of desegregation except pupil reassignment be accomplished by February 1, 1970, but allowed a delay in pupil reassignment until the beginning of the following school year in September. In *Carter v. West Feliciana Parish School Board*, the Supreme Court granted certiorari and summarily reversed three of the decisions; unlike *Alexander*, however, the chief justice and Justice Stewart dissented, protesting the summary disposition and arguing that the Court should show at least some deference to the lower courts' knowledge of local conditions. [6] Moreover, even the six justices who concurred in the reversal were divided; Justices Harlan and White would have allowed the local school boards eight weeks to demonstrate a need for delay, while Justices Douglas, Black, Brennan, and Marshall argued that no excuse for delay would be sufficient.[7]

Taken alone, the dispute in *Carter* could be viewed as reflecting a mere squabble over details, rather than a fundamental disagreement over basic principle. The justices themselves seem to have initially viewed the case in

---

4. *Green v. County School Board*, 391 U.S. 430, 439 (1968).

5. *Alexander v. Holmes County Board of Education*, 396 U.S. 18 (1969). The account which follows is taken from Bernard Schwartz, *Swann's Way: The School Busing Case and the Supreme Court* (New York: Oxford University Press, 1986), chap. 4; and Bob Woodward and Scott Armstrong, *The Brethren: Inside the Supreme Court* (New York: Simon and Schuster, 1979), 38–55.

6. *Carter v. West Feliciana Parish School Board*, 396 U.S. 290 (1970) (per curiam).

7. Lino A. Graglia, *Disaster by Decree: The Supreme Court Decisions on Race and the Schools* (Ithaca, N.Y.: Cornell University Press, 1976), 94–96.

those terms; for a short period thereafter, all of the members of the Court would remain committed to making a strong effort to maintain the tradition of unanimity in major school desegregation cases. This tradition would play a major role in the Court's initial evaluation of lower court decisions which required large-scale transportation of students in order to achieve racial balance.

Taking their cue from decisions such as *Griffin* and *Green*, the lower courts of the late Warren era began to issue orders that required massive restructuring of previously segregated school systems. The Warren Court never had an opportunity to rule on the propriety of such orders. During the presidential campaign of 1968, however, candidate Richard Nixon vigorously attacked what he described as the usurpation of the authority of local school boards. Ironically, however, it would be Warren Burger—Nixon's selection as chief justice—whose name would appear on the unanimous opinion in *Swann v. Charlotte-Mecklenburg Board of Education*,[8] the first Supreme Court pronouncement validating the use of such sweeping desegregation orders.

The Charlotte-Mecklenburg school system was a large, urban system in North Carolina; its population in 1969 was approximately 71 percent white and 29 percent African American. Prior to 1954, the school system had been racially segregated by law. In the wake of *Brown* and its progeny, the system of de jure segregation had been formally abandoned; however, in 1969 two-thirds of the system's African Americans attended schools with almost no white students. In large part, the racial composition of the schools reflected the segregated housing patterns of the city; thus, a simple requirement that students be assigned to schools according to geographic criteria would have left many African American students in virtually all-black schools. Faced with this reality, a federal district court ordered the grouping of two or three outlying, predominantly white schools with each of the all-black inner-city schools and the widespread transportation of students of both races in order to create school populations that mirrored the composition of the system as a whole.

After the case was argued before the Supreme Court, Chief Justice Burger departed from the standard procedure of having the justices cast formal votes at the initial conference. Instead, following the example of Chief Justice Warren in *Brown*, he suggested conducting the conference on *Swann* as a round-table discussion, with all of the justices having the opportunity to air their views on the case without being constrained by committing themselves to either affirmance or reversal. After this discussion, it became clear that a majority of the Court supported the basic thrust of Judge McMillan's order; although Justice Stewart had expressed some reservations, only Justice Black and the chief justice clearly took the opposing view. Nonetheless, taking advantage of the

8. *Swann v. Charlotte-Mecklenburg Board of Education*, 402 U.S. 1 (1971).

lack of a formal majority vote in favor of the McMillan plan, Burger assigned to himself the task of producing a draft opinion for the Court.

Burger's initial draft was almost unremittingly hostile to the district court's approach. While not completely ruling out the use of altered school zones and widespread transportation of students as remedies for past discrimination, the opinion plainly contemplated that the use of the neighborhood school concept would be the norm. The touchstone of Burger's argument was the view that "neither the Constitution nor equitable principles grants to judges the power to command that each school in a system reflects, either precisely or substantially, the racial origins of the pupils in the system" and that "nothing in the Constitution . . . precludes the maintenance of schools, all or predominantly of one racial composition in a city of mixed population, so long as the school assignment is not part of state enforced school segregation." Instead, Burger contended, "the objective [of remedial plans] should be to achieve as nearly as possible that distribution of students and those patterns of assignment that would have normally existed had the school authorities not previously practiced discrimination."[9]

Not surprisingly, Burger's draft provoked an immediate response from a number of justices. Justice Brennan was particularly forthright in advocating an opinion that would enshrine racial balance as the sine qua non of remedial orders in school desegregation cases. Predictably, Justices Douglas and Marshall also strongly objected to both the substance and tone of Burger's analysis. Justice Harlan also produced a draft which would have concluded that "mathematical racial balancing may be imposed on a school system where, in the district court's informed judgment, this remedy is necessary to achieve a stable desegregation plan." When Justice Stewart also produced a draft that supported McMillan's position (albeit in more muted tones), it became clear that no opinion which undermined the district court's plan could gain majority support.[10]

At the same time, the chief justice and Justice Black—the strong opponents of the McMillan approach—also had considerable leverage. In some ways, the situation in *Swann* paralleled that in *Brown* itself. In both cases, a majority clearly favored the liberal position, while a small minority on the Court opposed that position. At the same time, for political reasons, the members of the majority desperately needed a unanimous opinion; both cases dealt with highly controversial issues of race relations, and dissenting opinions would only increase the possibility of militant opposition to the majority's conclusion. This threat was exacerbated in *Swann* by the fact that the president of the United States had openly criticized the approach of the

9. Bernard Schwartz, *Swann's Way*, 217, 219, 220.
10. Ibid., 121, 107.

district judge. Thus, just as Chief Justice Warren chose to issue a bland opinion in *Brown* to achieve unanimity and persuade Justice Stanley F. Reed not to dissent, the *Swann* majority chose to make substantial concessions in order to gain the concurrence of the chief justice and induce Justice Black to remain silent.

The price of unanimity was an opinion of studied ambiguity. The *Swann* opinion—ironically, signed and delivered by Burger—explicitly rejected the view that the Constitution requires "any degree of racial mixing or balancing," instead declaring that "[t]he constitutional command to desegregate schools does not mean that every school in every community must always reflect the composition of the school system as a whole." At the same time, however, Burger also concluded that "[a]wareness of the racial composition of the whole school system is likely to be a useful starting point in shaping a remedy to correct past constitutional violations" and that "in a system with a history of segregation the need for remedial criteria of sufficient specificity to assure a school authority's compliance with its constitutional duty warrants a presumption against schools that are substantially disproportionate in their racial composition." Finally, returning to the theme that racial balance per se was not constitutionally required, *Swann* emphasized the limited duration of the supervision of the federal courts.

> At some point, these school authorities and others like them should have achieved full compliance with this Court's decision in *Brown I.* The systems will then be "unitary" in the sense required by our [previous] decisions.
>
> It does not follow that the communities served by such systems will remain demographically stable, for in a growing, mobile society, few will remain so. Neither school authorities nor district courts are constitutionally required to make year-by-year adjustments of the racial composition of student bodies once the affirmative duty to desegregate has been accomplished and racial discrimination through official action is eliminated from the system. [At that point] in the absence of a showing that either the school authorities or some other agency of the State has deliberately attempted to fix or alter demographic patterns to affect the racial composition of the schools, further intervention by a district court should not be necessary.[11]

Despite the internal tensions in Burger's opinion, it clearly established the propriety of *Swann*-type orders in school systems that had been rigidly segregated by law. By contrast, the ambiguities inherent in the opinion became more important as school desegregation litigation moved north-

---

11. *Swann v. Charlotte-Mecklenburg Board of Education,* 402 U.S. at 24–26, 31.

ward, to systems where de jure segregation was more episodic.[12] Ultimately, the Court would determine that even in these systems, district courts could ignore the principle of neighborhood schools in an effort to achieve racial balance. However, unlike *Alexander* and *Swann*, this conclusion would provoke open dissents that were unprecedented in school desegregation cases.

The increasingly sharp divisions on the Court were in part a function of the replacement of Justices Harlan and Black by Justices Rehnquist and Powell, respectively. Both of the new justices would prove to be among the Burger Court's most articulate and determined advocates of limitations on court-ordered desegregation plans. The 1972 decision in *Wright v. Council of City of Emporia* was the first to reflect the impact of the new appointees on school desegregation cases.[13]

Emporia involved the effort of a Virginia city to in effect secede from a county that was under a school desegregation order. The decision to secede was unrelated to the desegregation order itself; nonetheless, since the population of the new city's school system would be 52 percent African American, while the population of the unified county system was 66 percent African American, the secession would have had the effect of raising the percentage of African Americans in the noncity schools from 66 percent to 72 percent. Focusing on the lack of segregative intent, the four Nixon appointees concluded that the Constitution posed no barrier to the city's secession. However, the remaining five justices disagreed, holding that the school systems must remain merged.[14]

Speaking for the majority, Justice Stewart took pains to craft his opinion in the narrowest possible terms. He firmly disavowed any implication that racial imbalance per se violated the Constitution, or that racial balance was the sine qua non of school desegregation remedies. Instead, he relied on three arguments: first, that the increase in the percentage of African Americans in the noncity schools was likely to be exacerbated by white flight; second, that all of the formerly all-white schools in the merged system were located in the city and that these facilities in general were superior to the formerly all-black schools in the county; and third, that the African Americans in the noncity schools might *perceive* a racial motivation in the city's decision to secede and that this perception might create the kind of adverse psychological impact on which the Court had relied in *Brown* itself.[15]

---

12. The northern desegregation cases are described in detail in Paul R. Dimond, *Beyond Busing: Inside the Challenge to Urban Segregation* (Ann Arbor: University of Michigan Press, 1985).

13. *Wright v. Council of City of Emporia*, 407 U.S. 451 (1972).

14. Ibid. *Emporia* is discussed in detail in Graglia, *Disaster by Decree*, 146–52.

15. *Wright v. Council of City of Emporia*, passim.

In purely doctrinal terms, *Emporia* was of only limited import. At the same time, however, the structure of the decision prefigured the dynamic which would govern the Court's treatment of the more important issues to come. First, *Emporia* clearly demonstrated that the era of unanimity in school desegregation cases was over. Second, taken together with *Swann,* it presaged the pivotal role of Justices Stewart and Blackmun in determining the direction of the Court's jurisprudence in this area. While both Stewart and Blackmun had opposed the chief justice in *Swann,* neither was fully committed to the position of the core liberal justices on desegregation-related issues. This point was reflected in Stewart's efforts to closely circumscribe the parameters of the majority opinion in *Emporia,* as well as in Blackmun's choice to join the *Emporia* dissent.

Against this background, Blackmun would emerge as a pivotal figure in *Keyes v. School District No. 1,* the first critical northern desegregation case. *Keyes* was a dispute over the desegregation plan for Denver, Colorado. Approximately 66 percent of the students in the Denver school system were Anglos, 14 percent were African Americans, and 20 percent were of Hispanic descent. The non-Anglos were concentrated in schools where they formed majorities. Moreover, although the Colorado state constitution specifically prohibited school assignment based on race, the federal courts determined that the Denver School Board had taken deliberate segregative actions that had affected the racial composition of schools attended by substantial numbers of African Americans—particularly in the so-called "Park Hill" area of the city. After concluding that the schools in which non-Anglos were concentrated provided an inferior education, the district court decreed that a system-wide, *Swann*-type remedy was appropriate. In *Keyes,* the Court was called upon to determine whether the district judge had exceeded his authority.[16]

Keyes first came before the Court in 1971, as the Court was called upon to decide whether to stay the order of the district court pending appeal. The district court had refused to grant such a stay, but the court of appeals had disagreed. Justice Douglas sought to use the occasion to effectively eliminate the distinction between de facto and de jure segregation, a distinction that had been central to the compromise opinion in *Swann.* He proposed to grant the stay, accompanied by a statement that the racially imbalanced schools in Denver's core city provided an unequal educational opportunity

---

16. *Keyes v. School District No. 1,* 413 U.S. 189 (1973). The following account of the Court's internal deliberations in *Keyes* is taken from John C. Jeffries, Jr., *Justice Lewis F. Powell, Jr.* (New York: Charles Scribner's Sons, 1994), 292–308; Bernard Schwartz, *The Ascent of Pragmatism: The Burger Court in Action* (New York: Addison-Wesley, 1990), 259–66; and Woodward and Armstrong, *The Brethren,* 260–68. *Keyes* is also discussed in detail in Graglia, *Disaster by Decree,* 160–202.

and that this inequality was a sufficient predicate for a sweeping desegregation plan. Justices Brennan, Stewart, and Marshall joined with Douglas; however, the chief justice and Justices Black, Harlan, and Blackmun disagreed. Justice White, whose former law firm had once served as bond counsel to the Denver School Board, had reluctantly disqualified himself. Thus, the judgment of the court of appeals was affirmed by an equally divided Court, and the Douglas statement was never published.[17]

By the time that the Court turned to the merits of *Keyes*, Justices Harlan and Black had been replaced by Justices Rehnquist and Powell. Rehnquist was firmly committed to the position that the district judge had exceeded his authority in requiring the implementation of a district-wide desegregation plan. Powell's position, by contrast, was more complex and nuanced. On one hand, Powell saw the distinction between de jure and de facto segregation as an outmoded conception that unfairly placed burdens on the South while leaving the states in the North free to ignore the fact that their communities were equally segregated. On the other hand, he was a strong supporter of the concept of neighborhood schools and viewed widespread busing to achieve racial balance as counterproductive. Indeed, in *Swann* itself, he had filed an amicus brief urging this position on the Court.

For a time, it seemed that Powell might play a central role in the disposition of *Keyes*. At the initial conference, he joined the chief justice and Justice Rehnquist in concluding that the district court's plan could not be sustained; the remaining participating justices, by contrast, took the opposite view. In preparing his draft opinion, Justice Brennan was no doubt mindful of the fact that, with Justice White still not participating, he could not afford to lose a single vote and still command a majority of the Court. Thus, Brennan did not choose to directly attack the distinction between de jure and de facto segregation. Instead, he drafted an opinion which assumed that deliberate segregative acts were necessary to justify federal court intervention; the opinion also concluded, however, that "a finding of intentionally segregative actions in a meaningful portion of a school system . . . creates a presumption that other segregated schooling within the system is not adventitious." While in theory the school board would be given the opportunity to rebut the presumption, Brennan's opinion also made clear that it would not be enough for the school authorities to rely upon "some allegedly logical, racially neutral explanation for their actions"—for example, a neighborhood school policy. Thus, the presumption of intentional segregation was for all practical purposes irrefutable.[18]

17. This incident is described in Jeffries, *Justice Lewis F. Powell, Jr.*, 302.
18. Ibid., 208, 210

Initially, Justice Blackmun showed some reluctance to join the Brennan opinion; at the same time, however, Blackmun suggested that he, too, now had doubts about the vitality of the distinction between de jure and de facto segregation. Thus Brennan faced something of an anomalous situation; six justices were apparently willing to directly hold de facto segregation unconstitutional, but he had only four solid votes for a *Keyes* opinion that rested on a conceptually narrower ground. Brennan then offered to redraft the majority opinion to deal directly with the issue of de facto segregation if Powell would agree to endorse *Swann*-type remedies. Not surprisingly, Powell rejected this offer, and the Court was at a temporary impasse.

Ironically, Burger's efforts to turn the stalemate to his advantage had precisely the opposite effect. Noting the lack of a clear majority, the chief justice suggested putting *Keyes* over for reargument the next term and considering the case together with the Detroit desegregation case, which involved the propriety of busing students across district lines in order to achieve racial balance. Burger no doubt hoped that by linking *Keyes* with the issue of cross-district busing, he could persuade Blackmun and perhaps Stewart to join him in both cases. Burger, however, miscalculated badly. After Brennan distributed a sharply worded memorandum noting the differences between the Detroit and Denver cases, Blackmun chose to join Brennan's opinion, creating the necessary majority for support of the analysis of that opinion.

Faced with this reality, the chief justice abandoned his plan to dissent, choosing instead to concur in the result without opinion. By contrast, Justices Douglas, Rehnquist, and Powell filed separate opinions. While concurring with Brennan, Douglas also openly urged the abandonment of the distinction between de jure and de facto segregation, contending that the courts should act vigorously against all forms of racial imbalance. Concurring and dissenting, Powell agreed that de facto segregation should be found unconstitutional but at the same time attacked the use of busing as a remedy. Finally, Rehnquist flatly dissented, rejecting the notion that de facto segregation was unconstitutional and contending that the remedy should be limited to the Park Hill schools.[19] After *Keyes*, Powell abandoned his effort to eliminate the distinction between de facto and de jure segregation; thus, he would join the chief justice and Justice Rehnquist to form the core of the opposition on the Court to the expansion of the principles established by the Brennan opinion.

One of the most important issues that remained open after *Keyes* was the propriety of desegregation orders that required students to attend schools that were outside the district in which they resided. This question was critical in many urban areas where the student population of the city itself was

---

19. Ibid., 254–65 (Rehnquist, J., dissenting), 217–53 (Powell, J., concurring in part and dissenting in part), 214 (Burger, C. J., concurring in the result).

predominantly African American but that of the surrounding suburbs was almost entirely white. If meaningful racial balance was the ultimate goal, then a desegregation plan in those circumstances would necessarily involve transportation of students across established school district lines.

The Court first considered this issue in *Bradley v. School Board of Richmond*. There the district court had issued an order which would have forced the transportation of students from the city of Richmond, Virginia, to the surrounding suburbs, and vice versa. The Court of Appeals for the Fourth Circuit had reversed this order. When the case reached the Supreme Court, Justice Powell recused himself because of his previous service on the Richmond School Board. In Powell's absence, the Court divided equally, thereby affirming the judgment of the court of appeals without setting any precedent for future cases.[20]

By contrast, in 1974, *Milliken v. Bradley* produced a definitive ruling. In *Milliken* the issue was the legality of a desegregation order dealing with the Detroit metropolitan area, which included eighty-six separate school districts. The racial composition of the public school population of the area as a whole was 81 percent white and 19 percent African American; that of the city of Detroit, however, was 64 percent African American and 34 percent white. The district court found numerous segregative acts by the school board of the city itself, and on the basis of this finding ordered the implementation of a desegregation plan which required transportation of a large number of students from the Detroit school district to those of the surrounding suburbs, as well as from the suburbs to the city.[21]

In the Supreme Court, the defenders of the district court plan focused on the fact that the Fourteenth Amendment made the state as a whole responsible for the segregative acts of each of its subdivisions. Thus they contended that the boundaries of the city should not constrain the remedial power of the federal courts.[22] However, Justices Stewart and Blackmun joined Chief Justice Burger and Justices Powell and Rehnquist to form a narrow majority rejecting this contention. In his initial draft of the majority opinion, Burger sought to use *Milliken* as a vehicle to reverse the Court's approval of court-ordered busing. However, when it became clear that he could not hold a majority for this position, he settled on a narrower approach.[23] Thus, the majority opinion in *Milliken* ultimately focused on two points from *Swann:* first, that the Constitution does not guarantee racial balance per se in the schools; and, second, that the scope of the violation determined the scope of the permissible remedy.

20. *Bradley v. School Board of Richmond*, 412 U.S. 92 (1973).

21. *Milliken v. Bradley*, 418 U.S. 717 (1974).

22. This argument was at the core of the dissenting opinions in *Milliken*. *Milliken v. Bradley*, 418 U.S. at 762–81 (White, J., dissenting), 781–815 (Marshall, J., dissenting).

23. Jeffries, *Justice Lewis F. Powell, Jr.*, 312–13; Schwartz, *The Ascent of Pragmatism*, 264–65.

The majority concluded that, taken together, these principles required that interdistrict remedies be limited to situations in which segregative acts had a demonstrable interdistrict impact.

Milliken did not totally eliminate interdistrict remedies; for example, only Burger, Rehnquist, and Powell dissented from a summary affirmance of the imposition of such a regime on the school systems of the Wilmington, Delaware, area.[24] Nonetheless, *Milliken* did closely circumscribe the authority of federal courts to impose such remedies. Thus, it was rightly considered a major defeat by liberal activists. A slight change in the voting dynamic, however, produced a quite different result when in 1979 the Court clarified other ambiguities from *Keyes.*

Two related problems were central to the inquiry. The first was the extent of the segregative activity necessary to bring the *Keyes* presumption into play. *Keyes* itself seemed to suggest that even a quite limited showing of deliberate segregative acts would raise the presumption that other racial imbalance in the school system was the product of illegal government decisions. There, although remanding the case for further proceedings, the majority indicated that the presumption came into play where the school board had deliberately taken action to change the makeup of schools serving slightly more than one-third of the black student population of Denver and approximately one-tenth of the total student population, even though there was no finding regarding the extent to which the illegal school board actions had actually changed the racial balance within the affected schools. Some saw *Milliken* as an indication that the Court was preparing to require a showing of more extensive segregative actions as a predicate for a *Swann*-type order.

The other problem was the impact of the passage of time on the authority of the federal courts to force massive system-wide changes in order to bring about integration. Many of the segregative acts which might form the basis of the *Keyes* presumption had taken place prior to the Court's decision in *Brown,* which outlawed state-imposed segregation. By the late 1970s, however, pre-*Brown* acts were more than twenty years old. Some argued that the effects of individual actions taken prior to *Brown* were so attenuated that they should be given less weight in determining whether to presume that all racial imbalance in a school system could be traced to governmental activity. The credibility of this view was enhanced in 1976 by the decision in *Pasadena City Board of Education v. Spangler.* There, Justice White joined the members of the *Milliken* majority in holding that once a local school board had satisfied the requirements of the initial desegregation decree, the federal courts were powerless to remedy racial imbalance in the absence of new evidence of deliberate segregative acts.[25]

24. *Evans v. Buchanan,* 423 U.S. 962 (1975), *aff'g per curiam* 393 F. Supp. 1218 (D. Del. 1974).
25. *Pasadena City Board of Education v. Spangler,* 427 U.S. 424 (1976).

In 1979 the remaining *Keyes*-related issues were presented squarely to the Court in *Columbus Board of Education v. Penick*[26] and *Dayton Board of Education v. Brinkman.*[27] In both cases, the court of appeals had invoked the *Keyes* presumption to justify *Swann*-type desegregation orders. The procedural posture of *Dayton* made that case particularly critical; there the court of appeals had relied heavily on its conclusion that the trial court had been "clearly erroneous" in finding that some of the racial imbalance in the system was *not* the result of intentionally segregative acts by the city school board.

In the Supreme Court, the voting pattern of the justices closely resembled that which had produced the *Milliken* result. All of the *Milliken* dissenters who remained on the Court voted to find the imposition of the *Swann*-type order proper in *Dayton,* as did John Paul Stevens, who had replaced *Milliken* dissenter William O. Douglas. Conversely, four of the five members of the *Milliken* majority voted to strike down the *Dayton* desegregation order.[28] In a crucial shift from *Milliken,* however, Justice Blackmun rejoined his allies from *Swann* and *Keyes* and concurred in Justice White's opinion upholding the court of appeals. White began by arguing that, prior to 1954, the segregative acts of the Dayton Board of Education had been sufficiently widespread to warrant invocation of the *Keyes* presumption. He then reasoned that, at that point, the city government had come under an affirmative obligation to remedy the racial imbalance in the school system, and that acts which had the effect of even unintentionally impeding that goal were new constitutional violations. Under these circumstances, the five-member majority concluded, the imposition of a system-wide remedy was justified.

The *Dayton* and *Columbus* litigations marked the completion of the doctrinal development of school desegregation law under the Burger Court. The dynamic that generated the pattern of decisions was relatively simple. On critical issues, the liberals could consistently rely on four votes—Justices Brennan, Marshall, White, and either Justice Douglas or Stevens. By contrast, they were opposed consistently by only Justices Rehnquist and Powell. Thus expansions of liberal activism could be blocked only if Rehnquist and Powell could attract all of the swing votes. Ultimately, it was Justice Blackmun who became the central figure in desegregation law; after providing a necessary vote to give conservatives their one important victory in *Milliken,* his return to the liberal camp in *Dayton* created a majority for liberal activism.

---

26. *Columbus Board of Education v. Penick,* 443 U.S. 449 (1979).

27. *Dayton Board of Education v. Brinkman,* 443 U.S. 526 (1979).

28. Chief Justice Burger and Justice Stewart did, however, concur in the judgment that the order in *Columbus* should be upheld. *Columbus Board of Education v. Penick,* 443 U.S. at 468–69 (Burger, C.J. concurring in the result), 460–79 (Stewart concurring in the result).

Taken together, the results generated by this dynamic reflected a leftward drift in the case law during the Burger era. The combination of *Keyes* and *Dayton* virtually guaranteed a continuation of widespread, massive restructuring of northern school systems that had never maintained the type of dual school systems that had been prevalent in the pre-*Brown* South. Admittedly, liberal activists had not gained everything that they might have hoped for; but the legal power of the federal courts over racial imbalance had been extended far beyond the boundaries either firmly established by or clearly implied from Warren Court doctrine.

By contrast, on at least one other race-related issue, the Burger Court clearly did retreat from the plain implications of Warren Court doctrine. While continuing to maintain that the Fourteenth and Fifteenth Amendments generally imposed no constraints on purely private action, the Warren Court had greatly expanded the class of formally private activity that would be considered governmental action for purposes of constitutional adjudication. The Burger era saw a revivification of the state action doctrine as a significant limitation on the Court's willingness to find racial discrimination unconstitutional.[29]

The comparison between the late Warren Court decision in *Evans v. Newton*[30] and the early Burger Court decision in *Evans v. Abney*[31] provides a dramatic illustration of the shift in the Court's attitude. Both cases revolved around the will of Augustus Bacon; the will had devised a parcel of land in trust to the city of Macon, Georgia, to establish a park to be used by whites only. Once it had become clear that government maintenance of a segregated park was unconstitutional, the city began to allow African Americans to use the park as well. In an effort to maintain the segregated character of the park, a lawsuit was filed in state court, seeking to remove the city as trustee and replace it with private trustees, in order that segregation could be reinstated. Faced with the lawsuit, the city resigned, and private parties were duly appointed as trustees. Nonetheless, in *Newton*, a majority of the Court concluded that the park remained subject to the constitutional prohibitions against racial discrimination. Speaking for the majority, Justice William O. Douglas argued that the operation of the park should be considered government action for two reasons: first, the city remained "entwined in the management [and] control of the park"; and second, the park performed a "public function," like a fire department or police depart-

---

29. The Burger Court's approach to the issue of state action is discussed in detail in Ronna Greff Schneider, "The 1982 State Action Trilogy: Doctrinal Contraction, Confusion, and a Proposal for Change," *Notre Dame Law Review* 60 (1985): 1150–86.

30. *Evans v. Newton*, 382 U.S. 296 (1966).

31. *Evans v. Abney*, 396 U.S. 435 (1970). ·

ment. Thus, the Court concluded that, even after the appointment of private trustees, African Americans must be allowed to use the park.

In response to this decision, the state court held that the intentions of the testator had become impossible to fulfill and that the land should therefore revert to his residuary heirs. In *Abney*, a majority of the Supreme Court refused to overturn this decision, rejecting the view that the decision in effect imposed a penalty for integrating the park. Speaking for the Court, Justice Hugo Black noted that the construction of wills is essentially a state law question and concluded that the Georgia state court had applied race-neutral principles of trust law in reaching its decision.

The movement from *Newton* to *Abney* clearly reflected the influence of the personnel changes that took place at the end of the Warren era. No member of the *Abney* majority had joined the Douglas opinion in *Newton*. Instead, the majority consisted of the newly appointed Chief Justice Burger and Justice Blackmun; Justices Black, Harlan, and Stewart, who had dissented in *Newton;* and Justice White, who had concurred only in the result in *Newton*. Moreover, the *Abney* decision was by no means an isolated phenomenon; the replacement of Black and Harlan by Justices Lewis Powell and William Rehnquist only solidified the Burger Court's general antipathy to claims that facially private activities should be considered governmental action for constitutional purposes. For example, in *Moose Lodge v. Irvis*, only Justices Douglas, Brennan, and Marshall dissented from the holding that acceptance of a liquor license did not subject an otherwise private club to the strictures of the Fourteenth Amendment.[32]

However, the state action issue was of much less practical importance to the race discrimination jurisprudence of the Burger Court than the Warren Court. In the Civil Rights Act of 1964, Congress had outlawed private racial discrimination by statute in many contexts; moreover, in 1968, the Warren Court had held for the first time in *Jones v. Alfred H. Mayer Co.*[33] that Reconstruction-era civil rights legislation reached private as well as state-inspired discrimination. Taking its lead from *Jones*, in *Griffin v. Breckenridge*[34] and *Runyon v. McCrary*,[35] the Burger Court further expanded the reach of the post–Civil War statutes. Against this background, even where private racial discrimination was not held to violate the Constitution itself, it would nonetheless often be illegal under federal law. Thus, at least in race cases, the significance of the Burger Court's state action jurisprudence was quite limited.

---

32. *Moose Lodge v. Irvis*, 407 U.S. 163 (1972).
33. *Jones v. Alfred H. Mayer Co.*, 392 U.S. 409 (1968).
34. *Griffin v. Breckenridge*, 400 U.S. 88 (1971).
35. *Runyon v. McCrary*, 427 U.S. 160 (1976).

By contrast, other, more novel doctrinal issues arising during the Burger era were of far greater import. In large measures, the prominence of these new issues reflected a growing awareness of the complexity of race-related problems in the United States. During the Warren era, the primary focus of both the Court and Congress was on the elimination of formal, overt barriers to the advancement of racial minorities in American society. The implicit belief was that once these barriers were removed, African Americans and other minorities as a group would soon be on an equal economic and social footing with white Americans. The progress of racial minorities disappointed many of their supporters, however. For example, after the passage of the Civil Rights Act of 1964, it quickly became clear to the advocates of minority rights that, taken alone, a prohibition on intentional discrimination would create only limited employment opportunities for persons of color. Because of the position of African Americans in American society in the late 1960s and early 1970s, a high percentage lacked qualifications ordinarily required of white applicants for employment. The Voting Rights Act of 1965 had come closer to reaching the objectives of its supporters. A vigorous, largely successful federal effort to register minority voters had brought with it a substantial increase in the political power and influence of nonwhites in a number of areas. Nonetheless, African Americans were still underrepresented in many state and local governments in the 1970s.

Faced with this reality, and bolstered by the new political power of racial minorities, liberals pressed for even greater efforts to increase opportunities for African Americans and other nonwhites. First, they argued that both the Constitution and relevant federal civil rights statutes should be interpreted to bar not only facial and intentional racial discrimination, but also facially neutral practices that had a "disparate impact"—that is, the effect of placing racial minorities at a disadvantage. Second, they supported so-called "affirmative action"—plans that explicitly treated membership in a racial minority group as an advantage in the distribution of resources and benefits, and in some cases even guaranteed a degree of proportionate representation to nonwhites. Conversely, affirmative action plans (AAPs) faced judicial challenges from some conservatives who argued that they constituted illegal racial discrimination. The jurisprudence of the Burger Court would reflect the divisions of society generally on both of these issues.

Conservatives scored their clearest victory on the question of whether a showing of disparate racial impact alone was sufficient to raise the standard of review under the Fourteenth Amendment. In *Washington v. Davis,*[36] rejecting a challenge to the use of a test that disproportionately excluded African Americans from the opportunity to join the police force, the Court held that only facial or intentional discrimination was subject to strict scrutiny under equal

36. *Washington v. Davis,* 426 U.S. 229 (1976).

protection analysis. Speaking for the majority, Justice Byron White relied on both formal and functional arguments. First, he asserted that "we have difficulty understanding how a law establishing a racially neutral qualification for employment is nevertheless racially discriminatory and denies 'any person equal protection of the laws' simply because a greater proportion of [African Americans] fail to qualify than members of other racial or ethnic groups." Second, he noted that adoption of disparate impact analysis would call into question the constitutionality of a wide variety of tax, welfare, public service, regulatory, and licensing statutes. The holding in *Davis* was reinforced by the decision in *Personnel Administrator of Massachusetts v. Feeney*,[37] where, over the dissents of Justices Brennan and Marshall, the Court rejected a claim that the standard of review should be raised whenever the foreseeable impact of a governmental action was to place a protected class at a disadvantage. Although *Feeney* involved a claim of sex discrimination, the majority opinion was clearly broad enough to cover race cases as well.

Davis and *Feeney* represented clear victories for conservative positions; in terms of practical significance, however, they were more than counterbalanced by *Griggs v. Duke Power Co.*[38] *Griggs* was a challenge to the employment practices of an employer who, prior to the effective date of Title VII of the Civil Rights Act of 1964, had relegated African Americans to jobs in the Labor Department, the lowest-paying department in the company. After the effective date of the statute, the employer instituted a new policy requiring, first, that those who wished initial assignment to some other department both possess a high school diploma and pass two professionally prepared aptitude tests and, second, that those who wished to transfer from the Labor Department pass the Wonderlic Personnel Test and the Bennett Mechanical Comprehension Test. The burden of both the diploma requirement and the tests fell disproportionately on African Americans. Commentators of all stripes agree that Congress did not consciously intend to adopt impact analysis in Title VII;[39] nonetheless, a unanimous Court found that the use of these employment criteria violated the 1964 act, concluding that "[t]he Act proscribes not only overt discrimination but also practices that are fair in form, but discriminatory in operation." Speaking for the Court, Chief Justice Burger noted that African Americans continued to suffer from disadvantages stemming from the pre-*Brown* era and concluded that "Congress

37. *Personnel Administrator of Massachusetts v. Feeney*, 442 U.S. 256 (1979).

38. *Griggs v. Duke Power Co.*, 401 U.S. 424 (1971).

39. See, for example, Alfred W. Blumrosen, "Strangers in Paradise: *Griggs v. Duke Power Co.* and the Concept of Employment Discrimination," *Michigan Law Review* 71 (1972): 59–69; Michael E. Gold, "*Griggs*' Folly: An Essay on the Theory, Problems, and Origin of the Adverse Impact Definition of Employment Discrimination and a Recommendation for Reform," *Industrial Relations Law Journal* 7 (1985): 429.

directed the thrust of the Act to the *consequences* of employment practices, not simply the motivation."[40]

Griggs did not outlaw the use of all employment criteria that disproportionately excluded members of minority races; instead, it simply cast a burden on employers to provide a business justification for such practices. The opinion in *Griggs* itself sent mixed signals regarding the extent of that burden, ranging from "the touchstone is business necessity" to a suggestion that the employer's burden was to show a "demonstrable relationship to successful [job] performance."[41] Subsequent Burger Court case law did little to alleviate the uncertainty; while *Albemarle Paper Co. v. Moody*[42] and *Dothard v. Rawlinson*[43] appeared to cast a heavy burden on the employer, *New York City Transit Authority v. Beazer*[44] and the treatment of statutory issues in *Davis*[45] seemed to point in the opposite direction. The pattern of decisions reflected a fairly typical Burger Court dynamic: Justices Brennan and Marshall consistently supported a plaintiff-friendly view of impact analysis; the chief justice and Justice Rehnquist (who had not participated in *Griggs* itself) were more sympathetic to employers; and the remainder of the justices were less consistent, without any apparent recognition of the tension between the positions that they took in different cases.[46]

Despite the uncertainties remaining after *Griggs,* the Court's endorsement of disparate impact analysis not only had a profound effect on the development of the jurisprudence of Title VII, but also changed the political context in which discourse surrounding race relations took place. The decision gave credence to the idea that facially neutral action taken with no improper motive could nonetheless appropriately be viewed as illicit. Viewed from this perspective, *Griggs* was perhaps the most important race-related decision of the entire Burger era.

The juxtaposition of *Griggs* and *Davis* also exemplifies an important theme that recurred throughout the chief justiceship of Warren Burger. Taken together, the disparate impact cases are a prime example of the divergence between the Court's approach to statutory issues and its analysis of

---

40. *Griggs v. Duke Power Co.*, 401 U.S. at 431.

41. *Griggs v. Duke Power Co.*, 401 U.S. at 434.

42. *Albemarle Paper Co. v. Moody,* 422 U.S. 405 (1975).

43. *Dothard v. Rawlinson,* 433 U.S. 321 (1977).

44. *New York City Transit Authority v. Beazer,* 440 U.S. 568 (1979).

45. *Washington v. Davis,* 426 U.S. at 248–52.

46. The development of disparate impact analysis is discussed in detail in Steven L. Willborn, "The Disparate Impact Model of Discrimination: Theory and Limits," *American University Law Review* 34 (1985): 799–837; and Pamela L. Perry, "Balancing Equal Opportunities with Employers' Legitimate Discretion: The Business Necessity Response to Disparate Impact Discrimination under Title VII," *Industrial Relations Law Journal* 12 (1990): 1–88.

seemingly related constitutional issues. This pattern would be repeated in a number of contexts during the Burger era, including the treatment of race-related issues that effected the political process.

A good deal of the litigation focused on the issues raised by the use of multimember districts in elections for state and local governments. Often, such systems had initially been adopted without any consideration of racial issues. However, when combined with a consistent pattern of racial bloc voting, in practice multimember districts could dilute or negate the political power of the newly enfranchised African American citizens of the South.

Consider, for example, the case of a city whose population is 60 percent white and 40 percent African American. Suppose further that the city is governed by a council composed of five members. Under a regime in which each council member was elected from a separate, single-member district, one would normally expect that the African American community would be able to elect two members of its choice to the council. By contrast, if all members of the city council were elected at large, and city elections were marked by racial bloc voting, then it would be quite possible that none of the city council members would owe their election to African American votes and that none would truly represent the interests of the African American community.

Despite this potential problem, the Burger Court firmly rejected any suggestion that the use of multimember districts was unconstitutional per se. At the same time, however, the early, unanimous decisions in *Whitcomb v. Chavis*[47] and *White v. Regester*[48] concluded that the use of such districts would be held unconstitutional if they operated "to minimize or cancel out the voting strength of racial or political elements of the voting population."[49] This language seemed to suggest that a showing of discriminatory impact would be sufficient to support a finding of unconstitutionality. However, some ambiguity remained, in *Whitcomb,* the Court held that the plaintiff had not met its burden of proof, and in *Regester,* the facts would also have supported a finding of discriminatory intent.

Responding to *Whitcomb* and *Regester,* the United States Court of Appeals for the Fifth Circuit (which had the responsibility for hearing cases arising in most of the Deep South) developed a set of objective criteria for determining whether the use of multimember electoral districts was unconstitutional. In *Zimmer v. McKeithen,*[50] the court of appeals concluded that, in

47. *Whitcomb v. Chavis,* 403 U.S. 124 (1971).
48. *White v. Regester,* 412 U.S. 755 (1973).
49. *Whitcomb v. Chavis,* 403 U.S. at 143.
50. *Zimmer v. McKeithen,* 485 F. 2d 1297 (1973), *aff'd on other grounds sub nom. East Carroll Parish School Bd. v. Marshall* (424 U.S. 636 [1975] (per curiam).

evaluating multimember districts, courts should focus their primary attention on a lack of minority access to the candidate selection process, the responsiveness of elected officials to minority concerns, the weakness of the state interest in maintaining single-member districts, and the existence of past discrimination which precluded effective minority participation in the political process. In *City of Mobile v. Bolden,*[51] however, five justices concluded that the *Zimmer* criteria per se were insufficient to establish a constitutional violation. Speaking for himself, Chief Justice Burger, and Justices Powell and Rehnquist, Justice Stewart argued that only a specific finding of discriminatory intent was a sufficient predicate for a conclusion that the use of multimember districts violated either the Fourteenth or Fifteenth Amendment. Concurring in the result, Justice Stevens went even further, contending that the use of such districts was constitutional so long as they reflected the ordinary application of the political process, rather than an extraordinary effort to dilute the influence of minorities.

Bolden was met with cries of outrage from liberal forces, who saw the decision as a major setback for efforts to open the political process to members of minority races. Indeed—like *Washington v. Davis*—the case was often cited by critics of the Burger Court as a classic example of the Court's lack of sensitivity to the concerns of racial minorities generally.[52] Like *Davis,* however, *Bolden* can only be properly evaluated against the background of other, related decisions.

First, the Court's subsequent decision in *Rogers v. Lodge*[53] substantially limited the practical significance of *Bolden* as a source of constitutional standards. Decided two years after *Bolden, Lodge* was also a case in which the lower federal courts had responded to a complaint of vote dilution by ordering the abandonment of a system of at-large selection of local officials in favor of single-member districts. *Lodge* presented difficulties, however, because of the timing of the district court's judgment. The district court had entered its order prior to the decision in *Bolden;* thus, not surprisingly, its analysis was based almost entirely on the *Zimmer* criteria.[54]

Nonetheless, the opinion of the district court also alluded to the issue that was to dominate the debate among the justices in *Bolden.* First, the opinion took the view that (at least in theory) subjective discriminatory intent was a prerequisite to a finding that the use of the at-large system violated the Constitution. This concession, however, was effectively negated by the obser

51. *City of Mobile v. Bolden,* 446 U.S. 55 (1980).

52. See, for example, Laurence H. Tribe, *American Constitutional Law.* 2d ed. (Mineola, N.Y.: Foundation Press, 1988), 1506–12.

53. *Rogers v. Lodge,* 458 U.S. 613 (1982).

54. The text of the district court's opinion in *Lodge v. Buxton* can be found in the Joint Appendix in the record of *Rogers v. Lodge,* 458 U.S. 64a–98a.

vation that an objective finding of vote dilution under *Zimmer* raised an inference of discriminatory intent, obviating the need for a subjective inquiry into the existence of racial animus.[55]

The district court also concluded that while the at-large system had initially been adopted for neutral reasons, the failure of the state legislature to modify that system was a product of racial bias. While not citing any direct evidence to support this conclusion, the court reasoned that legislative action dealing with the structure of county government was effectively controlled by the representatives of that county, and that the local representatives (who owed their positions to white voters) had every incentive to avoid changing the at-large system to increase the influence of African American voters.[56]

When *Lodge* reached the Supreme Court, the reaction of the justices who had participated in *Bolden* was largely predictable. Justices Brennan, White, Marshall, and Blackmun—all of whom eschewed reliance on discriminatory intent in *Bolden*—were eager to accept the conclusions of the district court in *Lodge*. By contrast, Justices Powell and Stevens argued that the case should be reversed and remanded for more direct consideration of the issue of subjective intent. Somewhat surprisingly, at first Justice Rehnquist seemed willing to join the Brennan group; however, he was soon convinced by the arguments of Powell and Stevens. Finally, while the chief justice was bothered by some of the specific details of the challenged electoral process, he initially showed no inclination to accept the judicial imposition of single-member districts.[57]

This left the balance of power with Sandra Day O'Connor, who had replaced Potter Stewart—the spokesman for the *Bolden* plurality. Given her record on other issues, one might well have expected O'Connor to join the conservatives in *Lodge*. However, she inexplicably joined with the *Bolden* dissenters to create a majority in favor of affirming the judgment of the district court.[58] Faced with this fait accompli, Chief Justice Burger also abandoned Justices Powell, Rehnquist, and Stevens and joined Justice White's opinion for the Court. White characterized the district court's finding of discriminatory intent as no different than any other finding of fact, which must be upheld unless clearly erroneous. Thus, while leaving the intent requirement

---

55. *Rogers v. Lodge*, 458 U.S. 68a (Joint Appendix).

56. Ibid., 90a.

57. Conference notes, case file on *Rogers v. Lodge*, Lewis F. Powell Papers, Washington and Lee Law Library, Lexington, Va.

58. The Brennan and Marshall Papers provide no insight into Justice O'Connor's motivation. Justice Powell's conference notes list Justice O'Connor as a tentative vote for affirmance, but also describe her as troubled by the remedy and believing that at-large elections are neutral.

formally intact, *Lodge* effectively removed the *Bolden* standard as a significant check on lower federal courts in vote dilution cases.

The Burger Court's treatment of the Voting Rights Act of 1965 was even more significant.[59] The Voting Rights Act was one of the most sweeping and important pieces of civil rights legislation ever adopted by Congress. The act dealt with a wide variety of suffrage-related issues; however, its central purpose was to register large numbers of African American voters—particularly in the South—and to guarantee that they would have continuing, unfettered access to the political process. In order to effectuate this guarantee, the act required that states and "political subdivisions" that met certain criteria obtain "preclearance" prior to making changes in qualifications for voting or any standard, practice, or procedure relating to voting. Preclearance could be obtained either from the attorney general of the United States or by obtaining a declaratory judgment from the United States District Court for the District of Columbia which concluded that the change had neither the purpose nor the effect of denying or abridging the right to vote on the basis of race or color. By any standard, this provision was an extraordinary intrusion into state and local autonomy; nonetheless, in *South Carolina v. Katzenbach*,[60] the Warren Court held that Congress was granted the power to impose the preclearance requirement by section 2 of the Fifteenth Amendment. Moreover, in *Allen v. State Board of Elections*,[61] the Warren Court also held that changes which had even the most minor effect on voter access were subject to the preclearance requirement. While the pattern of decisions was by no means uniform, a majority of the Burger justices often joined decisions that expanded on *Katzenbach* and *Allen* and gave a broad reading to both the constitutional power of Congress and the terms of the act itself. Two of the most prominent examples are *City of Rome v. United States*[62] and *Thornburg v. Gingles*.[63]

Decided the same day as *Bolden*, *City of Rome* began with an effort by the city of Rome, Georgia (a state subject to the preclearance requirement), to obtain preclearance for both changes in the system for electing local officers and a

---

59. The Burger Court's approach to the Voting Rights Act is discussed in detail in Abigail M. Thernstrom, *Whose Votes Count: Affirmative Action and Minority Voting Rights* (Cambridge, Mass.: Harvard University Press, 1987); Nancy Maveety, *Representation Rights and the Burger Years* (Ann Arbor: University of Michigan Press, 1991); Richard L. Engstrom, "Racial Vote Dilution: The Concept and the Court," in *The Voting Rights Act: Consequences and Implications*, ed. Lorn S. Foster (New York: Praeger, 1985), 13–43; and Katherine L. Butler, "Denial or Abridgment of the Right to Vote: What Does It Mean?" in *The Voting Rights Act*, ed. Foster, 44–62.

60. *South Carolina v. Katzenbach*, 383 U.S. 301 (1966).

61. *Allen v. State Board of Elections*, 393 U.S. 544 (1968).

62. *City of Rome v. United States*, 446 U.S. 156 (1980).

63. *Thornburg v. Gingles*, 478 U.S. 30 (1986).

number of annexations of surrounding areas. Preclearance was denied for many of these proposed changes on the sole ground that they would have the effect of diluting the electoral power of African American voters. The city then sought to avail itself of the so-called "bailout" provision of the Voting Rights Act. Under this provision, a covered jurisdiction could escape the preclearance requirement by bringing a declaratory judgment action in the United States District Court for the District of Columbia and proving that for the past seventeen years no test or device had been used that had the purpose or effect of limiting the right to vote on the basis of race or color. By a six-to-three vote, the Court concluded that Rome could avoid the preclearance requirement only if the entire state of Georgia met the bailout requirements, that this construction was not subject to any constitutional objection, and that preclearance could constitutionally be denied solely on the basis of discriminatory effect.

As a threshold matter, on its face the language of the statute left some doubt as to whether the preclearance requirement had any applicability to cities. By its terms, the statute requires preclearance only of "a State or political subdivision" which meets the statutory criteria; moreover, the statutory definition of "political subdivision" does not include cities, but only "any county or parish [or] other subdivision of a State which conducts registration for voting." However, in *United States Board of Commissioners v. Sheffield,* over the dissents of Chief Justice Burger and Justices Stevens and Rehnquist, the Court held that cities in covered states were subject to the preclearance requirement, concluding that "we believe that the term 'State' can bear a meaning that includes all state actors within it and [given the structure and purposes of the Voting Rights Act] such a reading is a natural one."[64]

In *City of Rome,* Justice Powell—who had concurred only in the result in *Sheffield*—argued that since cities were to be considered "states" under the *Sheffield* analysis, they should be allowed to independently avail themselves of the bailout procedure. The majority, however, took a different view of *Sheffield,* concluding that the case stood for the proposition that some cities were covered because they were political units of covered states. Against this background, the Court confronted the claim that the statute as construed could not constitutionally be applied to prevent the city of Rome from effectuating the changes it desired.[65]

Two different arguments were deployed in support of this contention. Justice Powell had previously voiced his doubts regarding the constitutionality of the preclearance requirement generally; in *City of Rome,* he relied on general principles of federalism in arguing that the requirement could not constitutionally be applied to the city of Rome. Powell contended that, in

---

64. *United States Board of Commissioners v. Sheffield,* 435 U.S. 110, 129 n. 17 (1978).
65. *City of Rome,* 446 U.S. at 193–206 (Powell, J., dissenting), 168.

the absence of a bailout provision applicable to all covered entities on an individualized basis, the requirement unduly infringed on local prerogatives. By contrast, speaking for himself and Justice Stewart, Justice Rehnquist based their analysis on the contemporaneous holding in *Bolden*. Noting that authority to pass the Voting Rights Act could be based only on the enforcement provisions of the Fourteenth and Fifteenth Amendments, Rehnquist observed that *Bolden* established the proposition that only intentional dilution of minority voting power was unconstitutional. Relying on this principle, he concluded that where, as in *City of Rome*, the city had proven both that it had not engaged in racial discrimination in the past seventeen years and that the current changes had not been proposed for discriminatory reasons, Congress had no authority to prohibit a city from making changes based only on their discriminatory effect.[66]

Speaking for the majority, Justice Marshall took a much broader view of the scope of congressional enforcement authority. He relied on both *South Carolina v. Katzenbach*, which had explicitly approved the preclearance requirement, and *Katzenbach v. Morgan*,[67] in which a majority of the Warren Court had concluded that Congress had the power to expand the protections afforded by the Reconstruction amendments themselves. Based on these precedents, Marshall concluded that the application of the preclearance requirement was an "appropriate method of promoting the purposes of the Fifteenth Amendment."[68]

City of Rome went largely unnoticed in the political uproar that greeted *Bolden;* nonetheless, the decision was of enormous practical and doctrinal significance. The differing results can be traced to Chief Justice Burger and Justice Stevens, the only two justices who were in the majority in both cases. These votes are best understood as a reflection of the importance of doctrinal considerations in the decision-making process.

Stevens filed a concurring opinion explicitly noting the tension between his vote in *City of Rome* and his previous position in *Sheffield* and attributing the shift to his respect for precedent. While noting that it was possible to distinguish the two cases, he explicitly declined to rely on such a distinction, arguing instead that his "opinion that the *Sheffield* Court's construction of the Act is erroneous does not qualify the legal consequences of that holding."[69] While the evidence is less conclusive, Burger's vote also appears to have reflected his view of stare decisis.[70] Moreover, the shift from *Bolden* also

---

66. *City of Rome v. United States,* 446 U.S. at 206 (Rehnquist, J., dissenting).
67. *South Carolina v. Katzenbach,* 383 U.S.; *Katzenbach v. Morgan,* 384 U.S. 641 (1966).
68. *City of Rome v. United States,* 446 U.S. 175–77.
69. *City of Rome v. United States,* 446 U.S. 191 n. 3 (Stevens, J., concurring).
70. Conference notes, case file on *City of Rome v. United States,* Lewis Powell Papers, Washington and Lee Law Library.

exemplifies the same pervasive legal principle embodied in the juxtaposition of *Griggs* and *Davis*—that problems of statutory interpretation can raise different questions than seemingly analogous issues of constitutional analysis.

Stevens would also play a key role when the Court construed the 1982 amendments to the Voting Rights Act in *Gingles*. Much of the debate over the amendments was driven by the decision in *Bolden*. Focusing on the perceived evils of multimember electoral districts, liberals pressed vigorously for statutory language that would allow direct challenges to voting requirements and systems of representation that had the effect of reducing the political power of minorities. Conservatives, by contrast, argued against such language, asserting that it would effectively establish a right to proportional representation. Ultimately, a compromise was crafted, which provided that

> [a] violation of [the Voting Rights Act] is established if, based on the totality of the circumstances, it is shown that the political processes [of a] State or political subdivision are not equally open to participation by members [of a minority race] in that its members have less opportunity than other members of the electorate to participate in the political process and to elect representatives of their choice. The extent to which members of a protected class have been elected to office in the State or political subdivision is one circumstance which may be considered; *Provided,* That nothing in this section establishes a right to have members of a protected class elected in numbers equal to their proportion in the population.[71]

One point emerges clearly from the legislative history of this provision: it was intended to reject the intent standard of *Bolden* in favor of the effective participation test of *White v. Regester* and direct application of the *Zimmer* factors. However, given the imprecision of the *White* test itself, important issues remained unresolved. *Gingles* provided the Court with an opportunity to address these issues.

Justice Stevens joined the *Bolden* dissenters in establishing the prerequisites for a cause of action for a vote dilution claim against a system of multimember districts. Speaking for the five-justice majority, Justice Brennan concluded that such an action could be maintained if a minority group demonstrated *(a)* that the minority group is sufficiently large and geographically compact to constitute a majority in a single-member district, *(b)* that the minority group is politically cohesive, and *(c)* that the district's white majority votes sufficiently as a bloc to enable it to defeat minority candidates

---

71. 42 U.S.C. sec. 1973.

in the absence of special circumstances. By contrast, speaking for herself and the remaining members of the *Bolden* majority, Justice O'Connor contended that these criteria smacked of a system of proportional representation and that a test based on all relevant factors was more appropriate.[72]

Taken together, the Burger Court's treatment of the vote dilution cases represented nothing less than an overwhelming victory for liberal political forces. The cases also reflect the most important recurring theme of the Burger era—that the pattern of decisions was not generated by any single mode of analysis, but rather by the interaction between the approaches of justices with widely different views. The latter theme would assert itself even more clearly as the Court dealt with the issues raised by voluntary, race-conscious affirmative action plans (AAPs).[73]

The issue of the legality of AAPs took on increasing urgency as the Burger era progressed. At the time the four Nixon justices were appointed, the AAPs had substantial support from a wide spectrum of the political mainstream; indeed, the Nixon administration itself was an aggressive proponent of AAPs. Therefore, Nixon did not choose his appointees with this issue in mind. Thus, while affirmative action had become a key issue dividing liberals from conservatives by the time the question reached the Court in the late 1970s, it should not be surprising that the Nixon appointees would split on the issue, creating a badly fragmented Court.

Statutory problems created the first major hurdle for many AAPs. Title VII not only outlawed "discrimination" on the basis of race, but also forbade any covered employer to "classify his employees . . . in any way which would deprive or tend to deprive any individual of employment opportunities or otherwise adversely affect his status as an employee, because of such individual's race." On its face, this language might seem to outlaw AAPs; however, in *United Steelworkers of America v. Weber,* the Court held to the contrary.[74]

Weber was a challenge to a provision of the collective bargaining agreement between the Steelworkers' Union and the Kaiser Aluminum and Chemical Corporation (Kaiser). Designed to reduce racial imbalances in certain skilled positions, the agreement provided that Kaiser would reserve for black employees 50 percent of the openings in in-plant craft training programs until the percentage of African American workers in a plant was roughly equivalent to that of African Americans in the local labor force. The operation of the plan in one plant was challenged by a white worker who,

---

72. *Thornburg v. Gingles,* 478 U.S. at 50–51 (majority opinion), 85–100 (O'Connor, J., concurring in the result).

73. The development of the law of affirmative action is described in detail in Herman Belz, *Equality Transformed: A Quarter-Century of Affirmative Action* (New Brunswick, N.J.: Transaction Publishers, 1991).

74. *United Steelworkers of America v. Weber,* 443 U.S. 193 (1979).

absent considerations of race, would have been selected for a training program. He argued that the AAP violated the prohibition on racial discrimination embodied in Title VII.

By a five-to-two margin, the Supreme Court concluded that the Kaiser plan did not violate Title VII. Justice Brennan's majority opinion rejected the dissenters' claim that the legislative history of Title VII clearly established a congressional intent to outlaw all such programs; instead, noting that Congress's "primary concern" was with "the plight of the Negro in our economy," he argued that "[i]t would be ironic indeed if a law triggered by a Nation's concern over centuries of racial injustice . . . constituted the first legislative prohibition of all voluntary, private, race-conscious efforts to abolish traditional patterns of racial segregation and hierarchy." While not foreclosing all attacks on AAPs, Brennan concluded that the Kaiser plan was not prohibited because it was "designed to break down old patterns of racial segregation and hierarchy" and did "not unnecessarily trammel the interests of white employees."[75]

In a dissenting opinion joined by Chief Justice Burger, Justice Rehnquist accused the majority of adopting what he described as an Orwellian interpretation of Title VII. Rehnquist first noted that the language of the statute makes no distinction between AAPs and other forms of race-conscious decision making. He then disputed the majority's view of the legislative history, citing what he viewed as specific statements disavowing any intention to leave AAPs untouched. Thus, he concluded that the *Weber* plan was a clear violation of the statutory mandate.[76]

Concurring, Justice Blackmun seemed to agree with the dissenters' view of the legislative history of Title VII. After first noting that he shared "some of the misgivings" expressed in the dissent, Blackmun later conceded that several of the passages cited by Rehnquist did seem to indicate an intent to outlaw AAPs. Nonetheless, citing "additional consideration, practical and equitable," Blackmun voted with the majority and concurred in the opinion of the Court.[77]

Weber clearly removed the most important legal barrier to the adoption of AAPs by private employers. However, government-adopted AAPs also faced potential constitutional problems. Not focusing on the affirmative-action issue, *Brown* and its progeny typically stated generally that race was a suspect classification, and that racial classifications were therefore subject to strict scrutiny. One of the primary questions in the cases involving AAPs was

75. Ibid., 443 U.S. 202 [quoting 110 Cong. Rec. 6548 (1964) (remarks of Sen. Humphrey)], 204, 208.
76. Ibid., 219–55 (Rehnquist, J., dissenting). Chief Justice Burger also filed a separate dissent, ibid., 216–19 (Burger, C. J., dissenting).
77. Ibid., 209–16 (Blackmun, J., concurring), 209, 215.

whether this language should be taken at face value or whether it instead should be limited to discrimination against minority races.

Defunis v. Odegaard provided the Court with its first opportunity to deal with the issue. There, a rejected applicant to the University of Washington Law School challenged the school's affirmative-action admissions program. Lower courts had held the program unconstitutional and ordered the plaintiff admitted; thus, by the time the case reached the Supreme Court, he was in his final year of law school. Against this background, based upon the school's representation that it would not expel the plaintiff in any event, a narrow majority of the Court found the case moot and declined to reach the merits.[78]

No such escape was available in *Regents of University of California v. Bakke*,[79] which became perhaps the most ballyhooed constitutional case since *Brown v. Board of Education*. The facts of *Bakke* reflected the complexity of the problems raised by the issue of affirmative action generally. In many ways, the plaintiff, Allan Bakke, was a typical white-male success story of the 1960s and 1970s.[80] Born in 1940, the son of a mailman and a teacher, Bakke was a graduate of the University of Minnesota, where he maintained almost a straight A average. Bakke financed his college education by participating in the Naval Reserve Officer Training program; thus, after graduation he fought in the Vietnam War, returning unharmed in 1967. He then earned a master's degree from Stanford University and gained employment as an aeronautical engineer working in the space program.

Bakke's dream, however, was to become a doctor, and he was willing to make considerable sacrifices to achieve this ambition. Thus, although married with three children, in addition to his full-time job he took almost a full course load of medical prerequisites in biology and chemistry, working early mornings and evenings in order to make up the lost time at his job. Later, he worked off-hours as a volunteer in a hospital emergency room. Despite all of his efforts and achievements, medical schools remained unimpressed by Bakke's credentials; when he submitted applications to a dozen different schools in 1973, Bakke was rejected by all of them.

At this point, Bakke focused his anger and disappointment on the AAP of the University of California at Davis. Adopted as a reaction to the fact that almost no African Americans or Hispanics would meet the criteria that governed the admission of white students, the plan reserved

---

78. *Defunis v. Odegaard*, 416 U.S. 312 (1975).

79. *Regents of University of California v. Bakke*, 438 U.S. 265 (1978).

80. The details of Allan Bakke's personal life are taken from Bernard Schwartz, *Behind Bakke: Affirmative Action and the Burger Court* (New York: New York University Press, 1988), chap. 1; and J. Harvie Wilkinson, *From* Brown *to* Bakke—*The Supreme Court and School Integration* (New York: Oxford University Press, 1979).

sixteen of the one hundred places in each entering class for disadvantaged members of minority races. Upon learning of his rejection, Bakke sent a letter attacking both the propriety and legality of the AAP to Dr. Glenn Lowery, the chair of the admissions committee at Davis. Lowery referred the letter to one of his assistants, who informed Bakke that he had narrowly missed being admitted and urged him to reapply. Remarkably, the same assistant also encouraged Bakke to pursue a legal challenge to the Davis AAP.[81]

Bakke then reapplied to Davis, and as part of the regular process was interviewed by Dr. Lowery. Much of the interview focused on Bakke's expressed opposition to the AAP. Dr. Lowery's report to the admissions committee stated that these discussions led him to the opinion that Bakke was "a rigidly result-oriented young man who ha[d] a tendency to arrive at conclusions based more on his personal impressions than upon thought processes using available sources of information." This impression essentially doomed Bakke's application for admission; although the other five members of the committee gave Bakke high marks, Lowery rated him much lower, leaving his combined score insufficient for admission.[82] Bakke then filed a complaint in California state court, alleging that the maintenance of the AAP rendered his rejection by the Davis medical school illegal under Title VI of the Civil Rights Act of 1964 and both the federal and state constitutions.

Both the parties and the lower court seemed anxious to obtain a definitive ruling from the Supreme Court of the United States. Despite Bakke's unbroken record of rejections from other medical schools, the University of California at Davis conceded that he would have been admitted in the absence of the AAP, thereby obviating any standing objections. The treatment of the case by the California Supreme Court was equally remarkable. By 1976 the California courts commonly added state constitutional arguments to decisions which concluded that the federal Constitution invalidated some governmental action. By invoking such independent state grounds, the state court effectively shielded its decision from review by the United States Supreme Court. However, in striking down the Davis program in *Bakke,* the California court relied solely on federal law—notwithstanding the fact that Bakke had made state constitutional arguments and the trial court had specifically concluded that the use of the AAP violated the California constitution.[83] Thus, no procedural obstacle barred review of the decision by the Supreme Court.

---

81. Bernard Schwartz, *Behind Bakke,* 6–7.
82. Ibid., 8–9.
83. *Bakke v. Regents of the University of California,* 553 P.2d 1152 (1976).

The Court's deliberations on the petition for certiorari produced a rather strange alliance. Based on their subsequent support for the principle of affirmative action, one might have expected Justices Brennan and Marshall to be eager to reverse the California court's decision. Nonetheless, they opposed the petition for tactical reasons, hoping to forestall the Court's resolution of the issue until a more sympathetic case was presented. The chief justice and Justice Blackmun also opposed the writ; however, the remaining justices disagreed, and the parties proceeded to brief and argue the merits.[84]

The oral argument presented one of the great mismatches in the history of Supreme Court jurisprudence. The position of the university was defended by Wade McCree, the solicitor general of the United States, and Archibald Cox, a Harvard law professor who was the former solicitor general and Watergate prosecutor. Bakke, on the other hand, was represented by Charles Colvin, a partner in a small San Francisco law firm. Colvin may very well have been an expert trial attorney; however, *Bakke* was his first argument before the Supreme Court.

Colvin's inexperience was painfully obvious during the course of his presentation. He addressed the Court as if it were a jury, painstakingly recounting the history of the case and its factual record. Early in the argument, Justice Rehnquist indirectly but pointedly suggested that this approach was inappropriate and unhelpful to the Court; however, Bakke's attorney was undeterred. Finally, after twenty minutes, Justice Powell bluntly chided Colvin for belaboring the undisputed facts and declared, "We are here—at least I am—to hear a constitutional argument . . . I would like help, I really would, on the constitutional issues." The remainder of Colvin's argument was devoted to the legal questions in the case.[85]

In fact, at the initial conference on *Bakke,* the justices focused not on the Fourteenth Amendment issues, but rather on the relevance of Title VI, which prohibited racial discrimination in federally funded programs. This issue was complicated by uncertainty about the question of whether a private right of action could be inferred from Title VI. A majority of the justices believed that they needed additional guidance from the parties on this issue; thus, over the disagreement of Justices Brennan, Stewart, Marshall, and Powell, the Court requested additional briefs on the Title VI issue.[86]

The justices conferenced for a second time after receiving the supplemental briefs. By the time the conference took place, Justices Brennan, White, and Marshall had evinced support for the Davis program; by contrast, the chief jus-

84. Bernard Schwartz, *Behind Bakke,* 41–42.
85. The oral argument in *Bakke* is described in Jeffries, *Justice Lewis F. Powell, Jr.,* 480–82; and Bernard Schwartz, *Behind Bakke,* 48–54.
86. Bernard Schwartz, *Behind Bakke,* chap. 5.

tice and Justices Rehnquist and Stevens had indicated their opposition. At the conference itself, Justice Stewart announced that he supported the anti-Davis position. While a medical problem prevented Justice Blackmun from attending the conference itself, he subsequently voted with the Brennan group.[87]

This division left Justice Powell with the balance of power. In the words of his biographer, Powell considered AAPs "distasteful, unseemly, perhaps even unfair, but . . . also vital to an integrated society." Moreover, he feared that outlawing such programs would create social unrest. At the same time, he found the rigidity of the Davis program profoundly distasteful. Accordingly, even before the second conference, he circulated a memorandum which found the Davis program unconstitutional but clearly indicated that, in his view, other types of AAPs should survive legal challenges.[88]

Despite Powell's ambivalence, his vote seemed to give the anti-Davis group a clear, five-justice majority. However, at the conference Brennan argued that the California judgment seemed to require Davis to abandon all use of race in its admissions process and that Powell should vote to reverse that portion of the judgment. In fact, no such judgment existed. Bakke's suit was not a class action; moreover, while the California trial court had ordered Bakke's application considered without regard to race, that judgment had effectively been mooted by the California Supreme Court's order that he be admitted without the necessity of his application being reconsidered. Nonetheless, by accepting Brennan's invitation, Powell could achieve precisely the result that he desired; he could invalidate the Davis program while sending a clear signal that other AAPs would be able to pass legal scrutiny. Thus, Powell immediately accepted Brennan's suggestion.[89]

The result was that when the case was ultimately decided, it did not provide the kind of clear guidance for which many had hoped. By a five-to-four vote, the Court held that the specific affirmative action program was unlawful. At the same time, a different five member majority purported to reverse the "judgment" of the California Supreme Court that all consideration of race was unconstitutional—even though no such judgment was entered by the state supreme court. Moreover, the five-to-four divisions did not reflect views only on constitutional issues; although the chief justice and Justices Stewart and Rehnquist would have preferred to reach the constitutional issue, they reluctantly yielded to Justice Stevens's insistence that the anti-Davis opinion be based entirely on statutory grounds.[90] Thus, only Justice Powell—

87. Ibid., chaps. 8 and 11.
88. Jeffries, *Justice Lewis F. Powell, Jr.*, 470. His thought processes are described in detail in ibid., 468–99. The initial Powell memorandum can be found in Bernard Schwartz, *Behind Bakke*, appendix C.
89. Jeffries, *Justice Lewis F. Powell, Jr.*, 486–87; Bernard Schwartz, *Behind Bakke*, 96–97.
90. *Regents of University of California v. Bakke*, 438 U.S. at 408–21 (opinion of Stevens, J.).

the swing vote in *Bakke,* as in so many other Burger Court decisions—concluded that the challenged program was constitutionally objectionable.

Powell began his argument by asserting that all racial classifications should be judged by the standard of strict scrutiny. Thus, in Powell's view the Davis program could only be justifiable if the interest of the state was "constitutionally permissible and substantial" and the use of the classification was "'necessary . . . to the accomplishment' of [the state's] purpose or the safeguarding of its interest." He identified two state interests which were potentially of sufficient magnitude to justify the use of a racial classification: redressing past discrimination and maintaining diversity within the student body. Powell argued that the Board of Regents was an "isolated segment of our vast governmental structures" and that it lacked the necessary competence to make the type of findings which would justify the program in terms of the former interest. Moreover, he contended that the interest in diversity could be served by a less drastic means—the simple consideration of race as a factor in the admissions process. Powell therefore concluded that while some consideration of race in the admissions process was constitutionally permissible, the use of a quota violated the Equal Protection Clause.[91]

Justice Brennan wrote the most important pro-Davis opinion, which he signed jointly with Justices White, Marshall, and Blackmun (the "Brennan group"). These justices rejected the contention that affirmative action programs were to be subjected to traditional strict scrutiny; they did, however, conclude that the scrutiny of such programs should be "strict and searching" and that even compensatory racial classifications could pass muster only if substantially related to important government objectives. Unlike Justice Powell, the members of the Brennan group accepted the proposition that the Davis plan could be viewed as an appropriate vehicle to remedy past discrimination. Because they also believed that the Davis plan did not stigmatize any racial group, the Brennan group opinion concluded that the use of the plan was constitutionally permissible. Marshall and Blackmun added separate opinions, both of which emphasized the long history of racial discrimination in the United States.[92]

In an opinion joined by Chief Justice Burger and Justices Stewart and Rehnquist, Justice Stevens took a quite different view. Stevens focused only on Title VI of the Civil Rights Act of 1964; Title VI prohibits racial discrimination in any program or activity receiving federal assistance. Unlike Powell and the members of the Brennan group, Stevens declined to conclude that Title VI was congruent with the Fourteenth Amendment. Noting that race-conscious

91. Ibid., 268–319 (opinion of Powell, J.).

92. Ibid., 356 (opinion of Brennan, White, Marshall, and Blackmun, JJ.), 387–402 (opinion of Marshall, J.), 402–8 (opinion of Blackmun, J.).

AAPs were inconsistent with the plain language of the statute, Stevens concluded for that reason that the Davis plan violated federal law.[93]

If anything, *Bakke* left the law of affirmative action more confused than it had been before. *Fullilove v. Klutznick* did little to dispel the confusion. While much less widely publicized than either *Bakke* or *Weber*, *Fullilove* provided further evidence of the Burger Court's disarray on the constitutional issues related to AAPs. *Fullilove* was a facial challenge to a provision in the Public Works Employment Act of 1977, a provision which required that, in the absence of an administrative waiver, 10 percent of the federal funds granted for local projects must be allocated to businesses owned by members of specified minority groups. By a six-to-three vote, the Court held that this program did not violate the equal protection component of the Due Process Clause of the Fifth Amendment.[94]

The six-member majority split into two groups. Justices Brennan, Marshall, and Blackmun essentially reaffirmed the principles which the Brennan group had espoused in *Bakke*. By contrast, writing for himself, Justice White and Justice Powell, Chief Justice Burger produced a remarkable opinion which, while noting the need for "careful judicial evaluation" of all race-based classifications, failed to specify the standard of review to be applied. Repeatedly emphasizing that special deference was due to congressional judgments in this context—a theme also stressed in Powell's separate concurrence—the Burger opinion also focused heavily on the fact that the challenged provision was intended to remedy past discrimination. In this context, the Burger opinion concluded that the minority set-aside program could not be viewed as either fatally overinclusive or underinclusive on its face. The opinion left open the possibility, however, that the failure to grant an administrative waiver in a specific case might be unconstitutional.[95]

The dissenters also split into two groups. Justices Rehnquist and Stewart concluded that all racial classifications were unconstitutional. Justice Stevens, by contrast, found the process by which the challenged program was adopted to be offensive. Painting a sharply different picture than Burger and Powell, Stevens portrayed the set-aside program as the product of a simple political trade-off which failed to address the difficult problems that he viewed as inherent in the use of any racial classification. Contending that where such a classification is adopted "[i]t is up to Congress to demonstrate that its . . . statutory preference is justified by a relevant characteristic that is shared by the members of the preferred class," Stevens argued that this bur-

93. Ibid., 408–21 (opinion of Stevens, J.).
94. *Fullilove v. Klutznick*, 448 U.S. 448 (1980).
95. Ibid., 517–22 (Marshall, J., concurring in the judgment), cites to Burger and Powell opinions.

den had not been carried in *Fullilove*. Thus he concluded that the racial preference was unconstitutional.[96]

Several years later, in *Wygant v. Jackson Board of Education,* the Court
focused once again on the constitutional problems raised by AAPs. There the
Court considered the constitutionality of a provision in a collective bargaining
agreement governing layoffs of teachers. Crafted against the background of
chronic minority underrepresentation in the workforce, the provision provided that such layoffs were to proceed according to seniority "except that at
no time will there be a greater percentage of minority personnel laid off than
the current percentage of minority personnel employed at the time of the layoff." The effect of the proviso was that whites with greater seniority would in
some circumstances be laid off before minorities with less seniority. By a five-
to-four vote, the Court found this provision to be unconstitutional.[97]

Once again, the majority could not coalesce around any single opinion.
Justice Powell, joined by Chief Justice Burger and Justice Rehnquist, delivered the plurality opinion. Powell first reaffirmed his view that strict scrutiny
should be applied to all cases of racial discrimination. He then dismissed the
notion that racial preference could be justified as a means to ensure that
blacks and other minorities would be provided with appropriate role models,
concluding that racial classifications could not constitutionally be justified
simply as a remedy for societal discrimination. Powell did agree that the
school board might in some circumstances use racial classifications as a remedy for past discrimination by the school board itself. He expressed doubt,
however, that the school board had produced the "convincing evidence" of
past discrimination necessary to justify the use of race as a factor; moreover,
he concluded that subjecting whites to layoffs was an unduly intrusive means
of serving the compelling interest—a point which also formed the basis of Justice White's brief concurrence. Thus Powell found the classification unconstitutional.[98]

While agreeing that strict scrutiny was appropriate and that remedying
societal discrimination is not a compelling government interest, Justice
O'Connor differed with Justice Powell on two important points. First, she concluded that a pattern of minority underrepresentation alone could support an
inference of past discrimination and thus provide the basis for the use of a
racial classification as a remedial measure. Second, she explicitly reserved the
question of whether a system of race-based layoffs could ever be constitutional,
arguing instead that the standard used by the school board to determine the
appropriate level of minority representation was inappropriate.[99]

96. Ibid., 522–32 (Stewart, J., dissenting), 533–35 (Stevens, J., dissenting).

97. *Wygant v. Jackson Board of Education,* 476 U.S. 267 (1986).

98. Ibid., 269–84 (opinion of Powell, J.), 294–95 (White, J., concurring in the judgment).

99. Ibid., 284–90 (opinion of O'Connor, J.).

Speaking for himself and Justices Brennan and Blackmun, Justice Marshall reaffirmed his allegiance to the principles that had been espoused by the Brennan group in *Bakke*. In applying those principles to the AAP in *Wygant*, Marshall focused on both the importance of maintaining faculty diversity and the need to ameliorate the effects of past discrimination in the school system. These factors, he argued, provided the necessary constitutional predicate for the layoff provision.[100]

Justice Stevens dissented separately. While agreeing with the conclusion of the Marshall group, he did not adopt the same approach to the case. Instead, Stevens emphasized three points in arguing that the AAP was constitutional: the challenged provision served a valid public purpose, it was adopted through a fair procedure, and it was given a narrow breadth.[101]

In purely doctrinal terms, *Wygant* provides another clear example of conservative activism—the deployment of the Constitution to defeat liberal initiatives from other branches of government. At the same time, however, the practical significance of the decision should not be overstated. Given the strong political passions surrounding the issue of affirmative action, only the clearest mandate from the Court was likely to have a substantial impact on the decisions of other branches of government. The message sent by the badly splintered majority in *Wygant* hardly met this standard—particularly when read not only in the context of the previous decisions in *Weber, Bakke,* and *Fullilove*, but also in conjunction with the Court's contemporaneous action in *Local 28, Sheet Metal Workers Union v. EEOC*.[102]

In *Sheet Metal Workers* a trial court imposed a racial quota on a union that had been found guilty of a "pattern or practice" of discriminating on the basis of race. The quota was imposed only after the court determined that the violations had not been adequately remedied by earlier, less intrusive orders. It effectively gave advantages to some minority workers who were not victims of prior identified discrimination. Nonetheless, Justice Powell joined the *Wygant* dissenters in concluding that the imposition of the remedy was permitted by Title VII and not prohibited by the Constitution. Moreover, while not reaching the constitutional issue, Justice White indicated that he too believed that, in some circumstances, this kind of race-conscious remedy would have been permissible under Title VII. Against this background, it should not be surprising that there is no evidence that *Wygant* in any way discouraged the adoption or continuance of governmental affirmative-action programs.[103]

---

100. Ibid., 295–312 (Marshall, J., dissenting).

101. Ibid., 313–20 (Stevens, J., dissenting).

102. *Local 28, Sheet Metal Workers Union v. EEOC*, 478 U.S. 421 (1986).

103. Ibid., 444–82 (opinion of Brennan, J.), 483–88 (Powell, J., concurring in part and concurring in the judgment), 499 (White, J., dissenting).

Taken together, the race cases provide a microcosm of the structure of Burger Court jurisprudence generally. With the notable exception of *Swann* and *Griggs,* almost all of the decisions clearly reflect the deep ideological divisions on the Court. Neither side gained all that it wanted in the ideological struggle; however, crucial decisions such as *Keys* and *Griggs* clearly moved doctrine substantially to the left of where it had been when the chief justice succeeded Earl Warren. The Court's treatment of other equal protection issues repeated this pattern.

Table 11.1: Voting Patterns

	Bur	Dou	Bre	Mar	Whi	Stew	Bla	Reh	Pow	Stev	Oco
School Desegregation											
Alexander v. Holmes County Bd. of Educ. 396 U.S. 18 (1969) (delay in school desegregation)	BR	BR	BR	BR	BR	BR	NP	NP	NP	NP	NP
Carter v. West Feliciana Parish School Bd. 396 U.S. 290 (1970) (delay in school desegregation)	NR	BR	BR	BR	BR	NR	NP	NP	NP	NP	NP
Swann v. Charlotte-Mecklenburg Bd. of Educ. 402 U.S. 1 (1971) (systemwide busing)	BR	BR	BR	BR	BR	BR	BR	NP	NP	NP	NP
Wright v. Council of City of Emporia 407 U.S. 451 (1972) (secession of city)	C	U	U	U	U	U	C	C	C	NP	NP
Keyes v. School District No. 1 413 U.S. 189 (1973) (systemwide busing)	BR	BR	BR	BR	NP	BR	BR	NR	NR	NP	NP
Milliken v. Bradley 418 U.S. 717 (1974) (interdistrict busing)	NR	BR	BR	BR	BR	NR	NR	NR	NR	NP	NP
Pasadena City Bd. of Educ. v. Spangler 427 U.S. 424 (1976) (termination of desegregation order)	NR	NP	BR	BR	NR	NR	NR	NR	NR	NP	NP
Columbus Board of Educ. v. Penick 443 U.S. 449 (1979) (systemwide busing)	BR	NP	BR	BR	BR	BR	BR	NR	NR	BR	NP
Dayton Board of Educ. v. Brinkman 443 U.S. 526 (1979) (systemwide busing)	NR	NP	BR	BR	BR	NR	BR	NR	NR	BR	NP

	Bur	Dou	Bre	Mar	Whi	Stew	Bla	Reh	Pow	Stev	Oco

State Action

Evans v. Abney 396 U.S. 435 (1970) (reinterpretation of will)	NS	SA	SA	NP	NS	NS	NS	NP	NP	NP	NP
Moose Lodge v. *Irvis* 407 U.S. 163 (1972) (acceptance of liquor license)	NS	SA	SA	SA	NS	NS	NS	NS	NS	NP	NP

Disparate Impact

Title VII

Griggs v. *Duke Power Co.* 401 U.S. 424 (1971) (standardized tests and high school diploma)	IL	IL	NP	IL	IL	IL	IL	NP	N P	NP	NP
Albemarle Paper Co. *v. Moody* 422 U.S. 405 (1975) (standardized tests)	L	IL	IL	IL	IL	IL	IL	IL	IL	NP	NP
Dothard v. *Rawlinson* 433 U.S. 321 (1977) (height and weight requirement)	IL	NP	IL	IL	IL	IL	IL	IL	IL	IL	NP
New York City *Transit Authority* *v. Beazer* 440 U.S. 568 (1979) (exclusion of addicts on methadone maintenance)	L	NP	IL	IL	IL	L	L	L	U	L	NP
Washington v. *Davis* 426 U.S. 229 (1976) (standardized test)	L	NP	IL	IL	L	L	L	L	L	L	NP

	Bur	Dou	Bre	Mar	Whi	Stew	Bla	Reh	Pow	Stev	Oco
Constitutional Issues											
Washington v. Davis 426 U.S. 229 (1976) (standardized test)	C	NP	IL	IL	C	C	C	C	C	C	NP
Personnel Admin. of Mass. v. Feeney 442 U.S. 256 (1979) (veteran's preference)	C	NP	U	U	C	C	C	C	C	C	NP
City of Mobile v. Bolden 446 U.S. 55 (1980) (multimember districts)	C	NP	U	U	U	C	U	C	C	C	NP
Rogers v. Lodge 458 U.S. 613 (1982) (multimember districts)	U	NP	U	U	U	NP	U	C	C	C	U
Voting Rights Act											
United States v. Bd. of Commissioners 435 U.S. 110 (1978) (coverage of subdivisions)	NI	NP	BI	BI	BI	BI	BI	NI	BI	NI	NP
City of Rome v. United States 446 U.S. 156 (1980) (bailout of subdivisions)	BI	NP	BI	BI	BI	NI	BI	NI	NI	BI	NP
Thornburg v. Gingles 478 U.S. 30 (1986) (multimember districts)	NI	NP	BI	BI	BI	NP	BI	NI	NI	BI	NI

	Bur	Dou	Bre	Mar	Whi	Stew	Bla	Reh	Pow	Stev	Oco
Affirmative Action											
Constitutional Issues											
Regents of University of California v. Bakke 438 U.S. 265 (1978) (quota for medical school admissions)	IL	NP	C	C	C	IL	C	IL	U	IL	NP
Fullilove v. Klutznick 448 U.S. 448 (1980) (minority set-aside program)	C	NP	C	C	C	U	C	U	C	U	NP
Wygant v. Jackson Bd. of Education 476 U.S. 267 (1986) (race-conscious layoffs)	U	NP	C	C	U	NP	C	U	U	C	U
Statutory Issues											
United Steelworkers v. Weber 443 U.S. 193 (1979) (quota in training program)	IL	NP	L	L	L	L	L	IL	NP	NP	NP
Local 28, Sheet Metal Workers v. EEOC 478 U.S. 421 (1986) (remedial quota)	IL	NP	L	L	IL	NP	L	IL	L	L	IL

Key

BR	= Broad Remedy	IL	= Illegal under Statute	C	= Constitutional
NR	= Narrow Remedy	BI	= Broad Interpretation of Statute	U	= Unconstitutional
SA	= State Action			NP	= Not Participating
NS	= No State Action	NI	= Narrow Interpretation of Statute		
L	= Legal				

12

THE BURGER COURT AND
NONRACIAL CLASSIFICATIONS

The rapid evolution of legislative and judicial protection for minority races during the Warren era unleashed political and doctrinal forces that transcended racial issues. Emboldened by the success of African Americans in gaining special legal recognition of their plight in society, other groups began to argue that their situation was analogous to that of racial minorities, and that they too should be protected by both federal statutes and constitutional principles. The efforts of these groups ultimately created two different types of issues for the Burger Court to resolve. First, where Congress actually adopted statutes that protected nonracial groups, the Court was faced with a variety of questions of statutory interpretation. Second—independently of congressional action—the Court was forced to confront the question of which nonracial groups (if any) merited special constitutional protection.

In theory, the justices might have taken a simple approach to the latter question; noting the historical relationship between racial classifications and the Reconstruction amendments, they could have limited enhanced scrutiny to discrimination against minority races. However, only Justice Rehnquist was willing to adopt this approach (and even he, as we have seen, would have extended strict scrutiny to *all* racial classifications). The remaining justices approached the question differently, asking why racial discrimination was constitutionally disfavored, and whether the same rationale suggested that members of some other group should be protected by enhanced scrutiny of classifications that disfavored them. Not surprisingly, the members of the Court failed to reach consensus on this issue. Justices Douglas, Brennan, and Marshall enthusiastically embraced the cause of a wide variety of groups that sought special constitutional protection. The remaining justices, however, were not only more selective in identifying groups entitled to protection by enhanced scrutiny, but differed substantially among themselves on the appropriate standards to be applied.

Ironically, the Burger Court would limit the constitutional protections afforded to the one nonracial group in which the Warren Court showed a special interest—the poor. In cases such as *Harper v. Virginia State Board of Elections*,[1] *Griffin v. Illinois*,[2] and *Douglas v. California*,[3] the Warren Court held that the government could not constitutionally require indigent people to pay fees for access to the ballot box or appeals from criminal convictions. Initially, the Burger Court showed some willingness to extend this principle to other government functions; in *Boddie v. Connecticut*,[4] with only Justice Black dissenting, the Court held that indigents must be allowed access to divorce proceedings without payment of the fees normally required of litigants.

Boddie was not, however, the precursor of a trend. In *United States v. Kras*,[5] with Justice Brennan not participating and Justices Douglas, Stewart, and Marshall dissenting, the majority concluded that the state could constitutionally require indigents to pay the fifty-dollar fee generally imposed as a prerequisite for the filing of a bankruptcy petition. Speaking for the Court, Justice Blackmun argued that *Boddie* was distinguishable because a divorce proceeding was the only mechanism for dissolving a marriage, while debtors had plausible, nonjudicial alternatives available to adjust their legal relationships with creditors. The following year, in *Ross v. Moffitt*,[6] Justice Stewart joined the members of the *Kras* majority in effectively limiting *Douglas* to its facts, holding that indigents had no constitutional right to have counsel provided for a *discretionary* appeal to the state supreme court in a criminal case.

The line of cases from *Griffin* to *Moffitt* involved a somewhat unusual theory of equal protection. The indigent plaintiffs in those cases were not claiming the right to be treated the *same* as all other persons; instead, they claimed that their condition gave them the right to an *exemption* from generally applicable requirements. More often, groups sought to have a particular trait deemed irrelevant—to be treated the same as other groups in society. Their efforts to have the Court enshrine their claims in legal doctrine met with varying degrees of success.

Groups such as the elderly and the disabled were more successful in obtaining protection from Congress than from the Court. For example, Congress adopted legislation that protected older Americans from discrimination in federally funded programs and in the workplace generally. However, in *Massachusetts Board of Retirement v. Murgia*[7] and *Vance v.*

1. *Harper v. Virginia State Board of Elections*, 383 U.S. 663 (1966).
2. *Griffin v. Illinois*, 351 U.S. 12 (1956).
3. *Douglas v. California*, 372 U.S. 353 (1963).
4. *Boddie v. Connecticut*, 401 U.S. 371 (1971).
5. *United States v. Kras*, 409 U.S. 434 (1973).
6. *Ross v. Moffitt*, 417 U.S. 600 (1974).
7. *Massachusetts Board of Retirement v. Murgia*, 427 U.S. 307 (1976) (per curiam).

Bradley,[8] only Justice Marshall was willing to apply a heightened level of scrutiny in constitutional challenges to age discrimination.

The Court's response to the claims of disabled Americans was more complex. During the Burger era, Congress adopted a variety of statutes that were designed to more fully integrate disabled persons into American society. While the Court dealt with a variety of issues dealing with the rights of the disabled under both these statutes and the Constitution, the most significant decisions derived from claims made by mentally disabled people and their advocates.

In *Pennhurst State School and Hospital v. Halderman*, the Court was faced with the problem of interpreting the Developmentally Disabled Assistance and Bill of Rights Act. The central purpose of the statute was to establish a federal-state grant program to aid states in creating programs to care for and treat the developmentally disabled. In addition, the statute set forth a "bill of rights" for mentally retarded persons; it included "a right to appropriate treatment, services, and habilitation" in "the setting that is least restrictive of . . . personal liberty." In *Pennhurst*, the mentally retarded plaintiffs argued that this provision created substantive rights in their favor, as well as providing them with a private right of action to enforce those rights. Over the dissents of Justices Brennan, White, and Marshall the Court disagreed, concluding that the bill of rights provisions were simply a general statement of federal policy and did not create legally binding obligations on the states.[9]

Advocates for the mentally retarded were more successful in *City of Cleburne v. Cleburne Living Center*, where the plaintiffs sought to establish a group home for the mentally retarded in a residential area. Concluding that the group home would be a "hospital for the feeble-minded" within the meaning of the relevant ordinance, the local zoning authorities concluded that a special use permit was required for the operation of a group home and, largely because of the objections of the local populace, refused to grant the relevant permit. The Court unanimously found that the ordinance violated the Equal Protection Clause; however, the justices differed sharply on the appropriate standard of review to be applied.[10]

Focusing on what they viewed as the legacy of irrational prejudice against the mentally retarded, Justices Brennan, Marshall, and Blackmun argued that the Court should have subjected the denial of the permit to enhanced scrutiny. By contrast, speaking for the majority, Justice White purported to apply the rational basis test, noting the "real and undeniable dif-

---

8. *Vance v. Bradley*, 440 U.S. 93 (1979).

9. *Pennhurst State School and Hospital v. Halderman*, 465 U.S. 89 (1984).

10. *City of Cleburne v. Cleburne Living Center*, 473 U.S. 432 (1985).

ferences between the retarded and others" and contending that the recent
spate of legislation designed to aid the retarded belied any contention that
they needed special protection from the legislative process. Nonetheless, he
found that the denial of the permit was unconstitutional, concluding that it
rested on "an irrational prejudice against the mentally retarded."[11]

As Justice Stevens observed in a concurring opinion joined by the chief
justice, the rational basis test applied in *Cleburne* was plainly more stringent
than that of cases such as *Dandridge v. Williams*[12] and *United States Railroad
Retirement Board v. Fritz.*[13] Thus, the decision demonstrates that, in a sufficiently egregious case, even Justice Rehnquist was willing to seize on the
requirement of minimum rationality as a justification for overturning the
judgment of another branch of government. Equally important, *Cleburne* typifies the internal debate on the Court over the appropriate constitutional
treatment of groups other than minority races.

More often, this debate reflected broader forces that were transforming
the social and economic mores of the Burger era. Among the most important of these forces was the changing conception of the role of the institution of marriage in American society; this in turn was closely related to a
general reevaluation of sex roles in America. Traditionally, marriage had
been viewed as a stable, lifelong commitment between a man and a woman,
dissoluble only for very important reasons. The legal relationship established
by marriage was important not only in its own terms, but also as a convenient
yardstick to determine eligibility for a variety of government benefits.

Burger Court jurisprudence reflected considerable respect for the
importance of marriage in the abstract, with the majority of the justices
even characterizing the right to marry as fundamental. Thus, in *Zablocki v.
Redhail*,[14] only Justice Rehnquist was willing to countenance a Wisconsin law
forbidding marriage by a resident under court order to support minor children not in his or her custody, unless he or she proved compliance with the
support obligation and the children "[were] not and [were] not likely
thereafter to become public charges." Conversely, in *Califano v. Jobst*,[15] a
unanimous Court concluded that Congress need meet only the rational
basis test in using marriage as a criterion in determining eligibility for government benefits.

At the same time, a majority of the Court showed considerable hostility
to some of the traditional incidents of marriage. Historically, one of the most

11. Ibid., 444, 450.
12. *Dandridge v. Williams*, 397 U.S. 471 (1970).
13. *United States Railroad Retirement Board v. Fritz*, 449 U.S. 166 (1980).
14. *Zablocki v. Redhail*, 434 U.S. 374 (1978).
15. *Califano v. Jobst*, 434 U.S. 47 (1977).

important aspects of marriage was its significance for establishing the legal rights and responsibilities of a father toward children—particularly, the children born to the woman to whom the father was married. The children borne by the wife during the marriage were almost universally vested with economic claims against both the husband and the mother. In addition, the children were entitled to a variety of government benefits designed to replace the economic contribution of the husband in the event of his death. While it was generally expected that the wife's children would also in fact be the biological children of the husband, in many cases, the source of the claims against the husband and the government was not the biological relationship itself. Instead, the rights were founded in contract, with the child essentially becoming a third party beneficiary of the marriage contract between the husband and the child's mother.

In the late 1960s and 1970s, however, this conception of marriage and the appropriate legal relationship of fathers to children came under sharp attack from many elements of the American intelligentsia. The concept that marriage should be a permanent commitment between the husband and wife was undermined by a revolution in divorce law, a revolution which increasingly allowed either partner to leave the marriage on a unilateral declaration of "irreconcilable differences," or some similar formulation. Conversely, the social taboos against bearing children out of wedlock were weakened. Against this background, it became almost inevitable that many would argue that biology and social relationship, not contract, should be the basic determinants of the legal rights and responsibilities of fathers toward children.

This view would dominate the Burger Court's treatment of laws defining the rights of children born out of wedlock.[16] Thus, in *Gomez v. Perez*, over the procedural objections of Justices Stewart and Rehnquist, the Court struck down a Texas statute that granted only legitimate children a legally enforceable right to support from their biological fathers. The majority declared that "once a State posits a judicially enforceable right on behalf of children to needed support from their natural fathers there is no constitutionally sufficient justification for denying such an essential right simply because its natural father has not married its mother. For a State to do so is 'illogical and unjust.'"[17] However, the justices were deeply divided over other government classifications based on legitimacy. Justices Brennan, Marshall, and Stevens were consistently hostile to government efforts to differentiate

---

16. The Burger Court's analysis of the constitutional status of illegitimates is described in detail in Christine H. Kellett, "The Burger Decade: More Than Toothless Scrutiny for Laws Affecting Illegitimates," *University of Detroit Journal of Urban Law* 57 (1980): 791–811; and Earl M. Maltz, "Illegitimacy and Equal Protection," *Arizona State Law Journal* (1980): 831–51.

17. *Gomez v. Perez*, 409 U.S. 535, 538 (1973) (per curiam) [quoting *Weber v. Aetna Casualty and Surety Co.*, 406 U.S. 164, 175 (1972)].

between legitimate and illegitimate children, with Stevens declaring that such classifications should be subject to the strictest scrutiny because of the "social opprobrium" historically associated with illegitimacy.[18] By contrast, the remaining justices took the view that legitimacy might at times be an appropriate measuring stick to determine the "real" relationship between father and child.

The debate took place in two quite different contexts. One pair of cases—*Jiminez v. Weinberger*[19] and *Mathews v. Lucas*[20]—involved the distribution of government benefits where the claim of the illegitimate had no effect on the rights of other claimants. Both cases involved access to benefits provided to dependent children by the Social Security program. In *Jiminez*, the claim was based on the disability of the child's biological father, while *Lucas* was a claim for death benefits. In each case, all legitimate children were entitled to the benefit, as were illegitimate children who had been formally acknowledged by their fathers. However, the two programs differed in one important respect; while biological children who were not in the designated classes could never recover under the *Jiminez* statute, in *Lucas* the illegitimate child could receive the death benefit if the child could prove that the decedent was his/her biological father and that he/she was actually dependent on the father at the time of the father's death.

This distinction was critical to the chief justice and Justices Stewart, White, Powell, and Blackmun. In *Jiminez*, they agreed with Justices Brennan, Marshall, and Douglas, concluding that the statute had created an unconstitutional irrebuttable presumption; by contrast, in *Lucas* they joined Justice Rehnquist in holding that the constitutional challenge should be rejected. Speaking for the *Lucas* majority, Justice Blackmun conceded that the appropriate level of scrutiny was "not toothless," but nonetheless chose to defer to the expertise of Congress in specifying a "narrow set of objective and reasonable indicators [of dependency]."[21]

In cases such as *Jiminez* and *Lucas*, the claims of the illegitimate children had no impact on the potential rights of either legitimate children or any other claimants to government aid. Another group of cases, by contrast, involved at least potential competition for a finite set of resources between illegitimate children, on one hand, and persons whose claims were based on either a legal relationship or some biological relationship other than parent and child, on the other hand. The Court was once again deeply divided over the proper constitutional standards to be applied.

---

18. *Mathews v. Lucas*, 427 U.S. 495, 523 (Stevens, J., dissenting) (1976).
19. *Jiminez v. Weinberger*, 417 U.S. 628 (1974).
20. *Mathews v. Lucas*, 427 U.S. 495 (1976).
21. Ibid., 513–14.

The issue first came to the Burger Court in *Labine v. Vincent,* where a five-justice majority rejected a challenge to a Louisiana statute that denied illegitimates the right to inherit through intestate succession. Speaking for the majority, Justice Black emphasized the importance of contractually related family rights in creating legal obligations:

> There is no biological difference between a wife and a concubine, nor does the Constitution require that there be such a difference before the State may assert its power to protect the wife and her children against the claims of a concubine and her children. The social difference between a wife and a concubine is analogous to the difference between a legitimate and an illegitimate child. One set of relationships is socially sanctioned, legally recognized, and gives rise to various rights and duties. The other set of relationships is illicit and beyond the recognition of the law. Similarly, the State does not need biological or social reasons for distinguishing between ascendants and descendants.

Justice Harlan's concurring opinion took a similar tack, concluding that "[i]t is surely reasonable for Louisiana to provide that a man who has entered into a marital relationship thereby undertakes obligations beyond those he owes to the products of a casual liaison."[22]

Justice Brennan's dissenting opinion took a quite different view of the case. He argued that "the formality of marriage primarily signifies a relationship between husband and wife, not between parent and child" and suggested that because the biological relationship of the father does not vary based on legitimacy, the rights of legitimate and illegitimate children should be presumptively equal. From this perspective, Brennan concluded that "the central reality of this case [is that] Louisiana punishes illegitimate children for the misdeeds of their parents" and that the majority "uphold[s] the untenable and discredited moral prejudice of bygone centuries which vindictively punished not only the illegitimate's parents, but also the hapless, and innocent, children."[23]

The debate took a sharply different turn in *Weber v. Aetna Casualty and Surety Co.* There the Court dealt with a Louisiana system for allocating death benefits under the state's workers' compensation scheme. The statutes established a maximum benefit for each dependent child and made both legitimate and illegitimate children eligible to receive the benefits. At the same time, however, the statutes specified a maximum total benefit available for the death of any worker, and provided that unacknowledged illegiti-

22. *Labine v. Vincent,* 401 U.S. 532, 538, 540 (Harlan, J., concurring) (1971).
23. Ibid., 552–53, 557, 541 (Brennan, J., dissenting).

mates could only receive benefits if this maximum benefit had not been exhausted by payments to legitimate children and illegitimate children who had been legally acknowledged by the wage earner prior to his death. Only Justice Rehnquist dissented from the conclusion that the distinction between unacknowledged illegitimate children and other children violated the Equal Protection Clause. Speaking for the majority, Justice Powell (who had replaced Justice Black on the Court) drew heavily from the reasoning of Justice Brennan's dissent in *Labine*, declaring that

> imposing disabilities on the illegitimate child is contrary to the basic concept of our system that legal burdens should bear some relationship to individual responsibility or wrongdoing. Obviously, no child is responsible for his birth and penalizing the illegitimate child is an ineffectual—as well as an unjust—way of deterring the parent.[24]

This argument obscures important aspects of the issue in *Weber*. The statute clearly recognized that the unacknowledged, dependent illegitimate child had a cognizable claim to death benefits; the problem arose only because the statute established a maximum total benefit to be divided among all potential claimants. All of the children in the case had equal claims based on biology and dependence; the legitimate children, however, also had an *additional* claim, based on the contractual relationship between the deceased wage earner and their mother. The message of *Weber*, therefore, is that as a matter of constitutional law, the contractual claim must be deemed (if not completely irrelevant) entirely subordinate to claims based on biology. The decision thus stands as one of the clearest examples of Burger Court hostility to the use of traditional, formal legal categories.

As such, the majority opinion was clearly at odds with Justice Black's analysis in *Labine*. Obviously aware of this tension, Justice Powell sought to distinguish *Labine* on two grounds. First, he characterized *Labine* as resting in large measure on "the traditional deference to a State's prerogative to regulate the disposition at death of property within its borders." In addition, he noted that while the illegitimate children were denied the right to intestate succession in *Labine*, the father could have left them a substantial part of his estate by will. By contrast, on the facts of *Weber*, the wage earner could not have legally acknowledged the illegitimate—the point which Justice Blackmun described as dispositive in his concurring opinion. Thus, the two decisions were at least formally reconcilable.[25]

---

24. *Weber v. Aetna Casualty and Surety Co.*, 406 U.S. 164, 175 (1972).
25. Ibid., 170–71, 176–77 (Blackmun, J., concurring in the result).

Five years later, however, a majority of the Court jettisoned *Labine* in *Trimble v. Gordon*. In *Trimble*, like *Labine*, the relevant state law provided that illegitimate children could not inherit by intestate succession from their fathers; however, in *Trimble*, Justices Brennan, White, Marshall, Powell, and Stevens found the provision unconstitutional. Once again speaking for the majority, Justice Powell considered three state interests. The first—promotion of legitimate family relationships—was dismissed on the authority of *Weber*. Powell also rejected a second justification—the reflection of the presumed will of the intestate—as simply not a real motivating force behind the enactment of the challenged statute.[26]

Finally, the majority conceded that the state interest in providing a method for the orderly disposition of property at death, while reducing the incidence of spurious claims, was both substantial and furthered by the challenged statute. Nevertheless, the opinion suggested that this interest could be appropriately effectuated by the selection of some "middle ground between the extremes of complete exclusion and case-by-case determination of paternity."[27] Because the Court found that some categories of illegitimates could be recognized without jeopardizing the orderly settling of estates or the dependability of land titles which rest on intestate succession, the *Trimble* statute was held unconstitutional.

Despite the *Trimble* holding, it soon became clear that a majority of the Court did not view the Constitution as depriving the states of all power to make distinctions between legitimate and illegitimate children in laws dealing with intestate succession. In *Lalli v. Lalli*, over the dissents of Justice Stevens and the *Labine* dissenters who remained on the bench, the Court refused to invalidate a New York statute which allowed an illegitimate child to inherit by intestate succession from his father only if the child had obtained an order of filiation during the father's lifetime. No opinion commanded the support of a majority of the Court. While Justices Blackmun and Rehnquist would have overruled *Trimble* outright, the chief justice and Justice Stewart joined Justice Powell in an opinion which sought to distinguish it from *Lalli*. The plurality noted that, even in *Trimble*, the Court had recognized a state interest "of considerable magnitude" in providing for the just and orderly disposition of property at death, and concluded that the *Lalli* scheme was substantially related to this interest, as well as sufficiently "attuned to alternative considerations" to pass constitutional muster. Thus, the opinion rested on premises quite similar to those of *Lucas;* rather than accepting the proposition that legitimacy per se was a constitutionally

---

26. *Trimble v. Gordon*, 430 U.S. 762 (1977).
27. Ibid., 771.

acceptable criterion for intestate succession, the plurality in *Lalli* justified
the state law as an administratively convenient device to resolve postmortem
disputes over the question of whether a child born out of wedlock was in
fact a dependent biological child of the deceased.[28]

Taken together, the intestate succession cases provide another classic
example of the structure of Burger Court decision making. The *Labine* and
Trimble majorities rested on radically different theories of the appropriate legal
analysis to be applied to the problem. Thus, not surprisingly, no justice joined
both opinions; the difference in the results in the two cases was due solely to
the fact that Justice Powell had replaced Justice Black in the interim. However,
while his basic premises were much closer to the *Labine* dissenters than the
majority, Powell characteristically sought a middle ground—a middle ground
which led him to join the remaining members of the *Labine* majority and Justice Rehnquist in *Lalli* in upholding a limitation on the rights of illegitimates.
A more complex dynamic would emerge as the Court struggled with the issues
raised by sex discrimination.

The rapid evolution of the law of sex discrimination was one of the
most visible developments of the Burger era. Prior to Burger's appointment, the Court had given short shrift to claims that statutes differentiat-
ing between the sexes violated the Equal Protection Clause or its Fifth
Amendment counterpart. The state of the law in 1969 was defined by *Goesart v. Cleary*[29] and *Hoyt v. Florida*.[30] In *Goesart*, the Vinson Court applied the
rational basis test to uphold a state statute that forbade virtually all women
from working as bartenders, while in *Hoyt*, the Warren Court unanimously
upheld a law that included men on jury lists unless they requested an
exemption, while exempting women unless they volunteered. The *Hoyt*
Court declared that the state could reasonably take account of the fact that
the "woman is still regarded as the center of home and family life."[31]

The Burger Court, however, faced a quite different social and political climate as it confronted a series of issues related to sex discrimination. The 1960s
saw the rapid growth in the feminist movement, which challenged both traditional sex roles and the legal structures that reinforced those roles. At the federal level, feminists won important legislative victories as early as 1963 and
1964, with the passage of the Equal Pay Act and Title VII's prohibition of sex
discrimination in employment. The political strength of the movement continued to grow, and in 1972 the Equal Rights Amendment (ERA) was passed
by Congress with overwhelming bipartisan support. Moreover, initially it

28. *Lalli v. Lalli*, 439 U.S. 259, 268 (opinion of Powell, J.) (1978).
29. *Goesart v. Cleary*, 335 U.S. 464 (1948).
30. *Hoyt v. Florida*, 358 U.S. 57 (1961).
31. Ibid., 61–62.

seemed likely that the ERA would easily gain the thirty-eight state ratifications necessary to add it to the Constitution.

It was against this background that the Burger Court dramatically reshaped the constitutional status of sex discrimination.[32] The process began in 1971 with the decision in *Reed v. Reed*. There the Court unanimously struck down an Idaho statute requiring probate courts to prefer men over women as estate administrators in cases of "equal degrees of relationship" to the decedent. Speaking for the Court, Chief Justice Burger struggled to justify the result in terms of the rational basis analysis. Resorting to an older formulation of the rational basis test, he argued that the classification "must be reasonable, not arbitrary, and must rest upon some ground of difference having a fair and substantial relationship to the object of the legislation." Rejecting the state's justification of administrative convenience (based on the premise that men are, on the average, more likely than women to have significant business experience), Burger contended that "[t]o give a mandatory preference to members of either sex over members of the other, merely to accomplish the elimination of hearings on the merits, is to make the very kind of arbitrary legislative choice forbidden by the Equal Protection Clause."[33]

Two years later, in *Frontiero v. Richardson*, the liberal wing of the Court made a concerted but ultimately unsuccessful effort to raise the formal standard of review in sex discrimination cases. *Frontiero* was a challenge to a federal statute that dealt with the right of members of the armed forces to claim spouses as dependents for the purpose of obtaining a number of increased benefits. Servicemen were automatically entitled to claim their wives as dependents; a servicewoman, by contrast, could only claim her husband if she could prove that she actually provided the husband with more than one-half of his support. At the initial conference, Chief Justice Burger and Justice Rehnquist (who joined the Court after the decision in *Reed*) argued that the *Frontiero* statute was constitutional; however, the remaining justices disagreed, and ultimately even the chief justice agreed that the statute unconstitutionally discriminated against women. Nonetheless, the *Frontiero* Court ultimately failed to produce a majority opinion.[34]

---

32. The Burger Court's approach to gender-based classifications is described in detail in Ann E. Freedman, "Sex Equality, Sex Differences, and the Supreme Court," *Yale Law Journal* 92 (1983): 913–68; and Earl M. Maltz, "The Concept of the Doctrine of the Court in Constitutional Law," *Georgia Law Review* 16 (1982): 357–405.

33. *Reed v. Reed*, 404 U.S. 71 (1971).

34. *Frontiero v. Richardson*, 411 U.S. 677 (1973). The internal debate over the appropriate standard of review to be used in *Frontiero* is described in John C. Jeffries, Jr., *Justice Lewis F. Powell, Jr.* (New York: Charles Scribner's Sons, 1994), 507–9; and Bernard Schwartz, *The Ascent of Pragmatism: The Burger Court in Action* (New York: Addison-Wesley, 1990), 222–29.

Justice Brennan was assigned the task of preparing an opinion for the Court. The first draft that was circulated would simply have struck down the statutory discrimination solely on the authority of *Reed*.[35] Justice White, however, pressed for the designation of sex as a suspect classification, subject to strict scrutiny. White quickly gained the support of Justices Brennan, Marshall, and Douglas for his proposal. By contrast, Justice Powell opposed White's initiative, noting that the Equal Rights Amendment was currently under consideration by the states and that it would be inappropriate to in essence short-circuit the constitutionally mandated amendment process by judicially designating sex as a suspect classification. The chief justice and Justice Blackmun would later join an opinion by Powell which emphasized this point. Justice Stewart also refused to adopt White's position, choosing instead to file a brief statement simply citing *Reed v. Reed* and concluding that the discrimination in *Frontiero* was "invidious."

These developments left the advocates of strict scrutiny one vote short of a majority. Nonetheless, rather than seeking a compromise, Justice Brennan chose to file a plurality opinion making the argument that sex should be considered a suspect classification. Brennan based this conclusion on the nation's long history of sex discrimination, the underrepresentation of women in political policy-making roles, the fact that sex is an immutable characteristic, and the recognition by Congress that sex discrimination was a problem of national proportions.

One of the most notable features of the *Frontiero* debate is the juxtaposition between Brennan's use of congressional action to justify his position and Powell's deference to the ongoing process of ratifying the ERA. Implicitly at least, Brennan's opinion was a firm reaffirmation of the most basic tenet of the theory of the "living Constitution"—the idea that constitutional principles should change with evolving social mores, and that the Court was the institution best suited to make these changes. From this perspective, the fact that Congress had protected women through the Equal Pay Act of 1963 and Title VII of the Civil Rights Act of 1964, and had sent the ERA to the states for ratification, was a reliable indication of changes in society's attitudes toward women, and could appropriately be considered in the formulation of constitutional principles by the judiciary. By contrast, while Powell certainly did not completely reject the idea of the living Constitution, his worldview was less court-centered, and thus he was more anxious to await the outcome of the formal process of constitutional change by other institutions.

In any event, given the momentum that seemed to be carrying the ERA toward ratification in 1973, Justice Powell and his allies in *Frontiero* had every

35. Brennan's initial draft can be found in Bernard Schwartz, *The Unpublished Opinions of the Burger Court* (New York: Oxford University Press, 1988), 70–77.

reason to believe that a formal prohibition on sex discrimination would soon become part of the Constitution. However, in large measure because of the furor created by the decision in *Roe v. Wade*[36] the same year, the political dynamic abruptly shifted, and ERA proponents were unable to garner majorities in the three additional state legislatures necessary to add the amendment to the Constitution. Thus the Court was left to deal with issues of sex discrimination under the more general rubric of the Equal Protection Clause.

Against this background, despite the failure of a majority of the Court to endorse strict scrutiny in *Frontiero*, the Burger Court showed consistent hostility to laws that facially discriminated against women. After *Frontiero*, no such discrimination was found constitutional by a majority of the Court; no justice even authored a dissent on the merits in such a case.[37] Indeed, even Justice Rehnquist concurred in striking down the sex-based classifications in both *Weinberger v. Weisenfeld*[38] and *Kirchberg v. Feenstra.*[39]

By contrast, the Court remained deeply divided over the proper treatment of state action that discriminated against men. Such discrimination presented issues that were somewhat different from those raised by discrimination against women. Men were plainly not politically disadvantaged in American society; moreover, even some who proclaimed themselves opposed to sex discrimination in principle argued that laws which overtly favored women could at times be justified as a means to ameliorate the disadvantages placed upon women by society generally. Others, by contrast, argued that all sex discrimination was wrong in principle and that, in any event, even laws that on their face favored women would ultimately redound to their detriment by reinforcing the patriarchal structure of society.

Given the sharp divisions of opinion on this issue among the intelligentsia generally, it should not be surprising that the Burger Court also failed to reach consensus on the proper treatment of discrimination against men. Initially, with only Justices Brennan, Marshall, and White dissenting, the Court upheld a property tax exemption that favored widows rather than widowers, as well as a statute which provided that male officers in the military who did not achieve promotion would be discharged in a shorter time than women in similar situations.[40] By contrast, in *Craig v. Boren*, only Chief Justice Burger and Justice Rehnquist were willing to uphold an Oklahoma statute that allowed women between the ages of eighteen and twenty-one the

---

36. *Roe v. Wade*, 410 U.S. 113 (1973), discussed in chapter 13.

37. In *Vorchheimer v. School District of Philadelphia*, 430 U.S. 703 (1977), with Justice Rehnquist not participating, an equally divided Court affirmed a lower court judgment that allowed a school system to maintain sex-segregated schools for gifted children.

38. *Weinberger v. Weisenfeld*, 420 U.S. 636, 655 (1975).

39. *Kirchberg v. Feenstra*, 450 U.S. 455 (1981).

40. *Kahn v. Shevin*, 416 U.S. 351 (1974); *Schlesinger v. Ballard*, 419 U.S. 498 (1975).

right to buy 3.2 percent beer but denied that right to men of the same age. Speaking for the remaining members of the Court, Justice Brennan for the first time formally established an intermediate standard for review for *all* sex-based classifications, concluding that the Oklahoma classification was unconstitutional because it was not "substantially related to an important governmental interest."[41]

Although *Craig* definitively established the substantial relationship test as the standard of review for most gender-based classifications, a majority of the justices were more deferential in cases involving the traditional prerogatives of Congress. *Fiallo v. Bell* provides a classic illustration. *Fiallo* was a challenge to an immigration statute that granted preferential treatment to all persons whose mothers were citizens or permanent residents of the United States, as well as those who were the *legitimate* offspring of fathers who were citizens or permanent residents. However, *illegitimate* offspring could not claim special status based on a biological relationship to their natural fathers.[42]

In an opinion joined by Justice Brennan and "substantially" by Justice White, Justice Marshall noted that the statute not only discriminated on the basis of legitimacy and sex, but also effectively denied the parties the right to live together as a family—a right which the Court had deemed fundamental in other contexts. They also emphasized that the latter right was being denied not only to potential immigrants, but also to a group of citizens seeking to reunite their families. Against this background, Marshall concluded that the discrimination should be held unconstitutional.[43]

The other members of the Court disagreed, however. Speaking through Justice Powell, the majority emphasized that "the power to expel or exclude aliens [is] a fundamental sovereign attribute exercised by the Government's political departments largely immune from judicial control." Against this background, they concluded that "it is not the judicial role in cases of this sort to probe and test the justifications for the legislative decision."[44]

Similar considerations were also implicated in *Rostker v. Goldberg*,[45] the most politically prominent sex discrimination case of the Burger era. The litigation that culminated in the *Rostker* decision was spawned by the reinstatement of the requirement that eighteen-year-old males register for the potential draft of civilians into military service. Passed during the administration of President Jimmy Carter, the legislation was controversial for two quite different reasons. First, a substantial number of legislators opposed the

---

41. *Craig v. Boren*, 429 U.S. 190 (1976).
42. *Fiallo v. Bell*, 430 U.S. 737 (1977).
43. Ibid., 800–16 (Marshall, J., dissenting).
44. Ibid., 792 [quoting *Shaughnessy v. Mezei*, 345 U.S. 206, 210 (1953)], 799 (citation and footnote omitted).
45. *Rostker v. Goldberg*, 453 U.S. 57 (1981).

draft in principle; this group saw inclusion of women in the draft registration requirement as a means to defeat the entire concept. Second, feminists generally argued that excluding women from the requirement of draft registration was a classic example of discrimination which, while facially discriminating against men, in fact reinforced the subordination of women by implying that they were unsuited to perform the essential function of defending society against foreign enemies. These two groups joined forces in launching a constitutional attack on the registration statute, arguing that it unconstitutionally discriminated on the basis of sex.

Anticipating the constitutional challenge, supporters of the registration statute had testified in Congress that the draft was designed specifically to provide combat troops, and had noted that women were barred from combat under existing federal statutes and military policy. This point was emphasized in the committee report which accompanied the registration statute in the Senate. As part of their litigation strategy, the plaintiffs made a tactical decision *not* to challenge the ban on the use of women in combat. Against this background, with only Justices Brennan, Marshall, and White dissenting, the Court rejected the constitutional challenge in *Rostker.*

Speaking for all members of the majority, Justice Rehnquist declined to decide whether a lower standard of review might be appropriate in view of the deference that the Court traditionally pays to other branches of government on issues related to the military. Rehnquist argued that, in any event, the discrimination in the registration statute would survive under the substantial relationship test because women were excluded from combat roles. By contrast, Thurgood Marshall argued in his dissent that the *Boren* standard was in fact applicable to the case, and that the government could have achieved its goal in a gender-neutral fashion by requiring all eighteen year olds to register, and then (if it appeared that only combat troops were needed) drafting only men

The fact that a military-related judgment was involved in *Rostker* no doubt influenced the votes of some of the justices in the majority; however, even where no military or foreign policy issue was involved, no consensus emerged on the Burger Court on the appropriate factors to be considered in cases involving discrimination against men.[46] Nonetheless, throughout the post-*Craig* era, a majority of the justices remained committed to the view that all cases of sex discrimination were to be subjected to an intermediate level of scrutiny. The last real challenge to this principle came in *Michael M. v. Superior Court.*[47]

---

46. The interaction among the positions of the justices is explored in detail in Maltz, "The Concept of the Doctrine of the Court in Constitutional Law," 362–99.

47. *Michael M. v. Superior Court*, 450 U.S. 464 (1981). The internal dynamics of the *Michael M.* decision are described in Bernard Schwartz, *The Ascent of Pragmatism*, 229–31.

Michael M. was a constitutional challenge to a California statute which punished men for having sexual intercourse with women under the age of eighteen, but did not punish women for having sexual intercourse with men under the age of eighteen. At the conference on the case, Chief Justice Burger and Justices Stewart, Blackmun, Powell, and Rehnquist voted to reject the constitutional challenge, and the chief justice assigned the opinion to Justice Rehnquist. Rehnquist produced an opinion which sought to recharacterize *Craig* as a case that simply applied the traditional rational basis test with a somewhat "sharper focus" and which stated that the Court should not base its judgment on the actual motive for the adoption of a statute, but rather on the state's asserted justification. Focusing on the state's interest in preventing young women from becoming pregnant, he concluded that "a legislature acts well within its authority when it elects to punish only the participant who, by nature, suffers few of the consequences of his conduct" and "we cannot say that a gender-neutral statute would be as effective as the statute California has chosen to enact."[48]

Fearing that its reasoning diluted the concept of intermediate scrutiny, Justice Blackmun refused to join Rehnquist's analysis, thereby denying it the status of a majority opinion. Blackmun chose instead to file a rambling, almost incoherent concurrence devoted largely to criticizing decisions which allowed the government to limit the access of minors to abortion and questioning the wisdom of prosecuting the specific defendant in *Michael M.*[49] The opinion aptly symbolizes Blackmun's role in the development of the Court's sex discrimination jurisprudence; while he was one of the critical swing justices, his votes did not follow a discernible pattern.

The positions of a number of other justices in *Michael M.* also exemplified their views on discrimination against men more generally. Not surprisingly, the chief justice, who almost invariably concurred with Justice Rehnquist in rejecting constitutional challenges to such discrimination,[50] also joined his opinion in *Michael M.* Their most frequent ally among the remaining justices was Justice Stewart. In *Michael M.*, Stewart joined the plurality opinion but also wrote separately, reiterating his view that the proper inquiry was whether a statute "invidiously classifies similarly situated people on the basis of [sex]."

The dissenting opinions in *Michael M.* also reflected themes that would recur throughout the Burger Court's sex discrimination jurisprudence. For

48. *Michael M. v. Superior Court*, 450 U.S. at 468–69, 472 n. 7, 473 (opinion of Rehnquist, J.).

49. Ibid., 481–87 (Blackmun, J., concurring in the judgment).

50. The single exception was Burger's vote in *Wengler v. Druggists Mutual Insurance Co.*, 446 U.S. 142 (1980). However, the majority opinion in *Wengler* was based largely on principles of stare decisis, and in any event, Burger's position was in no way crucial to the outcome.

example, throughout the Burger era, Justices Brennan, White, and Marshall were consistently hostile to statutes that discriminated against men.[51] Thus, in *Michael M.*, they took issue with virtually every premise of the plurality opinion, arguing that the Court should examine the legislature's actual reasons for adopting a statute and that the state of California had failed to carry the burden of demonstrating that a sex-neutral statute would be less effective in deterring teen pregnancy than the means actually chosen.[52]

By contrast, Justice Stevens, like Justice Blackmun, was a swing voter in the sex discrimination cases. However, unlike Blackmun, his voting pattern reflected a coherent, well-thought-out approach, which he described in *Michael M.* itself. Stevens divided sex-based classifications into two groups— those which reflected physical differences between men and women, and those which did not reflect such differences. He viewed the first group of classifications as presumptively constitutional, but subject to invalidation upon a showing that the justification for the discrimination was "illusory or wholly inadequate." Conversely, where the challenged discrimination was not based on any physical difference between the sexes, in his view the state bore the burden of showing that the classification was not simply a by-product of traditional ways of thinking about sex roles. In *Michael M.* itself, Stevens conceded that the statute could plausibly be viewed as reflecting the fact that only women could become pregnant; nonetheless, he voted to strike down the statute because of the danger that the classication reflected "a habitual attitude [about sexual relations which is] nothing more than an irrational prejudice."[53]

Unlike the other swing justices, Powell chose not to write in *Michael M.*, choosing instead to simply concur in the plurality opinion. His positions in other cases, however, reveal an analytic framework that was not less developed than that of Stevens. Powell was generally sympathetic to statutory discriminations designed to compensate women for their inferior economic opportunities.[54] His approach to other issues was exemplified by his treatment of the claims of biological fathers of illegitimate children, fathers who sought to assert parental rights over their offspring.

---

51. The only exceptions were *Califano v. Webster*, 430 U.S. 313 (1977) (per curiam), in which the Court unanimously upheld a provision of the Social Security Act, a provision which was designed to compensate women for their disadvantageous position in the workforce; and Justice Marshall's vote in *Lehr v. Robertson*, 463 U.S. 248 (1983). Bernard Schwartz suggests that Brennan joined the majority in *Webster* in order to have an opportunity to write an opinion which could later be used to support constitutionality of race-based affirmative action. Bernard Schwartz, *Behind Bakke: Affirmative Action and the Supreme Court* (New York: New York University Press, 1988), 42.

52. *Michael M. v. Superior Court*, 450 U.S. at 479–96 (Brennan, J., dissenting).

53. Ibid., 498–99 n. 4, 501 (Stevens, J., dissenting). Stevens describes his approach in similar terms in *Califano v. Goldfarb*, 430 U.S. 199, 223 (Stevens, J., concurring in the result) (1977).

54. *Schlesinger v. Ballard*, 419 U.S. 495 (1975); *Kahn v. Shevin*, 416 U.S. 351 (1974).

In purely ideological terms, these cases raised issues that were closely related to those dealing with the rights of the illegitimate children themselves. The similarities emerged clearly in *Stanley v. Illinois*. There, a father of three children born out of wedlock sought to obtain legal custody of the children after the death of their mother. Notwithstanding the fact that he had an ongoing relationship with both the mother and the children, a state statute created an irrebuttable presumption that he was an unfit parent, and thus not entitled to custody. Over the dissents of Chief Justice Burger and Justice Blackmun, the Court concluded that the statute denied him equal protection by treating him differently from unmarried mothers, married parents, and divorced parents.[55]

Later cases, by contrast, focused specifically on the comparison between the rights of the biological father and those of the mother of the illegitimate children. By definition, neither of the natural parents was married at the time the children were born; thus, unlike the illegitimacy cases, the formal equal protection issue was not one of discrimination on the basis of legally created status. Rather, the question was whether the government could vary the rights of unmarried parents on the basis of gender. *Caban v. Mohammed*[56] and *Parham v. Hughes*[57]—each decided by a five-to-four vote on the same day in 1979—established the basic parameters of the constitutional limitations on the power of the state to make such distinctions.

The composition of the Court which decided *Caban* and *Parham* differed substantially from that of the *Stanley* Court. Justices Powell and Rehnquist had not participated in *Stanley*, and in the interim, Justice Stevens had replaced Justice Douglas. Each of the new justices had an important influence on the outcome of the cases. In *Caban*, the Court struck down a state statute that allowed biological mothers but not biological fathers of illegitimate children to block the adoption of the children by third parties; in *Parham*, by contrast, the majority upheld a law that allowed mothers to recover for the wrongful death of their illegitimate children but denied that right to biological fathers who had not formally legitimated their children.

A majority of the justices took positions that were analogous to those that they had taken in the intestate succession cases. The chief justice and Justices Rehnquist and Stewart voted to uphold both statutes, while Justices Brennan, Marshall, and White concluded that both were unconstitutional. Justices Blackmun and Stevens, by contrast, switched sides, with Blackmun (despite his dissent in *Stanley*) joining the Brennan group in *Caban* and *Parham*, and Stevens voting to uphold both statutes. While Blackmun gave

55. *Stanley v. Illinois*, 405 U.S. 246 (1972).
56. *Caban v. Mohammed*, 441 U.S. 380 (1979).
57. *Parham v. Hughes*, 441 U.S. 347 (1979).

no explanation for the apparent dissonance in his views, Stevens emphasized the physical basis for the difference between the treatment of mothers and that of fathers, noting that only the mother carries the child, and thus her identity will always be certain, whereas that of the father may be unknown.[58]

As in the intestate succession cases, this division left the balance of power with Justice Powell, who voted to strike down the *Caban* statute and uphold the state law in *Parham*. He sounded the same themes that had guided his approach in the intestate succession cases, arguing that the father in *Caban* was unable to remove his disability, while the father in *Parham* would have gained the right to maintain the wrongful death action if he had formally legitimated the child. Similarly, in *Lehr v. Robertson*,[59] he joined the *Caban* dissenters in voting to uphold a statute that granted biological fathers of illegitimates the right to be informed of adoption proceedings only if they acknowledged their paternity on a "putative father registry" or otherwise consistently acknowledged their paternity.

The themes that the various justices sounded in *Michael M.*, *Caban*, and *Parham* recurred consistently in Burger Court sex discrimination cases. Chief Justice Burger and Justice Rehnquist consistently voted to uphold classifications that favored women on their face; they were joined in all but the most egregious cases by Justice Stewart. Conversely, Justices Brennan, Marshall, and White almost invariably voted to strike down laws that discriminated on the basis of sex. With the retirement of Justice Douglas in 1976, this left the balance of power with Harry Blackmun, Lewis Powell, and John Paul Stevens, each of whom pursued his own idiosyncratic view of the proper approach.

Not surprisingly, the interaction among these different visions produced a complex pattern of decisions. In the period from 1976 through 1982, the Burger Court decided ten cases that the majority conceptualized as involving discrimination against men. The Court struck down four of the relevant statutes and upheld six. Only one of the cases was decided unanimously, while four were decided by a vote of five to four. In three cases, the justices could not even produce a majority opinion.[60]

Against this background, even a small shift in judicial sentiment could have important implications for the outcome of cases. The evolution of the law dealing with single-sex education dramatically illustrates this point. In 1977 the issue came before the Court in *Vorchheimer v. School District of*

---

58. *Caban v. Mohammed,* 441 U.S. at 405 (Stevens, J., dissenting).

59. *Lehr v. Robertson,* 463 U.S. 248 (1983).

60. *Califano v. Webster,* 430 U.S. 313 (1977), was the unanimous decision. *Califano v. Goldfarb,* 430 U.S. 199 (1977), *Parham v. Hughes,* 441 U.S. 347 (1979), *Caban v. Mohammed,* 441 U.S. 380 (1979), and *Michael M. v. Superior Court,* 450 U.S. 464 (1981) were decided on votes of five to four. There was no majority opinion in *Goldfarb, Parham,* or *Michael M.*

Philadelphia. In *Vorchheimer,* the city of Philadelphia maintained separate high schools for intellectually talented boys and intellectually talented girls. Acting on the assumption that the two schools provided equal educational opportunity, the court of appeals concluded that this arrangement did not run afoul of the Constitution.[61] With Justice Rehnquist not participating because of illness, this judgment was affirmed by an equally divided Court, as the chief justice and Justices Stewart, Blackmun, and Powell voted to reject the challenge and the remaining justices took the opposing view.[62]

Mississippi University for Women [MUW] v. Hogan[63] turned out quite differently. *Hogan* was a challenge to the constitutionality of Mississippi's maintenance of a nursing school open only to women. Chief Justice Burger and Justices Blackmun, Powell, and Rehnquist voted to reject the challenge, noting that other state-supported nursing schools were open to men and that the state was simply attempting to provide potential students with a choice between single-sex and coeducational training programs. If the case had been decided only one year earlier, one would have expected Potter Stewart to join this group and the constitutional challenge to have been rejected. However, Stewart had retired, and the newly appointed Sandra Day O'Connor examined the *Hogan* program with a more critical eye. Writing for the five-justice majority, O'Connor argued that, because there was no showing that women lacked adequate opportunities for training in nursing, the state could not justify the MUW program as compensation for past discrimination. Instead, she contended that the refusal to admit men to the program simply perpetuated the stereotypical view that nursing was a women's profession. Thus, invoking the substantial relationship test, O'Connor concluded that men must be admitted to the program.

Despite the decision in *Hogan,* the overall pattern of the sex discrimination jurisprudence of the Burger Court reflects one obvious point—a majority of the justices viewed sex discrimination quite differently than race discrimination. However, in some circumstances, imperatives of legal ideology required the justices to directly import concepts that had been developed to deal with the race issue. The Court's treatment of disparate impact claims clearly reflected the influence of these imperatives.

At the constitutional level, *Personnel Administrator of Massachusetts v. Feeney*[64] dramatically illustrates this point. *Feeney* was a challenge to a state civil service rule that gave absolute preference to veterans of military service. Ninety-eight percent of the beneficiaries of the statute were male;

61. *Vorchheimer v. School District of Philadelphia,* 532 F.2d 280 (3d Cir. 1976).
62. *Vorchheimer v. School District of Philadelphia,* 430 U.S. 703 (1977).
63. *Mississippi University for Women [MUW] v. Hogan,* 458 U.S. 718 (1982).
64. *Personnel Administrator of Massachusetts v. Feeney,* 442 U.S. 256 (1979).

moreover, for many years jobs that were filled primarily by women had been exempted from the operation of the statute. Nonetheless, the Court applied a rational basis test to reject the claim that the statute unconstitutionally discriminated against women.

Justices Brennan and Marshall dissented from this holding; nonetheless, all of the justices agreed that, since *Feeney* involved an equal protection challenge, the critical question was the proper application of the standards that had been enunciated in *Washington v. Davis*.[65] Speaking for the majority, Potter Stewart concluded that only a subjective intention to discriminate between men and women could justify invocation of the substantial relationship test; by contrast, Brennan and Marshall argued that the standard of review should be raised whenever a government decision maker was chargeable with knowledge that his action would place one sex at a substantial disadvantage.

Like *Davis* itself, however, the practical significance of *Feeney* was limited by the centrality of impact analysis to the Court's interpretation of Title VII of the Civil Rights Act of 1964. Some of the factors cited to support the use of impact analysis in *Griggs v. Duke Power Co.* related specifically to the position of African Americans in the social and political structure.[66] Nonetheless, because discrimination against race and sex were prohibited by the same sentence of Title VII, widely accepted conventions of statutory interpretation required that the same basic standards of proof be applied to allegations of race and sex discrimination, respectively. Thus, in *Dothard v. Rawlinson*, although differing on the precise nature of the burden of proof that *Griggs* placed on employers, all members of the Court agreed that sex discrimination claims were subject to impact analysis under Title VII.[67]

The paradigm of race discrimination also had a significant impact on the Court's analysis of claims that women had been subject to disparate treatment that violated Title VII—in particular, in cases dealing with "defined benefit" retirement plans. In their simplest form, such plans require employees to contribute a certain amount per month and in return provide a specified level of monthly benefits after the employee's retirement, benefits which continue until the death of the employee. Women, however, have a longer average life span than men; thus, if a woman who made the same monthly contribution as a man received the same monthly benefit after retirement, she would, on average, receive a greater return on her contribution. Prior to the adoption of Title VII, pension plans often sought to address this disparity by requiring a larger monthly contribution from women, thus reducing the amount of take-home pay available to female employees.

---

65. *Washington v. Davis*, 426 U.S. 229 (1976).
66. *Griggs v. Duke Power Co.*, 401 U.S. 424, 430 (1971).
67. *Dothard v. Rawlinson*, 433 U.S. 321 (1977).

In *City of Los Angeles Dept. of Water and Power v. Manhart*, Chief Justice Burger and Justice Rehnquist argued that Title VII did not prohibit this practice. They reasoned that requiring larger contributions from women was simply an actuarially sound method of ensuring that men and women would in fact receive equal returns on their contributions. The remainder of the Court, however, took a different view. Speaking for the majority, Justice Stevens acknowledged that the disparity in contributions was not based on a fictional or stereotypical view of sex roles, but rather on a real, physical difference between men and women. Nonetheless, he concluded that Title VII required equalization of contributions. In support of this view, Stevens first noted that the statute by its terms protected *individuals* from discrimination on the basis of sex, rather than simply providing that women as a class should be treated equally with men as a class. Therefore, he argued that "even a true generalization about the class is an insufficient reason for [disadvantaging] an individual to whom the generalization does not apply."[68]

Stevens bolstered his argument by an analogy to race discrimination. Noting that the average life span of African Americans was substantially less than that of whites, he observed that no one would argue that this fact justified a race-based differential in take-home pay. Thus, he concluded, the same principle applied to the sex-based differential at issue in *Manhart*.[69]

By contrast, in other contexts, the jurisprudence of race discrimination was of little aid in resolving sex-related problems. First, some statutory provisions did not deal with race at all, but instead related only to sex discrimination. Second, in some situations, the race cases simply did not provide clear analogies. In each case, the Burger Court was forced to develop a jurisprudential approach that was uniquely applicable to issues of sex discrimination.

One important problem involved the interaction between the Equal Pay Act (EPA) and Title VII. Adopted one year prior to Title VII, EPA by its terms singled out sex discrimination for special treatment, prohibiting employers from using sex as a criterion in determining compensation. However, the act had only a relatively narrow scope; it applied only where members of different sexes were performing "equal work on jobs the performance of which requires equal skill, effort and responsibility" and specifically excluded pay differentials "based on any other factor other than sex." Over the dissents of the chief justice and Justices Powell and Rehnquist, the Burger Court gave this exclusion a relatively narrow reading in *Corning Glass Works v. Brennan*,[70] nonetheless, the plaintiff's burden of proof under the EPA remained far more stringent than that generally required under Title VII.

---

68. *City of Los Angeles Dept. of Water and Power v. Manhart*, 435 U.S. 402 (1978).
69. Ibid.
70. *Corning Glass Works v. Brennan*, 417 U.S. 188 (1974).

One difficulty arising from this disparity was that the so-called "Bennett Amendment" provided that Title VII would not apply to any differences in compensation "authorized" by EPA. In *County of Washington v. Gunther*, Chief Justice Burger and Justices Stewart, Powell, and Rehnquist insisted that the Bennett Amendment required plaintiffs to meet the EPA equal work standard in order to recover for sex discrimination in compensation. Speaking for the majority, Justice Brennan disagreed; distinguishing between discrimination "authorized" by EPA and that which was simply not prohibited, Brennan concluded that the dissent's reading of the Bennett Amendment would "deprive [some] victims of discrimination of a remedy, without clear congressional mandate."[71]

Feminists had every reason to be satisfied with the Court's narrow reading of the Bennett Amendment. However, they were less enamored of the Court's treatment of other issues where the rules governing sex and race discrimination diverged. One such issue involved the interpretation of the concept of a "bona fide occupational qualification" (BFOQ)—an exception to Title VII's prohibition on sex discrimination that did not apply in race discrimination cases. In *Dothard*, only Justices Brennan and Marshall dissented from the conclusion that the BFOQ exception allowed the state of Alabama to require guards in its maximum security prisons to be of the same sex as the inmates of the prison.

While doctrinally important, *Dothard*'s practical significance was quite limited. Justice Rehnquist's majority opinion emphasized that the BFOQ exception was extremely narrow and suggested that the exception might not even be applicable to some maximum-security prisons. By contrast, the consequences of the Burger Court's treatment of pregnancy-related issues were potentially more far reaching; ultimately, however, congressional action would mitigate these consequences.

Geduldig v. Aiello established the basic Burger Court position on pregnancy-based distinctions.[72] *Geduldig* held that the state of California could constitutionally exclude disabilities related to pregnancy from the conditions covered by the state disability insurance program. Speaking for all members of the Court except Justices Douglas, Brennan, and Marshall, Justice Stewart concluded that the exclusion did not constitute sex discrimination, and that the state had a rational basis for excluding pregnancy-related disabilities from coverage. Two years later, the same majority used similar logic in *General Electric Co. v. Gilbert*, holding that Title VII did not require an employer to cover pregnancy in its disability insurance plan.[73]

---

71. *County of Washington v. Gunther*, 452 U.S. 161 (1981).
72. *Geduldig v. Aiello*, 417 U.S. 485 (1974).
73. *General Electric Co. v. Gilbert*, 429 U.S. 125 (1976).

Geduldig and *Gilbert* did not reflect complete indifference to classifications based on pregnancy. In *Cleveland Board of Education v. LaFleur*, only the chief justice and Justice Rehnquist were willing to countenance a requirement that all pregnant women take a mandatory maternity leave during the last five months of their pregnancies. Justice Powell argued that the classification failed the rational basis test; however, speaking for the other members of the majority, Justice Stewart instead relied on the novel, short-lived theory that the creation of an irrebuttable presumption of disability violated the Due Process Clause.[74] In addition, in *Nashville Gas Co. v. Satty* a unanimous Court limited the reach of *Gilbert*, holding that Title VII barred a company from requiring women who returned to work after taking maternity leave to forfeit accumulated seniority.[75]

One year after *Satty*, Congress adopted the Pregnancy Discrimination Act (PDA) with the explicit intention of overruling *Gilbert*. The PDA defined discrimination based on pregnancy as sex discrimination; however, both the language of the statute and the legislative history of the PDA itself could plausibly have been read to support the proposition that employers need not cover pregnancy-related expenses in medical plans for *dependents* of employees. However, in *Newport News Shipbuilding and Dry Dock Co. v. Equal Employment Opportunity Commission*, only Justices Powell and Rehnquist were willing to accept this argument; Chief Justice Burger joined the remaining members of the *LaFleur* majority in holding that this practice violated the PDA.[76]

On issues involving discrimination against women, *Newport News* and *LaFleur* were far more representative of Burger Court jurisprudence than *Geduldig* and *Gilbert*. Thus, despite their defeats in cases such as *Feeney* and *Dothard*, liberal political forces generally had reason to be well satisfied with the Court's sex discrimination jurisprudence. They had even more reason to applaud the Court's approach to another sex-related question—the politically explosive issue of abortion rights.

---

74. *Cleveland Board of Education v. LaFleur*, 414 U.S. 632 (1974).
75. *Nashville Gas Co. v. Satty*, 434 U.S. 136 (1977).
76. *Newport News Shipbuilding and Dry Dock Co. v. Equal Employment Opportunity Commission [EEOC]*, 462 U.S. 669 (1983).

Table 12.1: Voting Patterns

	Bur	Dou	Bre	Mar	Whi	Stew	Bla	Reh	Pow	Stev	Oco
Indigency											
Boddie v. *Connecticut* 401 U.S. 371 (1971) (fee for divorce)	U	U	U	U	U	U	U	NP	NP	NP	NP
United States v. *Kras* 409 U.S. 434 (1973) (fee for bankruptcy)	C	U	U	U	C	U	C	C	C	NP	NP
Ross v. Moffitt 417 U.S. 600 (1974) (fee for discretionary appeal)	C	U	U	U	C	C	C	C	C	NP	NP
Age											
Massachusetts Bd. *of Retirement v.* *Murgia* 427 U.S. 307 (1976) (mandatory retire-ment for police)	C	NP	C	U	C	C	C	C	C	C	NP
Vance v. Bradley 440 U.S. 93 (1979) (mandatory retire-ment from foreign service)	C	NP	C	U	C	C	C	C	C	C	NP
Disability											
Pennhurst State *School v.* *Halderman* 465 U.S. 89 (1984) (bill of rights for mentally retarded)	NI	NP	BI	BI	BI	NI	NI	NI	NI	NI	NP
City of Cleburne v. *Cleburne Living* *Center* 473 U.S. 432 (1985) (denial of permit for group home)	U	NP	U	U	U	NP	U	U	U	U	U

	Bur	Dou	Bre	Mar	Whi	Stew	Bla	Reh	Pow	Stev	Oco
Marriage											
Zablocki v. Redhail 434 U.S. 374 (1978) (limitation on right to marry)	U	NP	U	U	U	U	U	C	U	U	NP
Califano v. Jobst 434 U.S. 47 (1978) (marriage leads to reduction in benefits)	C	NP	C	C	C	C	C	C	C	C	NP
Legitimacy											
Gomez v. Perez 409 U.S. 535 (1973) (illegitimates have no right to support)	U	U	U	U	U	?	U	?	U	NP	NP
Jiminez v. Weinberger 417 U.S. 628 (1974) (limitation on death benefits)	U	U	U	U	U	U	U	C	U	NP	NP
Mathews v. Lucas 427 U.S. 495 (1976) (limitation on disability benefits)	C	NP	U	U	C	C	C	C	C	U	NP
Labine v. Vincent 401 U.S. 532 (1971) (no intestate succession for illegitimates)	C	U	U	U	U	C	C	NP	NP	NP	NP
Weber v. Aetna Casualty and Surety 406 U.S. 164 (1972) (limitation on worker's compensation)	U	U	U	U	U	U	U	C	U	NP	NP
Trimble v. Gordon 430 U.S. 762 (1977) (no intestate succession for illegitimates)	C	NP	U	U	U	C	C	C	U	U	NP

	Bur	Dou	Bre	Mar	Whi	Stew	Bla	Reh	Pow	Stev	Oco
Lalli v. Lalli 439 U.S. 259 (1978) (limit on intestate succession for illegitimates)	C	NP	U	U	U	C	C	C	C	U	NP

Gender

Constitutional Issues

	Bur	Dou	Bre	Mar	Whi	Stew	Bla	Reh	Pow	Stev	Oco
Reed v. Reed 404 U.S. 71 (1971) (gender preference for estate administration)	U	U	U	U	U	U	U	NP	NP	NP	NP
Frontiero v. Richardson 411 U.S. 677 (1973) (gender preference in allowance for dependents)	U	U	U	U	U	U	U	C	U	NP	NP
Craig v. Boren 429 U.S. 190 (1976) (only young women may purchase 3.2% beer)	C	NP	U	U	U	U	U	C	U	U	NP
Fiallo v. Bell 430 U.S. 787 (1977) (immigration preference for illegitimate children)	C	NP	U	U	U	C	C	C	C	C	NP
Rostker v. Goldberg 453 U.S. 57 (1981) (only males required to register for draft)	C	NP	U	U	U	C	C	C	C	C	NP
Michael M. v. Superior Court 450 U.S. 464 (1981) (only males liable for statutory rape)	C	NP	U	U	U	C	C	C	C	U	NP
Stanley v. Illinois 405 U.S. 645 (1972) (father of illegitimate irrebuttably presumed unfit)	C	NP	U	U	U	U	C	NP	NP	NP	NP

	Bur	Dou	Bre	Mar	Whi	Stew	Bla	Reh	Pow	Stev	Oco
Caban v. Mohammed 441 U.S. 380 (1979) (father may not block adoption of illegitimate offspring)	C	NP	U	U	U	C	U	C	U	C	NP
Parham v. Hughes 441 U.S. 347 (1979) (some fathers may not recover for wrongful death of illegitimate offspring)	C	NP	U	U	U	C	U	C	C	C	NP
Lehr v. Robertson 463 U.S. 248 (1983) (some fathers not entitled to be informed of adoption of illegitimate offspring)	C	NP	U	C	U	NP	U	C	C	C	C
MUW v. Hogan 458 U.S. 718 (1982) (single-sex nursing school)	C	NP	U	U	U	NP	C	C	C	U	U
Personnel Admin. of Mass. v. Feeney 442 U.S. 256 (1979) (veteran's preference)	C	NP	U	U	C	C	C	C	C	C	NP

Statutory Issues

	Bur	Dou	Bre	Mar	Whi	Stew	Bla	Reh	Pow	Stev	Oco
City of Los Angeles Dept. of Water and Power v. Manhart 435 U.S. 402 (1978) (differential pension benefits)	L	NP	NP	IL	IL	IL	IL	L	IL	NP	NP
Corning Glass Works v. Brennan 417 U.S. 188 (1974) (Equal Pay Act)	NI	BI	BI	BI	BI	NP	NI	NI	BI	NP	NP

	Bur	Dou	Bre	Mar	Whi	Stew	Bla	Reh	Pow	Stev	Oco
County of Washington v. Gunther 452 U.S. 161 (1981) (sex-based wage differential)	L	NP	IL	IL	IL	L	IL	L	L	IL	NP
Dothard v. Rawlinson 433 U.S. 321 (1977) (height and weight requirement for prison guards)	IL	NP	IL	IL	L	IL	IL	IL	IL	IL	NP
Dothard v. Rawlinson 433 U.S. 321 (1977) (sex-segregated prison guards)	L	NP	IL	IL	L	L	L	L	L	L	NP

Pregnancy

	Bur	Dou	Bre	Mar	Whi	Stew	Bla	Reh	Pow	Stev	Oco
Geduldig v. Aiello 417 U.S. 484 (1974) (exclusion of pregnancy from disability insurance)	C	U	U	U	C	C	C	C	C	NP	NP
General Electric v. Gilbert 429 U.S. 125 (1976) (exclusion of pregnancy from disability insurance)	L	L	IL	IL	L	L	L	L	L	NP	NP
Cleveland Bd. of Educ. v. LaFleur 414 U.S. 632 (1974) (mandatory maternity leave)	C	U	U	U	U	U	U	C	U	NP	NP
Nashville Gas Co. v. Satty 434 U.S. 136 (1977) (forfeiture of seniority after maternity leave)	IL	NP	IL	IL	IL	IL	IL	IL	IL	IL	NP

	Bur	Dou	Bre	Mar	Whi	Stew	Bla	Reh	Pow	Stev	Oco
Newport News Shipbuilding v. EEOC 462 U.S. 669 (1983) (denial of maternity benefits for dependents)	IL	NP	IL	IL	IL	NP	IL	L	0L	IL	IL

Key

C	= Constitutional	U	= Unconstitutional	?	= Unclear Position
L	= Legal under Statute	IL	= Illegal under Statute	NP	= Not Participating
BI	= Broad Interpretation of Statutory Protections	NI	= Narrow Interpretation of Statutory Protections		

13

ABORTION AND PRIVACY

During the tenure of Warren Burger, the Court intervened to assert its authority over many significant, emotionally charged political issues. However, in the public mind, one decision stands out as the symbol of the Burger era. That case is, of course, *Roe v. Wade*, the case which sharply limited government authority to regulate abortion.[1]

Prior to the mid 1960s, challenges to abortion regulations would have faced insurmountable doctrinal and political barriers to success. The jurisprudential difficulties were eased considerably by the Warren Court's 1965 decision in *Griswold v. Connecticut*. In *Griswold*, the Court struck down a Connecticut statute that prohibited the use of contraceptives. Speaking for the majority, Justice William O. Douglas sought to avoid the shadow of *Lochner v. New York* by arguing that, taken together, the provisions of the Bill of Rights created a "penumbral" zone of constitutionally protected privacy and the Connecticut statute infringed upon rights that were within that zone of privacy.[2]

Griswold and its progeny were an indispensable predicate to the ultimate pro-choice victory in *Roe*. In the absence of these decisions, it seems likely that the fear of "Lochnering" would have deterred a majority of the Court from taking on such a controversial issue as abortion. *Griswold*, by contrast, presented a challenge to a statute that was anathema to the entire liberal intelligentsia—the primary political constituency of the Warren Court. Thus, in *Griswold* itself, the justices in the majority did not see themselves as dealing with an issue about which there was legitimate controversy; instead, they saw the case as involving a statute that was not only wrong-headed, but anachronistic and oppressive as well. Even the dissenters went out of their way to express their distaste for the Connecticut statute, with Hugo Black declaring, "[T]he law is every bit as offensive to me as it is to my Brethren of the majority," and Potter Stewart labeling it "an uncommonly silly law."[3]

---

1. *Roe v. Wade*, 410 U.S. 113 (1973).
2. *Griswold v. Connecticut*, 381 U.S. 479 (1965); *Lochner v. New York*, 198 U.S. 45 (1905).
3. *Griswold v. Connecticut*, 381 U.S. at 507 (Black, J., dissenting), 527 (Stewart, J., dissenting).

The difficulty, of course, was that the concept of a fundamental constitutional right to privacy had implications that potentially extended far
beyond the dispute over contraception per se. In *Griswold* itself, the analysis
of the majority suggested some possible limiting principles; for example,
Douglas's opinion emphasized the fact that the Connecticut statute denied
married couples the right to use contraceptives. However, in *Eisenstadt v.
Baird,* with Chief Justice Burger dissenting and Justices Powell and Rehnquist not participating, Warren Court holdovers forged a majority holding
that the right to privacy prevented states from restricting the access of
unmarried as well as married couples to contraceptives.[4]

In any event, the abortion issue created more difficult problems for the
Court. First, the political context was quite different. Prior to the mid 1960s,
state laws uniformly prohibited nearly all abortions. Nonetheless, as early as
1959, the American Law Institute had endorsed the legalization of therapeutic abortions in limited circumstances, and the mid 1960s saw the beginning of organized legislative efforts to reform or repeal the statutory
restrictions on abortions. These efforts provoked intense, often bitter
debate, with very mixed results. However, while receiving substantial
national attention, abortion remained very much an issue of local politics.
Moreover, prior to 1973, support for or opposition to abortion rights was not
a major issue defining the distinction between either Democrats and Republicans or liberals and conservatives (although liberals were clearly more
likely to support reform or repeal of statutes that prohibited abortions).[5]

These factors were clearly reflected in the process leading to the nomination and confirmation of Justices Powell and Rehnquist. Richard Nixon
was avowedly opposed to the liberalization of antiabortion laws.[6] Nonetheless,
despite the fact that *Roe* and *Doe v. Bolton* were pending at the time of the
nominations, there is no evidence that he considered the views of either
prospective justice on the issue. Further, the matter was never even mentioned during the long and acrimonious debate over Rehnquist's confirmation by the Senate. In short, even on the eve of the decision in *Roe* itself, no
one seems to have realized that the controversy over abortion would produce
the defining moment of the chief justiceship of Warren Burger.

In 1971 the Burger Court had its first encounter with the abortion issue
in *United States v. Vuitch. Vuitch* was a challenge to a District of Columbia
statute that allowed only those abortions that were "necessary for the preser-

---

4. *Eisenstadt v. Baird,* 405 U.S. 438 (1972).

5. The evolution of the political debate over abortion is described in detail in David J. Garrow, *Liberty and Sexuality: The Right to Privacy and the Making of* Roe v. Wade (New York:
Macmillan Publishing Co., 1994).

6. Ibid., 483.

vation of the mother's life or health." Most of the justices in *Vuitch* limited themselves to consideration of the question of whether the statute was void for vagueness—the basis of the district court judgment which dismissed a criminal prosecution under the statute. Moreover, the case was complicated by a serious jurisdictional issue—the question of whether a direct appeal to the Supreme Court was appropriate under the circumstances of the case. Ultimately, the chief justice and Justices Black, Harlan, White, and Blackmun concluded that, so long as the term "health" was interpreted to included psychological as well as physical well-being, the statute was not unconstitutionally vague. Justice Douglas disagreed, and Justice Stewart argued that the statute could stand only if interpreted in a manner which made it impossible to prosecute physicians who had exercised their professional judgment in good faith.[7]

Two years later, in *Roe* and its companion case, *Doe v. Bolton*,[8] the pro-choice faction launched a more general constitutional attack on government authority to limit the access of pregnant women to abortions. *Roe* involved a Texas statute that prohibited all abortions unless the life of the mother was threatened by the continuation of the pregnancy; *Doe*, on the other hand, challenged a more modern Georgia statute that allowed abortions where the mother's life or health was seriously endangered, but required the operations to be performed in hospitals and set up special procedures for hospital approval of abortions.[9]

Of the seven justices who participated at the initial conference, only Chief Justice Burger and Justice White were willing to uphold the Texas statute. The reactions to the Georgia statute were more complex; while Justices Brennan, Stewart, and Marshall were once again willing to hold the statute unconstitutional on its face, Justices Douglas and Blackmun seemed more ambivalent, suggesting that a more complete record might be needed to adequately evaluate the constitutional issues. Despite the fact that he was clearly in the minority in *Roe*, the chief justice asserted the prerogative to assign both cases to Justice Blackmun. This brought an immediate protest from Justice Douglas, who believed that the cases were appropriately his to

---

7. *United States v. Vuitch*, 402 U.S. 62 (1971). The complexities of *Vuitch* and the Court's internal deliberations on the case are described in detail in Garrow, *Liberty and Sexuality*, 478–80, 493–94.

8. *Doe v. Bolton*, 410 U.S. 179 (1973).

9. The following account of the Court's internal deliberations on *Roe* and *Doe* is taken from Garrow, *Liberty and Sexuality*, 530–38, 547–60, 573–76, 580–87. Garrow's account is generally corroborated by John C. Jeffries, Jr., *Justice Lewis F. Powell, Jr.* (New York: Charles Scribner's Sons, 1994), 336–44; Bernard Schwartz, *The Ascent of Pragmatism: The Burger Court in Action* (New York: Addison-Wesley, 1990), 297–313; and Bob Woodward and Scott Armstrong, *The Brethren: Inside the Supreme Court* (New York: Simon and Schuster, 1979), 165–89, 229–40.

assign. Douglas was particularly disturbed by the *Doe* assignment; he had left the conference under the impression that he was a member of a four-justice majority which was in favor of striking down the Georgia statute, while Blackmun had joined Burger and White in dissent. Nonetheless, after consultations with Justice Brennan, Douglas decided to refrain from circulating a proposed opinion until after Blackmun had completed a draft.

Blackmun was a notoriously slow worker; thus, although the initial conference on the abortion cases took place on December 16, 1971, he did not circulate proposed opinions for *Roe* and *Doe* until May 1972. In both cases, the draft opinions concluded that the challenged statutes were unconstitutional; however, the tenor of the two opinions differed significantly. Hoping to persuade Burger and White to change their votes in *Roe*, Blackmun proposed to rest the judgment in that case solely on vagueness grounds. By contrast, his *Doe* opinion relied on a privacy theory to find the Georgia statute unconstitutional. At the same time, it left open the possibility that the state could constitutionally regulate or even prohibit abortions at some point during the pregnancy.

While Justices Douglas, Brennan, Stewart, and Marshall were not entirely satisfied with even the *Doe* submission, they feared that immediately raising their concerns would lead Blackmun to move for reargument—a reargument at which the newly appointed Justices Powell and Rehnquist might persuade Blackmun to change his basic position on the constitutionality of antiabortion statutes. Thus, they immediately signaled their concurrence in the *Doe* opinion, hoping to strengthen it further at a later stage in the process. Thus, Blackmun could now claim an official five-vote majority.

Nonetheless, stung by a draft dissent from White which pointed out the apparent inconsistency between the *Roe* draft and the *Vuitch* decision, Blackmun circulated a memorandum suggesting that both *Roe* and *Doe* should be reargued. He cited uncertainties about which case should be the vehicle for the lead opinion, as well as the question of whether the opinions should establish more definitive guidelines about the shape of future statutes. Blackmun also noted that in his view, cases of this sensitivity should be decided by a full, nine-member Court. Not surprisingly, the chief justice quickly noted his support for Blackmun's suggestion.

The justices who had noted their concurrence in the proposed *Doe* opinion were stunned and angered by the prospect of reargument. Douglas went so far as to threaten that, if the motion for reargument were granted, he would append an opinion that would openly accuse the chief justice of unfairly manipulating the Court's procedures in an effort to undermine majority views with which he disagreed. At this point, Justices Powell and Rehnquist entered the fray. Neither had been confirmed at the time that *Roe* and *Doe* were argued, and both had heretofore studiously avoided any participation in the Court's internal debates on the abortion issue. However, they now voted with the chief justice and Justices White and Blackmun, creating a five-vote majority for reargument. Douglas was persuaded not to launch his public attack on the tactics of the chief justice, and the reargument took place without incident.

At the conference which followed the reargument, the chief justice began by changing his position on *Roe* and expressing considerable ambivalence about *Doe*. The other justices who had participated in the first conference reaffirmed their positions. As expected, Justice Rehnquist noted his agreement with Justice White. By contrast, to the surprise of many, Justice Powell took the opposing view. Thus, the majority in favor of striking down the abortion laws was now more solid than ever.

Once again, Blackmun set out to craft a majority opinion. He now made *Roe* the lead case and determined that the opinion should clearly establish the parameters of permissible legislative action. Initially, the proposed opinion which he circulated would have left the states essentially free to regulate abortions performed after the first trimester of pregnancy. While Justice Douglas agreed with this approach, Justices Brennan and Powell argued that all previability abortions should be largely free from state regulation.[10] Ultimately, Justice Marshall suggested the compromise which emerged in the final opinion.

Much of the majority opinion in *Roe* is simply a tedious, detailed discussion of the history of abortion law since the time of the ancient Greeks; the only relevance of the discussion is that it seeks to demonstrate that differences in opinion on the issue are long-standing, and that strict regulation of abortions is of relatively recent vintage, dating from the late nineteenth century. Turning more specifically to constitutional theory, Blackmun declined to locate the right to choose an abortion in a broadly libertarian theory of constitutionally protected rights—a theory espoused in the concurrence of William O. Douglas. Instead, Blackmun argued that the right to choose an abortion should be included in the right to privacy because of the confluence of a variety of different considerations:

> The detriment that the State would impose upon the pregnant woman by denying this choice altogether is apparent. Specific and direct harm medically diagnosable even in early pregnancy may be involved. Maternity, or additional offspring, may force on the woman a distressful life and future. Psychological harm may be imminent. Mental and physical health may be taxed by child care. There is also the distress, of all concerned, associated with the unwanted child, and there is the problem of bringing a child into

---

10. While David J. Garrow credits Justice Brennan with initially making this suggestion to Justice Blackmun, John C. Jeffries, Jr., maintains that it originated with Justice Powell. Compare Garrow, *Liberty and Sexuality*, 582, with Jeffries, *Justice Lewis F. Powell, Jr.*, 341–42.

a family already unable, psychologically and otherwise, to care for it. In other cases . . . the additional difficulties and continuing stigma of unwed motherhood may be involved. All these factors the woman and her responsible physician necessarily will consider in consultation.[11]

Because of these factors, Blackmun concluded, access to abortions could only be restricted if the restrictions were necessary to serve a compelling governmental interest.

Blackmun then turned to the contention that the Texas statute was justified as a device to protect human life. After once again noting the wide range of opinions on the question of when (and if) a fetus should be considered a person, Blackmun concluded that the state could not justify its statute simply by adopting one particular view on the issue. Thus, although disclaiming any intention to resolve the "difficult question of when life begins" the majority opinion effectively concluded that, for constitutional purposes at least, human life does not begin at least until viability.[12]

Nonetheless, Blackmun did recognize two concededly legitimate state interests in regulating access—the protection of maternal health and the preservation of "the potentiality of human life." Blackmun concluded that neither of these interests was compelling during the first trimester of pregnancy and the state was required to leave the abortion decision to the pregnant woman and her doctor. Blackmun viewed the first interest as becoming compelling at the end of the first trimester of pregnancy, the point at which he believed abortions became more dangerous to the mother than carrying the fetus to term; beginning at this point, he determined that the state could impose regulation that "reasonably [related] to the preservation and protection of maternal health." Finally, Blackmun saw the second interest as compelling at the point of viability of the fetus, which he located at the end of the second trimester of pregnancy. The *Roe* opinion left the states free to proscribe all abortions in the third trimester, except those necessary to preserve the life or health of the mother.

Justices Stewart and White had switched sides since *Griswold*, and their separate opinions in *Roe* reflected their rationales. Concurring, Stewart noted simply that *Griswold* had definitively established the proposition that the Due Process Clause protected nontextual rights, and that in his view the right to choose whether or not to bear a child was one of those rights. By contrast, White's dissent reflected a strong distaste for abortion, decrying the view that "the Constitution of the United States values the convenience, whim or caprice of the putative mother more than the life or potential life

---

11. *Roe v. Wade*, 410 U.S. at 153.
12. Ibid., 158.

of the fetus" and arguing that the Court should not erect "a constitutional barrier to state efforts to protect human life" and provide "mothers and doctors [with] the constitutional right to exterminate it."[13]

Even those who agreed with the result in *Roe* and *Doe* often criticized the analysis of the majority opinion.[14] However, the technical deficiencies in the opinion did nothing to detract from the political impact of the abortion decisions. While *Roe* was by no means the first case in which the Court had attempted to definitively resolve a divisive social issue, its impact differed from other earlier controversial decisions in one crucial respect. In cases ranging from *Dred Scott v. Sandford* to *Brown v. Board of Education* and *Regents of Univ. of Cal. v. Bakke*,[15] the Court had focused its attention on questions that were already prominent in national politics. *Roe*, by contrast, transformed the nature of the abortion debate, projecting what had hitherto been a local issue onto the national stage. Stung by the decision, pro-life activists organized and worked to overturn it through the national political process—either by constitutional amendment or by changing the makeup of the Court itself. Conversely, pro-choice forces sought to bolster and expand *Roe* through the same political process. Abortion thus became a major issue in national political campaigns throughout the 1980s.

In Congress and the state legislatures, the political dynamic was quite complicated, with neither party entirely united on the issue. By contrast, at the level of presidential politics, attitudes toward *Roe* broke down along party lines; the Republican Party became closely associated with the pro-life position, while Democratic Party platforms were strongly pro-choice. Indeed, from the late 1970s through the 1980s, having the "correct" position on abortion became a litmus test for aspirants to national office in both political parties.

In this supercharged political atmosphere, compromise became almost impossible, with the most extreme elements of both the pro-life and pro-choice forces tending to dominate public debate. This phenomenon helped send the development of the constitutional law of abortion in a sharply different direction than the evolution of the Court's capital punishment jurisprudence, which took place over the same period. In both cases, the Court intervened to strike down all existing state laws dealing with a volatile political issue. In both cases, state legislatures responded by crafting new laws that they hoped would not be struck down by the Court. However, a

---

13. *Roe v. Wade*, 410 U.S. at 167–71 (Stewart, J., concurring), 221–23 (White, J., dissenting).
14. See, for example, Laurence H. Tribe, "The Supreme Court, 1972 Term—Foreword: Toward a Model of Roles in the Due Process of Life and Law," *Harvard Law Review* 87 (1973): 1–53.
15. *Dred Scott v. Sandford*, 60 U.S. (19 How.) 393 (1857); *Brown v. Board of Education*, 347 U.S. 483 (1954); *Regents of Univ. of Cal. v. Bakke*, 438 U.S. 265 (1978).

constitutionally acceptable set of capital punishment statutes gradually emerged from the dialogue that ensued between the judicial and legislative branches of governments; by contrast, outside the funding context, the period from 1976 to 1986 witnessed an almost unremitting hardening of the Burger Court majority's attitude toward state regulation of abortions.[16]

The simplest explanation for this difference is that the pivotal justices— Powell and Stewart—were simply more strongly opposed in principle to regulations of abortion than to capital punishment. Ironically, however, the very force of the pro-life reaction to *Roe* may also have contributed to the stiffening of constitutional standards. The capital punishment statutes drafted in the wake of *Furman v. Georgia*[17] were generally good-faith efforts to respond to the expressed constitutional concerns of the center justices. By contrast, the polarized atmosphere which existed in the wake of *Roe* generated a different political response. Pro-life legislators often seized on every conceivable ambiguity in Blackmun's majority opinion in an avowed effort to impose the maximum restrictions on access to abortion. The majority of the justices in turn reacted with a heightened suspicion of legislative motives and a hardening of attitude toward all restrictions on abortions. Thus, in addition to the pro-choice/pro-life conflict, the controversy over abortion became in part a contest between the authority of the pro-life legislatures and that of the judiciary itself.

Against this background, Justices Brennan, Marshall, and Blackmun remained steadfastly opposed to virtually all restrictions on abortions; by contrast, in a series of cases beginning with *Planned Parenthood v. Danforth*,[18] the chief justice most often joined Justices White and Rehnquist in supporting the constitutionality of state regulations. However, Justices Stewart, Powell, and Stevens joined the pro-choice group in most cases to create majorities striking down most regulations of second-trimester abortions—even some that were plausibly related to the protection of maternal health. Notwithstanding the language in *Roe*, even third-trimester limitations were also closely scrutinized, and at times invalidated. Stewart's replacement by Sandra Day O'Connor did little to stem the tide, as pro-choice forces retained a generally solid five-vote majority on the Court—a majority that further tightened the constitutional standards in *Akron v. Akron Center for Reproductive Health* and *Thornburgh v. American College of Obstetricians and Gynecologists*.[19] The Court's attitude toward state regulations had a profound effect on the vocabulary that shaped the

---

16. The post-*Roe* case law is discussed in Lee Epstein and Joseph F. Kobylka, *The Supreme Court and Legal Change: Abortion and the Death Penalty* (Chapel Hill: University of North Carolina Press, 1992); and Garrow, *Liberty and Sexuality*.

17. *Furman v. Georgia*, 408 U.S. 238 (1972).

18. *Planned Parenthood v. Danforth*, 428 U.S. 52 (1976).

19. *Akron v. Akron Center for Reproductive Health*, 462 U.S. 416 (1983); *Thornburgh v. American College of Obstetricians and Gynecologists*, 476 U.S. 747 (1986).

political debate over abortion; by 1986 even some statutes that would have been viewed as extremely permissive in the pre-*Roe* era were regularly characterized in the popular media as imposing stringent restrictions on access to abortion.

There were, however, two notable exceptions to Justices Stewart, Powell, and Stevens's consistent opposition to state restrictions on abortions. One of these exceptions involved public funding of abortions for poor women. Prior to the decision in *Roe,* abortion had not been specifically mentioned in the legislation that provided appropriations for Medicaid; nonetheless, the courts had uniformly held that federal funding was available for abortions in states where they could legally be obtained.[20] However, beginning in 1976 each Medicaid appropriation was accompanied by a version of the so-called "Hyde Amendment," which placed severe limitations on the availability of federal funds for Medicaid abortions. A variation of the Hyde Amendment, the variation which was ultimately challenged in the Supreme Court, prohibited all Medicaid funding for abortions, except in certain classes of cases where the pregnancy had resulted from rape or incest.

In *Maher v. Roe*[21] and *Harris v. McRae,*[22] the Court held that the state and federal governments, respectively, could constitutionally withhold funding for abortions under Medicaid, while at the same time subsidizing the medical expenses related to childbirth. Potter Stewart and Lewis Powell joined the three consistently pro-life justices to create the majorities in both cases. While both the *Maher* and *McRae* majorities recognized that governmental decisions may have made childbirth a more attractive option, the opinions argued that "[the government] has imposed no restriction on abortions that was not already there." Observing that *Roe* itself had recognized a legitimate state interest in preserving potential life, they argued that *Roe* required only that the state not place obstacles in the path of women seeking abortions, and that the government could constitutionally favor childbirth over abortion.

The three consistently pro-choice justices on the Court—William Brennan, Thurgood Marshall, and Harry Blackmun—took a more expansive view of *Roe*. They contended that the decision established a constitutional right to be free to choose between abortion and childbirth, and that the denial of Medicaid funding unconstitutionally penalized poor women who chose to have abortions. John Paul Stevens took a middle view, arguing that the purpose of Medicaid was to protect the health of poor women, and that therefore the government should be required to fund therapeutic abortions, but not abortions for other reasons.

---

20. See, for example, *Roe v. Norton,* 522 F. 2d 928 (2d Cir. 1975).
21. *Maher v. Roe,* 432 U.S. 464 (1977).
22. *Harris v. McRae,* 448 U.S. 297 (1980).

The only other context in which the three center justices were willing to countenance significant restrictions was in cases dealing with the right of minors to seek abortions without parental involvement. The issue first came to the fore in *Danforth*, where the state of Missouri sought to require written parental consent for all abortions performed on minors, except those that were necessary to save the life of the mother. With Chief Justice Burger and Justices White, Rehnquist, and Stevens dissenting, the Court held this requirement unconstitutional, reasoning that if the state lacked authority to prohibit abortions, it could not delegate such authority to any other person—in this case, the parents of the pregnant minor.

Not all of the members of the *Danforth* majority subscribed to this simple reasoning, however. Concurring, Justices Stewart and Powell suggested that, in their view, the vice in the Missouri statute was the lack of an alternative judicial procedure that would allow a minor to bypass the prerequisite of parental consent in appropriate cases.[23] Three years later, in *Bellotti v. Baird*, Powell and Stewart enunciated their view of the constitutional requirements in greater detail. In *Bellotti*, they concurred in a judgment striking down a Massachusetts statute that required the consent of both parents of a minor unless a judge chose to override the lack of consent "for good cause shown." At the same time, however, they concluded that a parental consent statute would be constitutional if it provided that the minor could, without notifying her parents, obtain a court order allowing the abortion if she could prove either that she was mature enough to make the decision herself, or that the abortion would be in her best interests.[24]

In an apparent effort to create binding law that would allow for at least some parental consent statutes, the chief justice and Justice Rehnquist abandoned their position in *Danforth* and joined Justice Powell's opinion. However, they failed to gain the crucial fifth vote needed to create a majority opinion. Apparently believing himself bound by the logic of *Danforth*, Justice Stevens joined Justices Brennan, Marshall, and Blackmun in voting to strike down the *Bellotti* statute without suggesting circumstances in which states could provide for parental consent. On the other hand, Justice White dissented, reiterating his distaste for any constitutional limitations on parental consent statutes.

Four years later, in *Planned Parenthood Association v. Ashcroft*, over the dissents of Justices Brennan, Marshall, Blackmun, and Stevens, a majority explicitly approved a statute that met the criteria established by Powell's *Bellotti* opinion. However, once again, the members of the majority failed to agree on a single rationale. The chief justice and Justice Powell reaffirmed

23. *Planned Parenthood v. Danforth*, 428 U.S. at 90–91 (Stewart, J., concurring).
24. *Bellotti v. Baird*, 443 U.S. 622, 624–51 (opinion of Powell, J.) (1979).

their allegiance to the *Bellotti* approach; by contrast, the newly appointed Justice O'Connor joined Justices Rehnquist and White in arguing that the requirement should be upheld because it did not create an "undue burden" on the minor's right to choose to have an abortion.[25]

By contrast, in 1981 a majority had managed to reach a very limited consensus on parental *notification* in *H. L. v. Matheson*. There, five justices concluded that a Utah statute which required parental notification "if possible" was constitutional as applied to a pregnant minor who was living with her parents and made no claim that she was emancipated or sufficiently mature to make the decision. However, Chief Justice Burger's majority opinion explicitly limited this conclusion to those facts. Justice Stevens would have gone even further; distinguishing sharply between notification requirements and consent requirements, he would have found the statute constitutional in all of its applications. Conversely, Justices Brennan, Marshall, and Blackmun would have concluded that the statute was unconstitutional on its face.[26]

In short, a majority of the Burger Court was willing to countenance some significant limitations on the right of minors to seek abortions. Even in these cases, however, the majority treated abortions quite differently than other medical procedures. In other contexts, except in the rarest circumstances, parents have absolute legal control over the ability of unemancipated minors to seek medical treatment. By contrast, the Burger Court majority held that a minor seeking an abortion could override the wishes of her parents if she demonstrated to a judge that the abortion would be in her best interest or that she was mature enough to make the decision for herself. Thus, far from evincing a significant retreat from the basic principles of *Roe*, the majority's treatment of minors in fact reflected the high place that the right to choose an abortion occupied in their pantheon of constitutional rights.

The abortion cases also dramatically illustrated the open-ended nature of the privacy right that underlay *Griswold*. It was almost inevitable that substantial efforts would be made to expand the right of privacy to cover other interests as well. Not surprisingly, these efforts produced sharp disagreement among the justices of the Burger Court, with characteristically fragile coalitions determining the outcome of constitutional challenges to laws which some groups viewed as unduly intrusive.

The battle over ordinances that limited the character of groups that were allowed to live together in single-family housing is typical. The first skirmish in this battle came in *Village of Belle Terre v. Boraas*, decided only a year

---

25. *Planned Parenthood Association v. Ashcroft*, 462 U.S. 476 (1983).

26. *H. L. v. Matheson*, 450 U.S. 398 (1981).

after *Roe. Belle Terre* was a challenge to a local ordinance which forbade more than two unrelated persons from occupying the same dwelling. Such ordinances are common in municipalities which fear an influx of college students into neighborhoods occupied by families; it is therefore not coincidental that the challengers in *Belle Terre* were six college students who sought to rent a dwelling in the village. The students contended that the ordinance violated their rights to privacy and free association.[27]

Thurgood Marshall agreed with this contention, asserting that the fundamental right of privacy included the right to choose "household companions—[to determine] whether a person's 'intellectual and emotional needs' are best met by living with family, friends, professional associates or others." Based on this view, he argued that the *Belle Terre* ordinance could not be upheld because it failed strict scrutiny. Seven members of the Court, however, rejected this position. No doubt influenced by his abiding concern for environmental regulations, Justice Douglas abandoned his accustomed liberal stance and spoke for the Court. Douglas emphasized the deference normally due to zoning regulations and dismissed out of hand claims that the ordinance violated fundamental rights, noting that there was no evidence that the ordinance was motivated by animosity toward unmarried couples per se. Applying the rational basis test, Douglas found the ordinance constitutionally unobjectionable.[28]

Three years later, a related ordinance met a quite different fate in *Moore v. City of East Cleveland*. Like the village of Belle Terre, East Cleveland had an ordinance that limited occupancy of a dwelling unit to members of a single family; however, the East Cleveland ordinance defined the term "family" quite narrowly, essentially limiting it to a traditional nuclear family. The ordinance was challenged by Inez Moore, a woman who lived together with her son and two grandsons, one of whom had come to live with her after the death of his mother; Ms. Moore was in violation of the ordinance because the two grandsons were first cousins, rather than brothers.[29]

A deeply divided Court found the East Cleveland ordinance unconstitutional. Lewis Powell, speaking for himself and Justices Brennan, Marshall, and Blackmun, argued that the ordinance should be subjected to enhanced scrutiny and that the state interests were insufficient to justify the restriction. While paying homage to the ghost of *Lochner* and noting the potential risks inherent in substantive due process analysis, Powell nonetheless contended that the Court should give special protection to those values that are "deeply rooted in this Nation's history and tradition," including respect for the sanc-

27. *Village of Belle Terre v. Boraas,* 416 U.S. 1 (1974).
28. Ibid., 16 (Marshall, J., dissenting), 7–8.
29. *Moore v. City of East Cleveland,* 431 U.S. 494 (1977).

tity of the family unit. Moreover, he asserted that "ours is by no means a tradition limited to respect for the bonds uniting the members of the nuclear
family. The tradition of uncles, aunts, cousins and especially grandparents
sharing a household along with parents and children has roots equally venerable and equally deserving of constitutional recognition." Concurring,
Brennan injected racial issues into the analysis, associating the traditional
nuclear family with the values of "white suburbia" and the extended family
with African American culture.[30]

Potter Stewart parted company with his allies in the abortion controversy to join Chief Justice Burger and Justices White and Rehnquist in dissent. Both Stewart and White argued that enhanced scrutiny should be
limited to the protection of interests that are "implicit in the concept of
ordered liberty," and that the right to share a single dwelling with relatives
did not rise to the level of fundamentality that had generated special judicial
solicitude for the right to marry and the right to determine whether or not
to beget a child. Further, Stewart responded to Brennan's implication that
the ordinance reflected racial prejudice by noting that the population of
East Cleveland was predominantly African American. Applying the rational
basis test, the dissenters would have found the ordinance constitutional.[31]

With the Court otherwise divided four to four, the balance of power
rested with John Paul Stevens. Stevens cast his vote with the Powell group;
however, he declined to hold that the East Cleveland ordinance should be
subject to enhanced scrutiny. Indeed, Stevens did not view the case as raising an issue of "privacy" at all. Instead, describing the stringency of the ordinance as "unprecedented," he concluded that it constituted a taking of
property without due process or compensation.[32]

The juxtaposition of *Belle Terre* and *Moore* provides an excellent illustration
of the complex interaction of ideological and doctrinal forces that produced
the pattern of Burger Court decisions. Both cases, however, raised issues whose
political implications were almost entirely local. By contrast, in *Bowers v. Hardwick*—one of the last cases decided in the Burger era—the Court was once
again invited to deploy the jurisprudence of privacy to resolve an explosive
social issue of emerging national concern. The issue was the constitutionality of
laws that prohibited sexual relations between members of the same sex.[33]

Prior to *Bowers,* the Court had not definitively addressed the question
of the extent to which the states could constitutionally regulate sexual

30. Ibid., 503 (footnote omitted), 504 (footnote omitted) (opinion of Powell, J.), 508–9
(Brennan, J., concurring).
31. Ibid., 549 (White, J., dissenting), 537 and n. 7 (Stewart, J., dissenting).
32. Ibid., 513–21 (Stevens, J., concurring in the result).
33. *Bowers v. Hardwick,* 478 U.S. 186 (1986).

practices per se. In *Doe v. Commonwealth's Attorney*, with Justices Brennan, Marshall, and Stevens dissenting, the Court had summarily affirmed a lower court decision that rejected a facial challenge to a Virginia statute that outlawed sodomy.[34] However, while such affirmances bind lower courts, they have little or no precedential significance in the Supreme Court itself. Conversely, the statement in *Paris Adult Theatre I v. Slaton* that sexual intimacy is "a key relationship of human existence, central to family life, community welfare, and the development of human personality," was clearly dictum, and thus equally nonbinding.[35]

Prior to *Bowers*, the most extensive discussion of the state's authority to regulate sexual activity came in *Carey v. Population Services International. Carey* was a challenge to a New York statute that prohibited all distribution of contraceptives to persons under the age of sixteen, allowed only licensed pharmacists to distribute contraceptives to persons aged sixteen and over, and barred any advertising or display of contraceptives. Only the chief justice and Justice Rehnquist dissented from the holding that all parts of the statute were unconstitutional; however, the discussion of the ban on distribution to minors provoked a sharp exchange among the justices, triggered by the state's assertion that the ban was justified as a means to discourage sexual activity among minors.[36]

While agreeing that the ban was unconstitutional, Lewis Powell expressed concern that the language of the plurality opinion was overly broad, declaring that "extraordinary protection [for] all personal decisions in matters of sex is neither required by the Constitution nor supported by our prior decisions." Speaking for himself and Justices Marshall, Stewart, and Blackmun, William Brennan responded that "the Court has not definitively answered the difficult question whether and to what extent the Constitution prohibits state statutes regarding [private consensual sexual activity] among adults" and that "we do not purport to answer that question now."[37] Rehnquist, by contrast, argued that *Doe v. Commonwealth's Attorney* conclusively settled the question in favor of the constitutionality of state authority to regulate sexual mores.

The issue was further complicated by the fact that sexual relationships are often consummated within the privacy of one's home. This factor brought not only *Griswold* into play, but also the Warren Court's decision in *Stanley v. Georgia*. There the Court held that the combination of First Amendment concepts

---

34. *Doe v. Commonwealth's Attorney*, 425 U.S. 901 (1976) (per curiam).

35. *Paris Adult Theatre I v. Slaton*, 413 U.S. 49, 63 (1973).

36. *Carey v. Population Services International*, 431 U.S. 678 (1977).

37. Ibid., 703 (Powell, J., concurring), 694 n. 17, 688 n. 5 (opinion of Brennan, J.), 718 n. 2 (Rehnquist, J., dissenting).

and privacy-related concerns provided constitutional protection for the right to read sexually oriented materials within the home—even if the state could constitutionally ban the sale of the specific materials as obscene.[38]

In *Bowers* itself, the Court dealt with these doctrinal arguments against the background of a gay rights movement that was gaining increasing momentum in the political process. Although the gay rights movement as a political force developed somewhat later than its feminist counterpart, by 1980 discrimination on the basis of sexual orientation had been outlawed by a number of local ordinances, and the movement had gained sufficient force to be specifically endorsed by the Democratic Party. Conversely, opposition to gay rights initiatives was an important tenet of the socially conservative groups that became extremely prominent in the Republican Party in the aftermath of the decisions in *Roe* and its progeny.

The specific chain of events that led to the *Bowers* decision began with Hardwick's arrest for allegedly violating Georgia's sodomy statute by engaging in sexual acts with another man in the bedroom of his own home. The local authorities dropped these charges without even presenting them to a grand jury; however, Hardwick then brought suit for a declaratory judgment in federal court, asserting that the Georgia statute was unconstitutional. Initially, Hardwick was joined in his lawsuit by a married couple who asserted that they were "chilled and deterred" from engaging in the statutorily prohibited conduct by the existence of the sodomy statute; however, because they could show no real likelihood of being prosecuted under the statute, the married couple was dismissed from the case for lack of standing. Thus, only Hardwick remained as a viable plaintiff when the case reached the Supreme Court. His argument was relatively straightforward; combining *Griswold, Roe,* and their progeny with *Stanley,* he argued that the right of privacy was broad enough to encompass the right to engage in consensual sexual relations in one's home, and that the state could show no interest sufficiently compelling to justify the limitations imposed by the sodomy statute.

The reactions of the justices to this argument were to some extent predictable. The argument was rejected by the justices who had most consistently opposed expansive readings of constitutionally protected privacy rights—Chief Justice Burger and Justices White and Rehnquist. They were joined by Sandra Day O'Connor, who, having replaced Potter Stewart, was conservative Ronald Reagan's sole appointee to the Burger Court. They were opposed by the three dissenters from *Doe v. Commonwealth's Attorney*—Justices Brennan, Marshall, and Stevens—together with Harry Blackmun, the only justice to clearly change his position in the decade following *Doe.*

---

38. *Stanley v. Georgia,* 394 U.S. 557 (1969).

Against this background, the vote of Lewis Powell became critical. Homosexuality was entirely foreign to Powell's experience; indeed, he purportedly told one of his clerks that he had never met a gay person. Nonetheless, Powell was forced to make a decision one way or another; after initially indicating that he would vote to strike down the Georgia statute, he ultimately concluded that the privacy-based substantive due process challenge should be rejected.[39] Thus, by a five-to-four vote, the Court declined to hold the Georgia statute unconstitutional.

Speaking for all members of the majority, Byron White first concluded that, because the married couple's complaint had been dismissed for lack of standing, the only issue before the Court was the constitutionality of the Georgia statute as applied to consensual homosexual sodomy. Distinguishing *Bowers* from cases involving either the right to procreate or the right to marital privacy, White noted the long history of antisodomy statutes and the fact that until 1961 sodomy was illegal in every state and the District of Columbia, and that it remained illegal in approximately half of the states. Given this context, he described the claim that the right to engage in homosexual sodomy was either "deeply rooted in this Nation's history" or "implicit in the concept of ordered liberty" as "at best, facetious." White then suggested that *Stanley*'s special protection for activities taking place within the privacy of one's home should be limited to First Amendment–related issues, and argued that the same logic that would protect consensual homosexual sodomy taking place within the home would also invalidate laws against adultery, incest, and other sexual crimes. Finally, White contended that the state could rationally base its laws on moral judgments.[40]

Although joining White's opinion, both Chief Justice Burger and Justice Powell also filed brief concurring opinions. Burger's opinion reflected a clear distaste for homosexual relationships, declaring that "to hold that the act of homosexual sodomy is somehow protected as a fundamental right would be to cast aside millennia of moral teaching." By contrast, while concluding, "I cannot say that conduct condemned for hundreds of years has now become a fundamental right," Powell also suggested that the actual imposition of any prison term for private, consensual homosexual activity would raise serious Eighth Amendment questions.[41]

Not surprisingly, the four dissenters took a quite different view of the nature of the issues presented by *Bowers*. Speaking for all of the dissenters, Jus-

39. The internal deliberations of the *Bowers* Court are discussed in detail in Garrow, *Liberty and Sexuality*, 659–61; and Jeffries, *Justice Lewis F. Powell, Jr.*, 521–24.

40. *Bowers v. Hardwick*, 478 U.S. at 194.

41. Ibid., 197 (Burger, C. J., concurring), 197, 198 n. 2 (Powell, J., concurring).

tice Blackmun argued that the case was not about a right to engage in homo-sexual sodomy, but rather about "the right to be let alone," and that the proper question was whether the state could constitutionally prohibit oral and anal sex generally. He contended that individuals had a constitutionally pro-tected fundamental right to structure their "intimate associations" with others, and that *Stanley* bolstered the proposition that the state could not constitu-tionally question a person's right to engage in consensual sexual activity within the confines of his own home. Finally, Blackmun argued that the enforcement of the traditional Judeo-Christian view of morality was not a legitimate state interest. Speaking for himself as well as Justices Brennan and Marshall, Justice Stevens concluded, first, that the government could not constitutionally pro-hibit oral and anal sex between persons of different sexes and, second, that the state had not supplied a sufficient reason for enforcing the statute against homosexuals while refusing to enforce it against those who engage in analo-gous practices in the context of heterosexual relationships.

Taken together, the results in the privacy cases are a microcosm of the internal forces that shaped much of Burger Court decision making: the polar extremes represented by William Rehnquist on one hand and William Bren-nan and Thurgood Marshall on the other hand; the gradual leftward drift of Harry Blackmun; and the pivotal role often played by a sometime vacillating Lewis Powell. The overall political impact of the Court's decisions in this area is also typical. While liberals did not obtain all that they wished from the Court—a fact clearly reflected in their intense negative reaction to *Bowers*—some of the values generally advocated by leftist politicians became newly enshrined in the Constitution. Moreover, even in areas where liberals did not triumph in the Court, they remained generally free to pursue their agendas through legislative action and state constitutional adjudication. In short, the Burger Court's jurisprudence of privacy law—like its approach to a number of other issues including school desegregation, sex discrimination, and aid to parochial schools—was clearly the most liberal in the history of the Supreme Court.

Table 13.1: Voting Patterns

	Bur	Dou	Bre	Mar	Whi	Stew	Bla	Reh	Pow	Stev	Oco
Abortion											
Roe v. Wade 410 U.S. 113 (1973) (restrictions on abortions)	U	U	U	U	C	U	U	C	U	NP	NP
Akron v. Akron Center for Reproductive Health 462 U.S. 416 (1983) (restrictions on abortions)	U	NP	U	U	C	NP	U	C	U	U	C
Thornburgh v. ACOG 476 U.S. 747 (1986) (restrictions on abortions)	C	NP	U	U	C	NP	U	C	U	U	C
Maher v. Roe 432 U.S. 464 (1977) (restrictions on funding)	C	NP	U	U	C	C	U	C	C	C	NP
Harris v. McRae 448 U.S. 297 (1980) (restrictions on funding)	C	NP	U	U	C	C	U	C	C	U	NP
Planned Parenthood v. Danforth 428 U.S. 52 (1976) (parental consent)	C	NP	U	U	C	U	U	C	U	C	NP
Bellotti v. Baird 443 U.S. 622 (1979) (parental consent)	U	NP	U	U	C	U	U	U	U	U	NP
Planned Parenthood Assoc. v. Ashcroft 462 U.S. 476 (1983) (parental consent)	C	NP	U	U	C	NP	U	C	C	U	C
H. L. v. Matheson 450 U.S. 398 (1981) (parental notification)	C	NP	U	U	C	C	U	C	C	C	NP

	Bur	Dou	Bre	Mar	Whi	Stew	Bla	Reh	Pow	Stev	Oco
Other Privacy Issues											
Village of Belle Terre v. Boraas 416 U.S. 1 (1974) (prohibition on unrelated people living together)	C	C	?	U	C	C	C	C	C	NP	NP
Moore v. City of East Cleveland 431 U.S. 494 (1977) (narrow definition of related people)	C	NP	U	U	C	C	U	C	U	U	NP
Bowers v. Hardwick 478 U.S. 186 (1986) (prohibition on same-sex relationships)	C	NP	U	U	C	NP	U	C	C	U	C

Key

C = Constitutional   NP = Not Participating   ? = Uncertain Position
U = Unconstitutional

14

THE BURGER COURT IN RETROSPECT

Any accurate evaluation of the jurisprudence of the Burger Court must distinguish between the Court's statutory and constitutional decisions. Burger-era statutory analysis was typically couched in traditional legal terms; at the same time, however, the decisions had a fairly consistent ideological orientation. On issues ranging from criminal procedure to labor relations law and antitrust law, the Burger Court moved the state of the law perceptibly to the right. There was, however, one notable exception to this trend; although its treatment of civil rights statutes was by no means ideologically uniform, the overall pattern of the Court's decisions had a decidedly liberal orientation. The most prominent examples are *Griggs v. Duke Power Co.*[1] and *United Steelworkers v. Weber,*[2] where the Court adopted the liberal position on critical issues, notwithstanding the fact that traditional methods of statutory interpretation rather clearly suggested a contrary result.

The pattern of decisions generated by the Burger Court in constitutional cases was much more complex. From a jurisprudential perspective, the Court's analysis can be most charitably described as consistently antiformalist in tone. Only Justice Rehnquist showed any consistent inclination to revive the emphasis on formal legal categories that had dominated pre-1937 constitutional jurisprudence. To be sure, some of the justices on the Court—most notably Justice Stevens, and to a lesser extent Justices White and Powell—sought to reinvigorate the idea that the Court should be strongly constrained by distinctively legal conventions. However, they disagreed strongly on what form those conventions should take; moreover, the remaining justices seemed to have little interest in the project. The result was that the constitutional opinions of the Burger era—like those of the Warren Court—often appear to be little more than thinly veiled examples of ordinary political discourse.

In political terms, the overall pattern of the Burger Court's constitutional jurisprudence is typically characterized as either centrist or moder-

---

1. *Griggs v. Duke Power Co.,* 401 U.S. 424 (1971).
2. *United Steelworkers v. Weber,* 443 U.S. 193 (1979).

ately conservative. This characterization reflects the perspective of left-of-center elements in the American political spectrum—the dominant force in the American legal academy during the late twentieth century. Liberals had become accustomed to ever-increasing support from the Warren Court; their evaluation reflects the fact that, during the Burger era, they were less consistently successful in convincing a majority of the justices to add new liberal values to their reading of the Constitution.

Other perspectives are at least equally plausible, however. For example, when measured against the overall performance of the Court since the adoption of the Reconstruction amendments, the jurisprudence of the Burger era appears quite liberal. In the period from the late nineteenth century through 1937, judicial activism was deployed largely (although not entirely) to enshrine *conservative* views into constitutional law. Admittedly, some aspects of Burger Court jurisprudence fit this description; the affirmative action cases are a prime example. However, the vast majority of the activist decisions of the Court instead adopted liberal political values. Conversely, most of the decisions that were characterized as "conservative" simply failed to constitutionalize the liberal position, instead leaving the other branches of government free to adopt whichever ideological viewpoint they chose.

Viewed in isolation, this phenomenon could be explained relatively easily. Although the idea of judicial deference is not connected analytically to conservative political ideology, opposition to judicial activism had become a central tenet of conservative politics by the late 1960s. Thus, conservative justices who might otherwise be inclined to constitutionalize their political viewpoint faced countervailing ideological pressure to abstain from doing so. Of course, as the affirmative action cases demonstrate, this countervailing pressure did not invariably deter the more conservative members of the Burger Court from concluding that their political positions were embodied in the Constitution. Nonetheless, the close political association between deference and conservatism rather clearly limited activist impulses among the more politically conservative justices.

The specific relationship between the constitutional jurisprudence of the Burger Court and that of the Warren Court is less easily explained. Without doubt, justices drawn from the conservative wing of American politics played a far greater role on the Burger Court than on its predecessor. Given this reality, one might have expected that the overall shape of constitutional doctrine would have taken a demonstrably conservative turn between 1969 and 1986. This expectation, however, is belied by the actual performance of the Court during this period. While precise characterization of Burger Court jurisprudence depends in part on questions of emphasis, no dispassionate observer would conclude that the Burger Court moved the overall shape of constitutional law significantly to the right.

Of course, the constitutional decisions of the Burger era were by no means uniformly liberal in tone. In addition to the decisions that actively constitutionalized conservative values (a possibility that would have been unthinkable during the regime of Earl Warren), the Burger Court abandoned or modified Warren Court precedents dealing with a variety of issues ranging from the First Amendment status of pornography to criminal procedure and constitutional protection for the poor. With the notable exceptions of cases dealing with affirmative action and pornography, however, these decisions typically did not dramatically alter the state of existing law; instead, they either refused to extend Warren Court reasoning or changed existing law only at the margins.

In large measure, this pattern can be viewed as a product of the institutional forces that worked to protect much of the Warren Court revolution. Admittedly, the Court has traditionally been more willing to modify existing precedents in constitutional cases than in cases raising statutory or common-law issues. Moreover, the doctrine of stare decisis suffered further erosion during the Warren and Burger eras. Nonetheless, the swing justices of the Burger Court continued to show some respect for preexisting doctrine, and the concept of precedent clearly influenced their attitude toward Warren Court case law in a variety of different contexts.

However, these institutional factors cannot explain the Burger Court decisions that created dramatic new liberal constitutional doctrine in cases dealing with the death penalty, abortion and women's rights generally, protection for illegitimates, commercial speech, and aid to parochial schools. Moreover, in areas where the precise import of existing law was somewhat uncertain, the Burger Court extended doctrines dealing with the dormant Commerce Clause and school desegregation well beyond the boundaries established by the Warren Court. Against this background, one can persuasively argue that the chief justiceship of Warren Burger produced the most liberal body of constitutional law in the nation's history.

In part, this apparent trend reflected changes in the basic canons of American political liberalism itself. Some of the principles that defined American liberalism during the regime of Warren Burger had not yet been fully embraced by liberals until the late 1960s or later. It would thus be anachronistic to suggest that the failure of the Warren Court to provide constitutional protection for these principles somehow reflected a lack of commitment to liberalism generally.

The evolution of the law of sex discrimination provides a classic example of this phenomenon. It was not until the mid to late 1960s that the feminist movement became a powerful force in postwar American politics. Thus, in 1961 Justice Brennan in particular saw no problem with joining the unanimous opinion in *Hoyt v. Florida,* where, in upholding a Florida statute which made jury service optional for women, the Court declared that "[because a] woman is still regarded as the center of home and family life . . . it is constitutionally [permissible] for a State . . . to conclude that a woman should be relieved from the civic duty of jury service unless she herself determines that such service is consistent with her own responsibilities."[3] By contrast, only a dozen years later Brennan would lead the liberal wing of the Burger Court in arguing that all gender-based classifications should be subjected to strict scrutiny, decrying "an attitude of 'romantic paternalism' which, in effect, put women not on a pedestal, but in a cage."[4] Thus, in response to changes in basic liberal ideology, Brennan had clearly changed his view of constitutional law and found this new position accepted in substantial part by a majority of the Court as well.

By contrast, even if they had come in the early or mid 1960s, Burger Court innovations dealing with issues such as capital punishment and aid to parochial schools would have been hailed as important victories by traditional liberals. To some extent, the Court's willingness to move beyond Warren Court doctrine in those cases reflects the continuing influence of Warren Court holdovers. Three of the Warren justices remained on the Court during the entire tenure of Warren Burger; until 1976 veterans of the Warren era actually formed a majority on the Burger Court. Thus, for example, in *Furman v. Georgia*,[5] all existing statutes providing for the death penalty were invalidated notwithstanding the fact that none of the four justices appointed by Richard Nixon favored this result. Similarly, until 1974 the continuing solid support of the Warren Court veterans for expansion of school desegregation orders guaranteed liberal victories in *Swann v. Charlotte-Mecklenburg Board of Education*[6] and *Keyes v. School District No. 1*.[7] The defection of Potter Stewart would lead to the signal conservative victory in *Milliken v. Bradley*;[8] however, Stewart's shift was soon neutralized by a countervailing decision by Harry Blackmun to abandon his erstwhile allies and, together with the newly appointed John Paul Stevens, join the remaining Warren Court holdovers to create a new liberal majority in *Columbus Board of Education v. Penick*.[9]

The pivotal role played by Justices Blackmun and Stevens in the school desegregation cases reflects one of the most important institutional features of the Burger Court: the fact that, although all were chosen by Republican presidents, the justices appointed after Warren's resignation varied widely in

---

3. *Hoyt v. Florida,* 368 U.S. 57, 62 (1961).

4. *Frontiero v. Richardson,* 411 U.S. 677 (opinion of Brennan, J.) (1973).

5. *Furman v. Georgia,* 408 U.S. 238 (1972).

6. *Swann v. Charlotte-Mecklenburg Board of Education,* 402 U.S. 1 (1971).

7. *Keyes v. School District No. 1,* 413 U.S. 189 (1973).

8. *Milliken v. Bradley,* 418 U.S. 717 (1974).

9. *Columbus Board of Education v. Penick,* 443 U.S. 449 (1979).

their commitment to conservative ideology. In a very real sense, these appointments reflected the political philosophy of the presidents who appointed them. Five of the justices chosen during the Burger era were selected by either Richard Nixon or Gerald Ford. While both of these Republican presidents were more conservative than the typical northern Democrat of their era, neither had the strong, generalized commitment to conservative domestic policies that marked (for example) Barry Goldwater and Ronald Reagan, the Republican presidential nominees who immediately preceded and followed them. Admittedly, Nixon was committed to the conservative position on desegregation and criminal procedure; however, on other issues such as affirmative action, his domestic policies were notably left of center. Gerald Ford—facing a Democratically controlled Congress as the unelected successor to a president who had resigned in disgrace—was further constrained by the political circumstances in which he found himself. Thus, it should not be surprising that, while Warren Burger and William Rehnquist were firmly ensconced in the conservative wing of the Republican party, John Paul Stevens was a classic representative of a group that was somewhat derisively referred to as "country club" Republicans—men from socially prominent families who owed allegiance not to some well-defined political ideology, but rather to the values shared by the segment of the affluent, educated classes to which they belonged. Although nominally a member of the Democratic Party, Lewis Powell's basic political orientation can be described in much the same terms.[10]

This point is clearly reflected in Powell's approach to constitutional adjudication. As the quintessential establishment lawyer, his opinions often embodied the same distaste for legal formalism that was a major theme of post-1937 legal scholarship; at the same time, his probusiness approach to regulatory statutes was exactly what one might expect from one whose career was spent representing business interests. As a lifelong resident of the South, he championed the values of federalism. As the former head of a local school board, Powell consistently emphasized the importance of public education in American society, while at the same time vigorously supporting the principle of local control and showing considerable hostility toward measures which provided government funds for private schools.

Powell's support for the basic concept of abortion rights also reflects the confluence of a variety of factors in his background. He was a well-educated, upper-class Protestant—the class of individuals whose support for the pro-

---

10. The influence of country club Republicans on the Burger Court is emphasized in Mark V. Tushnet, "The Burger Court in Historical Perspective: The Triumph of Country Club Republicanism," in *The Burger Court: Counter-Revolution or Confirmation*, ed. Bernard Schwartz (New York: Oxford University Press, 1998), 203–12.

choice position was overwhelming by 1973. Moreover, he had been personally involved in counseling an employee whose lover had died in the aftermath of an illegal abortion. Taken together, these life experiences were sufficient to outweigh any ideological commitment to the concept of judicial restraint that Powell may have possessed.[11]

While Powell's approach was critical to the overall development of Burger Court jurisprudence, other justices were influenced by analogous factors. Indeed, the experience of the Burger Court clearly supports the view that, in the absence of strong, widely accepted formal constraints on the discretion of the justices, constitutional law becomes little more than the aggregate of the idiosyncratic value judgments of the justices who happen to be serving on the Court at a particular time. This is perhaps the most important lesson that can be drawn from the chief justiceship of Warren Burger.

---

11. This analysis tracks that of John C. Jeffries, Jr., *Justice Lewis F. Powell, Jr.* (New York: Charles Scribner's Sons, 1994), 346–52.

APPENDIX

Correlations among Voting Patterns of Justices

These statistics are based upon the yearly account of the performance of the Supreme Court published by the *Harvard Law Review*. "The Supreme Court, 1969 Term," *Harvard Law Review* 84 (1970): 32–253 at 252; "The Supreme Court, 1970 Term," *Harvard Law Review* 85 (1971): 40–353 at 351; "The Supreme Court, 1971 Term," *Harvard Law Review* 86 (1972): 52–306 at 301; "The Supreme Court, 1972 Term," *Harvard Law Review* 87 (1973): 55–309 at 304; "The Supreme Court, 1973 Term," *Harvard Law Review* 88 (1974): 41–280 at 275; "The Supreme Court, 1974 Term," *Harvard Law Review* 89 (1975): 47–281 at 276; "The Supreme Court, 1975 Term," *Harvard Law Review* 90 (1976): 58–282 at 277; "The Supreme Court, 1976 Term," *Harvard Law Review* 91 (1977): 72–301 at 296; "The Supreme Court, 1977 Term," *Harvard Law Review* 92 (1978): 57–339 at 337; "The Supreme Court, 1978 Term," *Harvard Law Review* 93 (1979): 60–281 at 276; "The Supreme Court, 1979 Term," *Harvard Law Review* 94 (1980): 77–295 at 290; "The Supreme Court, 1980 Term," *Harvard Law Review* 95 (1981): 93–345 at 340; "The Supreme Court, 1981 Term," *Harvard Law Review* 96 (1982): 62–311 at 305; "The Supreme Court, 1982 Term," *Harvard Law Review* 97 (1983): 70–306 at 304; "The Supreme Court, 1983 Term," *Harvard Law Review* 98 (1984): 87–314 at 308, "The Supreme Court, 1984 Term," *Harvard Law Review* 99 (1985): 120–329 at 323; and "The Supreme Court, 1985 Term," *Harvard Law Review* 100 (1986): 100–311 at 305.

Burger

	Doug	Bren	Mars	Whit	Stew	Blac	Rehn	Pow	Stev	O'Con
69	46.2	52.7	60.7	68.5	76.1	na	na	na	na	na
70	37.4	44.2	49.6	68.1	64.2	89.9				
71	31.1	45.3	50.0	67.3	60.8	79.1	86.1	82.9		
72	37.2	46.5	48.1	75.9	59.5	85.7	84.7	84.0		
73	34.0	45.2	45.2	76.9	76.8	84.0	90.3	80.8		
74	32.8	52.9	52.9	70.8	65.7	79.6	80.3	79.8		
75	40.0	42.3	46.4	73.7	67.5	75.3	84.6	82.9	53.2	
76	na	36.9	37.4	65.2	64.7	74.3	78.4	69.8	51.4	
77	43.0	45.9	59.2	64.2	59.1	75.6	66.2	59.4		
78	43.4	40.6	67.6	66.9	69.6	80.3	79.1	61.2		
79	46.3	43.8	71.9	67.8	66.0	74.3	78.8	58.2		
80	50.0	43.8	68.6	70.2	59.3	79.9	74.8	49.6		
81	44.2	44.8	65.9	na	55.8	80.1	74.8	49.4	77.2	
82	57.4	48.4	79.6	64.8	82.1	84.3	57.4	80.7		
83	60.0	55.8	87.5	77.8	87.5	89.4	55.9	89.4		
84	55.3	51.7	85.9	72.5	89.3	80.8	60.1	88.6		
85	46.5	40.8	78.5	50.0	91.7	84.5	48.4	82.2		

Douglas

	Burg	Bren	Mars	Whit	Stew	Blac	Pow	Rehn
69	46.2	73.9	78.3	58.2	58.2	na	na	na
70	37.4	66.1	67.0	46.5	44.3	39.5		
71	31.1	62.6	63.8	45.0	53.1	32.7	38.2	26.9
72	37.2	64.8	66.5	41.4	48.1	37.9	45.5	30.7
73	34.0	68.6	67.5	46.1	42.2	36.2	38.8	27.8
74	32.8	63.8	55.2	39.7	44.0	39.7	33.4	31.0
75	40.0	40.0	40.0	20.0	40.0	40.0	40.0	40.0

Brennan

	Burg	Doug	Mars	Whit	Stew	Blac	Pow	Rehn	Stev	O'Con
69	52.7	73.9	90.5	78.5	65.6	na	na	na	na	na
70	44.2	66.1	80.3	60.5	50.8	48.7				
71	45.3	62.6	79.9	68.5	74.1	48.3	53.3	44.9		
72	46.5	64.8	83.0	55.4	62.4	53.8	55.3	74.4		
73	52.9	63.8	86.7	63.2	63.2	62.5	56.3	50.7		
74	45.2	68.6	91.6	63.5	57.0	48.7	53.0	40.6		
75	42.3	40.0	87.6	52.6	51.3	51.9	42.8	40.4	56.4	
76	36.9	na	93.6	51.4	53.6	50.4	49.3	36.8	56.8	
77	43.0	93.6	63.2	59.3	52.6	56.4	34.2	56.3		
78	43.4	87.5	63.7	53.7	58.8	44.7	34.1	62.9		
79	46.3	82.5	59.6	56.8	60.5	49.3	32.4	63.7		
80	50.0	85.4	63.5	51.1	63.7	52.7	41.0	56.3		
81	44.2	90.2	61.0	na	75.2	50.3	37.3	59.8	48.8	
82	57.4	83.2	57.4	74.7	53.5	46.9	70.4	54.7		
83	60.0	94.2	62.3	70.9	58.5	49.7	75.0	56.6		
84	46.5	91.0	54.8	80.3	55.8	43.9	67.9	59.6		
85	55.3	100.0	61.3	79.2	65.7	52.0	69.1	61.3		

Stewart

	Burg	Doug	Bren	Mars	Whit	Blac	Pow	Rehn	Stev
69	76.1	58.2	65.6	71.1	73.9				
70	64.2	44.3	50.8	55.6	67.2	70.6			
71	60.8	53.1	74.1	75.8	70.5	62.6	64.1	57.0	
72	59.5	48.1	62.4	61.2	60.3	63.5	69.5	59.9	
73	76.8	42.2	57.0	60.4	70.0	71.3	80.1	72.5	
74	65.7	44.0	63.2	69.1	59.8	70.0	78.5	72.3	
75	67.5	na	51.3	53.6	59.7	68.4	78.3	69.2	65.4
76	64.7	53.6	56.5	60.7	61.2	69.1	70.7	62.0	
77	64.2	59.3	58.3	61.2	55.3	62.3	56.7	65.2	
78	66.9	53.7	50.0	60.3	59.6	67.6	66.7	62.1	
79	67.8	56.8	51.8	64.1	55.5	74.5	67.3	64.1	
80	70.2	51.1	49.2	66.7	50.8	74.0	68.5	51.1	

White

	Burg	Doug	Bren	Mars	Stew	Blac	Pow	Rehn	Stev	O'Con
69	68.5	58.2	78.5	82.1	73.9					
70	68.1	46.5	60.5	61.5	67.2	70.3				
71	67.3	45.0	68.5	64.2	70.5	72.5	64.9	62.5		
72	75.9	41.4	55.4	53.8	60.3	76.7	77.9	75.2		
73	76.9	46.1	63.5	60.4	70.0	73.5	71.3	70.1		
74	70.8	39.7	63.2	64.0	59.8	77.4	72.3	70.8		
75	73.7	na	52.6	54.2	59.7	71.6	69.7	73.1	51.9	
76	65.2	51.4	55.0	60.7	70.9	70.7	67.2	60.4		
77	59.2	63.2	61.7	61.2	60.9	56.2	48.9	53.4		
78	67.9	63.7	61.3	60.3	73.7	65.8	64.0	62.9		
79	71.9	59.6	52.6	62.1	62.3	71.0	65.3	62.1		
80	68.6	63.5	57.2	66.7	66.2	69.7	64.4	61.8		
81	65.9	61.0	58.9	na	64.6	63.0	64.2	55.8	64.0	
82	79.6	57.4	56.5	67.3	73.6	77.8	55.6	70.8		
83	87.5	62.3	61.2	77.8	81.0	81.1	61.0	84.5		
84	85.9	61.3	57.9	77.0	79.8	81.8	63.5	82.4		
85	78.5	54.8	48.1	54.8	74.2	77.6	56.7	79.5		

Marshall

	Burg	Doug	Bren	Whit	Stew	Blac	Pow	Rehn	Stev	O'Con
69	60.7	78.3	90.5	82.1	71.1	na	na	na	na	na
70	49.6	67.0	80.3	61.5	55.6	55.8				
71	50.0	63.8	79.9	64.2	75.8	51.0	48.1	38.8		
72	48.1	66.5	83.0	53.8	61.2	52.3	57.3	42.0		
73	52.9	55.2	86.7	64.0	69.1	62.5	64.1	52.2		
74	45.2	67.5	91.6	60.4	60.4	50.0	54.0	42.5		
75	46.4	40.0	87.6	54.2	53.6	54.3	53.0	42.5	55.8	
76	37.4	na	93.6	55.0	56.5	49.6	50.7	39.0	56.9	
77	45.9	93.6	61.7	58.3	49.1	52.3	36.1	53.4		
78	40.6	87.5	61.3	50.0	60.9	43.5	33.6	61.9		
79	46.3	82.5	52.6	51.8	55.1	45.6	31.9	55.1		
80	43.8	85.4	57.2	49.2	56.6	49.2	34.8	54.4		
81	44.8	90.2	58.9	na	72.0	50.6	40.0	61.3	46.6	
82	48.4	83.2	56.5	70.2	45.6	37.3	61.5	40.6		
83	55.8	94.2	61.2	71.7	58.8	45.5	67.5	51.3		
84	51.7	100.0	57.9	75.0	62.7	47.6	65.3	59.3		
85	40.8	91.0	48.1	82.1	51.6	39.4	67.1	54.2		

Blackmun

	Burg	Doug	Bren	Mars	Whit	Stew	Pow	Rehn	Stev	O'Con
70	89.9	39.5	48.7	51.7	70.3	70.6	na	na	na	
71	79.1	32.7	48.3	51.0	72.5	62.6	72.4	81.0		
72	85.7	37.9	53.8	52.3	76.7	63.5	81.9	74.4		
73	84.0	36.2	48.7	50.0	73.5	71.3	74.8	79.9		
74	79.6	39.7	62.5	62.5	77.4	70.0	79.1	75.9		
75	75.3	na	51.9	54.3	71.6	68.4	77.3	72.1	56.4	
76	74.3	50.6	49.6	70.9	61.2	67.6	75.8			
77	59.1	52.6	49.1	60.9	55.3	60.7	50.4	50.4		
78	69.6	58.8	60.9	73.7	59.6	64.3	62.0	61.2		
79	66.0	60.5	55.1	62.3	55.5	63.0	53.4	52.0		
80	59.3	63.7	56.6	66.2	50.8	63.1	52.6	57.5		
81	55.8	75.2	72.0	64.6	na	56.4	51.2	61.0	60.7	
82	64.8	74.7	70.2	67.3	59.7	54.3	66.7	57.8		
83	77.8	70.9	71.7	77.8	78.3	68.9	66.3	75.2		
84	72.5	79.2	75.0	77.0	79.6	70.3	66.7	80.4		
85	50.0	80.3	82.1	54.8	58.4	46.8	64.1	59.6		

Powell

	Brug	Doug	Bren	Mars	Whit	Stew	Blac	Rehn	Stev	O'Con
71	82.9	38.2	53.3	48.1	64.9	64.1	72.4	75.7		
72	84.0	45.5	55.3	57.3	77.9	69.5	81.9	77.4		
73	80.8	38.8	53.0	54.0	71.3	70.0	74.8	72.5		
74	79.8	33.4	56.3	64.1	72.3	78.5	79.1	75.4		
75	82.9	na	42.8	53.0	69.7	78.3	77.3	75.7	64.5	
76	69.8	49.3	50.7	70.7	69.1	67.6	72.4	58.4		
77	66.2	56.4	52.3	56.2	62.3	60.7	55.4	54.7		
78	79.1	44.7	43.5	65.8	67.6	64.3	72.8	55.4		
79	78.8	49.3	45.6	71.0	74.5	63.0	70.7	57.5		
80	74.8	52.7	49.2	69.7	74.0	63.1	74.0	56.2		
81	74.8	50.3	50.6	63.0	na	56.4	75.6	56.8	72.0	
82	84.3	53.5	45.6	73.6	59.7	81.1	54.1	79.7		
83	89.4	58.5	58.8	81.0	78.3	82.4	55.6	84.9		
84	80.8	65.7	62.7	79.8	79.6	76.2	63.1	85.7		
85	84.5	55.8	51.6	74.2	58.4	87.7	56.1	87.1		

Rehnquist

	Burg	Doug	Bren	Mars	Whit	Stew	Blac	Pow	Stev	O'Con
70	na									
71	86.1	26.9	44.9	38.8	62.5	57.0	81.0	75.7		
72	84.7	30.7	39.6	42.0	75.2	59.9	74.4	77.4		
73	90.3	27.8	40.6	42.5	70.1	72.5	79.9	74.8		
74	80.3	31.0	50.7	52.2	70.8	72.3	75.9	75.4		
75	84.6	40.0	40.4	42.5	73.1	69.2	72.1	75.7	55.7	
76	78.4	na	36.8	39.0	67.2	70.7	75.8	72.4	52.4	
77	75.6	34.2	36.1	48.9	56.7	50.4	55.4	58.6		
78	80.3	34.1	33.6	64.0	66.7	62.0	72.8	60.9		
79	74.3	32.4	31.9	65.3	67.3	53.4	70.7	49.7		
80	79.9	41.0	34.8	64.4	68.8	52.6	74.0	48.9		
81	80.1	37.3	40.0	64.2	na	51.2	75.6	52.1	81.6	
82	82.1	46.9	37.3	77.8	54.3	81.1	51.9	85.7		
83	87.5	49.7	45.5	81.1	68.9	82.4	51.6	91.9		
84	89.3	52.0	47.6	81.8	70.3	76.2	60.1	90.5		
85	91.7	43.9	39.4	77.6	46.8	87.7	49.7	84.5		

Stevens

	Burg	Bren	Mars	Whit	Stew	Blac	Pow	Rehn	O'Con
75	53.2	56.4	55.8	51.9	65.4	56.4	64.5	55.7	
76	51.8	56.8	56.9	60.4	62.0	55.1	58.4	52.4	
77	59.4	56.3	53.4	53.4	65.2	50.4	54.7	58.6	
78	61.2	62.9	61.9	62.9	62.1	61.2	55.4	60.9	
79	58.2	63.7	55.1	62.1	64.1	52.0	57.5	49.7	
80	49.6	56.3	54.4	61.8	51.1	57.5	56.2	48.9	
81	49.4	59.8	61.3	55.8	na	61.0	56.8	52.1	53.4
82	57.4	70.4	61.5	55.6	66.7	54.1	51.9	58.4	
83	55.9	75.0	67.5	61.0	66.3	55.6	51.6	55.6	
84	60.1	69.1	65.3	63.5	66.7	63.1	60.1	63.3	
85	48.4	67.9	67.1	56.7	64.1	56.1	49.7	58.1	

O'Connor

	Burg	Bren	Mars	Whit	Blac	Pow	Rehn	Stev
81	77.2	48.4	46.6	64.0	60.7	72.0	81.6	53.4
82	80.7	54.7	40.6	70.8	57.8	79.7	85.7	58.4
83	91.9	56.6	51.3	84.5	75.2	84.9	91.9	58.5
84	88.6	61.3	59.3	82.4	80.4	85.7	90.5	63.3
85	82.2	56.8	54.2	79.5	59.6	87.1	84.5	58.1

SELECTED BIBLIOGRAPHY

MANUSCRIPT COLLECTIONS

Unfortunately, I was able to gain access to the papers of only four of the justices who served for long periods on the Burger Court.

William J. Brennan Papers, Manuscripts Division, Library of Congress.
William O. Douglas Papers, Manuscripts Division, Library of Congress.
Thurgood Marshall Papers, Manuscripts Division, Library of Congress.
Lewis F. Powell Papers, Washington and Lee Law Library, Lexington, Va.

OTHER PRIMARY SOURCES

New York Times
Newsweek
U.S. News and World Report

CITED SECONDARY SOURCES

A truly comprehensive bibliography of the vast secondary literature dealing with the Burger Court would itself fill a good-sized monograph. Accordingly, this list includes only cited sources. These sources in turn were chosen to provide the reader a springboard for further research, because they provide either in-depth background of specific cases or more exhaustive descriptions of the Burger Court's approach to specific issues.

Aranella, Peter. "Foreword: Rethinking the Functions of Criminal Procedure: The Warren and Burger Courts' Competing Ideologies." *Georgetown Law Journal* 72 (1983): 185–248.

Barrett, Edward L. "The Rational Basis Standard for Equal Protection Review of Ordinary Legislative Classifications." *Kentucky Law Journal* 68 (1980): 845–78.

Belz, Herman. *Equality Transformed: A Quarter-Century of Affirmative Action.* New Brunswick, N.J.: Transaction Publishers, 1991.

Bickel, Alexander M. *The Least Dangerous Branch: The Supreme Court at the Bar of Politics.* Indianapolis: Bobbs and Merrill, 1962.

Binion, Gayle. "Justice Potter Stewart: The Unpredictable Vote." *Journal of Supreme Court History* (1992): 99–108.

Blasi, Vincent, ed. *The Burger Court: The Counter-Revolution That Wasn't*. New Haven, Conn.: Yale University Press, 1983.

Blumrosen, Alfred W. "Strangers in Paradise: *Griggs v. Duke Power Co.* and the Concept of Employment Discrimination." *Michigan Law Review* 71 (1972): 59–110.

Boles, Donald E. *Mr. Justice Rehnquist: Judicial Activist*. Ames: Iowa State University Press, 1987.

Brennan, William J., Jr. "State Constitutions and the Protection of Individual Rights." *Harvard Law Review* 90 (1977): 489–504.

Brunet, Edward. "Streamlining Litigation by 'Facial Examination' of Restraints: The Burger Court and the Per Se–Rule of Reason Distinction." *Washington Law Review* 60 (1984): 1–32.

Chemerinsky, Erwin C. "A Paradox without Principle: A Comment on the Burger Court's Jurisprudence of Separation of Powers." *Southern California Law Review* 60 (1987): 1083–111.

———. "State Sovereignty and Federal Court Power: The Eleventh Amendment after *Pennhurst v. Halderman*." *Hastings Constitutional Law Quarterly* 12 (1985): 643–68.

Clark, Hunter C. *Mr. Justice Brennan: The Great Conciliator*. New York: Birch Lane Press, 1995.

Conrad, Alfred F. "Securities Regulation in the Burger Court." *University of Colorado Law Review* 56 (1985): 193–225.

Couzzi, William F., and Lee Sporn. "Private Lives and Public Concerns: The Decade since *Gertz v. Robert Welch*." *Brooklyn Law Review* 51 (1985): 425–78.

Craig, Barbara H. *Chadha: The Story of an Epic Constitutional Struggle*. New York: Oxford University Press, 1988.

Davis, Michael D., and Hunter R. Clark. *Thurgood Marshall, Warrior at the Bar, Rebel on the Bench*. New York: Birch Lane Press, 1992.

Davis, Sue. *Justice Rehnquist and the Constitution*. Princeton: Princeton University Press, 1988.

Decker, John F. *Revolution to the Right: Criminal Procedure Jurisprudence during the Burger-Rehnquist Era*. New York: Garland Publishing, 1992.

"Dedication to Justice Harry A. Blackmun." *Hamline Law Review* 8 (1985): 29–151.

Dimond, Paul R. *Beyond Busing: Inside the Challenge to Urban Segregation*. Ann Arbor: University of Michigan Press, 1985.

Douglas, William O. *The Court Years, 1939–1975: The Autobiography of William O. Douglas*. New York: Random House, 1980.

———. *Go East Young Man: The Early Years*. New York: Random House, 1974.

Epstein, Lee, and Joseph F. Kobylka. *The Supreme Court and Legal Change: Abortion and the Death Penalty*. Chapel Hill: University of North Carolina Press, 1992.

Field, Martha A. "*Garcia v. San Antonio Metropolitan Transit Authority:* Demise of a Misguided Doctrine." *Harvard Law Review* 99 (1985): 84–118.

Floyd, C. Douglas. "Justiciability Decisions for the Burger Court." *Notre Dame Law Review* 60 (1985): 862–946.

Foster, Lorn S., ed. *The Voting Rights Act: Consequences and Implications*. New York: Praeger, 1985.

Freedman, Ann E. "Sex Equality, Sex Differences, and the Supreme Court." *Yale Law Journal* 92 (1983): 913–68.

Friedman, Leon, and Fred L. Israel, eds. *The Justices of the Supreme Court: Their Lives and Major Opinions.* New York: Chelsea House Publishers, 1997.

Funston, Richard Y. *Constitutional Counter-Revolution? The Warren Court and the Burger Court: Judicial Policy-Making in America.* Cambridge, Mass.: Schenkman, 1977.

Garrow, David J. *Liberty and Sexuality: The Right to Privacy and the Making of* Roe v. Wade. New York: Macmillan Publishing Co., 1994.

Gertz, Elmer. Gertz v. Robert Welch, Inc.: *The Story of a Landmark Libel Case.* Carbondale: Southern Illinois University Press, 1992.

Goforth, Carol R. "A Jurisprudential Reflection upon the Burger Court's Approach to Procedural Due Process." *Arkansas Law Review* 42 (1989): 837–85.

Gold, Michael E. *"Griggs'* Folly: An Essay on the Theory, Problems, and Origin of the Adverse Impact Definition of Employment Discrimination and a Recommendation for Reform." *Industrial Relations Law Journal* 7 (1985): 429–598.

Gould, William B., IV. "The Burger Court and Labor Law: The Beat Goes On—Marcato." *San Diego Law Review* 24 (1987): 51–76.

Graglia, Lino A. *Disaster by Decree: The Supreme Court Decisions on Race and the Schools.* Ithaca, N.Y.: Cornell University Press, 1976.

Greenawalt, R. Kent. "The Enduring Significance of Neutral Principles." *Columbia Law Review* 78 (1978): 982–1021.

Haines, Charles G. *The American Doctrine of Judicial Supremacy.* New York: Macmillan, 1932.

Herman, Susan N. "The New Liberty: The Procedural Due Process Rights of Prisoners and Others under the Burger Court." *New York University Law Review* 59 (1984): 482–575.

Hutchinson, Dennis J. *The Man Who Once Was Whizzer White: A Portrait of Justice Byron R. White.* New York: Free Press, 1998.

Jackson, Vicki C. "The Supreme Court, the Eleventh Amendment, and State Sovereign Immunity." *Yale Law Journal* 98 (1988): 1–126.

Jaworski, Leon. *The Right and the Power: The Prosecution of Watergate.* New York: Reader's Digest Press, 1976.

Jeffries, John C., Jr. *Justice Lewis F. Powell, Jr.* New York: Charles Scribner's Sons, 1994.

"Justice Brennan: Foundation for the Future." *Pace Law Review* 11 (1991): 455–533.

"Justice Byron R. White Tribute." *Brigham Young University Law Review* (1994): 206–368.

Kahn, Ronald. *The Supreme Court and Constitutional Theory, 1953–1993.* Lawrence: University Press of Kansas, 1994.

Kellett, Christine H. "The Burger Decade: More Than Toothless Scrutiny for Laws Affecting Illegitimates." *University of Detroit Journal of Urban Law* 57 (1980): 791–811.

Kramer, Victor H. "The Case of Justice Stevens: How to Select, Nominate, and Confirm a Justice of the United States Supreme Court." *Constitutional Commentary* 7 (1990): 325–40.

Lee, Francis Graham. *Neither Conservative nor Liberal: The Burger Court on Civil Rights and Liberties.* Malabar, Fla.: Robert E. Krieger, 1983.

Lucas, J. Anthony. *Nightmare: The Underside of the Nixon Years.* New York: Viking Press, 1976.

Maltz, Earl M. "The Concept of the Doctrine of the Court in Constitutional Law."
    Georgia Law Review 16 (1982): 357–405.
————. "Illegitimacy and Equal Protection." *Arizona State Law Journal* (1980): 831–51.
————. "The Impact of the Constitutional Revolution of 1937 on the Dormant Com-
    merce Clause—A Case Study in the Decline of State Autonomy." *Harvard Jour-
    nal of Law and Public Policy* 19 (1995): 121–45.
————. "The Prospects for a Revival of Conservative Activism in Constitutional
    Jurisprudence." *Georgia Law Review* 24 (1991): 629–61.
Marion, David E. *The Jurisprudence of Justice William J. Brennan, Jr.: The Law and Politics
    of "Liberation Dignity."* Lanham, Md.: Rowman & Littlefield Publishers, 1997.
Maveety, Nancy. *Justice Sandra Day O'Connor: Strategist on the Supreme Court.* London:
    Rowan & Littlefield, 1996.
————. *Representation Rights and the Burger Years.* Ann Arbor: University of Michigan
    Press, 1991.
Michelman, Frank I. "Super Liberal: Romance, Community, and Tradition in William
    J. Brennan, Jr.'s, Constitutional Thought." *Virginia Law Review* 77 (1991):
    1261–332.
Nichol, Gene R., Jr. "Rethinking Standing." *California Law Review* 72 (1984): 68–102.
Nowak, John E., Ronald D. Rotunda, and J. Nelson Young. *Constitutional Law.* 2d ed.
    St. Paul, Minn.: West Publishing Co., 1983.
Perry, Pamela L. "Balancing Equal Opportunities with Employers' Legitimate Dis-
    cretion: The Business Necessity Response to Disparate Impact Discrimination
    under Title VII." *Industrial Relations Law Journal* 12 (1990): 1–88.
Pfeffer, Leo. *Religion, State, and the Burger Court.* New York: Prometheus Books,
    1984.
Regan, Donald H. "The Supreme Court and State Protectionism: Making Sense of
    the Dormant Clause." *Michigan Law Review* 86 (1986): 1091–287.
Rehnquist, William H. "The Notion of a Living Constitution." *Texas Law Review* 54
    (1976): 693–706.
Riggs, Robert E. "The Burger Court and Individual Rights: Commercial Speech as a
    Case Study." *Santa Clara Law Review* 21 (1981): 957–94.
Rudenstine, David. *The Day the Presses Stopped: A History of the Pentagon Papers Case.*
    Berkeley: University of California Press, 1996.
Saltzburg, Stephen A. "Foreword: The Flow and Ebb of Constitutional Criminal Pro-
    cedure in the Warren and Burger Courts." *Georgetown Law Journal* 69 (1980):
    151–209.
Savage, David G. *Turning Right: The Making of the Rehnquist Court.* New York: John
    Wiley & Sons, 1992.
Schneider, Bryan A. "Do Not Go Gentle into That Good Night: The Unquiet Death
    of Political Patronage." *Wisconsin Law Review* (1992): 511–46.
Schneider, Ronna Greff. "The 1982 State Action Trilogy: Doctrinal Contraction,
    Confusion, and a Proposal for Change." *Notre Dame Law Review* 60 (1985):
    1150–86.
Schwartz, Bernard. "Administrative Law and the Burger Court." *Hofstra Law Review* 8
    (1980): 325–401.

————. *The Ascent of Pragmatism: The Burger Court in Action.* New York: Addison-Wesley, 1990.

————. *Behind Bakke: Affirmative Action and the Burger Court.* New York: New York University Press, 1988.

————. *Swann's Way: The School Busing Case and the Supreme Court.* New York: Oxford University Press, 1986.

————. *The Unpublished Opinions of the Burger Court.* New York: Oxford University Press, 1988.

————., ed. *The Burger Court: Counter-Revolution or Confirmation.* New York: Oxford University Press, 1998.

Schwartz, Herman, ed. *The Burger Years: Rights and Wrongs in the Supreme Court, 1969–1986.* New York: Penguin Books, 1987.

Segal, Jeffrey A., and Harold J. Spaeth. *The Supreme Court and the Attitudinal Model.* New York: Cambridge University Press, 1992.

Shapiro, David L. "Mr. Justice Rehnquist: A Preliminary View." *Harvard Law Review* 90 (1976): 293–357.

Sickel, Robert J. *John Paul Stevens and the Constitution: A Search for Balance.* University Park: Pennsylvania State University Press, 1988.

Simon, James F. *Independent Journey: The Life of William O. Douglas.* New York: Harper & Row, 1980.

Spaeth, Harold, and Stuart H. Teger. "Activism and Restraint: A Cloak for the Justices' Policy Preferences." In *Supreme Court Activism and Restraint,* edited by Stephen C. Halpern and Charles M. Lamb. Lexington, Mass.: D. C. Heath and Company, 1982.

"The Supreme Court, 1969 Term." *Harvard Law Review* 84 (1970): 32–253.

"The Supreme Court, 1970 Term." *Harvard Law Review* 85 (1971): 40–353.

"The Supreme Court, 1971 Term." *Harvard Law Review* 86 (1972): 52–306.

"The Supreme Court, 1972 Term." *Harvard Law Review* 87 (1973): 55–309.

"The Supreme Court, 1973 Term." *Harvard Law Review* 88 (1974): 41–280.

"The Supreme Court, 1974 Term." *Harvard Law Review* 89 (1975): 47–281.

"The Supreme Court, 1975 Term." *Harvard Law Review* 90 (1976): 58–282.

"The Supreme Court, 1976 Term." *Harvard Law Review* 91 (1977): 72–301.

"The Supreme Court, 1977 Term." *Harvard Law Review* 92 (1978): 57–330.

"The Supreme Court, 1978 Term." *Harvard Law Review* 93 (1979): 60–281.

"The Supreme Court, 1979 Term." *Harvard Law Review* 94 (1980): 77–295.

"The Supreme Court, 1980 Term." *Harvard Law Review* 95 (1981): 93–345.

"The Supreme Court, 1981 Term." *Harvard Law Review* 96 (1982): 62–311.

"The Supreme Court, 1982 Term." *Harvard Law Review* 97 (1983): 70–306.

"The Supreme Court, 1983 Term." *Harvard Law Review* 98 (1984): 87–314.

"The Supreme Court, 1984 Term." *Harvard Law Review* 99 (1985): 120–329.

"The Supreme Court, 1985 Term." *Harvard Law Review* 100 (1986): 100–311.

"Symposium: *Asahi Metal Industry Co. v. Superior Court* and the Future of Personal Jurisdiction." *South Carolina Law Review* 39 (1988): 729–896.

"Symposium: The Jurisprudence of Warren Burger." *Oklahoma Law Review* 45 (1992): 1–168.

Thernstrom, Abigail M. *Whose Votes Count: Affirmative Action and Minority Voting Rights.* Cambridge, Mass.: Harvard University Press, 1987.

Tribe, Laurence H. *American Constitutional Law.* 2d ed. Mineola, N.Y.: Foundation Press, 1988.

———. "The Supreme Court, 1972 Term—Foreword: Toward a Model of Roles in the Due Process of Life and Law." *Harvard Law Review* 87 (1973): 1–53.

Tushnet, Mark V. "Following the Rules Laid Down." *Harvard Law Review* 96 (1984): 820.

———. *Making Constitutional Law: Thurgood Marshall and the Supreme Court, 1961–1991.* New York: Oxford University Press, 1997.

Van Alstyne, William W. "The Second Death of Federalism." *Michigan Law Review* (1985): 1709–33.

Wasby, Stephen L., ed. *"He Shall Not Pass This Way Again": The Legacy of William O. Douglas.* Pittsburgh: University of Pittsburgh Press, 1990.

Wechsler, Herbert. "Toward Neutral Principles of Constitutional Law." *Harvard Law Review* 73 (1959): 1–35.

White, Ethel S. "The Protection of the Individual and the Free Exchange of Ideas: Justice Potter Stewart's Role in First and Fourth Amendment Cases." *University of Cincinnati Law Review* 54 (1985): 87–128.

Wilkinson, J. Harvie. *From* Brown *to* Bakke—*The Supreme Court and School Integration.* New York: Oxford University Press, 1979.

Willborn, Steven L. "The Disparate Impact Model of Discrimination: Theory and Limits." *American University Law Review* 34 (1985): 799–837.

Woodward, Bob, and Scott Armstrong. *The Brethren: Inside the Supreme Court.* New York: Simon and Schuster, 1979.

INDEX OF CASES

BURGER COURT CASES

285

OTHER SUPREME COURT CASES

LOWER COURT CASES

SUBJECT INDEX

Black, Hugo L. (*continued*)
Supreme Court opinions: AFDC benefits, 144; contraceptives, 245; dormant Commerce Clause, 68; illegitimacy, 221; indigency, 216; *Pentagon Papers* case, 46, 47; race issues, 179–80, 189; sexually explicit speech, 98
Blackmun, Harry A.
appointment of, to Supreme Court, xii, 1
biography and career of, 18–20
as centrist, 20
as conservative, 19–20
personality of, 19
voting patterns of, 30, 58–60, 79–80, 95–96, 111–13, 123–24, 137, 149–50, 164–65, 174–75, 211–15, 239–44, 262–63, 272–78. *See also* specific content areas; specific cases in separate Index of Cases
Supreme Court opinions: abortion, 247–50, 253–54; affirmative action, 201; aliens' exclusion from civil service, 118; campaign financing, 109, 110; commercial speech, 101–2; Contract Clause, 89, 90; desegregation of schools, 182, 184, 187, 267; education of illegal aliens, 55; *Garcia v. San Antonio Metropolitan Authority*, 66–67; highway regulations, 76; illegal aliens, 56; illegitimacy, 220; *Pentagon Papers* case, 47; privacy rights, 261; *Roe v. Wade*, 19; sex discrimination, 230; *Topco* case, 87; *Usery* case, 66. *See also* specific content areas; specific cases in separate Index of Cases
Blasi, Vincent, 3
"bona fide occupational qualification" (BFOQ), 237
Boren standard, 228, 229
Bork, Robert, 23, 26, 37
Brandeis, Louis D., 14

Brennan, William J., Jr.
appointment of, to Supreme Court, 7
biography and career of, 14–15
judicial philosophy of, 26–28
as liberal, 2–3, 7, 13, 22
personality of, 15
voting patterns of, 24, 58–60, 79–80, 95–96, 111–13, 123–24, 137, 149–50, 164–65, 174–75, 211–15, 239–44, 262–63, 272–78
in Warren Court, 13, 15
Supreme Court opinions: abortion, 249, 253–54; AFDC benefits, 51, 144; affirmative action, 201, 206; campaign financing, 109n, 110; choice of law analysis, 128; Contract Clause, 90; death penalty, 152; desegregation of schools, 179, 183–84; education financing, 52; exclusionary rule, 156–57, 160; federal-state relations, 134; First Amendment, 46–47; food stamps, 54; habeas corpus, 161; highway regulations, 77–78; illegal aliens, 55, 56; illegitimacy, 221, 222; obscenity, 97; patronage system, 120–21; *Pentagon Papers* case, 46–47; personal jurisdiction, 131–32, 134; railroad retirement system, 53; rational basis test, 53; religion clauses, 166, 167, 170; sex discrimination, 226, 235, 237, 267; voting rights, 199–200. *See also* specific content areas; specific cases in separate Index of Cases
Brownell, Herbert, 8, 9
Bruce Church balancing test, 73, 75–77
Burger, Warren
appointment of, to Supreme Court, 1
assessment of, 10–13
biography and career of, 8–9
as conservative, 2, 18, 22, 30, 268
Nixon's choice of, as Supreme Court chief justice, 8, 9–10
personality of, 12

biography and career of, 25–26
as conservative, 13, 18, 22, 25–26, 30, 159
personality of, 25
voting patterns of, 58–60, 79–80, 95–96, 111–13, 123–24, 137, 149–50, 164–65, 174–75, 211–15, 239–44, 262–63, 272–78
Supreme Court opinions: abortion, 255; affirmative action, 208; at-large elections, 195, 195n. 58; dormant Commerce Clause, 71; *FERC v. Mississippi*, 66; review of state court decisions, 163; sex discrimination, 234; voting rights, 200. *See also* specific content areas; specific cases in separate Index of Cases
Office of Management and Budget, 139–40
Ohio, 133, 187–88, 256–57
Oklahoma, 132, 227–28

parochial schools. *See* private schools and colleges
patronage system, 120–21
PDA. *See* Pregnancy Discrimination Act
Pennsylvania, 234
pension plans. *See* retirement programs
Pentagon Papers, 44–48
personal jurisdiction issues, 128–36
Peters, John F., 9
pharmacist advertising, 101–3
Poff, Richard, 20
police, 190–91
political-question doctrine, 28
poor, 216, 239, 253, 266
pornography, 16–17, 97–100, 266
poverty programs, 31
Powell, Lewis F., Jr.
appointment of, to Supreme Court, xii, 1, 22, 246
biography and career of, 21–23
as centrist, 17, 22
as conservative, 17, 22
as Democrat, 268

judicial philosophy of, 29, 264, 268–69
personality of, 22
retirement of, 17
voting patterns of, 22, 58–60, 79–80, 95–96, 111–13, 123–24, 137, 149–50, 164–65, 174–75, 211–15, 239–44, 262–63, 272–78
Supreme Court opinions: abortion, 248–49, 252, 253, 254–55, 268–69; affirmative action, 204, 205–6, 208; aliens' status, 140; campaign financing, 109n, 110; choice of law analysis, 128; death penalty, 154; desegregation of schools, 183, 184, 185; dismissal of government employees, 146; dormant Commerce Clause, 70; education financing, 52; electoral procedures, 116–17; exclusionary rule, 160; federal-state relations, 121, 268; highway regulations, 75–77; illegal aliens, 55–56; illegitimacy, 222, 223, 233; lawsuits against federal officials, 43–44; patronage system, 120–21; personal jurisdiction, 131, 135; pregnancy issues, 238; privacy rights, 256–57, 258, 260; sex discrimination, 226–27, 228, 231; sexually explicit speech, 99, 100; standing to sue, 34; utility service, 147–48; voting rights, 197–98. *See also* specific content areas; specific cases in separate Index of Cases
prayer: in public schools, 171–72; in state legislatures, 172
preclearance requirement, 196–97
pregnancy, 237–38, 243–44, 253
Pregnancy Discrimination Act (PDA), 238
Price-Anderson Act, 35–36
privacy issues, 245–46, 255–61, 263. *See also* abortion
private schools and colleges, 83, 174–75, 196–71, 266, 267, 268